MANY EXCELLENT PEOPLE

A great many excellent people
. . . prefer to go elsewhere
rather than surrender rights and privileges
which they as citizens deem their own
and should enjoy.

Alamance Gleaner, 29 November 1900

I had rather live here [in Kansas]
in prefere[n]ce to North Carolina. . . .
You see, people are on more of equality—
not like it is in N.C.

J. W. Hinshaw, March 1883

The Fred W. Morrison
Series in Southern Studies

MANY EXCELLENT PEOPLE

POWER AND PRIVILEGE

IN NORTH CAROLINA,

1850–1900

PAUL D. ESCOTT

THE UNIVERSITY OF NORTH CAROLINA PRESS

Chapel Hill and London

© 1985 The University of North Carolina Press

All rights reserved

Manufactured in the United States of America

Library of Congress Cataloging in Publication Data

Escott, Paul D., 1947–

Many excellent people.

(The Fred W. Morrison series in Southern studies)

Bibliography: p.

Includes index.

1. North Carolina—Social conditions. 2. Social
classes—North Carolina—History—19th century.
3. Power (Social sciences) 4. North Carolina—Politics
and government—1865–1950. 5. North Carolina—Politics
and government—1775–1865. I. Title. II. Series.

HN79.N8E83   1985   306'.09756   84-28107

ISBN 0-8078-1651-5

All illustrations are courtesy of the
Division of Archives and History, Raleigh, North Carolina

To Lauren Elizabeth Escott

CONTENTS

TABLES

ILLUSTRATIONS

PREFACE

From its beginnings North Carolina seemed different from its Old South neighbors. Along the coast, colonists founded fewer large plantations and imported far fewer African workers than did the low-country planters to the north and south. In the backcountry small farmers with only a limited investment or belief in the slavery system far outnumbered would-be aristocrats. In the 1680s Governor Culpeper of Virginia dismissed North Carolina as "always . . . the sinke of America, the Refuge of our Renagadoes," and later patronizing Virginians like William Byrd referred to the colony as "poor Carolina."[1] According to an old chestnut North Carolina was "a vale of humility between two mountains of conceit."

Though these stereotypes are true in many ways, they also are misleading. For North Carolina did evolve a powerful class of men who viewed themselves as aristocrats, men who may have drawn their wealth from commerce and manufacturing as much as from the soil but who nevertheless held beliefs as antidemocratic as those of a tidewater gentleman or low-country lord. Compared to their neighbors in Virginia and South Carolina, or still more to European nobility, these men hardly seemed aristocratic—they were too simple, new, unpolished, and grasping. But their social position took its meaning from the conditions of life in a poor and undeveloped state. In that setting North Carolina had an aristocracy, and its leaders were powerful and hostile to democracy.

Despite recurrent challenge to the relatively closed and rigid social structure, this aristocracy has kept power tightly in its grasp for more than two centuries. In antebellum days the wealthy and influential were called the "gentry"; in 1949 political scientist V. O. Key, Jr., described the state's leadership as a "progressive plutocracy."[2] Though the terminology changed, the fact of dominance by a small group remained constant, as did certain traits of this elite. From colonial times onward, these leaders often chose paternalistic means of exercising power, and aristocratic attitudes took such a deep hold in the state that they remain very much a part of its life today.

An incident from the nineteenth century illustrates the complex truths about North Carolina's social structure. Juliana Margaret Conner visited Mecklenburg County and areas nearby in 1827 after her marriage to a North Carolinian. Raised in Charleston, she was accustomed to the polish and culture of a wealthy urban life. By contrast Charlotte was a "place not offering anything worthy of note or interest," and she found that "the society and manners are totally different from any which I have ever seen, they have none of the artificial distinctions which are kept up with such punctilious nicety in cities." Though the lands seemed "rich and highly cultivated," she noted that prosperous slaveowning farmers were too isolated to possess imported luxury goods and that ladies attending Hopewell Church made no attempt at city fashions or airs. "There were not 2 bonnets which differed in shape and color in the whole congregation[!]"[3]

For Charleston belle Juliana Conner, North Carolina obviously required some adjustment, but she formed a generally favorable opinion. "The manner of visiting renders all form superfluous," she commented, "it is kind and friendly and causes one to overlook the absence of more polish and refinement." With some disapproval she noted that leading families displayed "none of the elegance and taste which peculiarly belong to a city." Yet she balanced that fact by observing that "the style of living" had "a great abundance of all the necessaries and substantials of life" and that the farmers were "independent" and free from debt. On the whole the unpolished but comfortable conditions that she saw disposed her to philosophical approval. "We see no lordly castle towering in proud prominence over the more humble dwellings which surround it—no princely fortunes which so many labour to amass for one. . . . They preserve in this state pure republicanism—in practice as well as theory."[4]

Yet Juliana Conner had not fully described North Carolina's social structure, for she was an upper-class woman visiting among countrified but affluent families. A casual aside to one of her observations revealed the limitations of her perspective. Every visitor "is welcome and receives the same hospitality," she said, "provided he is what Pope calls the noblest work of God 'An honest man.' (I do not include the laboring class such as overseers, etc.)"[5] This last reservation was quite significant. It excluded most North Carolinians. Mrs. Conner's "pure republicanism" described social relations among the gentry rather than that group's contact with the rest of society. The great majority of people—small subsistence farmers, landless farm laborers, slaves, and others of "the laboring class"—ranked far below the gentry. If North Carolina's elite was modest and unprepossessing in comparison to Charleston's, on its own terms it remained quite exclusive. And behind the unpretentious facade of the self-chosen aristocracy, there had grown up a long-standing unwillingness to tolerate open opposition or share political power. The state was humble *and* aristocratic.

This book explores North Carolina's social system and the relations between common folk and elite figures during a crucial half century. Its central concern with the realities of class, race, and power developed naturally out of issues raised by earlier projects. My first major research in graduate school produced evidence of serious class resentment and class conflict within the Confederacy, and later research into slave narratives deepened my awareness of the importance of racial division in American history. North Carolina seemed an appropriate place to pursue these social cleavages. Although I have not pursued the additional and significant social division between men and women in any extended way, it is a component in all questions that underlie this book. These questions include: What happened to the fierce class resentment that arose during the Civil War? How did class conflict relate to the racial violence of the Ku Klux Klan? Did the Civil War, emancipation, and Reconstruction affect class structure and race relations in North Carolina? Did the New South truly represent a change from the Old? How did the forces of race and class interact during the transition from slave South to New South?

This book attempts to portray the major social groups in North Carolina—elite whites (such as planters, commercial farmers, businessmen and political leaders), ordinary white subsistence farmers and farm laborers, slaves, freedmen, industrialists, and factory workers—from 1850 to 1900. It focuses on patterns of social position and social power. It describes what the members of these groups believed and felt and analyzes major events affecting how they dealt with each other. Throughout the study these social groups are considered in the context of the society and social order of which they were part.

Between 1850 and 1900 a succession of major events seemed likely to transform the state. The Civil War, emancipation, Reconstruction, Populism, and the rise of New South industrialism all had a great impact on North Carolina's people and their social relations. My concern has been to analyze both changes and continuities in social attitudes, social structure, and power.

Though change occurred, my conclusions emphasize continuity in power relationships and in the elite's undemocratic attitudes. The men who benefited from the aristocratic customs and laws of 1850 fought tenaciously to protect their power and privilege during the Civil War and Reconstruction. Their successors, men who came to power in the New South, likewise battled to preserve their dominance and control over the lower classes, black and white. Fear of a biracial majority forming below haunted North Carolina's elite throughout the period and stimulated repeated repression. The forces of race and class were intertwined but with class as the dominant partner. Class enmity underlay racial discrimination, and elite figures proved to be the instigators of racial violence throughout the period. Thus the attitudes of an antebellum slave society cast a long shadow over the postwar years, and one theme of this book is the persistent influence of Old South values on the social practices of the "New" South.

Another theme, however, is the depth of self-respect and democratic aspirations among ordinary North Carolinians. As slaves and freedmen, small farmers and factory workers, these men and women sought equal treatment in their personal lives and often aided movements for greater justice in society. Their stubborn determination was surprising in light of their powerlessness. Despite the risks involved, ordinary Tar Heels repeatedly mounted fundamental challenges to the control of the elite. Protest against undemocratic attitudes and aristocratic social arrangements characterized these fifty years as strongly as did the pretensions of the elite.

In this study white yeomen farmers receive considerable attention. Although it seems even more difficult to find eloquent sources about them than about slaves, their story is important. Too often historians have made sweeping generalizations about the deference of common, rural whites toward the great planters or about interclass unity founded on racism. The yeomen's behavior was much more complex than that. They do not fit conventional concepts as either a racist appendage of the slaveholders or as a self-conscious class dedicated to overthrowing the elite.

North Carolina's yeomen were, in reality, a self-directed, stubborn, and independent group. Theirs was a traditional way of life based upon subsistence farming. It was neither luxurious nor easy, but it offered self-reliance and self-respect. The yeomen sought to pursue that way of life without interference from others. Repeatedly, however, events forced them into confrontations with other groups; history forced them to become a class despite themselves.

Although their characteristic posture was disengagement from other groups in society, they constituted a group with separate and distinct interests that were threatened. The yeomen were not bent on dominance over others, but they proved to be always ready to defend themselves. When in peril, they quickly became class-conscious and resistant. They fought fiercely and on occasions violently to maintain their traditions and their autonomy. Eventually they made a stand to save their treasured independence. Yet by 1900 their history had become a story of tragedy. Effects of that tragedy still linger today.

The fierceness with which yeomen defended their separate interests and way of life compels recognition of complex rules of coexistence within southern society. It forces us to consider both the yeomen and the South's class system in a fuller, more realistic manner. The behavior of yeomen was a key element in an intriguing social structure that contained both racial consensus among whites and vigorous class protest. Conflict took place on many levels within society, and ordinary whites as well as blacks fought for autonomy, despite the unequal terms of the contest and the repeated setbacks suffered by both.

I have profited from recent studies such as Jonathan Wiener's *Social Origins of the New South* and Dwight B. Billings, Jr.'s, *Planters and the Making of a "New South."* My book addresses many of the same questions asked by Billings, and some of the answers given are similar. The reader will notice, however, that the style of presentation is as different as historians' and sociologists' training. Billings's emphasis is on theory; this study, although not neglecting theory, approaches it by describing many particular events. My intent is to use them to show how North Carolina's social system actually worked. Because people's attitudes and acts can be very revealing of social reality, I have tried to embed the narrative in specific events.

Although the entire state of North Carolina is studied, five counties receive consistent attention, so far as the existence of records allows: Caldwell, Randolph, Alamance, Edgecombe, and New Hanover. These represent a spectrum of geographical, racial, economic, and political diversity. Caldwell County in the west, at the edge of the mountains, was predominantly white and steadily Democratic. Randolph County in the piedmont was a poor farming area, but it and nearby Alamance became centers of textile production and Republican political challenge. Edgecombe was a prosperous eastern plantation district that was heavily black, as was New Hanover County which contained Wilmington, the state's largest city and port. Thanks to the outstanding efforts of generations of archivists in North Carolina, a wealth of material is available on these areas, though the records inevitably are incomplete.

This study attempts to cover significant aspects of social and political history fully without treating every topic minutely. It tells the story of a conservative social system resisting change despite persistent challenge from democratic forces. It describes fifty years of change in a society that made little or no progress toward democracy.

Paul D. Escott
Charlotte, N.C.

ACKNOWLEDGMENTS

More than ever before I am in debt to friends and supporters who helped me to complete this study. The Rockefeller Foundation provided financial assistance that was vital; long ago, in 1979, it awarded a fellowship that gave me the freedom to begin the project and complete a sizable portion of the research. The Foundation of the University of North Carolina at Charlotte continued its support for my research with a summer grant in 1981. The College of Arts and Sciences at UNCC, through a reassignment of duties in the spring of 1983, allowed me to concentrate on writing the last half of the manuscript. Without the time and money that come through these kinds of support, scholarship would be impossible, or certainly long delayed.

Research also would be impossible without the skill and dedication during many years of North Carolina's archivists. I was indeed fortunate to be able to draw on the resources of the North Carolina Division of Archives and History, the Southern Historical Collection of the University of North Carolina at Chapel Hill, the Manuscripts Department at Perkins Library, Duke University, and the North Carolina Collection at UNC-Chapel Hill. Their staffs are as helpful as their collections are superb. For special acts of support I thank Jeffrey J. Crow, Terrell Armistead Crow, Freda Brittain, Barbara Cain, Neil Fulghum of the North Carolina Museum of History, Robert Topkins, Richard Shrader, Mattie Russell, and Alice Cotten. At UNCC I have relied upon a very helpful staff, especially Dawn Hubbs, Barbara Lisenby, Adie Davis, and Amanda Harmon. Mrs. Graham Barden generously made available to me the interesting papers of one of her ancestors, William J. Clarke.

The work on this book involved one special pleasure: staying with friends who opened their homes to me while I was doing research. For their hospitality and the pleasure it afforded me I am especially grateful to Jeff and Terri Crow, Malcolm Call, Pat and Ed Wagner, and Bob and Anne Durden.

Friends and colleagues in the historical profession have been generous with their time and expertise. Their suggestions and criticisms have aided me throughout the project and contributed a great deal to the final product. I am grateful, much more than this listing can show, to Jeffrey Crow, Robert Durden, Sydney Nathans, Peter Wood, Lyman Johnson, David Goldfield, Otto Olsen, Tony Scott, Jacquelyn Hall and her students (especially Wayne Durrill), Harry Watson, Bill Auman, and Gail O'Brien.

I thank Mary Bottomly, who typed most of the manuscript, for doing a skillful job that reflects her high standards and dedication to the history department. But I also thank her for taking an interest in the book and sharing with me comments that I valued. I appreciate Connie Higginbotham's help with the last portions of the typing and her good cheer.

MANY EXCELLENT PEOPLE

1

THE IDEA OF A REPUBLIC
VERSUS DEMOCRACY

In 1827, when Juliana Margaret Conner married and left Charleston to visit North Carolina, she found a state whose life was pervasively rural. "Visiting does not appear to be general," she observed, because "plantations are 3 or 4 miles distant and the intercourse is consequently not frequent." Even in the town of Salisbury, people's hours struck her as "almost primitive . . . [they rise early,] dine at noon and sup at sunset, and like good sober folks retire at 9." She felt that country life had "no excitement" and commented upon the simplicity of living among prosperous farmers. Their abundance consisted of good foods like "ham and chickens, vegetables, tarts, custards and sweetmeats, . . . corn or wheat cakes and coffee" rather than high fashions and imported luxury goods. She noted too that church was an important institution and meeting place. After one service she wrote, "Such an extensive connection I never saw—almost everyone was Uncle, Aunt or Cousin."[1]

In 1860 North Carolina retained this rural culture. Fewer than a million people inhabited the state, towns were small, and Wilmington was the largest city with approximately ten thousand residents. The great majority of whites (and roughly half of the blacks, who comprised 36 percent of the population) lived on small and isolated farms. Different sections of the state had little contact with each other, and most people knew little of the world beyond their own neighborhood and county. Without a major port or a large river to spur east-west commerce, trade often followed wagon roads into Virginia and river valleys into South Carolina. Many residents typically journeyed no farther than the nearest market town; some lived and died wholly within one county.[2]

The culture continued to be organized around family and kin. Any historian who reads manuscript census records from the nineteenth century, for example, easily sees how Patterson Township in Alamance County got its name: almost half the surnames listed were Patterson. People rooted themselves in a particular spot, their own family network, and their local culture. Many people moved out of North Carolina—indeed, in Tennessee Juliana Conner exclaimed that "you do not go anywhere without meeting" people from the Tar Heel State—but those who remained usually moved about little. Many writers have speculated that the self-selection of emigrants heightened North Carolina's tendencies toward conservatism, intrastate sectionalism, and provincialism.[3]

Despite the fact that North Carolina lacked Charleston's wealth and elegance and had a pervasive, humble, rural style of life, the society was not simple. It was complex, with a variety of social classes, each having its own values and outlooks, and a hierarchical structure of power that belied the seeming equality of a poor state. Both class and race divided the population in some ways that were obvious and some that were partly obscured. Within North Carolina a rigid structure of power existed alongside the aspirations of slaves for freedom and a hardy, even defiant, sense of individualism and self-worth among average white people. In many periods the potential for conflict among these attitudes went unnoticed, but the late antebellum years inaugurated what proved to be a half century of rising tensions, violence, and repression.

At the top of antebellum society were the members of the gentry. Planters (owners of 20 or more slaves), who constituted only about one-eighth of the slaveholding population, generally qualified for membership in the gentry, as did prosperous merchants, wealthy men of commerce, and educated professionals such as doctors, lawyers, and the high-church clergy.[4] Not infrequently a family or individual combined two or more of these roles. Physicians (of whom there were only 1,266 in 1860) often owned a plantation and slaves, and sons of planters sometimes aspired to join the bar (which had only 500 members). What distinguished the gentry was wealth and position more than lineage, slaveholding, or landownership. North Carolina could claim relatively few genuine, old, aristocratic families, and many middle-class people had risen into the elite. Similarly, wealth and certain attainments that went with it—the gentry claimed superior education, character, and manners—were more important than a particular form of wealth, such as a cotton plantation.

It is important to emphasize that the North State's elite embraced diverse economic backgrounds. Just as North Carolina was not a plantation state, its gentry was not characterized by an exclusively "seigneurial" or plantation ethos.[5] Planters certainly belonged to the gentry, but in a relatively poor, undeveloped, agrarian economy, such as North Carolina's, others who occupied positions of economic advantage could readily qualify. The general store was the basis of many fortunes—such as the Bennehan-Cameron wealth—and a means to augment many others. Owners of a flour and grist mill also possessed a facility needed by all their neighbors and could use it to climb to higher levels of affluence. As early as the 1830s prominent families like the Battles, Holts, Frieses, Moreheads, Schencks, and others were involved in textile manufacturing and in transportation. After the Whigs came to power in the state in 1836 (if not before), diverse forms of economic expansion were all respectable.[6]

Wealthy North Carolinians were entrepreneurs rather than seigneurs. Planters moved into commerce and industry while others traveled the reverse direction, all united in the search for profit. Older leaders such as Governor John M. Morehead and jurist Thomas Ruffin shared an interest in the coordinated development of railroads, water power, and coal and iron deposits.[7] Judge Ruffin assisted both railroad and textile ventures, and Paul Cameron, the largest slaveowner in the state in 1860, showed a persistent interest in industrial investments. Although he spoke in a paternalistic manner, Cameron invested in several cotton mills and never restricted himself to a purely plantation ethos.[8] Jonathan Worth was both slaveowner and owner and investor in textile mills. He shifted his assets rapidly, when necessary, among different enterprises and between different commodities such as cotton and real estate in order to protect and augment his fortune. Like leaders of the previous generation, he encouraged the promotion of industrial associations to stimulate manufacturing.[9]

Many local merchants, planters, or millers established sawmills or factories to expand their business. The Fries family of Salem branched out from flour milling into textile production, and the Patterson family of Caldwell County, Salem, and Greensboro carried the development of allied enterprises even further. In Caldwell County the Pattersons ran a grist mill, a textile mill, a store, a tan yard, an oil mill, and a wool-carding operation. Rufus Lenoir Patterson then established stores and textile mills in other parts of the state. In addition he once declared that, "A Rail Road to Patterson [in Caldwell County] is the bright dream of my life."[10]

If the gentry was diverse economically, socially it was surprisingly unified. Economic activities brought its members into contact with each other, and those who participated in politics met at party functions and at

Samuel Finley Patterson

the legislative sessions in Raleigh. In contrast to most North Carolinians, members of the gentry often traveled and sent their children away to academies and to the state's university. Prominent families socialized and intermarried. For example, Anne Cameron, daughter of the wealthiest man in the state, married into another large slaveowning family, the Collinses, of Washington and Tyrrell counties. Rufus Lenoir Patterson made an advantageous political match when he wed the daughter of Governor Morehead, and after her death he joined two prominent milling and manufacturing families by marrying Mary Fries. Families like the Pattersons entertained the children of other elite families in their homes, a practice that encouraged friendships and marital ties. And those who took part in county government quickly became familiar with members of their class in that area. Men active in public affairs over a long period of time, like Samuel Finley Patterson or Thomas Ruffin, came to know a wide network of prominent people.[11]

Below the gentry in status and power was a "middle" class composed of slaveowners with fewer than twenty slaves, commercial farmers, and merchants, manufacturers, artisans, and professionals on a smaller scale. "Middle" described this group accurately only in the sense that it lay between the upper and lower classes, for the middle class remained very small and was part of the elite, not the masses. But, as this book will show, the term accurately reflects the gentry's assumption that few people were respectable; in the eyes of the gentry, a small group of whites was middle class and the rest—roughly half of the white citizens of North Carolina— fell into an unreliable lower class along with free blacks and slaves.

Given the economic diversity of the gentry, the distinction between it and the so-called middle class was one of degree, not kind. These middling men were aspiring, but they lacked sufficient wealth, polish, or political success to be accepted as part of the gentry. They were propertied, however, and therefore they regarded themselves as thoroughly respectable members of the community and were recognized as such by the elite. Politically interested members of the middle class filled many local offices that the gentry did not occupy.

The average North Carolinian was a small farmer or farm laborer. Along with 72 percent of the white families in the state, yeomen owned no slaves, and they owned only modest amounts of land. In 1860 more than 69 percent of the state's farms contained fewer than one hundred acres, and almost 42 percent contained fewer than fifty acres. Many of these small farms were probably operated by tenants rather than landowners, although the vagaries of record keeping preclude a precise count. Whatever the exact figure, it is clear that most North Carolinians had only modest wealth and most landholders had very small holdings.[12]

Among the small farmers in the state, the yeoman class formed a vigorous and relatively successful element. Although yeomen were not wealthy enough to own slaves, they farmed their own land, usually a parcel of fifty to one hundred acres or less, and provided for their own needs. Most antebellum yeomen were subsistence farmers who fed themselves but did not direct much of their energies toward the commercial market. Cotton prices fluctuated, so the yeoman concentrated on supplying his family's needs and maintaining his independence, rather than risking a debt that could result in loss of his farm. If family members had some land and time left over, they might grow a little cotton to gain cash or work for a commercial farmer who was shorthanded. As a recent study of the Bennitt family (whose homestead is near Durham) has shown, yeomen also obtained cash by hauling goods and baggage, selling brandy or providing lodging to travelers, or making small quantities of basic commodities like clothes and shoes.[13] The income from these activities allowed purchases of medicines, books, clothes, or amusements at a general store to supplement the food derived from the family's grains, vegetables, fruit, and livestock (chiefly hogs).

Undoubtedly there were some yeomen who aspired intensely to become slaveowners. In one of the few yeoman's diaries that has come to light, a North Carolinian named John F. Flintoff recorded his struggles and desperate determination to become a slaveowner. In 1841 at age eighteen, he left Orange County for Mississippi, where he planned to work as an overseer and save money. Though he found the land "very good," the society was "irreligious," and his health became "very bad" with "chills and fever." Work for an uncle ended in quarrels and recriminations, and even at a camp meeting Flintoff found "but little warm feeling" to nurture his religious impulses. For a time he persisted, attending Centenary College near Jackson, but in 1846 he decided that "ma[na]ging negroes and large farms is soul destroying" and returned to North Carolina the next year. There he married and tried to raise his social status by purchasing "a negro boy 7 years old for 331 dollars," but, "impatient to get along in the world," he tried Mississippi again in 1852. This venture was a disaster. Sick, "low spirited," forced by his uncle to accept "hand pay," Flintoff returned in despair.

"I am well nigh heart broken," he wrote in 1854. Though he owned several slaves, mostly children, Flintoff admitted, "I have never owned one foot of land. I think I will have to sell some of my negroes to buy land this I must have I want *a home*." With the aid of his wife's family, he purchased a farm in Caswell County and began to raise tobacco. Gradually he worked his way out of a large debt without having to sell any of the slaves that he deemed so important to his status. After several years of making good crops and hauling wood during slack times, Flintoff finally achieved some peace of mind as a medium-sized slaveowner and tobacco farmer. It had been a nineteen-year struggle.[14]

Flintoff probably was atypical in many ways. Another yeoman's diary, found by Clement Eaton, revealed that Ferdinand L. Steel of Tennessee and Mississippi put the security of his small farm above cotton profits and slaveowner's status. He worked from 5 A.M. to dusk to raise food crops and grew only a little cotton for cash. In fact, Steel wanted to grow less of it. "We are too weak handed" to manage cotton, he wrote. "We had better raise small grain and corn and let cotton alone, raise corn and keep out of debt and we will have no necessity of raising cotton."[15]

But Steel shared with Flintoff some vital characteristics of the yeomen. Both had a fear and dislike of debt because they treasured their independence. The closeness of the frontier, the rural way of life, and American political values all reinforced the desire of the average yeoman to stand on his own two feet and be beholden to no one. Most yeomen were, in fact, independent, proud, and materially progressing, and if Steel did not attempt to become a slaveholder, he nevertheless probably shared Flintoff's conviction that he deserved social superiority to blacks. These facts fed an assertive individualism that was restrained but never weakened by religion and the family.[16] For both Flintoff and Steel life revolved around the family and kin, and both tried to dedicate their lives to evangelical religion. "Oh! may I live close to Jesus," cried out Flintoff; Steel joined a temperance society, studied religious books, and eventually became an itinerant Methodist parson. "My Faith increases," he noted happily, "& I enjoy much of that peace which the world cannot give."[17]

Ranking below the yeomen but like them in their attitudes of rural individualism were most of the landless whites. To be sure, some landless people lived in towns and worked as laborers or mechanics and artisans; the more skilled and prosperous among them probably were considered as respectable as the landowning farmer.[18] But most landless whites were rural people who worked as day laborers or farmhands. There were more than thirty-six thousand of them in 1860, or almost 30 percent of the adult white male population.[19] Some appear to have held stubbornly on to life-styles of hunting, herding, and droving that waned with the passing of the frontier. Living primitively in out-of-the-way areas, they hunted and occasionally rounded up livestock which they allowed to graze on the open range.[20] "Piney Woods" men squatted in the turpentine forests of New Hanover and other eastern counties and derived a living from the wilds, plus their cattle and bees, in return for occasional service to the landlord.[21] Some landless whites worked steadily as tenants, often on poor land; others labored more precariously as hired hands for low wages. The remainder probably formed the indigent class of "poor white trash" that has been frequently but almost always subjectively described.[22] However poor they were, most of these whites remained proud and believed, in accordance with Jacksonian politics and Christian faith, that they were as good as anybody.

Probably they were not as healthy as others in that era. For antebellum southerners health and life itself were never sure, even for the rich. Many of the yeomen, and perhaps most of the poorer whites and blacks below them, suffered from poor nutrition and disease. Travelers' accounts often painted a picture of a sickly, malnourished, listless population. One visitor in 1865–66 described most poorer whites as "sunk in sulkiness and apathy" and provided one possible explanation by quoting a farmer from the Cape Fear as saying, "More ager [ague—possibly malaria] round this year than he ever knew before." A typical, humble white woman was "barefooted," her face was "sallow . . . thin and dirty," "stained . . . with the juice of tobacco," and her skin lacked a ruddy, healthy color. Instead the "dingy white or clay color" of her dress "matched her complexion."[23]

Sidney Andrews, another postwar visitor, gave this description of "the native North-Carolinian as one sees him outside the cities and large towns":

> Spindling of legs, round of shoulders, sunken of chest, lank of body, stooping of posture. . . . There is insipidity in his face, indecision in his step, and inefficiency in his whole bearing. . . . His wife is leaner, more round-shouldered, more sunken of chest, and more pinched of face than her husband. . . .
>
> The complexion of these country residents is noticeable, and suggests many inquiries. If you say that half the men and nearly all the women are very pale, you strike at the matter, but fail to fairly hit it. Their whiteness of skin is simply the whiteness of ordinary tallow. It

is sallowness, with a suggestion of clayeyness. Unquestionably soap and water and crash towels would improve the appearance, but I doubt if they would give any bloom to the cheek. The skin seems utterly without vitality, and beyond the action of any restorative stimulants: it has a pitiful and repulsive death-in-life appearance. I am told the climate is in fault, but my judgment says the root of the matter is in the diet.[24]

Andrews probably was right. To the modern physician or public health officer his description reads like a catalog of dietary deficiency diseases. The "spindling legs" and "sunken chests" suggest rickets and the effect of inadequate vitamin D. The "pale," clayey, "death-in-life" color of the skin speaks of anemia due perhaps to malaria or the hookworm and other parasites that the "barefoot" North Carolinians could have picked up. With the water-borne and insect-carried diseases common in the nineteenth century, a limited diet based mainly on pork and corn did little to help the common people.

North Carolina's black population, both free and enslaved, endured living conditions inferior to those of the yeomen and poorer whites. Physically and socially, more than one-third of the state's populace had been relegated by harsh tradition and strict laws to a perpetually marginal and despised position defined by race. The few free blacks who prospered, like cabinetmaker Tom Day, were exceptions that proved the rule; most free blacks worked in the fields side-by-side with slaves for very low wages. A small number were lucky enough to find decent jobs as boatmen or artisans.[25]

During the antebellum period the law increasingly treated free blacks as subject to the same tight restrictions as slaves. "Little by little the Legislature stripped the free Negro of his personal liberties," wrote Guion Griffis Johnson, noting that after the 1820s free blacks lost the right to enter the state, to preach in public, to keep a gun without a special license, to buy or sell liquor, to attend public school, or to vote, no matter how much property they owned. When one of these restrictions was challenged, the Supreme Court ruled in *State v. Newsom*, 1844, that free black people "occupy such a position in society, as justified the legislature in adopting a course of policy in its acts peculiar to them." In fact, the Supreme Court declared that "free people of color cannot be considered as citizens, in the largest sense of the term."[26]

The courts moved in other ways to establish discrimination upon color rather than upon slave or free status. From 1746 it had been impermissible for any black or mulatto, slave or free, to testify against a white person, and even earlier a statute had decreed that the testimony of blacks was inherently inferior. Then, in 1794 in the case of "*State v. George* (a free negro)," a slave appeared as a witness, and the question arose whether it was "improper that a slave should testify against" George, because he was a freeman. The court allowed the testimony, and by 1843 it had become "clearly settled that a slave is a competent witness against a free negro," though never against any white.[27] Thus a line was drawn between black and white, not between slaves and freemen.

The slaves, of course, had lost to legal oppression most of the objective things that one person can take from another. They may have believed that they fared better than their brothers and sisters did in the factories-in-the-field of Mississippi and Alabama, but slavery offered no benefits beyond the qualities developed to endure and survive it. Like many whites, the slaves were religious, except they believed in a God who was no respecter of color. They believed that He would punish slaveholders for their wickedness, and a substantial part of the last generation in slavery seems to have believed, fervently, that God would deliver them from bondage. While they went about their assigned tasks, recalled one woman, "they prayed for freedom."[28]

The social gradations described above were more than aspects of status; they reflected the deeply entrenched hierarchy of power in society. The middle class was far from average; in terms of wealth it ranked well above the typical North Carolinians, who were yeomen subsistence farmers. Yet middle class conveys the appropriate connotations because, in North Carolina society, the advantaged people in this category completed the ranks of supposedly virtuous citizens and established the boundary beyond which the lower classes began.[29] As will be shown, those who held power looked with suspicion upon much of the white population. They assumed that power and wealth, if safe, rested in comparatively few hands.

Figures on landownership demonstrate the dominant economic position of the numerically small gentry and middle classes. (See tables 1–5.) Caldwell and Randolph counties were probably typical of many rather poor agricultural regions of the state. The great majority of farms had fewer than one hundred acres and took little part in commercial agricultural production. Yet the middle class and gentry owned a large majority of total acreage, and landholdings understated total wealth because the elite invested significantly in commercial and industrial ventures. Even in

TABLE 1

Concentration in Agriculture in Caldwell County, 1860

Farm Size Farm Acreage	No. of Farms	% of Farms	Estimated % of % of Farms
3–49 acres	235	41.5	9.0
50–99	183	32.3	20.0
100–499	140	24.7	61.5
500–999	7	1.2	7.7
1,000+	1	.2	1.8

Source: Tables 1–5 were constructed from data in the U.S. Census, Census of Agriculture for 1860. The third column was created by simple calculation. The fourth column was constructed according to the method explained in Fabian Linden's oft-cited article, "Economic Democracy in the Slave South." Linden's method follows Lewis Gray, is commonsensical, and yields useful estimates, but they are not exact and should be regarded as rough approximations rather than precise figures.

TABLE 2

Concentration in Agriculture in Randolph County, 1860

Farm Size	No. of Farms	% of Farms	Estimated % of Farm Acreage
3–49 acres	514	30.2	6.4
50–99	719	42.3	25.7
100–499	463	27.2	66.5
500–999	4	.2	1.4
1,000+	—	—	—

Alamance County, which was somewhat more representative of piedmont counties that produced important commercial crops, a large minority of farms were essentially subsistence operations, and larger units controlled most of the acreage. The imbalance in acreage according to farm size was, of course, much greater in slaveholding, plantation districts such as Edgecombe and New Hanover counties. There approximately half of the

TABLE 3

Concentration in Agriculture in Alamance County, 1860

Farm Size	No. of Farms	% of Farms	Estimated % of Farm Acreage
3–49 acres	129	14.6	1.9
50–99	285	32.3	12.1
100–499	448	50.7	76.0
500–999	17	1.9	7.2
1,000 +	4	.5	2.8

TABLE 4

Concentration in Agriculture in Edgecombe County, 1860

Farm Size	No. of Farms	% of Farms	Estimated % of Farm Acreage
3–49 acres	188	23.7	2.7
50–99	174	21.9	7.3
100–499	368	46.4	62.0
500–999	58	7.3	24.5
1,000 +	5	.6	3.5

TABLE 5

Concentration in Agriculture in New Hanover County, 1860

Farm Size	No. of Farms	% of Farms	Estimated % of Farm Acreage
3–49 acres	334	51.5	10.7
50–99	124	19.1	11.3
100–499	177	27.3	65.1
500–999	14	2.2	12.9
1,000 +	—	—	—

farms held only a small fraction of the land, about 10 percent. In New Hanover County 70 percent of the farms had less than 25 percent of the land.

Statistics on slaveholding magnify the above tendencies and reveal that wealth in slave property was highly concentrated. Even among the minority of slaveowners, ownership of slave property was quite concentrated, especially in plantation districts. (See tables 6–10.)

Moreover, significant restrictions and privileges were chiseled into the fundamental law of the state. North Carolina, along with a few other states, had successfully blunted the tide of democratic constitutional reform that swept across the South in the 1830s. Its Constitution of 1776 had established "a representative democracy in form but an oligarchy in spirit and practice," and the convention of 1835 made only modest changes.[30] Election of a governor became the choice of the voters, not the legislature, but few other democratizing measures prevailed.

White men who owned fewer than fifty acres of land—a large minority—still could not vote for state senator, whereas free blacks lost all rights of suffrage. Though all white adult male taxpayers could vote for members of the house of commons, a property requirement of one hundred acres disqualified more than half of them from running for the legislature. Property qualifications for senators were higher and for governor higher still. In 1860 more than 85 percent of the members of the general assembly were slaveholders (the highest percentage in the South), and more than 36 percent owned at least twenty slaves (one of the highest percentages in the South). Formulas for apportioning the legislature conceded something to the west's grievances against the east but nothing to democratic principle. The senate was to be chosen from districts paying equal amounts of taxes, thus overrepresenting wealthy areas; membership in the house of commons was based on the "federal ratio," which counted each slave as three-fifths of a person and thus overrepresented slaveholding areas. State funds for schools also were distributed in accord with the federal ratio.[31]

Moreover, the "oligarchic, undemocratic" system of local government lived on.[32] In an era when local government was very powerful, North Carolinians could not elect their local officials, except sheriff and clerk of court. Justices of the peace laid down county policies, elected various county officers, and made important decisions on tax rates, the location of roads, provisions for education and the poor, and many other social and economic matters. In their judicial capacity they judged most ordinary

TABLE 6

Concentration in Slaveholding in Caldwell County, 1860

No. of Slaves	% of Families in Total Population, White and Black	% of Families in Free Population	% of Slaves
none	86.8	85.0	0.0
1	3.4	3.8	4.1
2–4	4.2	4.8	13.5
5–9	3.8	4.3	28.8
10–19	1.0	1.1	15.4
20–49	.6	.7	21.8
50–99	.2	.3	16.5
100+	—	—	—

Source: Tables 6–10 were constructed from data in the U.S. Census, Census of Population, 1860, and by calculation from that data. For the percentage of slaves in holdings of ten or more, Linden's method of estimation was used, as in Tables 1–5. The author thanks Peter H. Wood for the suggestion that concentration of slaveholding, a measure of wealth, should be calculated in terms of the *total* population to give an accurate impression of the structure of society.

Note: To construct these tables a couple of justifiable assumptions had to be made. The census provides data on number of farms and size of slaveholdings; the author has assumed one family per farm and has assumed that, because many slaveowners in Wilmington (the only city covered by the tables) also owned plantations in New Hanover County, inclusion of the urban slave population in the total for slave population did not introduce gross error. Family size for whites in North Carolina was 5.2; to guard against overemphasizing the concentration of wealth in the entire population, 7.0 was used for black family size.

crimes and settled law suits and other civil matters vital to the affected parties such as the division of estates and disputes over boundaries. These justices of the peace, or "squires," were not elected but recommended by the county's representatives and appointed by the governor. Their term was for life. In many parts of the state a leading family, such as the Hawkinses of Warren County, the Riddicks of Gates and Perquimans counties, and the Speights of Greene County, dominated the county court and state offices for decades or generations. Samuel Finley Patterson chaired the Caldwell County Court for much of his adult life and continuously after 1845, except for brief intervals when he served as state senator, representative, or delegate to a constitutional convention. This "squirarchy" was so

TABLE 7

Concentration in Slaveholding in Randolph County, 1860

No. of Slaves	% of Families in Total Population, White and Black	% of Families in Free Population	% of Slaves
none	89.0	88.1	0.0
1	3.5	3.7	6.6
2–4	4.1	4.4	22.3
5–9	2.1	2.3	26.4
10–19	1.0	1.1	21.3
20–49	.3	.3	15.3
50–99	—	—	—
100+	.0	.0	8.1

TABLE 8

Concentration in Slaveholding in Alamance County, 1860

No. of Slaves	% of Families in Total Population, White and Black	% of Families in Free Population	% of Slaves
none	74.6	66.6	0.0
1	5.5	7.2	3.3
2–4	7.8	10.2	13.1
5–9	7.1	9.4	27.5
10–19	3.8	4.9	28.2
20–49	1.1	1.4	17.5
50–99	.1	.2	6.2
100+	.0	.1	4.2

powerful that justices "generally were able to control the vote of the county in the choice of representatives in the General Assembly and in state and national elections."[33]

It was a cozy system for the gentry and politically active middle-class families who ran the court. Members of the court passed the required

TABLE 9

Concentration in Slaveholding in Edgecombe County, 1860

No. of Slaves	% of Families in Total Population, White and Black	% of Families in Free Population	% of Slaves
none	77.1	54.8	0.0
1	2.3	4.4	0.7
2–4	5.2	10.3	4.3
5–9	5.5	10.9	10.7
10–19	5.1	10.1	19.8
20–49	3.5	7.0	29.9
50–99	.9	1.7	16.7
100+	.4	.8	17.9

TABLE 10

Concentration in Slaveholding in New Hanover County, 1860

No. of Slaves	% of Families in Total Population, White and Black	% of Families in Free Population	% of Slaves
none	74.9	58.5	0.0
1	3.3	5.5	1.2
2–4	5.8	9.7	6.1
5–9	6.7	11.1	16.2
10–19	5.4	8.9	26.7
20–49	3.3	5.5	35.4
50–99	.6	.8	11.5
100+	.1	.1	2.8

legal business around among themselves and occasionally judged indictments against one of their own number. Control of county politics was in so few hands that a prominent man, like Jonathan Worth of Randolph, could arrange to hand an office over to a friend and reclaim it after serving in a higher position.[34]

Because the squires were all prosperous and powerful by virtue of their lifetime office, the network of influence in a county worked through wealth. Anyone who sought office or wanted something done usually had to seek the support of a handful of local notables. For example, in Alamance County when Thomas Ruffin's son desired the electorate to have a better understanding of his father's views, he identified five key men to spread the proper message: "Messrs. Gab. Lea, John Newlin, Ed Holt, John Trollinger, and Dr. Montgomery." Holt was probably the largest textile manufacturer in North Carolina at that time and in 1850 owned thirty-five slaves besides; Montgomery was a well-to-do physician and manufacturer; John Newlin was a wealthy planter who owned forty slaves in 1860; Lea and Trollinger also were wealthy farmers. Together the five possessed real estate averaging $15,022 in value and personal property worth an average of $19,987.50.[35]

Any prudent man listened respectfully to the opinions of such individuals and to the sitting justices of a county court. The power of the justices required it, and the wealth of the justices and gentry gave them the means to offer or withhold many kinds of resources or assistance. This situation prevailed throughout county government. Virtually every wealthy local notable held an appointment as justice of the peace, although many justices did not take the trouble to participate regularly in county business. Men of considerable wealth ran the county courts at the end of the ante bellum period, even in relatively poor counties (see table 11). The typical white farmer of this era owned real and personal property worth no more than three hundred to six hundred dollars each.

Convinced of the rightness and social desirability of their powerful, privileged position, members of the gentry often spoke in paternalistic accents about those whom they controlled. The language of paternalism was especially common among large slaveholders when they discussed their slaves. "Since I last wrote you," Weldon Edwards told Thomas Ruffin, "I have sustained an irreparable loss" in the death of a "favorite servant." Edwards recounted the dead woman's "faithful" attendance when he had been sick and grieved that "the best medical skill could not save her." "I am sure I shall never be able to supply her place," Edwards concluded.[36] It was common for planters to ask each other about health conditions "in your family of slaves" and to speak of human chattel as part of their families, black and white.[37]

Paul Cameron was possibly more eloquent but not essentially different from other planters in the way he spoke of the approximately one thou-

TABLE II

Average Wealth of County Court Members, circa 1860

County	Real Estate	Personal Estate
Caldwell	$13,122	$12,504
Randolph	3,077	6,511
Alamance	10,374	25,717
Edgecombe	17,125	33,750
New Hanover	7,343	19,560

Source: County court minutes and U.S. manuscript census records. The data covered the years from 1857 to early 1865, with slight variation from county to county due to gaps in the extant records.

Note: Because justices were appointed for life, the list of persons holding that office in a county would be lengthy. This table is based on lists of those justices who sat as a court of pleas and quarter sessions. They were the individuals who together made policy and ran the county's affairs.

sand slaves his family controlled in North Carolina. After a period of sickness he wrote, "I fear the negroes have suffered much from the want of proper attention and kindness under this late distemper . . . no love of lucre shall ever induce me to be cruel, or even to make or permit to be made any great exposure of their persons at inclement seasons." At another time he described to his sister his sense of duty: "I cannot better follow the example of our venerated Mother than in doing my duty to her faithful old slaves and their descendants. Do you remember a cold & frosty morning, during her illness, when she said to me 'Paul my son the people ought to be shod' this is ever in my ears, whenever I see any ones shoes in bad order; and in my ears it will be, so long as I am master."[38]

This paternalism depended upon the subjection of the slaves, for owners sounded solicitous only so long as they believed their slaves were firmly under control. In a democratic nation, however, members of the gentry could never be quite as sure of their control of other whites, and therefore the lower orders in the white population were potentially dangerous. Even though the elite had a tight grasp on power in North Carolina, it saw poorer white people as a threat.

John Stafford, who owned real property valued at four thousand dollars (the equivalent of several hundred acres), was an example of an elite figure who worried that his property might be insecure. Assuring Thomas Ruf-

Paul C. Cameron

fin that he held sound views, Stafford warned, "Let blood once be shed
. . . amongst a people divided as we are by different politics, sects, interests, and sentiments and soon those sowers of the wind will be able to
reap rich Harvests of the whirlwind . . . there is no class in North Carolina
that can raise a larger male force than that class that possess but little else
than moral polution having no property to destroy, no conscience to
overcome, no God to fear, they can make fearful strides in the way of
distruction." Weldon Edwards, an experienced political leader, summed
up the dangers against which the privileged minority of North Carolinians were determined to struggle: "The democratic proclivities of the age
pervade our whole country—nothing can arrest our downward tendency
to absolute Government—the idea of a Republic is cherished by but
few."[39]

Stafford and Edwards had discerned, accurately, that democratic aspirations were alive in the hearts of many ordinary citizens, despite the formidable power of the gentry. Wealth and power may have been highly
concentrated, but a great diversity of attitudes and outlooks persisted
nevertheless. People cherished divergent or even diametrically opposed
values, and the diversity of perspectives went beyond the opposed views of
slaves and masters. Within the white population lay essential differences
that had potentially great implications.

Undoubtedly the absence of local democracy and the restrictive constitutional mechanisms that placed other offices in the hands of the elite had
discouraged some yeomen. No one likes to beat his head against a wall for
no purpose, and average Tar Heels were fully able to comprehend that the
wealthy and influential had placed effective power beyond their reach. It
was reasonable for some who grew discouraged to devote their attention
to family or personal goals, to ignore politics, or to adopt a strategy of
trying to shield their lives from the intrusions of a nondisinterested government. Such attitudes are widespread among powerless people today.[40]
But generally large numbers of North Carolinians turned out for political
events; they had become a thrilling spectator sport in the age of Jackson,
and they remained an important source of entertainment in a rural society.
Moreover, the humble yeoman characteristically used political occasions
to assert his claims to equality and respectful treatment. Paul Cameron
once learned to his disadvantage that the average voter expected certain
signs of esteem from any office seeker. Lightheartedly reviewing his acts
of "folly" and "foolish[ness]," Cameron prominently noted this failing: "I
sought to be elected in Orange County *without* the use of whiskey."[41]

What kept democratic attitudes alive in the face of a hierarchical, un-democratic government and social structure? Jacksonian democracy had thrived in the South, and the pervasive democratic values of America were part of the answer, as Weldon Edwards had ruefully observed. For the American Revolution had set loose upon hierarchical societies the idea of natural, inherent human rights, and the words "all men are created equal" swiftly made the Declaration of Independence an imperishable document. As America grew, it filled up with men and women eager to grasp new opportunities of equality. The surging democracy that Alexis de Tocque-ville described had, just a few years previously, carried thousands of simple citizens into the White House, where they raucously celebrated the inau-guration of Andrew Jackson. The election of this hero of the common man, writes one scholar, "marked the coming of age in the United States of a new political idea—the idea that people had a right to a voice in choosing their rulers and lawmakers, not because they possessed special qualifications of education or of wealth, but simply because they were people."[42] Elites might contain the democratic impulse, but they could not remove it.

The influence of frontier traditions also was extremely important in a sparsely settled state that retained a strong, rural ambiance (there were only 20.4 persons per square mile, on the average, in 1860). On the frontier individuals had taken care of their own needs and provided for themselves; most North Carolinians continued in fact to live in economic independence on their family farms. On the frontier men also had settled their own scores without reliance on others, for a man was not worthy of respect if he failed to rise to a challenge; this frontier attitude about violence also remained influential. Whereas the wealthy fought duels, commoners settled disputes in fistfights or worse. Judge William Battle was shocked in 1851 to see how thoroughly the informal code of honor supplanted the law. A Burke County lawyer named William Waightstill Avery shot and killed another man in the courtroom in front of the judge and dozens of spectators; ten days later a jury of citizens speedily acquitted Avery of murder because the victim previously had cowhided Avery on a public street, thus calling into question his honor.[43]

Encounters with others had an extra bite amid the isolation of rural life, and conflict in such communities, whose members all were known to each other, became very personal. People managed their own affairs, and their own district became their world. They knew well their problems, their friends, and their enemies. As they contested issues with other individuals, they were prone to take the law into their own hands. To many the rules of law were distant and abstract compared to the small realm that was home, a realm in which they sought to establish their will. One visitor found such attitudes in a man who spoke openly of avenging himself on "six or seven creeturs up in my district." "I don't speak fur nothin' but my deestric,'" the man specified, "an' what I tell ye is what me an' my neighbors 'll stand to."[44] Thus community standards, hammered out through the clash of wills, could take the place of formal statutes, and the direct action of assault could inject a rough form of equality among individuals into the social order.

But there was another important agent of democratic values in the culture of many yeomen. Evangelical religion exercised a powerful influence over many North Carolinians, impelling them to concentrate upon religious priorities whose sacred character superseded all worldly strivings. This religious world created its own, autonomous standards beside which the pretensions of secular powers were, by definition, dross. A sizable portion of the state's ordinary citizens followed evangelical faiths and thus participated in an emotionally compelling way of life that stood apart from society's rules of hierarchy.

Methodists and Baptists dominated evangelical circles in much of North Carolina. In 1860 Alamance County had seven Methodist churches and two Baptist congregations; Caldwell County had sixteen Methodist and fifteen Baptist churches; for Edgecombe the figures were eight and nine; and for New Hanover and Randolph they were eighteen and fourteen and fifty-one and seven, respectively. Various other dissenting sects, such as the Christians, Presbyterians, or Lutherans as well as Primitive and Missionary Baptists claimed adherents throughout the state, but the higher-status Episcopalian churches were rare outside plantation areas. Randolph County had an unusually varied mixture of religions that included a strong community of Friends.[45]

An important quality of evangelical congregations was the seriousness of their devotion to pious living and the rigor of their discipline. Both Methodists and Baptists, for example, believed that the church had a responsibility to monitor the conduct of its members. Methodists periodically examined the character of delegates to their conferences and of exhorters, licensed preachers, and other officers; those found wanting lost their place or failed to have their licenses renewed. New members generally were admitted "on trial" before gaining acceptance into "full communion." The Baptists likewise supervised the behavior of their communicants in virtually any area of personal or business life. Baptist churches, each acting independently as an autonomous body, appointed committees of their members to investigate rumors or charges of sinful behavior. Called into the presence of the congregation, a wrongdoer had to hear the committee's report and answer to the membership, on pain of expulsion.[46]

The evangelical sought through conversion and faith to enter into a new and holier life, and therefore any signs of falling away from God's path were relevant. The Mount Zion Baptist Church in Alamance County scrutinized a dispute between two members "about some unmarked hogs" as readily as it appointed "a Committee of females . . . to inquire into a Report in circulation against Kisia Wheeler for the sin of fornication." The nearby Mount Olive Baptist Church heard "A report laid in by the Commity [Committee] Against Brother Levi Crutchfield for Drinking two Mutch and Swaring"; it also investigated "A Charg" that "Brother J. F. Cheek . . . was the Father of A [il]legitimate child" and delegated "Brother Alston Smith . . . to see Brother John Edwards for reported absence." Orange County's Mount Herman Baptist Church expelled a number of members in the 1850s for "neglect in attending Church Meetings" as well as for more notorious sins. Similarly, the nine churches in the conference of Lenoir Crescent Methodist Church regularly reported the number of expulsions as well as conversions and heard appeals in which the member under question had to appear in person.[47]

Given the individualism of the ordinary farmer, it was not remarkable that Brother Oliver Foster after being absent "for some time" from Mount Zion Baptist Church defiantly told the investigating committee "that he had as good right to stay away as others." But most church members had committed themselves fervidly to a new way of living and therefore regarded their summons before the congregation as a serious crisis. Kisia Wheeler admitted her fornication and "Requested the church to forgive her." Her repentence resulted in a successful "motion [that] the church forgive her." Similarly an Orange County Baptist "made his confession" of drunkenness and was "forgiven" with a "Serious Charge" from the "Moderator . . . to abstain from even the appearance of that evil." Although Edward Edwards, a Caldwell County Methodist, had been expelled from the church at Lenoir for profanity, his "particular temperament . . . the very vexing cause . . . his great desire to remain . . . and the probability of his doing better in the future" won him a pardon. The first time Alamance County Baptists investigated Sister Anne Kimery for "sinful conduct," she "confessed she had done wrong," sought forgiveness, and remained in fellowship. A year later, however, the congregation excommunicated her "for not Complying with the Requirements of the Church and for sinful Conduct and fornication."[48]

In the eyes of the church faith, zeal, devotion to righteous living, and other spiritual qualities counted, not secular social status. Committees had a duty to investigate according to God's law, and though they might find a rumor to be false, they took stands against wrongdoing no matter what the position of its perpetrator. Some politically influential men belonged to the Lenoir Crescent Methodist Conference, and they found that the rituals of politics could conflict with the requirements of the church. In 1850 the Quarterly Conference resolved that "no member . . . will hereafter support or vote for any candidate for office who shall treat to ardent Spirits"; it judged the distilling of liquor a violation of the "Rule of Discipline." Because treating was virtually obligatory in politics yet forbidden in religion, the politically ambitious Methodist faced a difficult choice. By 1853 the conference had demonstrated the strength of its resolve on three occasions: it found a steward of the church guilty of "treating and allowing treating to be done" and dismissed him from his office; and twice, by increasing majorities, it reaffirmed the church's policy.[49]

Evangelical religion symbolized an alternative, more democratic set of values in a rigid hierarchical social order. Beginning with the Second Great Awakening after 1800, evangelicalism brought "a new sense of worthiness and hope to people at every level of society. . . . Faith and worship instilled a sense of competence and dignity into ordinary people in the South." The thrust of evangelicalism was to democratize religion and make salvation available to all, not just a few elect. One of its tendencies was to breach racial barriers and involve black and white together in worship (a phenomenon which occurred in some of the churches described above). In fact, evangelicalism had a "soaring ambition to unite and relate all individual experiences in ways which blur and obscure the larger society with its resistant substrata of habit and injustice." Another tendency of evangelicalism was to lead people to renounce the "temptations . . . vain amusements . . . and the allurements of the world"; indeed it sometimes denounced wealth, power, and prestige as worldly vanities unimportant before God. More explicitly than any other source, evangelical Christianity proclaimed to antebellum Southerners "that wisdom and authority and fame belonged to people equally and could be appropriated and celebrated by anyone with the gumption and virtue to do so."[50]

This faith was a powerful element in North Carolina (and southern) culture. It worked against and moderated the aristocratic tendencies in the social order. To the extent that it reached people at all levels of society, it tended to blur the line between aristocracy and democracy, hierarchy and equality. In this way it rendered society a more ambiguous and complex whole. But evangelicalism had not united all levels of society or created a uniform consciousness. The social order remained highly divergent and stratified, and therefore the functional significance of evangelicalism lay in its strengthening of democratic values.

At some times and in some circumstances white North Carolinians felt almost no class tension or separation, but the potential for such awareness was strong. As the decade of the 1850s progressed, a series of events drew attention to class issues and aroused both resentment among the poor and fear among the elite. Questions of suffrage and taxation became prominent in politics, and as people debated free suffrage and ad valorem taxation of slave property, they stimulated a consciousness that perceived class issues in the decision about secession. The 1850s set the stage for the class tension and conflict that became prominent in the 1860s.

David S. Reid injected class issues into state politics in 1848 when he was the Democratic candidate for governor. In a debate with the Whig candidate, Charles Manly, Reid "exploded the free suffrage bombshell" by calling for abolition of the fifty acre property requirement for voting for state senator. Reid was opposed to this undemocratic restriction on principle, but "many of the leading Democrats had serious reservations" and "aristocratic eastern leaders acquiesced . . . [only] in the hope that it would end the long period of party defeat." Caught by surprise, Charles Manly declared his opposition to free suffrage, and Democratic editor William Woods Holden quickly and skillfully began to portray the Whigs as selfish aristocrats. Holden's newspaper, the *North Carolina Standard* declared to "the honest yeomanry of North Carolina" that the Whigs "were opposed to popular rights" whereas the Democrats were "always the friends of the people and on the side of equal rights." The "free suffrage" issue proved "popular with the masses," and although Manly squeaked by with a majority of fewer than a thousand votes, the Democratic party had found new vigor in the issue.[51]

Thereafter class issues remained prominent in politics although the stands of parties became less clear-cut. Reid backed free suffrage strongly again in 1850 while the Whigs showed more respect for the power of democratic appeals. They tried to satisfy western reformers in their party by declaring their willingness to abide by a popular referendum not only on suffrage restrictions but also on the election of judges and local officials as well. Reid's unambiguous stand helped him to win, but perhaps not as much as Holden's simultaneous appeal to conservative eastern planters. The Democratic editor charged that Manly was "betraying eastern interests by supporting a change in the basis of legislative apportionment from property to white population." Voting results showed that the Democrats benefited most in 1850 from their tactic of "pandering to reactionary eastern slaveholders." Both parties thereafter displayed "progressive western and conservative eastern blocs"; indeed the strongest call for democratization of North Carolina's system of government came in "An Address to the People . . . on the Subject of Constitutional Reform" which was issued in 1851 by thirty-seven legislators. All of them were from the west, and all but one were Whigs.[52]

Meanwhile the undemocratic character of North Carolina's constitutional system kept free suffrage from becoming a reality for several years. A cumbersome procedure for amendments required two successive three-fifths majorities in the legislature before a referendum could be held, and not until 1856 did the necessary continuity of support occur. By a vote of 50,007 to 19,397 the voters approved free suffrage in 1857, thus showing the strength of popular support for democratic change. Free suffrage had won "the largest majority on any political issue in North Carolina up to that time," but there was considerable opposition "in the eastern Democratic slaveholding counties" and among some eastern Whigs as well.[53]

No sooner had the suffrage issue been laid to rest than a clamor for higher taxation of slave property arose. Under the 1835 Constitution an equal capitation tax had to be laid both on free males of ages twenty-one through forty-four and on all slaves between the ages of twelve and fifty (whose owners would pay the levy). But the constitution gave slave-owners considerable protection. Younger and older slaves escaped taxation, and because the tax was a flat rate, it did not reflect any increase in the value of a slave. Moreover, the requirement that the capitation be equal for free men and slaves shielded slaveholders from heavy taxes on their slaves because "the nonslaveholding majority could raise the tax on slaves only by raising the tax on itself."[54] With class issues present in state politics, the state debt increasing, and the value of slaves rising steeply in the 1850s, proposals for ad valorem taxation of slaves soon became a major issue.

During the 1858–59 legislative session reformers urged ad valorem taxation. Though they did not succeed, support for the measure grew and began to cross party and even sectional lines. "A coalition of nonslaveholders and small slaveholders along with a group of progressive planters" began to form, and in 1859 this coalition captured a dominant place in the new Opposition party, which formed from the remains of the Whigs and Know-Nothings. Mechanics, artisans, day-laborers and some professionals formed a Wake County Working Men's Association to push the cause of ad valorem taxation, and in 1860 reformers in the Opposition party overcame the wishes of easterners and nominated John Pool for governor. Although Pool was a wealthy planter from eastern Pasquotank County, he vigorously supported ad valorem.[55]

Class feeling increased to an extent that alarmed many conservatives. Jonathan Worth was a fundamentally conservative member of the elite, but years of living in Randolph County had reconciled him to the necessity of adjusting to demands of the nonslaveholding majority. "Policy even more than justice" required a change in the tax system, he wrote, for, "Should slave owners insist on preserving this portion of our constitution, I think they will array against them a feeling among ourselves, more to be dreaded than Northern Abolitionism."[56] Daniel Barringer, prominent in politics since the 1830s, wrote Thomas Ruffin about his concern over where the agitation for higher taxes on slaves would lead. "One thing is certain," Barringer commented: in light of the sectional crisis over slavery "it will require all the prudence and wisdom we can command to give it a . . . safe direction."[57] Similarly, Kenneth Rayner, a Whig planter from Hertford County, wrote Ruffin about his fears that

> There will be a desperate effort made to *revolutionize* the state, upon the *ad valorem* principle of taxation. The attempt will be made to carry it in the West, by getting up a furor against the *negroes* in the East. In the East, it is to be urged on the ground of its being a *poor man's* law. Much as I dislike the word, you may rely on it we are in a *crisis* . . . [L]et the conservative men without reference to *past* issues confer together for the purpose of preserving the State.[58]

The crisis grew, however, with class issues ringing out loudly throughout the gubernatorial campaign. To oppose Pool the Democrats nominated their incumbent, Governor John W. Ellis, and defeated William W.

Holden's attempt to get the party to endorse ad valorem. While the Opposition made ad valorem the major issue, urging a change to "equal" taxation, the Democrats opposed any change in the way slaves were taxed. Because the class issue was hurting them, however, the Democrats invented a confusing and effective countercharge. Ad valorem taxes, Democrats cried, would result in a tax on every piece of property down to the poor man's "tin cups." Did yeomen, Ellis asked, want the poor man's necessities taxed on the same basis as the rich man's luxuries? Did they want the "family bible" and the farmer's "road wagon" taxed like the "gambler's cards" and the rich man's "pleasure wagon?"[59]

The "tin cups" strategy and a stress on the dangers of Abolitionism enabled the Democratic party to hold its lines and win by a greatly reduced margin. But the Opposition had made impressive gains and reinforced the prominence of class issues. "Besides identifying slavery as oppressive to the laboring class, the Opposition branded the institution as the main prop of the 'aristocratic' Democratic party."[60] Class concerns would not go away, and neither would the issue of ad valorem taxation.

Ultimately the implications of secession compelled conservatives to yield on taxation. Secession, opposed by a large majority of North Carolinians until the last minute (see chapter 2), raised too clearly the possibility of denunciations of a "rich man's war"; some gesture was needed to unite white North Carolinians of all classes, rich and poor. As W. S. Pettigrew, a planter who served in the secession convention, wrote to his brother, reform was desirable "as it will have a tendency to unite our people—the nonslaveholders—more closely with us in this contest with the north for our very existence." Accordingly in 1861 the secession convention passed a version of ad valorem, yet even this law was cleverly worded. It stipulated that the tax on slaves could not exceed the tax on land; the poll tax, moreover, was tied to the land tax. Thus the tax on slaves could not be increased without raising the poll and land taxes. The elite again had protected itself against the possibility that poorer citizens would run the tax on slaves too high.[61]

The 1850s had brought the issue of white political equality into politics. The majority—unorganized, unaccustomed to challenging power, and without leaders of their own—had nevertheless spoken in a loud voice. Their full-throated support for free suffrage and growing demand for ad valorem taxation demonstrated their hearty self-respect, if not their readiness to compete more strenuously against privileged groups. The gentry had displayed skill and a determination to thwart democratic principles. Though divided into rival political parties, members of the elite proved alert to threats to their position and reacted to them with sophistication.

Both the interest in democratization and the implacable opposition to it continued throughout the next fifty years as these two forces became major themes in the life of the state. The impulse toward democracy struggled to take form and achieve self-conscious direction; the defense of undemocratic privilege adopted more extreme measures in the face of internal pressure and external shocks. Both forces remained prominent in politics. Part of the reason for their salience in the 1860s was internal— aristocracy and democracy had coexisted uneasily within antebellum North Carolina, creating the potential for an "irrepressible conflict" within.[62] And part of their prominence derived from the divisive effects of a devastating and unpopular war. For the Civil War, when it came to North Carolina, greatly intensified both subjective feelings about injustice and objective differences between the lives of rich and poor.

AN UNPOPULAR WAR
AND POVERTY

The experience of the Civil War varied widely for North Carolinians. Most soldiers on the front lines—lonely, hungry, and face-to-face with death—found less excitement and glory in the war than did the ardent secessionists and southern patriots who could follow events from the safety of their homes. These partisans of the South were themselves worlds apart from the many highly placed North Carolinians who found the war a disaster and came to damn Jefferson Davis and the "Destructives" who supported his policies. Slaves watched expectantly for the end of bondage and the arrival of freedom; tens of thousands of white citizens struggled literally to survive. There even were isolated individuals so absorbed in their personal concerns that they barely noticed the war: an evangelical Methodist named John Frederick Mallett recorded desperate struggles with "my own wicked heart of unbelief and sin" in a wartime journal that scarcely mentions the war.[1]

But for North Carolinians in general the Civil War was a time of tremendous upheaval, a sequence of events that turned their world upside down. After entering the Confederacy with great reluctance and deep misgivings, North Carolina became a mainstay of the cause as accidents of geography and troop movements caused the Confederate government to demand from it constantly increasing support. As their burdens increased, citizens grew more critical and discontented until major opposition flourished in the state. Serious discontent was evident in politics but perhaps even more in violent resistance to wartime policies and laws. The war aggravated class conflicts, propagated bitter political and social dissension, and took a huge toll in human lives and suffering. By 1864 or 1865 it appeared that the most profound longings of the slaves were to be satis-

fied, but the hopes and dreams of most whites—rich and poor, pro-Confederate or pro-Union—were shattered. The war damaged North Carolina's society and left many white citizens ill-prepared either to forget the
grievances of the past or take up the challenges of the future.

On the eve of the conflict North Carolina had a few fiery secessionists,
but the overall political climate was remarkable for its pro-Union sentiment. Like the rest of the upper South, North Carolina had participated
comparatively little in the cotton boom of the Gulf states, and it had many
ties to the northern economy and to the Union. Moreover, the persistence
of two-party competition in the state reduced some of the anxiety that led
to radical measures; in one-party states of the deep South, defeat of the
Democrats might seem calamitous because the South's fate seemed to
depend on that party, but Tar Heels knew from experience that parties and
policies could change with every election.[2] Thus they approached the
issues of the 1860 election with concern but not with panic.

Former governor Charles Manly was enraged by the attack on Harper's
Ferry—"I want to knock down a John Browner so bad I *dunno* what to
do," he said—but not because he felt a hostile North was threatening the
South. To Manly the enemy was "Fanatics" on both sides, and he believed
that, "The People will save [the Country.] It can't be possible that the
Advocates of Treason, murder and stealing can overturn and destroy this
great Confederacy [the United States]." The Democrat Rufus Lenoir Patterson similarly fumed that, "If this Union *is* dissolved—that man Yancey
[William L. Yancey of Alabama] will be the cause of it." Fire-eating secessionists like Yancey were pursuing "ulterior objects in which the *citizens of
N.C. cannot be interested*," and the South's grievance about the territories
he viewed as a "miserable abstraction." In Patterson's opinion, "The monstrous absurdity about our rights being taken away in the territories etc.
being sufficient cause for breaking up the best government in the world
cannot deceive those who are really patriots." With a similar dose of realism Jonathan Worth declared that, "If he [Lincoln] should pledge himself
to execute the Fugitive Slave Law, and do it, I care nothing about the
question as to Squatter Sovereignty." And with analytical insight Worth
pointed out that southern theories of nullification would also logically
support northern nullification of the fugitive slave law; under such a
theory "there is virtually no Union to dissolve."[3]

"The election of 1860," notes a major text, "showed that the overwhelming majority of North Carolina citizens were unionist—opposed to
secession."[4] Although John C. Breckinridge won a narrow majority, he

had been regarded "as the nominee of the regular official democratic party," and his supporters had staunchly denied that he favored disunion.[5] Many votes for Breckinridge were as unionist as all of those cast for his opponents, John Bell and Stephen A. Douglas. The electoral victory of Abraham Lincoln caused some, like Paul Cameron, to become "very anxious . . . [because] the 'Black Republicans' will get the Government into their hands!"[6] But most voters undoubtedly agreed with Rufus Lenoir Patterson, who declared, "I am unwilling to see our country ruined because a Bl'k Rep. President is elected . . . I am for giving him *a trial*." Even W. W. Holden, whose intemperate editorials had demanded southern rights, began to reverse his position as he considered what Patterson called "the anarchy, confusion, strife and desolation of civil war."[7]

The reality of secession by other southern states dismayed North Carolinians. "Our country is destroyed forever!" moaned Charles Manly. "This great nation which yesterday was the glory of its citizens and the admiration of the world has in 90 days sunk down to ruin and contempt by the machinations of the Devil and Bankrupt Politicians." "I try to keep myself employed," wrote Paul Cameron, "but I find my mind nearly all the time occupied with the State of the Country and it makes me very unhappy. I love the Union." Jonathan Worth even opposed the calling of a convention to consider the crisis or secession, and on 28 February 1861, a majority of the state's voters agreed with him.[8] They refused to hold a convention because it might lead to secession. Judge Thomas Ruffin, former Governor John M. Morehead, and others attended the Peace Conference called by Virginia and supported several proposed amendments to the Constitution; these sought to divide gains on contested issues evenly between proslavery and antislavery forces in order to save the Union. B. F. Moore, an experienced political leader, felt the state's voters would approve all the amendments by a majority of six to one.[9]

Social and class fears were present in North Carolina, as they had been in states that seceded earlier. After a tour of Hertford, Bertie, and Gates counties Kenneth Rayner was appalled at "the mischief done last summer by the advocates of 'ad-valorem.' . . . The people who did not own slaves were swearing that they 'would not lift a finger to protect rich men's negroes.'" And Matthias Manly believed that slaveowners had to "take [their] stand" or face the imminent "necessity . . . of *running away from their slaves*." But for most of the elite, the dangers of staying in the Union still seemed less than those that would follow secession. "Slavery is doomed if the South sets up a Southern Confederacy," concluded Jonathan Worth. He reasoned that the Confederacy's northern border would immediately acquire the attractiveness of Canada and that runaway slaves would stream into the North. With that situation and with "all hating us, it is madness to think of anything else only to cut the throats of the negroes or have our own throats cut."[10]

Nevertheless, the war began, and North Carolinians had to choose which side to support. As Southerners most whites chose the South without hesitation. "We are all one now," declared a converted unionist, and North Carolina quickly assembled a convention that severed its ties with the United States. Zebulon B. Vance wrote that although he had been pleading for the Union with upraised hand, when news of Fort Sumter arrived his hand fell "slowly and sadly by the side of a Secessionist."[11]

The sadness Vance felt was remarkably widespread; it was also a remarkably clairvoyant feature of North Carolina's commitment to the Confederacy. From the top of society to the bottom people mourned the fate of the Union. Jonathan Worth regarded "the dissolution of the Union as the greatest misfortune which could befall the whole nation and the whole human race," and John F. Flintoff bemoaned the fact that "the Union . . . is cut asunder . . . we are lamentably in war," a "war with our Northern friends."[12] Many had no illusions about the future. Charles Manly felt that no government reconstituted from the Union would "be worth a Button." "No other divided government," wrote Jonathan Worth, "can ever be built up so good as the United one we are pulling down." "I think the South is committing suicide, but my lot is cast with the South." Rufus Lenoir Patterson knew that, "Dissolution is a remedy for no evil—it will bring ten thousand evils where we now have one." And John Flintoff, who had less to lose, may have felt the possibility of loss more acutely. "My prospects in life [are] to all human appearances broken up," he lamented, and he prayed to God for strength to bear the fact that he would not obtain "what I have worked, prayed yea longed for"—prosperity and peace.[13]

Flintoff's gloomy predictions were correct, for the war blasted the prospects of many North Carolinians. From Fort Sumter to Appomattox, most of the state remained inside Confederate lines, and as the Confederacy lost territory on its periphery, it had to rely more heavily on the resources of its core. Thus North Carolina, with a large majority of non-slaveholders, furnished far more than its share of soldiers and disproportionate amounts of money, food, equipment, and other needed commodities. Virtually the entire military population served at some point, yet there was another side to the story. It also was true that North Carolina led the South in desertions and signs of disaffection. Forced to make exceptional sacrifices for a cause that had not commanded their enthusiasm, North Carolinians suffered, complained, and eventually resisted. Along with unusual contributions to the cause, the state made exceptional protests.[14]

Almost as soon as Tar Heels had seceded, unity began to fade and political bitterness began to grow. Secessionists ostracized some of their opponents; William Holden lost the state's printing contract and the Fries family stopped speaking to Rufus Lenoir Patterson. "I have never known such bitterness as they can cherish in this place" [Salem!], wrote Patterson's wife. "If you dare differ with certain persons in politics, . . . they take it as a personal insult and grow cold."[15] The division between secessionists and former unionists deepened as parties formed. Secessionists organized a largely Democratic "Confederate" party, whereas old Whigs and Democrats who had clung to the Union until the last possible moment coalesced as "Conservatives." Initially these parties argued over Jefferson Davis's appointments, each side feeling that Davis had overlooked the deserving and neglected North Carolina. As the policies of the Richmond administration stiffened, becoming more controversial and onerous, this original split developed into a profound difference of perspective between Conservatives and the Confederates, whom the former called "Destructives." The Conservatives recoiled from the unexpected measures of the Davis government and saw the willingness of prosecession Destructives to accept Confederate policies as another sign of their recklessness and disregard of the public good.[16]

As it happened, the war brought a succession of unpopular, hotly debated Confederate policies. Jefferson Davis became a resolute nationalist, convinced of the need to use all powers of the central government and determined to prosecute the war in an efficient, unified manner. To achieve these ends he took strong steps—insisting on central control of the army, initiating conscription, and calling for the suspension of habeas corpus, the imposition of martial law, higher taxes, impressment of slaves and supplies, a tax-in-kind, control of shipping and transportation, and many other measures. These policies shocked the principles of states' rights advocates and revolutionized the relationship of Southerners to their national government. Never before had a central authority reached so deep into southern society or affected so directly the daily lives of its citizens. Along with rampant inflation, blockade-induced shortages, and the chaos, destruction, and reverses of war, these policies made the Confederacy a shockingly untraditional, unsouthern experience.[17]

At first, of course, many prewar social patterns retained their prominence. When the Alamance Regulators organized to defend the South after Fort Sumter, men from the wealthiest and most influential families won all four officers' positions. In time military skill began to take precedence over social position, but the old, entrenched local hierarchy remained in place in April 1861.[18] So, too, did the power of the network of local notables. Men who wanted a transfer or sought special treatment for a relative contacted influential figures like Samuel Finley Patterson in Caldwell County or Thomas Ruffin in Alamance.[19] Throughout the war poorer men were wise to ask such persons to intercede for a son who "left [the army] in a mad fit unthauted of the consequence" or for a soldier whose family needed him home on furlough or detail. Thomas Ruffin, Jr. even asked his father to look in on the mother of a dead soldier who had "always been so respectful towards me, and so ready to be advised by me."[20]

But unsettling change and disillusioning reverses came quickly. In August 1861, U.S. forces captured the outer banks, and invasion of parts of eastern North Carolina soon began. Throughout the rest of the war federal troops held coastal areas including New Bern, Fort Macon, and much of the sound region from which they launched periodic raids inland. The reality of war made its presence felt to Tar Heels at an early date and deepened thereafter.[21]

Early in 1862 enthusiasm had fled from one of the most highly placed Tar Heels, Thomas Bragg, who was Jefferson Davis's attorney general. "Dangers surround us," he wrote in his diary, and with heavy irony he noted that, "The permanent Gov't. so called, (pardon the expression whoever may chance to see it) is being organized. . . . It will be a singular coincidence if our rapid fall shall date from the expiration of the 'Provisional Government.' Yet for aught that I can see it will be so." On 20 February 1862 Bragg soberly concluded that "our cause is hopeless." Nor was his pessimism exceptional. He noted "much discontent . . . in No. Ca." and heard of "general panic" along with "a good deal of disloyalty." "Our people seem to have lost the spirit which animated them in the outset of the contest," wrote Bragg, and Walter F. Leak, a member of the state's secession convention, expressed fears "that our people will not bear a draft for the war or 3 years to fill up the quota of troops required."[22]

In October 1862, newly elected Governor Zeb Vance informed Jeffer-

Zebulon B. Vance

son Davis that "the original advocates of secession no longer hold the ear of the people" and that, despite "all the popularity with which I came into office, it will be exceedingly difficult for me to execute" the conscript law. Vance wasted no time in expressing some of the strong dissatisfaction in the state. He declared his unalterable opposition to suspension of habeas corpus and protested the conscription of any justice of the peace, constable, or town police officer. Writing to Weldon N. Edwards, president of the convention (which had not yet permanently adjourned), he urged action to control "extortion and speculation" which had produced "the enormous prices at which provisions are selling." "The cry of distress comes up from the poor wives and children of our soldiers . . . from all parts of the State," wrote Vance. Soon he was petitioning Jefferson Davis for special exemptions from conscription or for furloughs to allow troops to return to their farms. Conscription had taken "a large class," Vance argued, "whose labor was . . . absolutely necessary to the existence of the women and children left behind."[23]

Inequities in the war effort became a source of strong complaint. As conditions deteriorated, yeomen families and the poor began to suffer well in advance of the rich, and they often felt that they were making a larger contribution. When the Confederate Congress voted slaveowners or overseers of twenty Negroes an exemption from the army, the outcry was so loud that even the state's general assembly protested this "unjust discrimination." Yet, this legislative resolution had no effect on the social and political hierarchy within North Carolina. Given the aristocratic structure of local government, the wealthy and influential had superior opportunities to obtain exemptions or safe, "bomb-proof" assignments. Eventually Zeb Vance exempted more than 14,675 state employees from Confederate service, and most of these fortunate individuals probably had above-average connections. In April 1863, a patriotic planter serving in the army put it bluntly: "The young men of wealth in our State have shown entirely too much reluctance to going into the field. Look around and see how few of those of your acquaintance are facing danger and enduring privations."[24]

Yet, members of the elite felt that they had many just complaints, too. Catherine Devereux Edmondston, the wife of an eastern planter, had been belligerently prosecession. Nevertheless, she became totally hostile to Confederate seizures of cotton and was convinced that her husband was too old and delicate to benefit the army. Many political leaders could not adjust themselves to the "despotic conduct" of the Richmond government and fought on principle against all the measures that were turning the country, as they saw it, into "a great military despotism."[25] Some bills they considered unwise had even become law in North Carolina.

To members of the gentry, one of the worst acts of the legislature was the "stay law," a legal moratorium on the payment of debts. In every state of the Confederacy wartime legislatures passed such bills in response to the ground swell of support from ordinary citizens, whose earnings potential was deeply affected by the war. But to some of North Carolina's conservative leaders, a stay law contravened basic principles on which society was built. "It disorganizes Civilized society," complained Jonathan Worth. "The Stay law is a revolutionary measure," declared B. F. Moore, "radical, unwise, demoralizing, disgraceful. . . . It is the beginning . . . of continued efforts to discharge all debts."[26]

To men of this mentality, the stay law represented the triumph of "the profligate, the spendthrifts, reckless, insolvents"; it showed that the wrong kind of men had gained some power and influence. The problem, believed Weldon Edwards, was the tendency toward "a numerical majority. Ours is not a Government of majorities—tho' . . . Demagogues . . . are rapidly imbuing the Public Mind with that sentiment." Former governor Manly agreed: "If our Independence were established tomorrow the Confederacy would not last six months. The national debt would be too tempting for Demagogues and repudiation would follow, sure as day. Universal suffrage is the Devil."[27] To the dismay of poorer North Carolinians, the aroused gentry secured repeal of the stay law after only four months. They also beat back subsequent efforts to enact a modified version of the stay law, and as a result thousands of hard-pressed citizens had to fear debt and financial ruin along with war's destruction.[28]

While these controversies swirled about among the civilian population, a large group of disillusioned, dispirited North Carolinians developed in the army. Although the Old North State had its share of valiant, long-suffering heroes who gave their all to the cause and never wavered, it seems clear that most men found service in the army—especially the Confederate army—demoralizing. The son of an Edgecombe County magistrate pressed his father and sister to get together some papers that might win a medical discharge. "I hope soon to get them that I may get out of this miserable Army again and be free once more." One member of an affluent family from New Hanover County wrote that "a soldiers life . . . is the roughest existence possible. . . . No man in this whole army of 40,000 [the Army of Northern Virginia] can say, with truth, that *any* part of his previous life was not preferable to his life here." The soldiers were "half-fed, badly clad, and *almost entirely* barefooted" in the month of January, he noted. A relative of this man advised friends to stay out of the army "if it be possible" for he had "been there long enough to know that it is Hell."[29] Obviously such conditions affected poor men as severely as the rich, and the poor lived also with greater fears for the welfare of their families back home.

Besides bad conditions, the soldiers had to endure the carnage of battle. "Any one who goes over a battlefield after a battle," wrote John Brodnax in 1862, "never cares to go over another. . . . I don't care if I am never near another fight again during the war. It is a sad sight to see the dead and if possible more sad to see the wounded; shot in every possible way you can imagine." Another man stated: "I have heard such sounds, and seen such sights, as to make my flesh almost crawl when I think of them. Such suffering, agonizing and terrible in the extreme, I never had the least idea of before. And the sorrow was not confined to our men merely but to those miserable Yankees who were strewn all around. The woods and roads were alive with dead men, many of them unburied, some of the Yankees only partially buried, one with a head left out of the ground, another the feet sticking out."[30]

If, after the first year, the war offered hope to any group of North Carolinians, it offered it to the slaves. For them the experience of war followed a different emotional curve, one which was depressed at the beginning but rose steadily until the day of Jubilee. Although most had to repress their joy during slavery's last days, some began to enjoy freedom before 1865, and all could share the anticipation of realizing a life-long dream.

On the eve of the conflict, the general assembly dramatically tightened restrictions on black people. To protect the slave system from attack, North Carolina made the circulating of "incendiary" literature and conspiracy to rebel with a slave capital offenses. Slaveowners lost the privilege of freeing any slave in their last will and testament, bounties for capturing runaway slaves were increased, and free blacks were prohibited from any further buying or hiring of slaves (who usually were family members). White citizens felt that the times required such steps, and the wealthy planter W. S. Pettigrew asserted that there had been plans for an insurrection by three hundred slaves in Washington County.[31]

Obviously, with such restrictions in place, slaves had to be circumspect during the early days of the war. But there was no way that all information about the war could be kept from them. "There were stories of fights and freedom," recalled a former slave named Mary Anderson. "The news went from plantation to plantation and while the slaves acted natural and some even more polite than usual, they prayed for freedom." Those in eastern North Carolina had special reasons to hope after the federal invasion occurred. Hundreds were captured from slavery almost immediately, and by July 1862, several thousand more had fled their plantations and crossed over into Union territory.[32]

"The slaves unanimously refuse to be removed [from eastern plantations]," noted a Rowan County attorney named David Schenck. "If it is insisted upon, they flee to the swamps. They are fully aware of the causes of the invasion and know that it involves their freedom. Thousands of them are now said to be roaming in insubordination through the country." E. J. Blount of Pitt County likewise warned Governor Vance that any organized attempt to protect slave property by moving slaves inland would trigger widespread flight. Charles Manly was only one slaveowner who believed that "the best of the negroes" went to the Yankees; Kenneth Rayner reported the flight of "my boy John, that kept my keys and was entrusted with everything." Rayner noted that "A great many negroes have run off in Hertford [County]" and in 1863 asserted that two thousand "tried to slip through [CSA] Gen. Hill's lines, and get off, but were driven back by our soldiers."[33]

What the slaves were running to, of course, was freedom and their first chance to pursue some of freedom's opportunities in federally occupied territory. Several hundred blacks of all ages started attending school in New Bern in 1862. Although Lincoln's military governor, Edward Stanly, ordered this first school closed, educational efforts resumed in 1863 under Horace James, superintendent of Negro affairs. Blacks who poured into New Bern and surrounding areas organized their own churches and institutions; black women even founded "The Colored Ladies Aid Association of North Carolina" to support more than five thousand Negro troops who entered federal service in the state.[34]

Those who were unable to enter Union lines gradually became an increasing problem for their owners. Masters complained of disobedience and restlessness that was especially pronounced in areas close to the Yankees or following federal raids. They complained of the slaves' "laziness" and "willfullness," or said they "simply were not working." Women who had to manage slaves in the absence of their husbands or sons often found the task difficult. Owners who fled from the coastal plain had to make arrangements to move and reemploy their slaves or to keep them working under the supervision of someone who stayed behind. In the latter case some usually ran off, and dislocations often brought about serious inconveniences for the gentry, such as loss of a good cook or house servant. Rumors of insurrection and the behavior even of "loyal" slaves showed whites what slaves thought of the institution of slavery, and some whites expressed intensified racism as a result.[35]

Even more visible, however, was the increasing opposition to the war. Because Vance had been a Unionist and was a Conservative along with others who opposed the Destructives, secessionists viewed his election, with some justice, "as counter-revolutionary in its tendency."[36] Soon after Vance's triumph the legislature sent another Conservative, former Whig William A. Graham, to the Confederate Senate in place of the secessionist George Davis. Kenneth Rayner complained that Davis had lost his seat because he was "a true and warm Southern-rights man"; Rayner believed that the Conservatives intended to claim that they were the first to favor reconstruction, if disasters sank the Confederacy. Meanwhile Holden's *North Carolina Standard*, according to Thomas Bragg, was "doing what it can to break down the Adm'n and to create discontent—the fellow is opening the way for submission and the ascendancy of the former Union men, as he is denouncing the makers of the War, the original secessionists."[37]

The *Standard* did not have to "create" discontent, however; such feelings were widespread, strong, and growing. North Carolinians were suffering severely from the conflict. Jonathan Worth reported in January 1863 that many people seemed "on the verge of starvation. Nearly every man I saw . . . is openly for re-construction on the basis of the Constitution of the U.S., if these terms can be obtained." Soldiers wrote strong letters to Governor Vance expressing their problems and resentments. A volunteer named O. Goddin stressed that he had "left a wife with four children . . . [and] made the sacrifices thinking that the Govt. would protect his family and keep them from starvation." Instead the government had favored slaveowners with the notorious "twenty nigger law" and had allowed prosperous men to furnish substitutes. "Healthy and active men who have furnished substitutes are grinding the poor by speculation [raising the prices of necessities] while their substitutes have been discharged after a month's service as being too old or as invalids." Private Goddin put the issue bluntly:

Now Govr. do tell me how we poor soldiers who are fighting for the "rich mans negro" can support our families at [pay of] $11 per month? How can the poor live? I dread to see summer as I am fearful there will be much suffering and probably many deaths from starvation. They are suffering now. . . .

I am fearful we will have a revolution unless something is done as the majority of our soldiers are poor men with families who say they are tired of the rich mans war & poor mans fight, they wish to get to their families & fully believe some settlement could be made were it not that our authorities have made up their minds to prosecute the war regardless of all suffering. . . . A mans first duty is to provide for his own household the soldiers wont be imposed upon much longer.[38]

Many soldiers and citizens had reached their limit. Brigadier General W. D. Pender complained in April 1863, of "the state of affairs that exists in the North Carolina regiments of the army." Large numbers of men were deserting and Pender feared "the matter will grow from bad to worse." Letters from home "are received by the men, urging them to leave"; in addition a recent decision of North Carolina Chief Justice Richmond Pearson against the conscript law had convinced men that the law was unconstitutional and unenforceable in the state. "Conscripts and deserters go unmolested in Yadkin County," said Pender, and the same was true elsewhere. The tendency to evade conscription, resist impressment, or refuse to pay taxes grew. Even the aspiring slaveholder John F. Flintoff condemned "this blood[y] and cruel war" with its tax-in-kind and "very heavy" money taxes. Instead of submitting to conscription he hired an older substitute. Although Flintoff was healthy and only forty, he declared himself "almost broken hearted" when the government finally ended substitution and required all men eligible for the draft to serve. "What injustice," he cried with unintentional irony, "hav[ing] to go myself after hiring a substitute over 50 years old. This is very hard and unjust."[39]

Some of those who resisted the war began to organize. In 1861 a secret order known as the Heroes of America (HOA) formed to oppose the Confederacy. Its activities required the dispatch of hundreds of troops to the "Quaker-belt" counties of Randolph, Davidson, Forsyth, and Guilford in 1861 and 1862, and late in 1863 its influence began to spread beyond the piedmont. The HOA protected and aided draft resisters and deserters and occasionally cooperated with U.S. forces. Working actively though behind the scenes in politics, the HOA achieved the election of some of its own members and other propeace candidates. Ultimately it "counted perhaps 10,000 members in North Carolina and . . . played an active part not only in resisting the Confederacy but also in wartime and Reconstruction politics in the state."[40]

Far more openly William Holden began to organize political pressure for peace. Vowing to "tell [the people] the truth as far as we know it," Holden's *North Carolina Standard* came out for peace in the summer of 1863. Declaring that, "What the great mass of our people desire is a cessation of hostilities, and negotiations," the paper presented some unpleasant but persuasive facts. "The enemy has slowly but surely gained upon us. . . . We have lost Missouri, Maryland, Kentucky, Tennessee, the Mississippi Valley, Texas, Louisiana, Arkansas, and considerable portions of other states. . . . We cannot hope to add materially to our forces. . . . Our enemies . . . have a large army in the field, and their President has just called for three hundred thousand more. He will get them. . . . It is time to consult reason and common sense."

Holden believed that if negotiations were to begin, "the conflict of arms would not be renewed, and . . . *some* settlement would be effected." He reminded the people *"that they are sovereign*—that they are the masters of those who administer the government— . . . and they must not be afraid to utter their opinions freely and boldly. If they want continued, wasting, bloody war, let them say so; if they want peace, let them say so." The *Standard* then endorsed a letter writer's suggestion that the voters choose congressmen who would work for the appointment of commissioners to meet with "'others on the part of Lincoln, to make an honest effort to stay the effusion of blood by an honorable adjustment.'" To deflect criticism Holden claimed that if the North rejected peace, "desperation would then nerve every Southern arm. . . . But . . . it may do much good, and can do no harm to talk—to negotiate." The *Raleigh Daily Progress* also declared itself in favor of "any peace that is honorable . . . because we believe that peace now would save slavery . . . [and] because there has been enough of blood and carnage."[41]

In response to the *Standard's* call, peace meetings were held throughout North Carolina. Within eight weeks one hundred meetings took place and produced numerous resolutions. In Guilford County, for example, citizens met in August 1863 and drew up a protest against the Confederacy's treatment of North Carolina, the "unjust and tyrannical" tax-in-kind, and the continuing heavy demand for conscripts. Then they declared "that we

are in favor of a Peace Convention . . . [and] an immediate armistice. . . .
In our opinion . . . the best thing the people of North Carolina can do, is
go for the principles of Washington, Jefferson, Madison, Monroe, Jackson
etc., and for the Constitution as it is."[42] Although Holden spoke of "negotiations with a view to separation," he also declared that the state
should stand by the Confederacy only "as long as it is to the interest of
North Carolina to do so, and no longer."[43]

The fall elections showed how popular the idea of a negotiated peace
was with the people. Eight of the state's ten elected congressmen opposed
the administration; only one Democrat gained a seat; no original secessionist triumphed; and five of the winning candidates had run on a peace
platform. The message was so clear that on 30 December 1863, Governor
Vance wrote a frank letter to Jefferson Davis. Discontent had advanced so
far, Vance argued, "that it will be perhaps impossible to remove it, except
by making some effort at negotiations with the enemy." Urging the president to make a peace initiative, Vance tried to convince him that even an
unsuccessful attempt might unite southerners and would demonstrate to
"the humblest of our citizens . . . that the government is tender of their
lives and happiness, and would not prolong their sufferings unnecessarily
one moment."[44]

Zeb Vance knew that he had reached a crossroads. With a friend he
shared his belief that Holden sought "to call a convention in May [1864]
to take N.C. back to the United States." Vance then decided, reluctantly
and almost despairingly, to break with the editor and "a large number of
my political friends. . . . I can never consent to [Holden's] course . . . it
would steep the name of North Carolina in infamy." Yet Vance believed
that Holden correctly read the heart of the people. Independence would
require more "blood and misery, . . . *and our people will not pay this
price.* . . . I am convinced of it." Even after later events confirmed for
Vance that "the great *popular heart* is not now & never has been in this
war," he still believed that "duty" required him to stand by the
Confederacy.[45]

Other experienced politicians agreed that the people hungered for
peace. The fact that the Confederacy had no two-party system inhibited
opposition; supporters of the government could denounce the peace men
as "disloyal—and for this reason many who concur [in Holden's views]
have not the moral courage to avow their sentiments." Still, Jonathan
Worth was "sure [that] . . . a majority of the people of North Carolina"
supported Holden, and he drafted a petition calling for a state conven-

tion. In Worth's part of the piedmont, he believed, "*at least two-thirds* of the people . . . concur [with Holden] . . . with this difference[,] that they go much farther . . . than he does."[46]

Conservatives like Worth, John Pool, and Alfred Dockery believed the South could obtain liberal terms through voluntary reconstruction, but they also may have hoped for peace because they feared the growing potential for social revolution. Attorney David Schenck was alarmed that the rank and file of the convention movement was "the lowest population of the country—contemptible either by their ignorance, or generally by their vicious character, such men as never dared speak in times of peace." The legislator Andrew C. Cowles also believed it was vital to keep lower-class whites from gaining control of the peace movement. "Many foolish and bad men," he warned, "are assembling at Still Houses under the plea of peace meetings and organizing . . . with the avowed purpose of resisting 'with Arms' the laws of the state . . . and with a secret purpose of committing such depradations upon the property of their neighbors as their necessities or malignity may suggest." Such men had to be "loped off" from the peace movement, said Cowles, and he advocated "striking down . . . every ignorant and malicious upstart who assumes the leadership even of a district squad."[47]

For his part Holden encouraged all peace sentiment and decided to build a gubernatorial campaign upon it. "It was not my wish to run for Governor," Holden wrote to Calvin Cowles, but he explained that he did so after friends appealed to him and Vance went over to the Destructives. Holden had perceived the fundamental decision that caused Vance so much agony. "It is my opinion," said Holden, "that Gov. Vance had made up his mind deliberately to go with Davis and the Destructives ever since his visit to Richmond last August." In subsequent months "his appointments . . . have all been Destructives," and Holden also felt that Vance had failed "to stand by the civil law" and against military usurpations.[48]

Holden's decision was a mistake. He ignored the personal unpopularity that his shifts in political direction were creating, but, more importantly, he failed to take into account Vance's political acumen and the sage advice offered by the governor's allies. Vance did not have to lash himself to the mast of the sinking Confederate ship and go down nobly to principled defeat. He still had considerable personal influence with Conservatives and truly formidable powers on the stump, where his humorous speeches were already famous.[49] Moreover, John Gilmer pointed out that Vance could use his record to counter Holden's efforts "to identify you with the

ultra and extreme men of the Confederacy." Gilmer urged Vance to publish his December letter to Davis, which favored "national proposals for
peace, & the sparing of the further effusion of blood."[50]

In short, Vance could run as a peace candidate. J. M. Leach, a propeace
congressman, warned Vance not to alienate "the 60 or 70,000 voters . . .
that think as I do." He then argued cogently that negotiations would at
some point precede peace and urged the governor "to see the civil laws
and rights of the Citizen maintained and defended at all hazards." More
positively, another ally declared that: "The hearts of the people are ripe for
peace and any move you may make in that direction will be endorsed by
them and you sustained."[51]

Some advice Vance wisely rejected. Jefferson Davis insisted that negotiations were impossible "until the enemy is beaten out of his vain confidence in our subjugation." Urging Vance not to deal gingerly with "traitors," Davis pressed him to defy rather than conciliate the leaders of the
peace movement. To show his determination Davis again asked congress
to suspend habeas corpus, after which Holden's newspaper suspended
publication. Similarly, an ally in Edgecombe County informed Vance that
many in the plantation districts were not inclined to vote because they saw
"very little difference" between the governor and Holden. To win more
ultra, planter votes, he clearly implied, Vance should take a hard line.[52]

But Vance knew that political realities did not allow the course Davis
recommended, and he accepted John Gilmer's judgment that he could
criticize the original secessionists and still gain their support.[53] After all,
in North Carolina, Vance was the only candidate acceptable to staunch
Confederates who had any chance of winning. Already the state's secessionists and Confederates had had to adopt an uncritical posture toward
the Richmond government that was highly unusual in the South. Elsewhere ultras had been confident of the revolution and eager to guide its
course. They quickly became bitter critics of centralization and excoriated
Jefferson Davis. But in North Carolina secessionists feared for the revolution and knew how fragile the state's support for the Confederacy was. Of
necessity they had supported Davis while Conservatives lambasted the
administration's departures from states' rights.[54]

Thus Vance and his supporters worked to identify the governor with
peace. In the words of one historian, the campaign "tended to make all
voters friends of peace." Branding Holden as "the *war* candidate," Vance
argued that the editor would take North Carolina out of the Confederacy
only to involve her in civil war with her neighbors, "a new war, a bloodier

conflict than that you now deplore." When the legislature assembled in May, Vance called on its members to define fair terms of peace and instruct the state's congressmen to press for peace and independence after the South's next military victory. With overwhelming newspaper support, and aided by his oratorical skills, Vance seized the mantle of peacemaker and defeated Holden, 58,070 to 14,491.[55]

The surprised editor suspected fraud, particularly in the army's ballots, and his crushing defeat was surprising, because even the governor's supporters had discovered broadly based enthusiasm for Holden. For example, B. F. Gaither had been dismayed by the "disloyalty and Holdenism" in Rutherford and McDowell counties and had expected Holden to "carry Burke and Caldwell Counties by large majorities" due to lower-class support: "no one of intelligence and influence [is] for Holden but Tod [Caldwell] and he is not open about it." Even on the eve of the election some of Vance's friends felt that "most persons . . . did not support Vance with any cordiality" and might vote for him "under duress, as it were."[56]

Something like duress was suggested by the stern and propeace letter of a poorly educated soldier to the governor. "This is twice I have voated for you," wrote the soldier, "and if you dont seend out some proclamation now for peace and that soon I will [not] cast one more or I shall want to cast one to put you out of thare and thare is al around hear that will put you out too . . . I want you to make some eforts and see if you cant doo that very thing that Mr. Holden was going to doo." The victory of peace candidates for lower offices also confirmed that North Carolina's weariness with the war had not abated.[57]

Indeed, the soldier who wrote Vance showed unmistakably just how desperate for peace he was. "I understand very well the reason why peace cant be made," he said, "it is on the account of the blacks." Having raised a crucial issue for the South, he declared that he owned some slaves and said that fact in no way lessened his desire for peace. "Before I will stay in this war and fight day and night I will give up the last one . . . If you ware [were] preest down like I am you['d] doo so too or allmost any thing ellce . . . men is suffering death hear anyhow without being shot and then to stand all of this and have to be shot at last—I wont stand it[!]"[58]

Race relations became as prominent in people's minds as peace after Vance's reelection. The war ground on, and it became even more obvious that the Confederacy could not win its independence. Peace was likely to come through defeat, but then what would happen to slavery? Although North Carolina's slaveholders feared emancipation, many had not given up hope of keeping their slaves. Ironically, the fact that Tar Heels had not led the way out of the Union, but had been dragged out, seemed to make them hopeful that they could salvage something from the wreck. They were not conscious of having taken a revolutionary leap; they did not see themselves as traitors to the nation but as loyal citizens forced to endure exile. They reasoned that their discontent in the Confederacy proved their good intentions, and they seemed to feel that surely the North would not hold against them a blunder of others that they would be glad to undo. Thus, the hope that slaveowners might be able to hold onto their slaves never died.

When Jefferson Davis attempted to abolish slavery, he discovered how committed to the institution North Carolinians were. After Lincoln's re-election, Davis concluded that the South faced a choice between defeat with forced emancipation or voluntary emancipation with the possibility of independence. Always for independence, Davis proposed first a government purchase of slaves for use as laborers and then the arming and deployment of slaves as soldiers. The reward for faithful service would be freedom, and Davis also wanted the states to legislate freedom for soldiers' families. These steps, to Davis's mind, would provide the Confederacy with vital manpower that would otherwise fall to the U.S. They also might remove the main barrier to foreign recognition and assistance.[59]

Davis's plan aroused a storm of opposition, and nowhere was there less apparent enthusiasm than in North Carolina. To be sure, a few Tar Heels believed that God was ending slavery to punish southerners' sins, but most prominent men seemed determined to try to keep slavery alive. David L. Swain, president of the University of North Carolina, wrote Vance that Davis's proposal "meets with little favor in this quarter." Swain believed that many legislators would favor reconstruction to alliance with England and France at the cost of abolishing slavery. To Jonathan Worth the president's idea could not appeal to the slaves as much as northern promises and was ridiculous—it "caps the climax of tyranny and non-sense." John Pool worked very actively in the North Carolina Senate to block Davis's plan, and both houses of the general assembly voted, in solid fashion, against Confederate emancipation.[60]

William A. Graham led the opposition in the Confederate Senate and held out hope of great results from the approaching Hampton Roads parley between Confederate commissioners and President Lincoln. The North, Graham believed, would insist on restoration of the Union, but "I am convinced would for that, guarantee slavery as it now exists, and probably make other concessions, including . . . perhaps some compensation." State senator Robert P. Dick also believed that "prudent negotiation and speedy peace may yet postpone the doom of slavery."[61] Obviously these leaders were reluctant to sacrifice for Jefferson Davis what they believed they could secure from Abraham Lincoln.

Contrary to modern misconceptions, Graham and Dick were not acting on illusions. Lincoln was willing to consider the prolongation of slavery, or at least a postponement of its demise. At Hampton Roads, Lincoln restated his view that the Emancipation Proclamation was only a war measure whose postwar effect the courts would have to decide; possibly some or none of the slaves would gain permanent freedom. He also allowed Secretary of State William Seward to suggest that with a speedy reentry into the Union, southern states could defeat the Thirteenth Amendment. Lincoln did not contradict Seward, suggesting only a prospective ratification (which would take effect after five years), and he promised to be liberal on confiscation and to seek a $400 million indemnity for southern slaveholders when slavery was ended.[62]

After the Hampton Roads conference knowledge of Lincoln's views spread among North Carolinians, who even saw through the tactics of Jefferson Davis. The Confederate president, still resolute for independence, urged his nation's commissioners to report to congress "that Lincoln and Seward insisted on abolition and submission." This they refused to do, feeling that, although Lincoln had ruled out independence, the door to further discussions should not be closed. Davis himself then informed congress that the U.S. had refused any terms save "those which the conqueror may grant" and insisted on "unconditional submission . . . coupled with the acceptance of" the Thirteenth Amendment. S. F. Phillips felt that Davis had "contrive[d] a trick of *playing at making peace*" while actually trying to produce events that would make the South "furious for War." Believing that Lincoln would have granted "gradual emancipation," Phillips and other North Carolina congressmen and legislators favored calling a convention. Congressman John A. Gilmer expected the general assembly to convene a convention in May to reenter the Union "in time to vote against the abolition amendment."[63]

Surrender came before May, however, so military events rather than a convention decreed that North Carolina would reenter the Union. The war's end left the state's citizens with many powerful emotions. There was relief that "the fighting part of the war is over," to use John Flintoff's words, but many must have wondered about the peace, "such a peace as it will be." Some, like Rufus Lenoir Patterson, felt relief that slavery was destroyed—"Let it go," Patterson said—but obviously others still hoped to hang onto the institution. Staunch unionists welcomed the return to the United States. "Having always been opposed to the secession movement," wrote Samuel Finley Patterson, "I shall be content with a return to the old government under which *I* never felt I was oppressed."[64]

But there was a great deal of bitterness, too. Conservatives and Confederates had fought each other fiercely—Jonathan Worth, for example, had approved Holden's peace movement because "somebody must breast the storm of Secession hate," and he denounced "this accursed war, and the wicked men, North and South, who inaugurated it." Similarly, Rufus Lenoir Patterson hated "secession and its head and chief" so much that he preferred that Davis and cabinet officer Judah Benjamin "be caught and *hung*." On the other hand, many Confederates shared A. M. McPheeters's view that Holden was a "*bad man—entirely* devoid of principle." The war's destruction had embittered many against the North, none perhaps more so than some white Tar Heel women. More than forty thousand of their sons, brothers, husbands, and fathers had died, more than in any other southern state. After encountering the enemy, Janie Smith wanted "dissolution carried to the heart" of the U.S. and northern "widows and orphans left naked and starving just as ours were left. . . . If ever I see a Yankee woman, I intend to whip her and take the clothes off her back." And Catharine de Rosset Meares of Wilmington found "the sense of captivity, of subjugation . . . so galling that I cannot see how a manly spirit could submit to it. . . . Oh, it is such degradation to see our men yield voluntary submission to these rascally Yankees. Better stand on the last plank and die in the last ditch."[65]

But the greatest source of bitterness was the poverty that had descended on hundreds of thousands of North Carolinians. Even a relatively prosperous, middle-class farmer like John F. Flintoff had suffered greatly from the devastation of the South's economy and the physical destruction of war. Flintoff expressed very common feelings when he wrote in his diary the words, "evrything appears to be dark and gloomy . . . the country the property and money is almost worthless. We are very poor people who were once rich. . . . The South is a wreck. . . . The people have had scarcely bread to supply them till harvest . . . there is very little meat anywhere to be had."[66]

The conditions Flintoff described were not just an end-of-the-war phenomenon. Poverty had engulfed thousands of North Carolina yeomen early in the war and extended its cruel grip to many thousands more thereafter. In terms of social impact and significance, nothing played a larger role during the entire Civil War.[67] North Carolina's ordinary farmers, farm workers, and artisans had always been proud and self-reliant people. Suddenly they were plunged into need and robbed of the ability to provide for themselves. This rapid transformation of their fundamental social situation had a major psychological effect, moving many to fight for the restoration of their previous condition.

The causes of wartime poverty were numerous. The south's meager industrial capacity and the northern blockade soon had a painful impact. "We are getting scarce of almost every article of necessity, from a needle to a scythe blade," wrote one citizen in 1862. As prices rose people denounced speculators and extortioners for alleged profiteering on disappearing commodities. Farming tools especially were in short supply after blacksmiths volunteered or went off to the army as conscripts; in North Carolina's rural society, many districts depended on one or two smiths who alone had the ability to keep tools in repair. Many other artisans—such as millers or tanners—were also sorely missed.[68]

The Confederate government itself made conditions far worse through impressment—the taking of needed supplies and materials by the army. This "harsh, unequal, and odious" practice began in 1861, and after the fall of 1862 the army depended almost totally upon it, despite the fact that government officials knew it was "the sorest test of [the people's] patriotism." Indeed, many North Carolinians regarded impressment officers as "robers" and could not believe that any "orders from [the] Gen'l" justified an orgy of "robing and plundering. . . . We have a bad way of getting a long and if those fellows are allowed to remain here they will ruin our people." Other Confederate troops often destroyed citizens' property, and Governor Vance in exasperation declared: "If God Almighty had yet in store another plague worse than all others which he intended to have let loose on the Egyptians in case Pharoah still hardened his heart, I am sure it must have been a regiment or so of half-armed half-disciplined Confederate cavalry."[69]

The most basic cause of poverty was the loss of laborers essential to many family farms. North Carolina was primarily a yeoman state; most of its white population were nonslaveholders who raised their own food and had no slaves to do that for them. Because 125,000 men and boys served at some point in the war—virtually the entire military population plus some overage and underage males—the war constituted a massive drain on farm labor. "By taking too many men from their farms, [government officials] have not left enough to cultivate the land, thus making a scarcity of provisions," complained one private to Zebulon Vance. The governor agreed and frequently urged Richmond to send men home for planting and harvest and to exempt hard-hit areas of the state from further calls for troops.[70]

Of course natural calamities could occur in time of war as much as at any other time, and bad weather also had a serious impact on crops. In 1862 John Flintoff wrote in his diary, "The wheat crop is very poor . . . the prospect for food looks gloomy." Early in 1863 he exclaimed that "wheat [is] selling at 5 to 6 dollars per bu[shel,] corn 3 to 4[,] meat 60 to 70 cts per lb. . . . The hardest times we have ever seen." Then, to make things worse, the corn came "up very badly"; a spell of "wett" weather preceded "very dry" conditions that made the "land very hard—hardly [can] plow." In 1864 there was "scarcely any rain this winter, winter oats nearly all dead the wheat very thin a poor crop will be made." That summer seventy-seven days of drought caused "the poorest chance for corn I ever saw. . . . I think we can [make only] about ⅓ of a crop of corn the prospect is indeed alarming." The price of corn soared to thirty, then fifty dollars a bushel while wheat kept pace and bacon rose from fifteen cents to ten dollars per pound. For sugar and coffee Flintoff simply recorded the word, "none."[71]

There is no question that thousands, indeed tens of thousands, of Tar Heels went hungry for food. As early as 1862 Walter Gwynn wrote to Thomas Ruffin, "I fear . . . starvation, meal is three dollars per bushel and other *necessaries* of life in like proportion. I have witnessed great distress, among the lower and poorer classes." Citing poor crops Kenneth Rayner agreed that "suffering among the poor . . . is dreadful to contemplate." By 1863 Joseph A. Worth in Fayetteville expressed his alarm "about the chances for people to live much longer if this war continues. . . . If more men are called to the field, . . . many *must* starve." By 1864 "much suffering among the people exists . . . in Chatham county one of the best counties in the state for provisions a great many have not had any meat for months. Clothing is very scarce. People known as the poorer class are almost destitute."[72]

This kind of suffering had profound effects. The sudden and drastic decline in their economic condition shocked yeomen who had always provided for their own needs. Their conditions had become intolerable, and they had lost their social autonomy. This change produced anxiety, desperation, resentment, and determination to do something about the problem. Everywhere poorly educated citizens took up pen and paper and poured out their grievances to Jefferson Davis and Zebulon Vance. Sometimes their letters were apologetic. "Sir, I wish you to pardon me for taxing your patience with this note," wrote one woman to Governor Vance, and a man said, "I Beg to Be Excused a private Soldier a writing to a man of your Rank for I hate to do So." Always their needs were the same: "i wante you . . . and Mr. Davis to . . . send home the poor solgers"; "I have received a letter from home yesterday and [my family] are sufering very much for the want of provisions or money to by with"; "there are many others besides myself who have neither brother, husband, nor Father at home . . . and no slave labor to depend on."[73]

But it was also obvious, even in the apologetic letters, that poorer North Carolinians were aware of their rights and of claims of their loved ones that were superior to national obligations. "Necessity compelled me to [write,]" said one correspondent. "I have to make Some effort for there [their] Relief," declared another. More pointedly two men in Burnsville urged Governor Vance to override the county court, which had dispensed relief money to all soldiers' families instead of "entirely to the destitute. [This] gives a great deal of the money into families such as the Rays and many others that are as you know independent livers." Such injustice needed to be changed and "the money be expended rightly." Before long disproportionate numbers of Tar Heel soldiers were leaving the armies and going home to care for their wives and children. If challenged about their authority to travel, some merely patted their rifles and said, "This is my furlough."[74] The poverty of the masses fed the alarming increases in class resentment, desertion, and resistance to authority.

The local gentry and the county courts were aware of this phenomenon, and under the prodding of wartime circumstances they made unprecedented efforts to extend government aid to the poor. There is no evidence that the counties included free black people in their programs, but they responded in a steadily increasing way to the plight of ordinary whites. Within the first year of the conflict most county courts established one or more purchasing agents, who were responsible for finding and securing food for families of soldiers and for the poor. County expenditures for relief soared beyond inflation; quickly they became the major item in the budget, and other, less pressing programs, including education, lost their funds as the needs of poor relief grew larger.[75]

In Randolph County, for example, John M. Worth was the "County

Commissioner for the Relief of Indigent Soldiers Families." Before November 1863, he reported expenditures of $31,653.53 for the relief of families, but in the fourteen and one-half months that followed he spent the far larger sum of $166,121.70. One purchase of grain cost $50,000; several thousand dollars were spent to acquire scythe blades, cotton cards, and other necessary commodities; and the rest of the money went for monthly distributions of cash. The Caldwell County court likewise raised a special poor tax although the suffering there seemed lighter at first. When "great scarcity of grain and other provisions" appeared, the justices quickly appealed to Governor Vance for help in obtaining food.[76]

The state legislature provided aid when it became obvious that need exceeded the capacity of local government. Three times the legislature voted $1 million for poor relief, $500,000 on another occasion, and finally another $3 million. This infusion of money kept many local programs alive. The state bought grain and meat in eastern counties and sold 17,000 bushels of corn and 125,000 pounds of bacon to local governments in 1863. Between August and November 1864, Orange County, to give one example, received $45,866.85 for the poor, of which $31,464.77 came from the state. After raising their county taxes, the county courts attempted "to borrow any amount of money necessary" and some tried to issue bonds to buy food.[77]

County governments also took the lead in pressing the Confederacy to inaugurate a larger and more effective relief system. As the counties ran out of food and money with which to buy it, the Confederate government started collecting the tax-in-kind, which in five months of 1863 produced $5,189,087.25 worth of food. Soon county courts were petitioning the Richmond authorities, pleading that "crops . . . are unusually short" and that "it is indispensably necessary to purchase . . . corn from the Government." For a time the Confederacy allowed counties to buy back part of the tax-in-kind at reduced rates, but eventually the demands of the armies dried up this source of civilian food. In February 1864, congress empowered the army to seize half of every family's yearly supply of meat. By the end of 1864 Confederate officials were taking "three-fourths of all the surplus corn [in eastern North Carolina] for the . . . Army." Piedmont counties, like Orange, which had six hundred women and eight hundred children younger than eight on relief, could get no provisions locally and sought help from the Confederacy in vain.[78] State aid also disappeared— the state proved unable to provide at least $4 million of the $6.5 million which it had appropriated.[79]

This left an enormous need unmet. The women and children in Orange County, for example, represented 19.7 percent of the adult white women and nearly 35 percent of the white children in that age category. Randolph County's huge expenditures for relief could have purchased corn for 1,258 women and an equal number of children. This figure represented 34.4 percent of the adult white female population, and even a reduction of the estimate on the assumption that some of the money went for purchases of meat leaves a large proportion of relief recipients. Records from the eastern counties of Duplin and Cumberland show that enough corn was purchased to support 666 women and the same number of children and 1,022 women and children respectively. In other words, in Duplin County 32.9 percent of the adult white women were on relief and 40.7 percent in Cumberland. Even if thousands of refugees from the federally occupied coastal counties flooded into Duplin and Cumberland—which would have increased the total population and reduced the percentage on relief—it is obvious that the problem of hunger and poverty was extremely severe.[80]

Overall the counties spent $6 million on poor relief.[81] Despite the rapid depreciation of Confederate money, theirs was an unprecedented response to the problems of the lower classes. Only the enormity of the need, the revolutionary effects of war, and the fact that the poor but individualistic yeomen soldiers would not fight if their families were neglected can explain this level of activity from generally unresponsive, aristocratic governments. Breaking sharply with traditional practices, the county courts had tried to assist the nonslaveholders on whom the Confederacy depended and to meet desperate human needs.

If it is clear that the counties tried, however, it is equally clear that they and the state and national governments failed. Effective taxes remained regressive: in 1863 small farmers were paying far more in the tenth of their crops required by the tax-in-kind than highly paid individuals were assessed through the income tax; and the exemption from taxation of first $300, then $500, and finally $1,000 of an individual's estate never kept up with the Confederacy's inflation rate of nearly 7,000 percent.[82] Moreover, the government simply did not obtain enough food for the poor. The destruction and dislocation of war were too great, and the needs of the army took too high a priority relative to civilian needs.

But relief for the poor was inadequate in concept as well as quantity. Ordinary North Carolinians were accustomed both to a certain level of physical existence and to a certain style of social relations. Food handed

out by the gentry who ran the county courts could not restore the precious independence of small farmers; indeed, it negated what yeomen
viewed as a social necessity even as it alleviated a physical need. The gentry
had no way to restore the yeomen's social condition even if it tried to
minister to their physical need. As a result tens of thousands of ordinary
citizens suffered severely during the Civil War. Their hunger and anguish
strengthened the peace movement and helped explain Governor Vance's
efforts to shield the state from Confederate demands. At a minimum their
deprivation also stimulated desertions as men returned from the armies to
care for their families.

But in addition the poverty that gripped the yeomen moved them to
take action. It moved them to defend their sense of right and challenge the
authority of the aristocracy; it encouraged resistance to Confederate laws
as men sought to recover what they had lost; it stimulated latent class
resentments and intensified perceptions of social injustice. In a variety of
ways it heightened the frustrations that contributed to widespread violence within the state and between North Carolinians. In places this violence even assumed the form of stealing that was not regarded as theft by
popular opinion—that is, it led to conflict so deep that robbery became
social banditry. The Civil War in North Carolina was more than a disastrous intersectional war—it was also an internal war.

INTERNAL WAR

Almost from the beginning of the Civil War there were signs that popular dissatisfaction in North Carolina went far beyond the norm. Tar Heels had felt such reluctance to secede and grew so critical of Confederate policies that discontent soon turned to resistance. Not only did North Carolinians fight in southern ranks against the North, they also fought against the Confederacy and among each other in battles that were fierce, widespread, and occasionally even large-scale. In addition to war's destruction and poverty, the state had to endure robbery, pillaging, battles between Home Guards and deserters, and other violent civil disorders. The hierarchy and subordination that were so vital to the state's elite threatened to dissolve entirely in the turmoil and upheaval of war.

Despite the reflex of loyalty to the South that swept North Carolina into the Confederacy after the firing on Fort Sumter, worrisome signs of dissent soon appeared. Interestingly enough, the first symptoms of disunity came from all parts of the state. Governor Henry T. Clark, who preceded Zebulon Vance during 1861 and 1862, admitted that "a few are disaffected" in mountainous counties on the western border. Blaming this trouble on the influence of Tennessee Unionists, Clark was sufficiently concerned about the "few" to call on the Confederate secretary of war for aid in suppressing treason. At the same time a loyal Confederate in Bertie County, on the shore of Albemarle Sound, warned that his area was "infested by Torys & disloyal persons." His analysis of the problem stressed the class divisions that so often coincided with other lines of cleavage. Although the county contained many slaves, there were "but few men of wealth compared to the number of nonslaveholding persons."[1]

In Alamance County in the piedmont unionist activities pointed toward the possibility of serious class conflict over the war. A "Union Meeting" took place "near the Regulation Battle ground," and the protesters in attendance made plans to fly a United States flag at the site six weeks later, practically on the anniversary of the Regulators' final challenge to oppressive government on 16 May 1771. Thus protestors against secession and its leaders were likening themselves to the Regulators who rose against the greed and abuse of power of predatory, upper-class officials almost a hundred years before. The class warfare that erupted then had threatened to tear the colony apart, and some of the men who heard of the 1861 protest hurriedly requested a meeting with the archconservative jurist, Thomas Ruffin.[2]

Several months later the members of Ruffin's family shared their concern about "indications of decided disaffection" in Alamance. "At a recent constable election, one of the candidates announced himself as still devoted to the union and his supporters voted for him with ballots having on them the Eagle, as emblematic of their attachment to the Union." Even more ominous was something that happened shortly thereafter. In the southern part of the county "some of the militia have on the field refused to muster under the Flag of the Confederate States and have defended themselves from arrest with arms in their hands." Fearing that such opposition might spread, William K. Ruffin advised against "mak[ing] public that there is *any* disappointment among our people."[3]

But it was too late for silence—the phenomenon was already abroad. One of Jonathan Worth's daughters wrote in March 1862, that ten miles from Asheboro a demonstration had taken place "in a community where there were very few men with any education. They had a kind of prayer meeting where some 50 men raised a white flag & said they were for peace. The captain of that district, John C. Hill, [a] rather illiterate man gave the command that all who were in favor of peace [were] to follow in the procession, over 50 persons obeyed & they marched after the white flag, had prayer for peace & then dispersed." In Davidson County, which adjoins Randolph on the west, a similar "peace demonstration" occurred. Both might have been sparked by Governor Clark's attempt to draft militiamen for Confederate service, but they showed as well an underlying hostility to the direction in which the government was moving.[4]

At the same time Rufus Lenoir Patterson, normally a calm observer of events, felt disturbed by the manner in which class feelings were growing. He feared that "a set of low-bred agrarians" was whipping up class enmity in Forsyth County. "Every man who is pursuing an honest calling & realizing *profits* is denounced by these people," lamented Patterson, whose mercantile activities were extensive, "& they are crying out, 'Oh, for the

Josiah Collins III

old Union that Lincoln might confiscate the property of the *rich* and give it to the *loyal* poor.'"[5] Not all unionists had such class purposes, but this dimension of internal conflict showed up elsewhere as well.

In the east, along the border of Washington and Tyrrell counties, lay the vast plantations of the Collins and Pettigrew families. Nearly a hundred years before Josiah Collins I had imported African slaves and put them to work for years draining the swampy land around Phelps Lake. Their labors had eventually created a productive but isolated baronial estate called Somerset, over which Josiah Collins III presided. The Pettigrews had developed a similarly impressive plantation nearby, while much poorer white agriculturalists and herdsmen eked out a living from wetlands that they lacked the capital to improve. Before the war the wealthy and poor whites had coexisted peacefully; occasionally the poorer folk had their grain ground at the planters' mills or sold some chickens to the Collinses if the latter were planning a large banquet.

Soon after the war began, however, unusual events exposed the bitter feelings that had lain beneath the surface of previous routines. Federal invasion of the coast forced white planters to flee and allowed lowlier blacks and whites to express emotions that they had hidden through the years when they had no power. William Pettigrew's slaves "stampeded" upon the news of a Federal advance, and this ingratitude so enraged Pettigrew that he surrounded the slave quarters with troops, seized the slaves by force, and endeavored to remove all of his human—and all too willful—property to Chatham County. With 328 slaves, Josiah Collins III had too many bondsmen to remove, and because it was difficult to find employment for all of them away from the lake, he tried to keep many working there under the supervision of an overseer.

The attempt worked badly. Seeking the freedom that Yankee soldiers told them about, the Collins slaves abandoned their supposedly innate servility. "In speaking of you," a friend reported to Josiah Collins III, "they call you 'Old Collins.' They say that if ever you go or send down there for them they intend to leave." Overseer George Spruill explained that none had left Somerset by 16 May 1863, "but I have had to wearke Evry skiam [scheme] to keep them hear. . . . The[y] tore dowan and steal and take any thing the[y] pleas. i can not say a worde. i keepe talking to them[,] have gived off hogs and Cattle to Each family [and] by those meanes i have kept them on the lake. . . . the[re] are no Dependance in no nigro when the weard fredom is given . . . the[y] doo not cear [care] for you at all."[6]

The behavior of poorer whites was even more surprising to Collins. As soon as United States troops appeared, white supporters known as Buffaloes materialized and began to aid the North and punish prominent Confederates. Their conduct toward the richest families was especially pointed. One outraged landowner wrote to Josiah Collins that "young Wm Adkinson has got possession of my Carriage & Buggy and has a pair of your best mules & is driving over the County. He has furnished his House with Mr. C. L. Pettigrew's furniture. I wrote him that the day of retribution would come, & he might prepare himself for it." Such warnings had little effect, however. As another man wrote to Collins, "[your] furniture the 'Buffs' have in a great measure divided among themselves. Mr. Warren Ambrose . . . has furnished his house to a most extravagant s[t]ate. They have taken away all the horses, mules, cattle, hogs & sheep except very few. . . . Many of the country people have supplied themselves with corn from your plantation."

Another writer reported that Buffaloes "tore up things generally" at Somerset and forced the overseer "to let off water to run the mill whenever they pleased. . . . Hamilton Davenport is driving about in yr. mountain wagon & . . . Buffaloe houses all around the country are supplied with books & furniture taken fr. houses of loyal citizens who have come away." Hamilton Davenport and other Buffaloes who drew pay as members of a partisan company, the U.S. First North Carolina Union Volunteers, were the same individuals who had sold chickens and eggs to Josiah Collins III or done occasional odd jobs at Somerset. Their normally humble mien around the Collinses had disappeared, and the Pettigrews similarly learned that poorer whites were "ensconced in their dwelling houses" and claiming parts of their land.[7]

Obviously, motives of class resentment were prominent in the actions of these Unionists, but the state had its share of politically motivated Unionists as well. Bryan Tyson of strongly pro-Whig and antisecession Randolph County saw the war as a disaster, and to end its "cruel" effects he favored "going back into the Union, provided we can get our rights." In September 1862, Tyson drew up a broadside that proposed an armistice followed by reunion and the deposing of Abraham Lincoln. If reunion could be achieved, however, he was even willing to allow Lincoln to serve out his term, and Tyson labored to publish his argument in book form for distribution to North Carolina's legislators. Not an abolitionist, Tyson later criticized Lincoln for blocking the major goal—reunion—in order to make the war a crusade against slavery. Most Tar Heel Unionists shared those priorities, although at least one of Tyson's correspondents came to believe that slavery was "an evil thing" and donned a federal uniform "to help defend our flag and demolish slavery."[8]

The secret unionist order, the Heroes of America, spread through North Carolina and into other southern states after 1862. Coordinating various types of anti-Confederate activity, the order aided deserters, recruited soldiers for the North, encouraged "mutual cooperation and support" in resisting Confederate demands, and lent its support to the independent and more broadly based peace movement. Employing a body of ritual adapted from Freemasonry and drawing on biblical imagery, the HOA encouraged its members to place a red string in their lapels or on their doors and windows as a protective sign of identification on the day of ultimate Union victory. Whereas some of the "Red Strings" were highly political people who later became involved in Reconstruction, others joined the order out of generalized discontent over the course of the war and a desire to limit its disastrous impact upon their lives.[9]

The more personal kind of unionism was likely among those who had always been most reluctant to risk the war. "On Cane Creek you know that the people . . . are nearly all for the union," wrote an Alamance County man. "We was all ordered to camp & the foundrys are all stoped & things are in a verry bad condition. . . . I had to leave my family & go in the army or leave the country to keep from going in the Confederate army." A Randolph County man who declared that he was "forsed in to t[h]is war varry mutch aganst my will" served in the army only four of twenty-one months after being conscripted in July 1862; the rest of the time he hid out near home, like another man who "lay out in the woods 19 months" rather than fight. "I did not believ that the rebelion was right," he wrote another deserter from Randolph, "and my friends told me to leave the first chance I got."[10]

The ordinary motives of hunger, fear, anxiety, disillusionment, and the determination to aid one's family led a much larger number of citizens into resistance to the Confederacy. Lonely and worried about the shortage of food and high prices back home, one soldier asked his father to "take good cear [care] of mi things till i come home if i ever doo. Tel Jorge never to come to the war i wod li out fust . . . eanoch can tel yo how bad it is to be here and no [know] yo can't go home." As the fortunes of the Confederacy plummeted, personal hardship increased and the combination convinced many that the Confederate cause could have no good result. "I see the foly of the undertaking of the South," wrote one man, and another reported that "Ther is more union [sentiment] in Randolph [now, November 1863] th[a]n ther was when the war commensed. . . . every tim the union army whip it make the union that much more increasing. About the tim of the Getysburg battle nearly all the people was union."[11]

Indeed, desertion increased markedly in the summer of 1863 following Confederate military disasters. Demoralized about the cause, angered by unfair policies like the "twenty nigger law," and worried about their suffering families, large numbers of Tar Heel soldiers left the ranks. When pursued they tended to gather in rugged, isolated mountain counties, swamps, woods, or in areas where popular disgust for the war provided them with sympathy or support. During that summer approximately five hundred congregated in Wilkes County, three to four hundred in Randolph, and substantial numbers in Catawba, Yadkin, and Iredell.[12] Although these men generally sought only to be left alone or to aid their families, there was the potential for violent resistance if authorities tried to enforce the law and make arrests. And that day was nearing, for the Confederacy's assistant secretary of war concluded that "the condition of things in the mountain districts of North Carolina, South Carolina, Georgia, and Alabama menaces the existence of the Confederacy as fatally as either of the armies of the United States."[13]

Before many violent confrontations with deserters occurred, however, a telling form of civilian violence arose: the food riot. In March 1863, the *Salisbury Carolina Watchman* reported the details of "A Female Raid." According to the paper, "Between 40 and 50 soldiers' wives, followed by a numerous train of curious female observers, made an attack on several of our businessmen . . . whom they regarded as speculators in the necessaries of life." These women "demand[ed] an abatement in prices" or threatened to "forcibly tak[e] possession of the goods they required." Calling on first one merchant and then another, the women demanded to buy flour at a price they considered fair. When one storekeeper protested that he had paid twice as much for the commodity, "They then said they were determined to have the flour, and would take it, unless he would sell. . . . Accordingly [they] went to work with hatchets on the store room door." Reconsidering, the storekeeper donated ten barrels to the women. They moved on, visiting one store after another until they had presented their demands to seven other merchants. Although the supplies of two were exhausted, the women collected thirteen more barrels of flour, a barrel of molasses, two sacks of salt, and twenty dollars. They specifically accused one storeowner of "having run up flour from $40 to $50" when they visited him. The next morning, in a meeting reported by the newspaper, these women settled upon a fair method of dividing the captured food among themselves.[14]

Several things about this "female raid" were highly significant. The women involved demanded and stole food publicly, in open daylight, and with no attempt to conceal themselves. They unhesitatingly declared their purpose and gave specific arguments to justify their acts. Daring the authorities and seemingly unafraid of public opinion, they did not hide after the raid but assembled once more to divide the spoils. Obviously the forty or fifty soldiers' wives who led this food "riot" were neither out of control nor in the grip of a thoughtless passion; they believed that what they were doing was right and they challenged the community to object to their actions. They saw themselves as redressing a social wrong, and it seems likely that many of the "numerous train of curious female observers" were not merely curious but supportive.

In fact, public opinion was substantially behind the women, as evidenced by the newspaper report itself. Noting that "this movement was aimed as a blow at the practice of speculating in provisions," the paper admitted that it was also caused "by pinching want. . . . There are many families in this town and vicinity who have not tasted meat for weeks, and some times, months together. Of course they have had no butter, molasses, or sugar. Many of them have no gardens and consequently no vegetables of their own raising; and the scarcity and high price of potatoes, peas, beans &c. render it extremely difficult if at all possible, for them to obtain these articles. What, then, have they to support life? Bread and water!" After thus justifying the women's action, the paper went on to condemn the county commissioners for inadequate efforts at poor relief. "Do they suppose they will escape the fury of the devil their mal-administration has helped to arouse?" The paper then added: "Men of position are already suspicioned of countenancing, if they did not secretly provoke, the proceedings."[15]

In other words this robbery from merchants was a case of "social crime," or illegal activity that was not regarded as wrong, but rather applauded, by popular opinion. The women were thieves, but they were "*not* regarded as simple criminals by public opinion."[16] Instead they were excused, admired, and even supported because they had championed the neglected and avenged a wrong. Their act was actually a form of rebellion designed to restore basic human rights of common people whom the war had injured.

Tar Heel women, who viewed the hunger of children and families most directly, continued to protest social injustice during the rest of the war. Because women were supposed to be subordinate to their husbands and were not even allowed to vote by society, their outspoken protest called special attention to their grievances. It inverted normal social roles, over-turning both the sexual hierarchy and the political order to ventilate griev-ances rising up from below. At an almost unconscious level, such female protest may have continued ancient European folk traditions of the chari-vari and other rituals of protest.[17] In any case the women spoke up—there was another raid on stores, this time in High Point, and a North Carolina legislator saw "quite a crowd of women" demonstrating for Holden and peace in March 1864. "They were all for Holden," he reported, "and 'kantankerously' opposed" to any of his political foes.[18]

In 1864 and 1865 this "kantankerousness" again took purposeful form as food "riots." Fifty women "marched in a body" to a government ware-house in Yancey County and seized sixty bushels of wheat. In mountain-ous Yadkin County early in 1865 "a band of *women*, armed with axes, came down on [Jonesville], to press [seize] the tithe corn &c." According to an upper-class woman who related the incident, the women "brought wagons along to carry it off" and confronted a lone official who tried to protect the corn. "You know women generally want to carry their point, and it was with great difficulty that our hero could withstand them." But by chance, at a crucial moment, "an old drunk man" came along and caused the horses to bolt and run away with the wagons before the women could seize the corn. Undaunted, they or some other women soon made a successful raid on Hamptonville, where "they took as much as they wanted without meeting with any resistance." Again, the lack of resistance suggested wide popular support, and even the disapproving upper-class woman who reported these events felt sympathy for the wom-en's plight. "'Tis a melancholy truth," she wrote, "that there is not enough corn in the county for its inhabitants to subsist on."[19]

These sorties by poor and hungry women were relatively peaceful af-fairs, but numerous incidents of violence began to take place in connec-tion with the growing numbers of deserters. Both state and Confederate officials reacted predictably to the appearance of identifiable areas where deserters found haven—they organized military actions to clean out the "deserters' country." A number of operations took place in 1863 in piedmont counties like Randolph, Moore, Chatham, and Montgomery and in various parts of the mountains. At first such operations seemed quite successful—"the deserters were dispersed over a large [expanse] of country sparsely settled and generally only a few acting together," Randolph's Jonathan Worth advised Governor Vance; seizing their horses was "a most efficient means of bringing them in."[20]

But this solution proved to be no more than temporary. The number of deserters continued to grow. Even men who enjoyed a safe detail at the saltworks in Wilmington fell ill with a malady that "nothing but home, it seems, will cure"; virtually none returned from furloughs, and those with medical leaves "generally [got] them extended by physicians." Worse still was the fact that the military actions undertaken to suppress desertion often seemed to aggravate the very problems that caused it. J. H. Foust of Randolph County complained to Zeb Vance around Christmas 1863, that approximately one thousand troops who were hunting deserters in the area had become a serious problem. They had been ordered to live off the land, and consequently they were consuming large amounts of scarce food, thus deepening the suffering among the common people. Citizens in Yadkin County circulated a petition asking Governor Vance to withdraw the forces that were supposed to do good instead of harm there, and other complaints arrived, such as one denouncing "excesses committed by a Lt. Hobinson . . . in Clay and Cherokee Co.s acting as he claims under orders of Col. Palmer." Troops sometimes lost their discipline, also, and were guilty of mistreating the citizens they encountered.[21]

However, authorities like Governor Vance felt pressure from the other side as citizens complained about the stealing that was done by deserters and fugitives who had become outlaws. A number of correspondents from Wilkes County wrote in 1864 that deserters tended to pass along the Blue Ridge into the county. "Mobs of deserters and disloyal men and women," they asserted, "are Robing and plundering the good and Loyal Citizens of their Guns and their Scanty stock of provisions." Others from Watauga explained that robberies were increasing and that the deserters and bushwackers had committed murders in their efforts to stay free and maintain themselves. J. H. Haughton of Pittsboro lamented that deserters were committing many "depradations" in Chatham County, filling up Montgomery County, and putting the lives of enrolling officers in danger.[22] Thus both efforts to suppress deserters and the growth of their numbers continued.

As 1864 advanced, desertion and violence spread all over North Carolina. Governor Vance received pleas for help from Richmond and Chatham counties in August; in the latter instance he learned that deserters
had "threatened to burn Pittsbraugh [Pittsboro]." Another man claimed
that "Robbing houses and stealing and shooting down Cattle in the
woods has become to be the order *of the day*." Although many felt problems in Randolph County had been solved in the fall of 1864, by January
1865 Jonathan Worth reported that "theft, robbery, and almost every
other crime are common in almost all the rural districts" and were increasing. "We bolt & bar our doors every night, not knowing what hour they
[Bushwackers] may make their appearance," declared a member of Caldwell County's gentry. By February and March 1865 reports were common
of bands of three to four hundred deserters "committing the most tyrannical outrages," of "bold & defiant" deserters who "had a fight . . . with our
Cavalry," and of "Union men . . . defying the Confederate authorities."[23]

In addition to the areas mentioned above, frequent complaints of robbery and violence came from counties such as Avery, Wilkes, and Jackson
in the mountains; Forsyth, Moore, and Montgomery in the piedmont;
and Cumberland, Robeson, Bladen, Columbus, Johnston, and Edgecombe in the east. The problem had expanded all over the state and
become a general phenomenon. Order was dissolving and disorder
spreading like an epidemic in the last months of the war. Not only had
violence become a daily affair, but also the forces of illegal opposition to
authority had become so formidable that in many places the power to
enforce obedience was in doubt. Bemoaning the fact that a judge had not
dared to hold court in Pittsboro and Asheboro, Jonathan Worth admitted,
"it is an acknowledgment to the deserters that they have overawed the
courts."[24] If the courts, which could command the presence of armed
forces of the state, were so threatened, it was far more clear to the ordinary
citizen that the state was struggling with a massive tide of violence within.

In fact, as the breadth of the evidence indicates, North Carolina experienced internal war as well as the anguish of war with the forces of the
United States. Citizens within the state had resorted to violence to achieve
change. By turning their backs on the established political process, they
revealed a breakdown in the legitimacy of the social order. Their actions
pointed also toward the existence of a startling amount of collective frus-
tration and aggression in the population at large. Deeply divisive conflict
was at work within.[25]

Why did the authority of the political system of North Carolina deteriorate to such a point that internal war prevailed? What did this phenomenon mean? It is important to analyze these questions carefully, for the rise of internal war during the Confederate period revealed a fundamental characteristic of the antebellum social system that in normal times had remained hidden from view.

Any thorough analysis of North Carolina's internal war must begin with the impact of disorienting social processes. Even before the abnormal conditions of wartime made themselves felt, the state had gone through profound changes. After debating the choice between secession and the attractions of the Union, Tar Heels had withdrawn from the only government most of them had known and pledged their allegiance to a new nation, the Confederacy. These actions, even if they had been unanimous, raised basic issues and tended to focus people's attention on the question of the legitimacy of the government. Airing such matters in itself undercut patterns of automatic acceptance of authority and unthinking obedience to the laws. Then the effects of war heightened the departure from normality. There is some truth in the overly general observation that "political violence is generated by rapid social change." The militarization of society, shortages, inflation, impressment, and the spread of poverty all introduced rapid changes into the normal routines of life. Moreover, they constituted "erratic and uneven rates of social change" that made adjustment more difficult.[26] Because the war transformed daily life, it was natural to feel a separation from customary modes of behavior and obedience. The chaos and confusion of the times contributed to a feeling that all was unpredictable and that the traditional rules were suspended.

In this context certain preconditions or facilitating tendencies helped to give rise to internal war. Social theorists have argued that "internal wars are due to the inadequate circulation of elites" and that they are "responses to oppressive government."[27] Certainly North Carolina had a firmly established, stable elite structure with a slow rate of turnover or recruitment into the upper echelons. The political controversies of the 1850s signaled that there was some popular dissatisfaction with this system, and some types of quiet protest may have spoken even more loudly. Of the five counties that received special attention in this study, only the two eastern, plantation counties had the heavy voter turnouts that had been characteristic of the nation since Andrew Jackson's era. Alamance County had a voter participation rate of 65 percent in 1856, somewhat low for that period, and Caldwell County in the mountains averaged only slightly more than 50 percent through the 1850s. Populous but poor

Randolph County never had a majority turnout in presidential elections from 1848 through 1860; approximately 44 percent voted in 1852 and an even smaller proportion in 1856.[28] These figures suggest that there had been at least a degree of alienation from the political system, which offered almost no local elections and choices of limited substance, even in an age of popular enjoyment of politicking.

The social system of a location like Somerset plantation presented some of the undemocratic aspects of North Carolina's society in exaggerated form. There hierarchy was especially evident, and the events of wartime suggest that it also was more than usually resented. The culture of the yeomen contained beliefs and institutions that strengthened the democratic spirit. If yeomen and wealthier planters or merchants usually got along together without collisions in normal times, the potential for conflict nevertheless was present, and this possibility represented another precondition that changed circumstances significantly.

Geography, both physical and social, was a third precondition or facilitating tendency for internal war. It is notable that North Carolina's internal violence clustered in the same regions during both the Revolutionary War and the Civil War. Conflict occurred, despite different issues and background conditions in the 1770s and 1860s, in the same locales: mountainous districts; sparsely settled, wooded areas of the piedmont; and the swamps, pocosins, and Carolina bays of the coastal plain.[29] Such geographical features, which offer concealment and impede pursuit, have always been an advantage for insurgents.

Social geography was of special significance in the Quaker Belt counties of Randolph, Guilford, Forsyth, and Davidson. Both Moravians and members of the Society of Friends were numerous there, and these groups were pacifist and tended to be unionist. Moreover, other residents probably had developed some uncharacteristic attitudes due to their long association with and toleration of the Quakers. A conscientious objector and Friend named Thomas Hinshaw, for example, encountered unusually sympathetic treatment when he was arrested for refusal to serve in the army and refusal to pay the objector's tax, which he believed aided killing. None of the Randolph County soldiers he met would strike or abuse him, even when ordered to do so by an angry lieutenant who wanted to punish Hinshaw as a slacker and draft dodger. Soldiers even pleaded with a judge not to imprison Hinshaw and inconvenienced themselves rather than let him spend a night in jail.[30] The Quaker attitudes also stimulated an unusually strong resistance to war and disapproval of a war to preserve slavery. In antebellum days many Quakers had migrated from the state to avoid living under a slave regime, and again between 1860 and 1868 there was a 60 percent decrease in the number of Quakers in North Carolina.[31] Although one resident denied that Quakers especially were leaving or being mistreated, a man who went to Indiana wrote during the war that, "I found all of Randolph Co out heare. . . . It Seames like all of the Boys has left Randolph they is some comes evry week."[32]

Another factor that has been very influential across cultures in the stimulation of internal wars is apparent incompetence on the part of rulers. The course of the war itself and the severe sacrifices entailed added up in many people's minds to a damning indictment of elite ineffectiveness. In human terms the war was grotesquely prodigal of both life and happiness, and as results went from bad to worse many ordinary North Carolinians wondered how anyone could justify its continuation. For thousands of families whose condition can be inferred from the shocking statistics on poor relief, the war had brought unprecedented suffering, and understandably some people raged against a government that had brought its people to disaster. This emotion probably was prominent among the motives of women who raided stores to obtain food for their families. It also was strong among those who witnessed the "militia and caveldry" taking food or destroying the crops of suffering families. One man complained, "Large numbers of people have been stript of everything."[33]

In addition, a crucial aspect of the failure of the elite was the fact that many of its policies seemed inequitable. Impressment was both capricious and unequal, and the tax-in-kind and measures such as the taking of half of any family's meat supply seemed excessive to poor people as long as there still were families of much greater wealth with far more to gain from the war. Moreover, the shorter terms of service given to those who could supply all their equipment, the acceptance of substitutes, and the exemption of planters and overseers patently contradicted the idea of equality.[34] Society had allotted many privileges to the upper class before the war, but fighting introduced the issue of life and death and heightened the stakes for everyone. Thus it was not surprising that in Randolph County, for example, conscripted men refused to leave after wealthier militia officers got exemptions and were allowed to stay home. Privileged militia officers became targets of hate, especially when they took part in roundups of poor men for dangerous service that the rich could avoid.[35] "Our soldiers cant understand why so many young magistrates are permitted to remain at home," wrote one foot soldier to Governor Vance, "and especially so many militia officers there being no militia and two sets of officers." This kind of class resentment, inherent but often latent in the antebellum social order, played a powerful role in wartime resistance.[36]

What effect did attempts to subvert the political structure have on the internal war? As the existence of the Heroes of America shows, organized efforts at subversion were a factor, and some officials feared that this "secret party . . . is threatening to overt[h]row our Gove[rn]ment."[37] Yet for many reasons the conclusion is inescapable that subversion was of minor importance. It involved possibly ten thousand people (some of whom merely belonged), whereas much larger numbers were involved in grassroots resistance to the Confederacy or various acts of internal war; it contributed nothing new to the pattern of dissent and conflict that was already established; it supported rather than instigated Holden's independent peace movement; and it had no special and particular impact on society that was as marked as the effect of other kinds of violent resistance. Even its success in electing a number of officials came where resistance was already widespread and followed from that. Moreover, the deserters and bandits who fought against the Confederacy and state authorities were not trying to subvert the government and replace it with something else—they wanted instead merely to be left alone. Subversion was one small aspect of internal war, not the key to it.

Ironically, repression was a key, for efforts to put down opposition must be both judicious and effective. In Confederate North Carolina repression backfired; it increased people's alienation from government without removing the sources of challenge to law. The major reason that repression magnified opposition was that it was excessively harsh and carelessly targeted. Many Tar Heel yeomen who had reservations about the Confederacy were inclined to keep to themselves rather than to seek out opportunities for opposition. Severe and unexpected repression transformed them into determined opponents. Perhaps the assertive individualism shared by North Carolinians of all classes and political outlooks encouraged Confederate supporters to condemn and react punitively toward those who thought differently. Or perhaps the uncertain status of the Confederacy convinced the zealous that they had to act decisively, for from the beginning repression was unnecessarily harsh.

In Randolph County in the fall of 1861, for example, an order went out to arrest one Thomas Dougan. The Confederacy then was in its infancy, and in a state that had opposed secession until the bitter end it was predictable that a few supporters of the old government would criticize the new. Thomas Dougan was one of these critics, though his offense seemed quite harmless. In conversation he had uttered the opinion that "secessions are Rascals & traitors and would be whiped." Dougan had done nothing to convert this feeling into disloyal action, yet when others assailed him, his individualism produced a more resistant spirit. Declaring that he "would say what he pleased[,] it was a free country," Dougan was hailed into court, charged "for using language in favor of the federal government," and forced to give a $1,000 bond in legal proceedings that dragged on for two years. At his trial Dougan, now stubbornly opposed to an oppressive government, entered a defiant plea: "I deny the charge but if i was guilty it was no offense." Learning nothing from this incident, the local authorities continued to prosecute—and alienate—citizens for such heinous offenses as "feeding a deserter" who was a relative.[38]

As the war went on some citizens became convinced that the leaders of the Home Guards, who often searched for deserters, were hypocritical and prone to persecute those who deserved respect. A woman named Phoebe Crook upbraided Governor Vance for the fact that militia officers and magistrates who had "remained at home ever since the war com-menced" had found a way to keep themselves safe. They were arresting "old grey headed fathers" and sending them to the front. They even "shoot . . . down without halting them . . . [men] that has served in the army, some of them for 2 or 3 years."[39] An even more remarkable report of hypocritical use of the law came from Watauga County on the state's western border. The privileged Home Guards had been "raiding over the county for more than a year shooting men for not [going] to the army and deserting," yet they had no more devotion to the cause than many desert-ers. Although the Home Guards supposedly were "doing King Jefferson [Davis] good servis," they actually collected few troops "and Jefferson all ways drew a blank. Therefore he sent his sub king or vice gerant and conscripted those [of the Home Guard] that was liable." Soon there was "considerable excitement," for "all except two [I] understand has run the bloccade [and are] now in Abrahams dominions."[40]

Due to the harsh actions of local enforcers of Confederate authority, who tended to have high social status, many ordinary citizens turned against the government, and in some cases violence bred violence, produc-ing "a general lack of receptivity to legitimacy of any kind."[41] A guilt-stricken member of Surry County's Home Guard confirmed that loyal men often went too far and injured the innocent. "I have been on *duty* . . . & have just gotten home from a campaign in Alleghany where we . . .

destroyed innocent men's property and left poor women and children in a destitute condition, taking even their meat & bread from the[ir] hands. Yes I think the Devil himself would blush at some of the deeds that are done in a country that was once free from such outrages. . . . [When troops arrive] you had as well be at the Devil, they spare *none*."[42]

Missions against deserters often led to personal cruelty and violence. Judge Thomas Settle investigated the mistreatment of the wife of a well-known deserter named Bill Owens. The leader of a militia company admitted to Settle that, "I slaped her jaws . . . tied her thumbs together behind her back & suspended her with a cord tied to her two thumbs thus fastened behind her to a limb so that her toes could just touch the ground . . . & [later] put her thumbs under the corner of the fence." Then the unrepentant officer declared, "If I have not the right to treat Bill Owens, his wife & the like in this manner . . . I will go to the Yankees or anywhere else before I will live in a country in which I cannot treat such people in this manner." Nor was this man's attitude unusual. Deeply disturbed, Settle told Governor Vance that about 150 women, "some . . . in delicate health," had been "dragged from their homes" and mistreated in Chatham, Randolph, and Davidson counties. "Women have been frightened into abortions almost under the eyes of their terrifiers," he found.[43]

The actions of men against men often had a rougher quality. In January 1863, in Madison County, a party of soldiers murdered thirteen suspected Unionists, including some who were boys of thirteen or fourteen. That same year conflicts between pro-Confederate authorities and Unionists or deserters had reached the point of killing in Randolph County. "A party of cecesh and soldiers" killed a one-armed Unionist named Neill McDonnold and shot another, reported a Union sympathizer. After mentioning two other executions (one in Chatham County), this man then drew the lesson: anti-Confederates had decided that "when they could they would defend themselves. . . . Often would [the authorities] take a man to kill him but the union men would go and take him by force of arms." People remembered such violence and formed grudges; later they tried to settle the score, sometimes after the passage of decades. Even elite figures began to think of individual violence as a substitute for the legal process of the state. "To shoot [robbers] in the act, as Leak did," declared Jonathan Worth, "is perfectly justifiable."[44]

Thus repression had a powerful, though unintended, effect. But another, usually potent, mechanism of elite control failed to have any power. Faced with the threat of internal war, governments the world over have attempted to use diversionary mechanisms; that is, they have raised issues designed to overcome resentment and deflect or divert discontent into safer channels. In the Confederate period this tactic had no effect in North Carolina, as resistance and internal war continued steadily to spread. Political leaders from Jefferson Davis on down labored assiduously to arouse people's fear of racial equality or direct their anger away from the government and onto the Yankees. The federal troops, Davis often argued, were cruel barbarians who flouted every rule of civilized warfare. After the serious Confederate defeats at Gettysburg and Vicksburg in July 1863, Davis and many other leaders warned shrilly that northern victory would mean racial equality, the degradation of southern whites, and lives utterly devoid of dignity or honor. "Fellow citizens, no alternative is left you but victory or subjugation, slavery, and . . . utter ruin," trumpeted the Confederate president, and Zeb Vance asserted that the North would treat southerners in the manner of "a master who promises them *only life*." Despite the extremity of these threats, disaffected areas, resistance, and internal conflict grew, for, as one man put it, "the people do not fear their condition being worsted. The time has gone by that the people can be madened by such newspaper and pulpit slang as Yankee confiscation, appropriation of pretty women & c."[45]

What, then, could the authorities do? Removing the causes of disaffection was beyond their capabilities, yet they retained the major advantage of commanding all the legal means of force of the state. Compared to the Confederate armies, bands of deserters or bandits were small, poorly supplied, and unorganized. Although the government could not maintain order constantly, it was able to repress opposition whenever it was willing to divert scarce resources from the war effort to internal problems. Zeb Vance's brilliance in stealing the banner of peace from Holden and arguing against Holden's tactics also helped to keep opposition underground. Thus it remained a strong but surreptitious movement that sprang up in the shadows and interstices of authority but never laid claim to equal legitimacy in the light of day. As the Civil War neared its end the power of legal authorities waned and their influence became more intermittent. The desperate state of the battle against the North reduced attention to internal problems, but the government was never powerless.

Neither was the opposition. In fact, support for deserters, draft resisters, food rioters, and bandits became so substantial among the lower classes that some local leaders feared a fundamental loss of control. The frightening reality confronted them that what the gentry viewed as crime was to much of the public merely social crime—acts of resistance that were justifiable, approved, and possibly even applauded. The lawless were becoming respectable, cherished privileges were turning into marks of oppression, and theft was transforming itself into an act of social justice. Silently the bases of social control were slipping away as the growing popularity of resistance undermined the foundations of authority.

To many, an alarming sign of this erosion was the cooperation of blacks and whites in robbery and resistance. In September 1864, one man wrote to Governor Vance that "some deserters & some negroes that has absented themselves from the employment of their owner" had formed a marauding band. A woman from Randolph County anxiously warned that "our negroes are nearly all in league with the deserters." And a refugee from Wilmington described interracial banditry between Fayetteville and Lumberton that caused outraged citizens to organize "a Company to hunt them." After two or three days this company caught "the four negroes that were with them . . . & dispers[ed] the remainder." The fear that this interracial challenge had aroused was clear in the citizens' next action: "the negroes they shot."[46]

But, although this breach of racial lines had drawn residents together to oppose banditry, elsewhere citizens were not showing the same opposition to illegal acts. On the contrary, a commander of the Home Guards sent into Guilford County to arrest deserters found that "the people (all belonging to the 'Society of Friends') positively deny there being any such in this neighborhood." Worse still, the local Home Guards "positively refus[ed] to assist me in any way whatever." Saying, "I can do nothing," the commander asked Governor Vance to let his men return home. Similarly, in Davidson County late in 1864 a legislator who had accepted an assignment to round up deserters found that a local judge interfered with his effort and concluded that deserters would "be sure to crowd a county where they receive so much 'aid and comfort.'" In these cases popular sympathy with war resisters was blocking the enforcement of the laws.[47]

At the same time a colonel reported to Governor Vance that "the situation of Wilk[e]s County is bad beyond a doubt all the section of county north of the [Yadkin] river is very disloyal." This officer was even "satisfied" that militia and Home Guard officers had "been encouraging desertion and have gone under with the disloyal sentiment with at least one-half of the people of the county. I am convinced that a good many magistrates have succumbed." Indeed, while he was advising that "troops will certainly have to be kep[t] here," citizens were writing letters to Vance arguing that such a force was not necessary. A loyal correspondent claimed that a petition against the stationing of troops "was gotten up by the deserters friends."[48]

The same situation prevailed in neighboring Yadkin County, where "a band of deserters and fugitive conscripts" murdered "two of our best citizens, magistrates of the county." According to the man who reported the deaths, "a strong feeling against the conscript law among the uninformed part of the citizens" had been the background to resistance and then violence. So hostile was public opinion that deserters "always had many more active friends than they [the militia officers] had and could always get timely information of every movement to arrest them and so avoid it." Now the citizens "readily conceal the murderers and convey intelligence to them," and loyal men feared that it would be "exceedingly difficult" to capture them, even with a large force.[49]

This defection of popular loyalties to deserters, robbers, and others who were resisting Confederate authority struck at the heart of social control and order. It placed all official power under a cloud. Ultimately, in two of the five counties that received close study, something like a "moral economy of the crowd" became dominant. Rebellious outlaws gained the support of ordinary citizens; together they put class-based perceptions of fairness before the law and forced the authorities to give way before popular views of natural justice.[50] The common people pressured the ruling elite into making concessions and acknowledging their demands for relief in return for a cessation of the war on property. Deserters and others who were resisting the government, supported by a large portion of the supposedly loyal citizens, won exemption from the laws that bore so heavily upon them. In the face of this hostile public opinion, magistrates and lawmakers made deals with deserters and outlaws; theirs was a desperate step to avert rebellion and protect the sanctity of property.

In Caldwell County, for example, robbery had continued to increase. "Affairs in our vicinity grow worse every week," wrote Edmund W. Jones, one of the richest landowners, to Vance, and soon bandits burned the house of a physician prominent in county affairs and robbed members of the influential Lenoir family. Rufus Lenoir Patterson moved his family to the relative safety of Salem; Tories had captured Home Guards, he reported, in groups of eighteen and fifty. The loyal forces that were not captured often seemed unreliable. "Our home guard does but little, if any good," wrote Edmund Jones. "Many of them would favor a tory as soon as a rebel—some of them much sooner."[51]

By March 1865, Rufus Lenoir Patterson had decided that something must be done to restore order and end the violence. Arguing that the Confederacy was near its end but that conflict inside the county could go on indefinitely, Patterson urged his father to arrange an end to the internecine conflict. "I pray you may compromise matters in our county," he wrote. "By all means stop the cavalry & let all honest men come home. *Put down robbery.*" Samuel Finley Patterson, as chairman of the county court, convened a special meeting that authorized Rufus L. Patterson and five others to appeal to Governor Vance "to allow the Home Guard of our County to remain home . . . and also to allow recusant conscripts to come in and join the Home Guard." Although this wording was indirect, Samuel Finley Patterson made the Court's purpose clear in a later letter to his son: "[We are] endeavoring to compromise matters with the Bushwackers."[52]

On 22 April another special meeting of the county court convened, with eighteen worried magistrates present, to ratify the terms of a settlement. The justices approved an agreement between

> certain recusant conscripts, and other citizens of the county of Caldwell who are unwilling to perform Military service under the Confederate Government, and who to avoid the same are obliged to absent themselves from their Homes, on the one part; and a portion of the Military Authorities of the Confederate government, under the command of Capt. N. A. Miller, on the other part, to the following effect: that the said Military Authorities or forces be withdrawn from service; that no further effort be made to enforce the conscription law in the county; that the said recusant conscripts and others be permitted to return quietly to their homes and pursue their lawful occupations unmolested; that restitution of all captured or stolen property be made, as far as possible, by both parties and that both parties shall hereafter demean themselves as quiet, orderly citizens.

The court gave further evidence of its fear for property in a final condition: "it is understood, that the said recusant conscripts and others who have heretofore been or are now associated with them have pledged themselves to aid and assist other citizens in putting down and suppressing robery and plundering and all manner of lawlessness, and will honestly endeavor . . . to restore and reestablish law and order in the county."[53]

On 16 February 1865, J. M. Worth concluded that similar arrangements were necessary in Randolph County. Writing to his brother Jonathan (who at that time was state treasurer), Worth stated, "I feel that I cannot possibly make you fully appreciate our horrible condition." Not only was robbery constant, but the Home Guards were unreliable: "Many of them are afraid and many more are in *heart* with the deserters." Since August the Home Guards' commander had regarded one-half of them as untrustworthy, and in February others reported that some members had harbored men they were supposed to arrest. J. M. Worth suggested that "some arrangment . . . be made with the military authorities to offer the better class of the deserters some terms so they will organize and drive the Robbers from the Country. . . . It is terrible to have to offer terms to Deserters but it would relieve the County and state of great trouble and save life and property and allow the citizens a quiet sleep."[54]

No doubt Jonathan Worth's values revolted too at the prospect of offering terms to deserters, but his realism proved stronger. Within four days he had conferred with Governor Vance and obtained his approval of the arrangement to suppress robbery. Part of the plan called for guaranteeing the Home Guard that they could stay in the county "if they will go to work and put this thing down and keep them down." But resistance to authority was so widespread that on 28 February J. M. Worth reported that the Home Guards had balked. They were called out to organize, but "not one 5th of them appeared . . . every one is disposed to stand hands off and unless the masses encourage the Home Guard it will be another failure." By early March he had concluded that a show of force was needed to effect the compromise. Six hundred troops arrived, but an agent to promise safety to any deserters who cooperated still had not appeared. "I want to urge with all the power I can," J. M. Worth wrote his brother, "that Gov. Vance send a man as promised to take charge of what I have been calling the better class of deserters. If he does not do it we are gone."[55] Without a compromise, even six hundred troops were ineffective.

Finally the arrangements were complete, and relative peace returned to Randolph County. The deserters in both Randolph and Caldwell had wrung major concessions from a proud and powerful elite, thanks to the support of large numbers of law-abiding but disaffected citizens. By acting on their own concepts of social justice, the lower classes had shown their power. In Caldwell County, after Samuel Finley Patterson entered the agreement "on the minutes of the court," he sent "several copies . . . to the leading bushwackers. —This seems to have given them great satisfaction, as well as the recusant conscripts who were in the woods." Their satisfaction was understandable, for they had forced a rigid social order to yield and had obtained redress for their grievances through concessions that abrogated the law.[56]

Thus the crisis of internal war destroyed interclass unity and revealed a fissure that had run beneath the surface of the antebellum social system. The proud and independent yeomen had managed their own affairs and held to a Jacksonian, indeed an American, faith that they were as good as anybody. Their evangelical religion and their slow but steady economic progress had nourished a strong devotion to democratic values. At the same time they had lived in quite an undemocratic state and coexisted with aristocratic leaders who exercised major control over social processes. The yeomen could not help but know these facts, yet in the antebellum era they often had been able to ignore them.

The prewar social system, despite growing signs of conflict, had been able to maintain an appearance of calm because the yeomen customarily had enjoyed a large degree of functional independence. Their daily routines of subsistence farming and livestock raising took place in a sparsely settled, rural world that left them fairly isolated from the larger society. Most yeomen did not frequently confront the facts of class privilege, and they were free to seek salvation in company with a self-governing, evangelical congregation or to devote their attention to family ties, hunting and recreation, or other activities of their choice. In normal times many of these people tolerated power realities that were difficult to change, and thus a combination of yeoman independence and aristocratic privilege was usually possible. The rich largely dominated what the poor largely ignored, and both groups concentrated primarily on their own affairs. This meant that there had been an unrecognized condition to yeoman cooperation with authority. In effect the price of North Carolina's autocratic government was substantial independence for the lower classes and acceptable living conditions among them.

During the war all the essential conditions of coexistence were violated. After a long prewar period of economic improvement for nonslaveholders and slaveholders alike, ordinary North Carolinians experienced a sudden and drastic deterioration in their standard of living.[57] For tens of thousands penury and hunger became constant companions. Government, which traditionally had borne lightly upon the people, now reached deeply into society, imposed unprecedented burdens, and demanded painful sacrifices. Moreover, government took these actions in ways that were inequitable and discriminatory and without successful results; thus it seemed both oppressive and ineffectual. Nor could efforts to aid the yeomen offset these deficiencies. Poor relief, even in adequate quantities, would have been unsatisfactory because it meant the end of people's precious independence and a demeaning reliance on those who arrogantly claimed superiority. The conditions of wartime added up to an attack on the core of yeoman culture. Given the assertive individualism that characterized them, it was predictable that they would rebel and struggle against the decline in their status.

The independent thinking and outspoken resentment of many ordinary North Carolinians are evident in a rare letter of protest from a Randolph County man named Emsley Beckerdite to the editor and politician Marmaduke Robins. Although he wrote "in a homely back woods stile," Beckerdite lost no pointedness thereby. Blasting the irresponsibility of the newspapers, he recalled that, "according to [them], cecession was to be peacable. Cotton was to be King, and if by any possibility war should ensue, it was to be a *mighty* little thing. The Yankees would not fight &c., &c., &c." Then he asked, addressing himself to a basic question, "Was ours a republican government? You answer in the affirmative. Then I ask again if the people, the bone and sinew of this once great country were ever legitimately consulted upon the question of cecession. You would not like to risk your well earned title to intelligence by answering affirmatively." The war, Beckerdite charged, was the responsibility of a minority and its "ignorance, madness or selfish policy."[58]

Then he proceeded to describe frankly the feelings of the common people who were bearing the resulting burdens. "I have not known a man in the last two years [1863 and 1864] who would not willingly have given all he had and would have pledged all that his friends had to keep out of the army. . . . I tell you plainly that the people of the Confederate states would welcome with ovations any power upon earth that was able to deliver them from Conscription impressments taxation and the other ills imposed upon them by those who have deceived them." Beckerdite even declared that racial justifications for continuing the war could not stand: "We cannot afford to give up the white race for the negro." Then he drew the implication of his arguments very plainly. "The common people, the bone and sinew of the southern states are looking to other sources than the Confederate authorities for deliverance."[59]

These independent, individualistic people looked to themselves for deliverance. They refused to be pushed too far, and once the essential conditions of cooperation had been violated, they adamantly resisted all attempts to force their compliance. After the common people's personal independence had been taken away and their sense of justice violated, they paid no attention to diversionary mechanisms. The elite's cause suffered from the large-scale defection of stubbornly independent individuals who continued to act in an individualistic way. Relatively few engaged in highly organized subversion or laid plans to overthrow the government, but many thousands drew the line at further cooperation and acted instead upon their own concepts of fairness and social justice. They demonstrated that there were limits to society's power over them, and after those limits had been reached they replaced acquiescence with disobedience.

In a very real sense society had embraced not just a white community and a black one but several separate communities of whites. The yeomen constituted a class that was dedicated to the preservation of its way of life. The painful experience of war had deepened the yeomen's sense of their identity as opposed to other groups and shown that they were quite capable of violence in defense of their class position. But the yeomen's social attitudes tended to emphasize disengagement rather than engagement with society. Normally they preferred not to impose their desires on other groups but to continue an independent style of life free from extensive involvement with, or dependence on, others. When necessity required they acted strongly to protect their independence.

Both yeomen and gentry had oriented themselves toward their own group and had dealt with others from a distance. Feisty and sure of themselves, Tar Heels were both reserved and assertive; they sprang to the defense of whatever they valued but otherwise asked to be left alone and generally were willing to accord others the same treatment. In terms used by sociologist John Shelton Reed to describe contemporary social relations, southern whites lived in "different communities" and "pretty well succeed[ed]" both in "ignoring one another" and in "disguis[ing] indifference as cordial respect."[60] The Civil War exposed lines of division that had been invisible in normal times.

The disunity and class hostility that emerged in wartime horrified North Carolina's elite. They saw all too clearly how weak and tenuous were the cords of social control on which they relied. The wartime behavior of many yeomen confirmed the gentry's deepest fears about the unreliable and dangerous character of the masses, the mob. The war left many elite figures with recollections of frightening experiences, such as this one described by a member of the Randolph County Court: "Our house tonight is a scene of confusion—everything is torn to pieces— . . . safe broken & a large amount of money taken besides so many other things it is impossible to enumerate. . . . Do not let a human being know this letter was written."[61] Deserters and bandits had waged a war on property that often made the elite the targets and that ultimately, in a few districts, seemed to place all property in peril.

Most of all, it seemed to the gentry that the principle of hierarchy was threatened as it had not been for decades. The strains of war had loosened controls, and in the changed environment the influence of "bad men" and "ignorant and malicious upstart[s]" had soared.[62] Undeniably, lawless elements had been in as much control of certain areas as the legally constituted, upper-class authorities. Thus, it seemed imperative that proper order be restored to society and the dangerous impulses of the masses contained once more.

Ironically, the triumph of the United States armies did more to accomplish this in a few months than the anxious efforts of Confederate authorities had done during two years. Imposing a rigid discipline, federal troops vigorously "put . . . down . . . armed mobs of Confederate soldiers, deserters, & c," observed David Schenck in Lincolnton. Reports from the mountains and other parts of the state indicated that "things are quiet." Even at Somerset plantation the power of the conquering army had discouraged any departures from good order and strict legality. Josiah Collins's son George gave up hope of recovering most articles that had been stolen, but he marveled at the safety and quiet that prevailed "as in former days." Moreover, he noticed that "the very fellows who talked most openly against us are now coming to us as usual fawning & whining for favours."[63]

But these unexpected benefits of defeat could not lull the gentry into a false sense of security. The wartime problem of poverty remained serious,[64] and common sense told politically experienced men that the effects of internal war would be long lasting. The aristocrats had seen their suspicions of the lower orders confirmed, and the poorer classes had shown their hostility to government by and for the rich. Class conflict was sure to be a theme in postwar society.

4

RECONSTRUCTION: RESISTANCE
TO WHITE DEMOCRACY

The end of the Civil War brought the beginning of a period of uncertainty in politics and social relations. Although it was clear that North Carolina and other states of the defeated Confederacy would have to rejoin the Union, no one knew what this reconstruction would mean—in federal-state relations, race relations, politics, or legal and constitutional adjustments. Stung by their wartime experiences, elite North Carolinians feared an erosion of social control or an attack upon established patterns of hierarchy. Some leaders realized that change was unavoidable and started adjusting to a new world, but others instinctively desired to preserve and restore old methods of control.

Their fear of change revealed that Reconstruction was more than a contest over racial equality—it was a battle against the principle of equality itself. Indeed, in the first two years after the war, during presidential reconstruction, the major political struggle within North Carolina concerned the extent of democracy among whites. Before meaningful equality for blacks became an issue, most of the state's traditional leaders had begun to draw together in defense of the fundamental principle of hierarchy against democracy. To them the immediate danger was a shift of power from prominent to supposedly undeserving whites, and on virtually every issue they sought the most conservative answers and attempted to minimize change.

Initially the conservatives' stand against change was successful, as they beat back democratizing tendencies and reestablished the customary machinery of government from the state level down to local county affairs. But then the course of Reconstruction changed due to events in Washington, D.C. Northern Republicans, worried that Andrew Johnson's reconstruction program was losing the peace, sought to modify it through the Fourteenth Amendment. After southern states rejected the proposed amendment, northern voters became fearful also and endorsed sterner measures. Congress asserted its power over national policy and required universal male suffrage, new constitutional conventions, and new, more democratic governments in the South. These laws, imposed by the superior force of the federal government, overwhelmed North Carolina conservatives. "Radical" democracy became the rule. When this change came through external decisions, elite Tar Heels resented it with extra bitterness because it snatched away ground that they had recently secured once again from lower-class blacks and whites within the state. Thus the defense of hierarchy and opposition to "the mob" were central to later resistance to Radical Reconstruction. Continuing class tension set the stage for racial conflict that was more overt and violent yet intrinsically related to the underlying opposition to democracy.

Social and political developments in postwar North Carolina took place against a backdrop of pervasive hardship and economic difficulty. The poverty of wartime did not quickly disappear, and many ordinary white citizens of the state continued to struggle to support themselves. Instead of seeking equality, they were worrying about survival. Though hard times forced poor people to devote their energy to making a living and, in the confused atmosphere of changing Reconstruction policies, probably diminished their involvement in politics, the potential for popular protest was real. Experience demonstrated that the existence of suffering people could translate into powerful pressures from below.

In May 1865, Samuel Finley Patterson wrote that many of the family's white employees in Caldwell County were "very hard run for something to eat," and he rented "10 acres of *very* good land" to two of his most valuable workers in order to insure their service. Drought ravaged agriculture in 1866; "the wheat crop was a sad failure," and official papers from the governor's office spoke of "the failure of both the corn and wheat crop in many of the Western Counties . . . [and] the almost destitution of many among the masses . . . and even among those who possess large real estate in that grain growing portion of the State." By February 1867, North Carolina was importing substantial quantities of grain to relieve distress.[1]

It does not appear that poverty reached the terrible levels of wartime, but officials feared "extreme suffering—if starvation itself can be prevented" in areas where the previous summer's drought had hit hard. They sent one thousand bushels of corn to Randolph County, another thousand to Union County, and hundreds to other parts of the state. One official believed that suffering was greatest in Union and Stanly counties "owing to an utter failure of the crops," and the state gratefully accepted aid from as far away as Maryland and New York. Local wardens of the poor reported 700 whites and 322 blacks impoverished in Union County, 520 and 250 in Stanly, and totals of 275, 193, 174, and 164 in Guilford, Duplin, Clay, and Carteret among others.[2]

Even in 1868 an Orange County man was complaining that "times is mighty hard down here." With corn selling at $7.50 per barrel and wheat at $2.00 per bushel, "a pore man is hard run to live. . . . The winter is tremendous rough." Later that year another man observed that people were "all most without money and corn," and the general stagnation of business in the postwar South discouraged even middle-class businessmen and professionals, who belonged in the most propertied and secure third of the population. Frederick L. Childs heard such bad news from Wilmington that he went to New York in search of opportunity, and a friend of his wrote from Hillsboro in 1867 that "there is not much encouragement now a days in the pursuit of any business in our poor desolate land."[3]

Nevertheless, people made an effort to put things back together and to reorganize both economic affairs and government. Former Union men and foes of the Confederacy spoke up about the kind of reorganization they desired. According to resolutions adopted in June 1865, nearly three thousand citizens from Surry, Yadkin, Alleghany, and Stokes counties assembled in Mount Airy to state their views on postwar politics. Asserting that North Carolinians would not have ratified secession at the polls, they welcomed the return of the Union, declared their loyalty, and indicated their readiness to work with the government of Andrew Johnson. In a positive spirit they resolved to put internal violence behind them, pledging not to seek revenge despite "the many acts of wanton violence committed upon their persons, property, and liberty." But they also put secessionists and Destructives on notice—forgiveness would not preclude a close scrutiny of their advice in the future.[4]

Similarly, the broadly based opposition to the war in Randolph County organized a citizens' meeting at the Asheboro courthouse in June. With prompt and practical purpose, this meeting selected sixty names to recommend to President Johnson's Provisional Governor, William Holden, for appointment as justices of the peace in Randolph. The list of nominees included Zebedee Rush, the reputed "High Priest" of the Heroes of

America in Randolph County, prominent leaders of the peace movement such as Jesse D. Cox and William Gollihorn, and outspoken critics of the war such as Emsley Beckerdite. Several magistrates who had been active in county affairs during the war received continued support, but others such as Isaac H. Foust, who had been the target of a deserters' raid, were passed over. This meeting and its leaders showed the potential for democratic change that existed, if ordinary citizens became organized.

Opposition to the war had run so deep in Randolph—it was one of only three counties to give Holden a majority in 1864—that many of the county's substantial citizens had broken with the Confederate establishment. Dr. B. A. Sellers, who chaired the meeting, was a wealthy man by county standards; he was worth $10,800 in real estate and $13,750 in personal property in 1860. Thomas Branson, another nominee of the meeting, was the youthful son of a farmer who in 1860 owned $6,350 in land and $6,300 in personal property. But Branson had shown that he merited lower-class support; in 1864 he was the leading signer of a demand that the county's legislators join in support of the peace movement.[5] Branson and men like him seemed ready to support a new regime, one with more sensitivity to deep discontent among the common people.

But in most of the state, where unrest had not equaled the extraordinary levels reached in Randolph County, members of the old elite slowly but naturally formed a determination to hold onto the privileges and power they had always enjoyed. Initially they struggled with powerful, painful emotions as they confronted the consequences of defeat. Perhaps more than any other group, the war's end left them reeling from the enormous destruction of battle, the emancipation of their slaves, and the upheaval that lay ahead. In monetary terms they had lost fortunes—for Paul Cameron the minimum estimate would be the dollar value of approximately one thousand slaves his family had held in North Carolina plus another eight hundred or so in the deep South; Thomas Ruffin, who had owned one hundred slaves in 1860, put his losses in excess of $250,000; and smaller slaveowners still lost major fortunes compared to the average yeoman. "We are a most terribly punished people," moaned Cameron, who was so disheartened by the wreck of his antebellum world that he declared his eagerness to sell his remaining property and "get off with *a half of its value* to some new field of industry and hope," if family duties would permit him to do so. B. G. Worth, Fayetteville newspaper publisher E. J. Hale and his sons, and others considered emigration, often reaching tentative decisions to leave. But within a few months these prominent men were seeking their pardons from the federal government and looking toward the protection of their positions.[6]

To most of the gentry opportunities naturally seemed less sure outside the state where they had already achieved great success. In addition, their hostility to change in an aristocratic system was too deeply ingrained to permit surrender of their powers without a fight. At bottom most elite Tar Heels felt contempt for the democratic aspirations of lower-class men, whom they judged to be inferior and envious. Writing early in 1865, when the Confederacy's fate was clear and class resentments in the state were strongly apparent, W. W. Lenoir, for example, condemned the "low ebb" in "the morality and virtue of some of my white neighbors" in Haywood County. He judged their class-influenced politics "disgusting . . . the exhibition of a malicious and disappointed feeling towards those who they were weak enough to believe would be brought to their own level."[7] What yeomen saw as social justice was malicious envy in the eyes of aristocrats, just as class-based political appeals in the 1850s had been "demagoguery."

A remarkable insight into the mind of the elite was provided on the eve of Reconstruction by Calvin Wiley, North Carolina's leading educator, who had been on familiar terms with a succession of governors and many other political leaders. At the end of January 1865, he forced himself to confront the imminence of northern victory and searched his soul for an explanation. For a public figure in the Confederacy he reached a rather unusual conclusion: the South had sinned "in the *management* of slavery" (though not in slaveholding itself) and the God of battles was chastising the South, "calling on us to reform the institution."[8] This conviction caused Wiley to embark on a crusade to reform slavery as a precondition for victory, but it also prodded him to imagine the disastrous result that would follow from a failure to repent. His ominous prediction revealed some deeply rooted antidemocratic assumptions about society.

In his apocalyptic vision of the future after defeat, Wiley saw a rapid and inevitable slide into despotism. The danger was social, and it was patent: "The negroes, in our country, & the meanest class of white people, would constitute a majority." Base-born blacks and whites would form a dangerous combination. Feeding on the opportunity presented by their numbers, a despot would arise, usurping the place of the upper class and enforcing his power through reliance on "a vast & brutal soldiery." Such a tyrant would probably gain the support of a few leaders who felt they could gain from his domination, but the real basis of his power would be the inherent desire for revenge of the lower orders. Lower-class whites and the Negroes would unite in a "common sympathy of hatred for the [now] intermediate classes, once the masters of the country & hence dreaded by its tyrant & hated by his minions, who were once socially & politically degraded."[9] These were the social realities upon which North Carolina society rested, Wiley feared; consequently he saw an imperative need to reestablish aristocratic control on more stable foundations.

The editor of the *Raleigh Daily Sentinel* voiced the same concern for restraining the lower classes in August 1865. "Those who prate so loudly against the aristocracy of wealth, or of position," warned the paper, were dangerous. Although such "harpies" did not admit it, "they are levellers," proclaimed the *Sentinel*, and "their doctrines or teachings are agrarian." The *Sentinel* denounced malicious "taunts upon the [wealthy] few, as a 'negro aristocracy,' 'cotton aristocracy,' 'rich, proud nabobs,' [or] 'property holders'" and argued that they were both detrimental to the public good and mistaken. Applying to North Carolina certain well-worn assertions about American opportunity, the paper denied that there were any privileged classes. "It is a libel upon American society to charge it in any of its phases, with the 'aristocracy of wealth,'" the editor wrote. "There is no such thing really among us." Although the *Sentinel* echoed a familiar formula of the gentry by identifying the basis of America's aristocracy as "intelligence, virtue, and enterprise," it quickly returned to the theme of democratic opportunity. "The road to preferment, to position and influence . . . is wide open to every one. The poorest boy or girl that walks our streets, may aspire to the highest position and . . . gain it."[10]

It is doubtful that anyone in North Carolina accepted that statement as literally true in regard to women; without a doubt many men of the yeomen and landless classes had found it to be less than accurate. One man who had managed to rise only to find his progress blocked by aristocrats was William W. Holden. More than any other individual he had resuscitated the Democratic party of the 1840s and guided it to a position of dominance in the 1850s. Brilliant in strategy and deft in communicating with the electorate through slashing articles in his *North Carolina Standard*, Holden had labored tirelessly for the party until, at length, he had sought the reward of public office. Yet in 1858 the wealthy and prominent leaders of the democracy denied him both the gubernatorial nomination and a place in the United States Senate. Sympathetic papers described his opponents as the aristocrats in the party, and Holden himself published a deeply felt comment on the elite's disapproval of his humble background.[11] For Holden had been illegitimate, born out of wedlock to a poor woman.

Illegitimacy was no small thing in North Carolina. Despite the diverse economic backgrounds and relatively modest fame of leading families in the state, members of the gentry believed in their superiority; moreover, they associated respectability and wealth with personal character. When Jonathan Worth broke with "a close friend" in the late 1850s, the most bitter charge that he could level at the man was that he behaved as "a conceited, ill-bred upstart" and had "no breeding." Language of this sort would have resulted in a duel but for the refusal of the Quaker Worth to defend honor in the widely accepted manner.[12] In the eyes of North Carolina's aristocrats, their class naturally produced leaders, not because it virtually precluded outside competition, but because it was the reservoir of talent, intelligence, and virtue. No one could be entirely free of suspicion who had risen from unseemly or humble background, as had Holden.

Or Andrew Johnson for that matter, the new president of the United States. Johnson had been born to a poor family in North Carolina and had grown up in Raleigh. Illiterate until his wife taught him to read and write, Andy Johnson the tailor went on to make an impressive political career for himself in Tennessee, but certain Tar Heels overlooked neither his origins nor what they indicated about him. Incredulous at Johnson's exalted position and the low level from which he sprang, even David Swain (forgetful of his own rise in life) spoke contemptuously of the poor boy who became president. While crediting Johnson with tact, Swain quoted a remark of the English writer Alexander Pope and then added, "I ask pardon of his shade, for applying it to a taylor's apprentice . . . who did not make such an impression on those more highly favored by fortune as to be remembered by any one."[13]

A female member of Wilmington's wealthy de Rosset family was more blunt. "Think of Andy Johnson," she wrote, "[as] the president. (I will not say *our*.) and Holden—governor. With such men, in such places, what will become of us—'the aristocrats of the South' as we are termed?"[14] Others shared both her outrage and disquiet.

There was rational basis for anxiety among the aristocrats. Andrew Johnson had built his entire career upon attacking the aristocracy and championing the common men who suffered from their snubs and their tight grasp on power, wealth, and opportunity. Although Holden had attempted to become a member of the elite and gain full acceptance in its inner circle, he came from the masses and exhibited a remarkably keen perception of their feelings and motives. His ambition for offices higher than he "deserved" and his leadership of the peace movement marked him further as a "demagogue" and a dangerous man. When Johnson excluded men whose wealth exceeded twenty thousand dollars from his amnesty proclamation, he signaled an intention to punish the rich, and, according to one of the principals, upon giving Holden his commission as provisional governor Johnson said, "Now, Holden, you have got these aristocrats in your power, give them hell."[15] Miss de Rosset was right to ask, "With such men, in such places, what will become of us—'the aristocrats of the South'?"

In some ways Holden did attempt to create a new regime in North Carolina. As Andrew Johnson originally intended, Holden set out to identify and raise into influence a new leadership class, one that was more reflective of nonslaveholders and ordinary white farmers. He reached out to knowledgeable men who had been critical of secession, the war, and the policies of the Destructives; from Rufus Lenoir Patterson, for example, he asked for advice and "a list of good and loyal men for Justices in the Counties of Wilkes, Caldwell, Ashe, and Watauga."[16] And he drew on the detailed knowledge of state and local politics that he himself had gained from years as a party operative, candidate for office, and leader of the peace movement. This thorough grounding in the state's affairs enabled Holden to lay the foundation for change by renewing power at its source: the personnel of local government.

His responsibility and opportunity as provisional governor was to reconstitute the governing bodies of the state, from county courts through a constitutional convention to the election of a new legislature and executive. Despite the immensity of the task, Holden succeeded in appointing many new people as justices of the peace. In the plantation district's Edgecombe County, he managed to make only seven new appointments out of seventeen, but in New Hanover County, which had greater diversity due to the presence of Wilmington, thirty-one of forty-four appointees had no previous experience as magistrates. Nineteen of the thirty justices appointed for Caldwell County were new men, and twenty-seven of thirty-nine appointees (almost 70 percent) in Randolph County were new to office.[17] In a system of local government that was highly traditional and rigid, these were wholesale changes that pushed the established oligarchs aside.

Of course, many of Holden's appointees were fairly substantial, proper-

William W. Holden

tied men, for the middle and upper classes, rather than the poor, had produced most party activists. But the change intended by Holden was clear in the slate of justices for Randolph County, where strong antiwar sentiment and unionism had furnished abundant material for a new government. Following the recommendations of the Unionists' June meeting quite closely, Holden made thirty-three of the men they nominated justices, or 85 percent of his appointments. Zebedee Rush of the Heroes of America and Thomas Branson, supporters of the peace movement, became magistrates, and ten of the twelve justices who had previously served carried the endorsement of the June meeting.[18] In local government, Holden's broom had cleared a new path.

Yet, in a basic sense, Holden's actions were far from revolutionary. He sought a reorientation of North Carolina's government rather than an overthrow of the entire system. In the area of race relations, Holden immediately acted to wound the hopes of black people and deflate any expectations they had for change. Admonishing freedmen to remember the "superior intelligence of the white race," he flatly declared that they were not qualified "to discharge all the duties of the citizen." By this he meant voting, for just as Holden had advocated peace to save slavery in 1863, his paper in August 1865 took a stand of "unqualified opposition to what is called negro suffrage." In fact, Holden remained opposed well into the fall of 1866, and he placed heavy, public emphasis on the freedman's obligation to work hard, obey the law, and shun idleness.[19]

He also stood firmly as a guardian of property and order against all types of unrest. Two weeks after taking office he was asking U.S. military authorities to furnish ammunition "as speedily as you can" to county police in Halifax and Northampton; the danger was simply "a large class of idle population in those counties." Even when disturbances involved Unionists and others who were Holden's natural allies politically, the provisional governor spoke out strongly against unrest. Although Holden's "sympathies [were] with the ultra Union men . . . [who were] unjustly . . . treated during the late rebellion," he sternly reminded the magistrates of Yadkin County that under the president's proclamation of amnesty there was "no room for . . . violence." In September 1865, a federal commander notified Holden that sixty men in Randolph County had attacked and beaten a man in the presence of Sheriff Z. F. Rush (son of Zebedee Rush) and Justice of the Peace Sellars, both of whom did nothing. Apparently this was another case of Tar Heels evening the score from wartime conflicts, because complaints had already reached Holden that "some of the magistrates of Randolph are causing persons to be arrested . . . for acts done by the militia while in service hunting deserters." Holden had already ordered such arrests to stop, and within a few days he repeated his injunction against violence.[20]

No doubt Holden disappointed some of his supporters in the matter of appointments, for he did not attempt to bar all of his opponents or even to reduce the influence of prominent men who might adopt his views. The olive branch that Holden offered to Rufus Lenoir Patterson enabled that family to maintain its baronial control of politics in Caldwell County. Secure in the good graces of the provisional government, the Pattersons continued to wield enormous influence at home. When Rufus expressed interest in serving as county representative to the constitutional convention, his father Samuel Finley Patterson assured him that there was "no talk of any opposition." Rufus was unable to visit Caldwell "several days before the election" as his family had advised, so his father and cousin simply went into Lenoir on Saturday, mixed with the people, and then had the sheriff assemble a crowd in the Court House. The family patriarch announced Rufus's candidacy and offered to explain his son's views. The audience raised no public objection, and Samuel Finley Patterson added this postscript to his letter: "I will attend to having your certificate of election made out and forwarded in due time."[21] Eventually Rufus Lenoir Patterson became a Republican, but in the meantime some in Caldwell County surely felt that little had changed.

Almost 100 citizens of Cleveland County found fault with Holden's actions and petitioned the governor "to remove from Office . . . disloyal men whom you have appointed." Another 140 in Alamance County complained of bad appointments, particularly that of Jesse Gant, a wealthy farmer and previous officeholder who in 1860 had owned thirty-seven slaves. Holden made seventeen additional appointments in Alamance to ensure a unionist majority, but he refused to remove anyone. He also helped some prominent planters gain pardons, writing out a request on the spot for Paul Cameron and Thomas Ruffin when Cameron challenged Holden's refusal to support his case.[22]

Eventually complaints by Unionists reached President Johnson, who asked Holden if it was true that "the true Union men are totally ignored." Denying the accusation, Holden admitted that some mistakes were possible in almost four thousand appointments; still he insisted that he tried to prefer "persons who were originally Union men, and persons who were in favor of restoring the authority of the federal government." This last category, however, could be a very broad one, and conservative historian J. G. de Roulhac Hamilton was correct in observing that Holden "was less proscriptive than might have been expected or, in fact, than was expected . . . in view of the events of the preceding five years." He also supported the interests of planters through the state's agent in Washington, who apologized for federal delays in returning to "our people in the Eastern portion of the State . . . their property, now improperly held by the Freedmen's Bureau."[23]

Yet none of this was conservative enough for some influential figures from the old elite. At the extreme there was an inability to accept the idea that North Carolina's wartime government, a treasonous, rebel government in northern eyes, had been illegitimate or that President Johnson's Provisional Government could be legitimate and proper. David Swain and Nathaniel Boyden, president of the North Carolina Railroad, both wrote to Thomas Ruffin and deprecated the confusion arising from new sets of officeholders; they objected to the creation of any new officials and felt the wartime government should continue without change.[24] In addition, public issues concerning money and the limits on democracy arose.

Given the hard times that prevailed in the state, many ordinary Tar Heels desperately needed a breathing space in which to reestablish themselves economically. Heavy taxes or creditors beating on their doors might spell ruin. As a Union County man wrote to Governor Holden, "if we ar[en']t [al]lowed the Home Stid [homestead tax exemption] on old dept [debt] the union party will bee Dun with . . . all the Deptes [debts] upt to the Serrender ought to Bee ded [dead]."[25] But to members of the gentry, debt was a form of property, creditors' property. Interference with the collection of debts was a threat to order. Stay laws were wrong and repudiation anathema.

Jonathan Worth and conservative men like him believed that the Confederate debt should be paid and feared that the Reconstruction convention would repudiate that debt and then renounce other state obligations as well. Rufus Lenoir Patterson shared these fears when he sat in the convention in October 1865. Although "the Convention [was] more Conservative than I at first supposed," Patterson remained "very much afraid that Republicanism will triumph in NC." He sat on the committee that recommended no action on the war debt, but worried, "there is no telling . . . what the radicals will do." When Thomas Settle of Rockingham County made "a *warm* speech in favor of *Repudiation*," Patterson condemned him as "seeking political preferment" through "demagogical speeches." Another delegate to the convention observed that "a great deal of the talent & most all the wealth of the State" favored honoring the debt but recognized that, at the least, due to pressure from the electorate, "a strong Stay Law will be passed . . . either by Convention or Legislature."[26]

The *Raleigh Daily Sentinel* voiced establishment opinion in August 1865, when it asked, "Shall North Carolina repudiate—ignore a just debt contracted by her people or her constituted authorities? The very thought is humiliating, withering. Nor does it do to say, that the debt was illegal. . . . The question is was the debt contracted under her assumed authority?" The *Sentinel* deplored the fact that several counties elected delegates because they favored repudiation, and its editor called for a return to stable, conservative government. Justices of the peace "should be the conservators and guardians of the public morals . . . [they] should be always selected from the best men of the country." Similarly the *Sentinel* defended limitations on democracy: the abolition of property qualifications for office, proposed by Holden's *Standard*, would be "monstrous." As for free suffrage, enacted in 1857 after a long struggle, "the intelligence of North Carolina to-day would if possible, strike it from the Constitution and restore the old regime."[27]

Not only were these opinions extremely conservative, but also they were unrealistic in the context of national politics, for the North was soon to require that southern democracy move forward rather than backward. Victor Barringer, a professor at Davidson College and brother of Confederate General Rufus Barringer, had warned in the pages of the *Sentinel* that the victorious North would demand Negro suffrage. Deploring this opinion, the paper clung to its own view that mere acceptance of emancipation was "an immense sacrifice to offer upon the altar of peace and Union." Many members of the convention were not ready to make other sacrifices. After declaring secession null and void, prohibiting slavery, and submitting both measures to the voters, they felt they had done enough. When President Johnson, upon inquiry from Holden, insisted on repudiation of North Carolina's wartime debt, a majority complied, but many were angry and resentful.[28]

The issue of the debt helped to cause a split between Jonathan Worth and Holden. Although Worth had worked closely with the provisional governor earlier in the summer, he took a position as state treasurer that North Carolina should not repudiate the debt. Only two days after the convention voted for repudiation, Worth announced as a candidate against Holden for governor. Worth also was angry that Holden had opposed the pardons of a few prominent Whigs while aiding some secessionist Democrats, and he disapproved of Holden's shifts in political direction. Seeing himself as a man of consistency and principle, Worth sensed that Holden's inconsistent course had made him vulnerable.

Because only three weeks remained before the election, the campaign was short. Although Worth did not favor defying the president on the debt, his conservative fiscal views were plain, and he stood behind his record as a staunch friend of the Union before his state seceded.[29] Thus the state treasurer was clearly the more conservative candidate, yet one who could be defended before the North.

Worth had correctly gauged the emotional opposition that Holden aroused. Furthermore, Worth was in an enviable political position. His affection for the Union and distaste for the war had been sincere enough to make him very acceptable to wartime Conservatives yet restrained enough not to offend former Confederates. Although Holden's daring advocacy of peace had insured his victory in the strongest unionist counties, such as Randolph, Wilkes, and Bertie, Worth could take some pro-Union votes from him elsewhere. More importantly, Jonathan Worth was far more popular with secessionists and Destructives than Holden. These people loathed Holden as a traitorous former ally and unprincipled demagogue. Although Worth had bitterly deplored the Destructives' acts, they accurately saw him as a consistent and conservative man free of dangerous tendencies. Only five days after he became a candidate, Worth was gloating over a strange, new political alignment that would aid him: "It is generally conceded that I will beat [Holden] largely in the East."[30]

The irony of this realignment was lost on Jonathan Worth. He welcomed his victory by almost six thousand votes out of sixty thousand even though it came "largely" from the hands of those who had been his wartime opponents. Several eastern counties that voted heavily for Worth voted simultaneously against repeal of the ordinance of secession. Camden, Currituck, Duplin, Edgecombe, Gates, Jones, and Pitt counties all refused to repudiate secession, and they all supported Worth by lopsided margins, giving him 82.3 percent of their combined vote. This fact illustrated to some Unionists that Worth was not "the candidate of the *Union men of the state*."[31]

Worth won partly because Holden had failed to seize that title for himself. Holden had little time to build a grass-roots organization, but he also had not tried to transform wartime divisions into new political align-

Jonathan Worth

ments. Still hoping for acceptance from a gentry that had largely turned against him, Holden had tried to reorient politics not revolutionize it. He made no stirring appeal to poorer whites who had shown their alienation from the wartime government. He did not give a clear enough signal to thousands of ordinary Tar Heels, struggling under the destruction and poverty caused by war, that a new, more democratic day had dawned. Unorganized and weighted down by personal calamities, many of them had not gone to the polls; turnout was even lower than in 1864. An opportunity to redefine politics along lines of the class consciousness raised by the war had not been taken. Instead, Jonathan Worth had begun to pull prominent critics of the war into an alliance with staunch conservatives.

The prospect of embracing "the wicked men . . . who inaugurated" the war failed to trouble Worth because he failed to see Reconstruction in terms of Unionist vs. secessionist. To him North Carolina was a loyal state that had been forced out of the Union by unfortunate circumstances. As a conservative man and an original Whig, he envisioned both a minimal Reconstruction and the resumption of traditional party politics in the state. Indeed, as one observer noted, "the old parties are both alive, and neither of them a whit . . . less pugilistic." Worth saw himself as a Whig opposing Holden the Democrat, a man of principle opposing a somewhat unscrupulous office-seeker; if Holden's foes within the Democracy came over to his side, they were so much the wiser. To baffled outsiders who saw Holden's defeat as a sign of hostility to Reconstruction, Worth could sincerely make the claim that, "the old Whig party of the State . . . was the real Union party."[32]

Thus Jonathan Worth entered upon a reconciliation with Destructives and conservative Democrats, and he immediately took stands on financial questions that deepened this alliance. In his first message to the legislature he recommended "repeal of the stay law which I have always regarded as unconstitutional and unwise, pernicious . . . and demoralizing." Although he expected this recommendation to be "disregarded" by the people's representatives and "disapproved" by the press, Worth was determined to stand on principle, and he remained steadfast in support of creditors' interests. In April 1866, he stated his conviction that there were "persons" in the state who wanted to find a rival candidate for governor "who would go for out and out repudiation" of the antebellum state debt, if they could find anyone "so shameless." To his son-in-law Worth confided, "I believe the great body of the people are opposed to paying [the debt]."[33]

In his appointments to government Worth also found common ground with former Confederates and Democrats. When a friend suggested several names for seats on the state Literary Board, he assured Worth that the men suggested were "all of that conservative, honest class [of] which you can boast." In other words, they were all from the gentry. An old Whig like Worth believed, as did the aristocratic Democrats who had opposed Holden, that only such men should govern, for only such men were fit to govern. The idea of disfranchising Confederate leaders, which Congress was writing into the proposed Fourteenth Amendment, was anathema to Worth and many established leaders. Calvin Wiley branded as "radical" the constitutional changes adopted by Missouri and Tennessee to disfranchise prominent Confederates; such an approach would amount to "disfranchising the better half of the state."[34] Jonathan Worth believed in "the better half."

As governor he quickly restored this class to power in local government. Reversing the changes made by Holden, Worth appointed justices of the peace who reflected the persistent influence of old families as strongly as Holden's appointees had signaled a break with tradition. The possibility of change, which was present in Holden's governments, disappeared. In Caldwell County thirteen men who had been active on past courts took charge of county affairs once more, along with only five new faces, and Samuel Finley Patterson reclaimed his accustomed role as chairman. In Randolph County fifteen justices emerged as the decision-making cadre, and nine of these were old hands on the court. Out of fifty-two Randolph appointments in all, Worth elevated men nominated by the unionist meeting of June 1865 in only 52 percent of the cases, a significantly lower percentage than that among Holden's appointees. The loss of records for Alamance County prevents comparison with Holden's actions, but of fifteen justices who frequently attended county court under Worth, four had been active before the Civil War and another seven bore the family names of former justices. Jesse Gant, who had aroused the ire of 140 Unionist petitioners, now presided as chairman. In Edgecombe ten of the nineteen most active justices had served previously and in New Hanover twenty-four out of thirty-two magistrates maintained the habit of power, with the Honorable William Wright returning to the chair.[35]

In social and economic terms these appointments meant that the wealthy old elite of planters plus a few merchants and professionals returned to power. Comparison of the average wealth of these county courts before the defeat of the Confederacy and under Worth's governorship

TABLE 12

Changes in Average Wealth of County Officials, 1860–1867

County	Years	Real Estate	Personal Estate	Years	Real Estate	Personal Estate
Caldwell	1860–65	$13,122	$12,504	1866–67	$8,127	$7,724
Randolph	1860–65	3,077	6,511	1866–67	3,293	5,989
Alamance	1857–60	10,374	25,717	1866–67	10,523	26,388
Edgecombe	1860–65	17,125	33,750	1866–67	23,333	24,300
New Hanover	1860–65	7,343	19,560	1866–67	$13,050	

Source: County court minutes, U.S. Census of Population for 1860 and, in a few cases, 1870, and tax lists of New Hanover County for the years 1856 and 1865–66.

Note: The county court minutes for Alamance County are not extant for the years 1861–65, so the years 1857–60 were used as the comparison period. The New Hanover County tax lists account for the single figure on wealth appearing in the table. Data on wealth were found for 11 of 17 justices in Caldwell County, 7 of 15 in Randolph County, 10 of 15 in Alamance County, 6 of 19 in Edgecombe County, and 29 of 31 in New Hanover County.

shows little or no change (see table 12). Despite use in some cases of data from the 1870 manuscript census, which reflected the substantial loss of wealth in slaves, the average wealth of justices dropped very little or in some cases rose. Thus Jonathan Worth brought back the squirearchy.

To Worth it was satisfying to think that "the virtue and intelligence of the State and of all political parties is for me," even if he worried that in 1866 the opposition might field a candidate skilled in the "demagogue arts." But a few North Carolinians resented the wholesale return of the old order. D. F. Caldwell of Greensboro exemplified the potential for change in local affairs that Worth snuffed out. A man of influence in Guilford County, Caldwell had braved violence to win election to the state house in 1864 as a peace candidate. After the war he developed plans that featured aid for Unionists who had suffered during the war and education, especially for the children of "conscripts" killed in battle. He also considered an expanded system of local government that would "educate the people by letting the boys have a chance to act as constables, coroners, commissioners, magistrates, etc., etc."[36]

When Caldwell discerned the reactionary course that Worth was taking, he wrote the governor an angry letter of criticism in July 1866, upbraiding him for allying with secessionists and forgetting his old friends. Worth's appointees, Caldwell protested, were trying to ruin Union men who did not agree with them. "Nor do I think it wise or prudent," warned Caldwell, "to aid a miserable old sullen aristocratic clique to continue their sway in N.C. forever." In vain he cautioned Worth against the influence of "[former] Gov. Graham, Judge Manly, Ruffin, and hosts of such men."[37] But Worth used his long personal association with Caldwell to pull him slowly into the Conservative ranks. There Caldwell's ideas for democratic reform came to nothing.[38]

Meanwhile, the events of national Reconstruction were pushing the conservative Worth into an even tighter embrace with reactionary elements. As the conflict between President Johnson and Congress grew heated, Worth became adamant in his support of Johnson and the status quo. The governor raged against the northern legislators, especially the minority of Radical Republicans, and encouraged North Carolinians to stand behind the president. Enlisting as an ally in the political struggle to defend Johnson's program, Worth asserted tirelessly that North Carolina was completely peaceable and loyal and ignored all evidence to the contrary.

In fact, violence was widespread and serious throughout Jonathan Worth's governorship. According to a very thorough study of the subject, the levels of violence in early phases of Reconstruction came close to equaling the later lawlessness of the Ku Klux Klan, which has attracted far more attention. Postwar violence took several forms, including conflict between Unionists and Confederates, attacks by self-styled Regulators upon tax collectors and tax records, and especially persecution of freedmen and those who aided the freedmen (to be discussed in the next chapter). Despite claims to the contrary, law and order did not return to North Carolina after the war; instead wartime patterns of extra-legal, violent activity continued to be an unusually frequent feature of life.[39]

Revenge was a prominent motive in the violence among whites. The combative, individualistic yeomen and the privileged aristocrats were making the postwar readjustment "just what they made the Rebellion—" noted one keen observer, "a personal issue with another class of the people." And undeniably many incidents of personal revenge had both personal and class dimensions. The traveler John Dennett reported from Chatham County that, "I everywhere hear stories of assaults made upon persons who were formerly in the service of the Confederate government, and especially upon such as were engaged in picking up deserters." A magistrate in Asheboro (Randolph County) told of "more than a hundred houses owned by secessionists which had been broken into and robbed within the past few months." He had a shrewd explanation: "Them out-layin' boys had learned a little bushwackin' when the secessioners learn'd 'em to live in the woods." According to Sidney Andrews, wartime Union-ists were still rebelling "against the little tyranny of local politicians," and "not a few" of these lower-class whites "claim that the farms of the leading Rebels should be apportioned out among those who fought Rebels." For their part, the secessionists were equally determined. When asked about the power of the antisecessionists, Dennett's Pittsboro landlord re-sponded, "wait two years and then you'll see. We've got to get back into the Union . . . first of all get back and [then] get our own State into our own hands."[40]

Because he was intent upon restoring North Carolina to the Union without modification of Johnson's program, Jonathan Worth denied this reality. Any group that undercut his position drew his ire, including con-servative newspapers. In January 1867, Worth was outraged that an edito-rial in the *Tarboro Southerner* stated that "*organized* companies of malefac-tors in Pitt [and] Greene" counties had defeated the militia. Worth admitted that "there are lurking robbers and murderers" but deplored the description of organized resistance because it would damage the state's position before Congress. Similarly he condemned the *Goldsboro News* and the *Newbern Commercial* for reporting "gross murders, robberies, etc." Earlier, in the summer of 1866, four hundred citizens of Forsyth and Stokes counties petitioned B. S. Hedrick in Washington, D.C. and com-plained that local officials were unfairly prosecuting Union men and wink-ing at offenses of rebels. Hedrick, who was informally assisting Worth with the state's affairs in the capital, warned him "that numerous indict-ments are being found against the Union men," especially in western and mountain counties. Despite similar reports from others, the governor chose to believe that such complaints represented a conspiracy instigated by William Holden for the purpose of reviving martial law over the state.[41]

By July 1866, Worth had grown so bitter about the North's desire for change in the South that he thereafter cooperated with conservatives op-posed to virtually any change within the state. B. S. Hedrick supplied Worth with a steady flow of accurate, insightful information about north-ern public opinion and about trends in Congress, but the governor ig-nored it all. His essential conservatism, which had led him to oppose secession and the war because they were dangerous and unwise, now made him unable to adjust to change in the old order. The Fourteenth Amendment, he declared, could only restore "a worthless Union . . . [of] mutual detestation and abhorrence. . . . No Southern State, where the people are free to vote, will adopt it. . . . I would submit to confiscation or any other calamity which brute force can impose before I would be guilty of the self-degradation of voting for this amendment."[42]

Worth had accurately predicted the position of most established southern politicians, whom Andrew Johnson had led to believe that Reconstruction would be simple and brief, and in this atmosphere of hardening positions even small democratic changes met with attack. The convention that convened in 1865 had been part of President Johnson's program of Reconstruction, but by 1866 conservatives "desired its dissolution because a large number of its members were adherents of Holden."[43] When this convention completed its work and proposed a revised constitution, conservatives launched a battle against some of its modestly democratic features.

Thus the first struggle of Reconstruction within North Carolina concerned the extent of democracy among whites. Amidst the confused atmosphere of disagreements between president and Congress and changing national policies, prominent members of the old guard determined to arrest the liberalizing tendency that had slowly gained ground in the state during the 1850s. Their arguments against the proposed constitution showed that they actually wanted to reverse course and strengthen the elites that had been threatened during the war. As that experience showed, power needed to be more securely placed in the hands of "the better half."

The principal task of the constitutional convention of 1865–66, aside from incorporating earlier changes, had been to adjust North Carolina's fundamental law to the facts of war, emancipation, and defeat. That required repudiation of secession and the acknowledgement of the end of slavery. Various clauses that depended on the newly extinct institution had to be modified, and one such clause involved representation. Seats in the house of commons had been apportioned to the counties in accord with the federal ratio, which counted a slave as three-fifths of a white person. The white convention's most telling reaction to emancipation was to prohibit black people from voting or holding office, but because it could no longer count them as slaves, the convention decided to adopt the "white basis," that is to base representation in the house upon the number of white people. That change, which would benefit western districts, was the most significant movement in a democratic direction. The only other liberalizing revision provided for the election of county magistrates for terms of six years.

In all other respects the proposed constitution remained soundly conservative. The residence requirement for governor and legislators was five years, and property qualifications for officeholders continued in the amounts of two thousand dollars worth of land for governor, three hundred acres or a freehold worth one thousand dollars for state senators, and one hundred acres or land with a three hundred dollar value for members of the house. Thus, as before, a large portion of the state's white population would be legally too poor to qualify for service in the legislature and blacks would be prohibited. In addition no amendments could be made in the future except by a convention.[44]

But this constitution was not conservative enough. State legislator Edward Conigland detected in the document influences of "the popular doctrine, namely the indefeasible right of a mere numerical majority to have all power vested in their hands." Writing to Thomas Ruffin, Conigland declared that he was one of many who had not accepted such ideas and stood ready to defend "true principles of government." A stalwart defense was needed, Conigland feared, for "a spirit of radicalism is at work which will not cease until the [state] Judges are made elective for short terms, and until all property qualification for office is destroyed." Conigland regretted the shift to election of county magistrates, and a telling indicator of his extreme conservatism was that he criticized B. F. Moore, an opponent of elective judgeships, for supporting the replacement of Confederate judges with new officials.[45]

Conigland found many sympathizers among the elite; in the reaction against congressional Reconstruction, even the modest changes drawn up by Andrew Johnson's government in 1865 now seemed too liberal. The traditionally dominant political classes of the state—the gentry and the middle class—were growing determined to accept nothing beyond the mild adjustments of presidential Reconstruction. Moreover, the popular forces that would naturally support the white basis and local democracy lacked organization. William Holden was their likely and best-known leader, but he had not yet begun to organize a Republican party among Tar Heels. Without strong leadership and beset by economic difficulties, many yeomen and landless whites faced a confusing, unfocused political scene.

Thomas Ruffin provided the rallying cry for conservatives, however, in

Thomas Ruffin

a thundering denunciation of the proposed constitution. In a long article published in various newspapers, Ruffin attacked the very legitimacy of the "so-called" convention and the "so-called" constitution that it had written. "Your Convention was not a legitimate Convention and had no power to make a Constitution for us. . . . It was called without the consent of the People of No. Ca." Even President Johnson, now the South's ally, was guilty of "clear and despotic usurpation" in requiring a convention, and Johnson's exclusion of "the best Men" of the state from political participation meant that the people did not choose the document's authors. "How dare they" write fundamental law for the state, Ruffin exclaimed. Denying that secession and defeat could carry any practical penalties, he argued that there was no middle ground between the intolerable view that North Carolina was conquered territory utterly without law, on the one hand, and the view that all laws and officials remained in power regardless of secession, on the other.[46]

Ruffin also revealed the cherished principles of aristocratic thought in an offended dismissal of the "white basis" as "the very worst basis of representation, that could have been selected." According to this experienced jurist there was an essential difference between natural rights and political rights. The "natural rights inherent in freedom" entitled people to "security in person and property" under the law; but political rights were "conventional" not "natural" because they involved "powers *over* the Constitution and laws" and were granted "according to the sense of the Community of the fitness of particular classes." Before granting the right of suffrage, the community had to consider "the homogeneity of the classes" and the safety of both the government and the most "intelligent, virtuous, and valuable portion of the population." Just as "women and minors . . . [even] of the most favoured race" could not vote because giving them that right would be "impolitic and unsafe," Ruffin held that Negro voters should be excluded "for all time to come, if not forever."[47]

Offering an alternative to the white basis, Ruffin then articulated a philosophy of aristocratic privilege couched in the most encompassing, if deceptive, paternalistic terms. Like women and minors, black people were "bound by the laws that may be made and therefore, as much interested in them" as whites. Therefore lawmakers ought to be "men who are their neighbors, know their wants and condition and sympathize with them both in their wants and wishes." Only if representation were based on the number of whites plus nonvoting blacks could society "guard the interests of all, whether voters or not." Former slaveowners and plantation districts should gain representation in the legislature so that their representatives could "guard the rights" of black citizens—by deciding "whether they shall be educated" and by finding ways to "make them contented and as happy as their subordinate and dependent condition will allow."[48] In a nutshell, Ruffin believed that for the benefit of blacks power should shift even further toward the formerly slaveowning whites.

Holden's *North Carolina Standard* attacked the selfish class interests behind Ruffin's view and charged that men of his stamp wanted to force payment of the "rebel debt." An article in the *Old North State* called on "the people of Western North Carolina to rally" against Ruffin's "extreme *Eastern* view," but admitted that conservative opposition to the constitution in the East was "very general." One of the strongest replies to Ruffin, which was not published until after the referendum, came from B. F. Moore, who emphasized how unrealistic the old judge's views were in light of the fact that the war had occurred. But "Orange" (probably Samuel F. Phillips, speaker of the house) warned "conservative gentlemen" through the *Sentinel* that this constitution was as good as they could get—within ten years there would be "the white basis in both Houses, or a negro-suffrage in both, the abolishment of all property qualifications for office, the election of Judges . . . and many other inventions of that American Democracy which is surging and hissing, at a white heat, throughout this continent."[49]

In private Ruffin scorned Phillips as a demagogue "of the first water," a man who "retains the coarseness of his origin" despite talents and education. Other conservatives shared this strong reaction against supporters of the constitution. In fact some opposed the constitution even more totally than Ruffin. One writer to the *Wilmington Journal* focused on the amendment giving each county and district the right to elect justices of the peace. If the legislature subsequently removed trial by jury in petty misdemeanors, these cases would rest with elected magistrates, possibly "bad m[e]n." "A reign of terror may be inaugurated under this new Constitution," asserted the writer, who concluded, "to this dangerous innovation I can never give my assent."[50]

In large numbers conservatives withheld their assent, while many ordinary white men who were the logical supporters of the constitution failed to cast a ballot. On 2 August 1866, the proposed constitution went down to defeat, 21,552 votes to 19,570, in the smallest ballot of any election during the Civil War or Reconstruction. Only 41,122 voters participated compared to more than 112,000 in the 1860 gubernatorial election and

approximately 72,000 in the 1864 race for the same office.[51] Undoubtedly the wealthier classes who had long dominated politics turned out to
protect their interests, whereas the common people remained unorganized and as yet uninvolved in the shifting issues of Reconstruction. Indeed, many white yeomen and farm laborers were leaving North Carolina
to seek opportunity elsewhere. The brother-in-law of Jonathan Worth
reported more immigration to Indiana than "for many years . . . thousands and still they come." Very few, this man added, were "of the better
class."[52]

Despite defeat of the constitution, many observers still believed that
class issues were potent. E. J. Warren of Washington, N.C. who opposed
Worth but viewed himself as a conservative, declared, "there is no better
theme for popular orators than the proposed new constitution." "The
West will be aroused and indignant at [its] rejection," he predicted, and "a
candidate who will take his stand upon the white basis . . . will . . . have
some chance of success." Worth himself expected attack from this quarter;
he predicted that "the small band of Radicals" in North Carolina would
"nominate Genl Logan of Rutherford and . . . mix up some white basis
issue." When the election for governor rolled around in October 1866,
however, Holden and his allies could do no better than to nominate Alfred Dockery, who refused to run. Worth thus won reelection in another
poorly attended election, which drew only 44,994 voters.[53]

Thus a socially conservative elite fearful of democracy succeeded in
reestablishing itself in North Carolina. But ironically, it secured its position within the state at the very moment when that position became most
tenuous nationally. The stubborn intransigence of men like Worth and
Ruffin was turning the northern public against President Johnson's program, and Weldon Edwards recognized that the northern congressional
elections late in 1866 meant "utter ruin and abject degradation" for southern whites determined to yield not one inch. As the internal clamor for
relief from debt continued, external political events turned against white
conservatives, and a new northern Congress came to Washington determined to keep Andrew Johnson from losing the peace.[54] After 1866, this
Congress required a new beginning in Reconstruction, one which extended the principles of democracy much farther than they had ever
reached in the South before. Equal rights among all classes of whites
became a subsidiary issue.

But North Carolina's gentry did not forget. Its opposition to "unqualified" whites had been a serious effort based on utter conviction, and the aristocratic attitudes that underlay the ephemeral victories of 1866 continued to shape elite thinking through the rest of Reconstruction. Consider, for example, the shocked disapproval of rising attorney David Schenck, who saw two Negro men included in a jury pool in Catawba Superior Court during 1867. The panel, Schenck raged, "was the most inferior in intelligence I ever saw in N.C.," but not solely because of the presence of the two "unadulterated Africans." More basic was the fact that the panel had been drawn "from the tax payers in general without regard to freehold qualifications," that is from a pool including lower-class people of both races who were inherently unfit to govern. "The negroes were about of average intelligence with the whites," Schenck observed.[55]

"What is called 'Manhood Suffrage'" was completely distasteful to men who believed, with Walter F. Leak, in "a *qualified* right [of suffrage], which looks to morals and intelligence. Political rights, in a great degree like *social* position, should never be conferd, but should be *earned*; leaving to the Negro *as well as to others* to take that position which his character and intelligence assign him." To North Carolina's gentry the character and intelligence of the masses of whites were permanently deficient. Jonathan Worth warned a Philadelphia businessman that, "all laboring for wages here, white or black, are poor and improvident," and advised obtaining laborers by paying them "promptly by *the week* or by the *day* and at very low wages." Such stern exploitation made sense because "Providence has so ordered it that a majority of mankind are improvident . . . and hence the non-property holder will be antagonistic to the property holder. Civilization consists in the possession and protection of property."[56]

Just as it had before the Civil War, North Carolina's traditional elite shared Worth's fear of "the universal suffrage principle . . . as undermining civilization." Congress's Reconstruction policy was subversive of the essential hierarchy in society: "Agrarianism and anarchy must be the result of this ultra democracy." After the lower orders received the vote in 1868, Jonathan Worth grimly observed, "Nobody surrenders power. If there be any rational hope of future good government here it must be looked for in Revolution." His judgment on the shift in national policy was more eloquent but no different than that of most political and social leaders. "I abhor the democratic tendency of our government," wrote Worth. "The tendency is to ignore virtue and property and intelligence—and to put the powers of government into the hands of mere *numbers*." To proud elitists such contravention of aristocratic values was galling and intolerable, an outrage that compelled them to redouble their fight to secure rigid hierarchy and reliable social control. For, as Jonathan Worth put it in 1868, "At present the basis of our government is Ignorance. The dregs of society . . . rule the State."[57]

RECONSTRUCTION: THE BATTLE
AGAINST BLACK FREEDOM

Benjamin Harrington was one of the "dregs of society." He was a freed-man, one of more than 330,000 black North Carolinians who no longer were chattel. He was glad of his new legal status and eager to assume the rights of a citizen. But in the early years of Reconstruction he did not "rule the state." In fact, he encountered strong opposition as he tried to manage even the most personal family matters in his life. The opposition came from whites who formerly held power over him and even from those whites who were supposed to be his friends, and his experience was representative. For North Carolina's black people found that the white world firmly resisted the substance of black freedom.

Benjamin Harrington's troubles began in 1866 when his former master, William D. Harrington, succeeded in having two young Negro boys apprenticed to him by authority of the Freedmen's Bureau. The two boys were Hugh Harrington and Scott Harrington, ages fourteen and twelve. The problem was that Benjamin Harrington wanted his sons to live with him, and he took them to his home.

William D. Harrington, on the other hand, wanted his young workers back, and he brought before Manchester N. Weld, agent of the Freedmen's Bureau, a charge that "Benj. Harrington (col'd) had enticed" two apprentices away in violation of their contract. The bureau was determined to instruct black people in the observance of valid contracts, so Weld ordered Benjamin Harrington to return the boys to their master. Benjamin took "no notice" of the order; worse, he showed a defiant spirit. When Weld had an assistant deliver a legal document to Benjamin Harrington, he "refused to obey the summons" and sent back this message: "If he [Weld] has any more business with me than I have with him, he can come to me." On 1 October 1867 Harrington again refused a military summons, saying, "You need not come Coloneling around me, for I won't go for none of them."

Though the Freedmen's Bureau often helped blacks, Weld felt that his authority was being undermined. The issue, he wrote a superior, was "who shall rule in this dist[rict]—the United States Government or Mr. Sambo?"[1] Constantly assailed and pressured by former slaveholders, Agent Weld was not ready to be challenged or defied by former slaves. His actions, as well as his language, showed that black people faced a formidable task in seeking the full benefits of freedom.

Ranged against them were the manifold effects of two hundred years of prejudice and oppression, for as one historian has put it, emancipation did not eradicate an intangible but real "institution." This was the institution of caste prejudice, an institution that prescribed the "'proper' ways to manage all the intercourse between the races" so that Negro inferiority was always upheld. In both law and custom the South had erected a massive structure of white supremacy, complete with its own "ritual," its "deeply instilled emotional attitudes," and its "prescribed behavioral patterns." From the seventeenth century onward, laws, supported by custom, had stigmatized black people and dictated that they always be subordinate and deferential to whites. "Not all the slaveholding states had specific laws regarding the insult or assault of a white person by a Negro, but, in any event, unwritten law took care of the matter."[2]

North Carolina's legal records documented the powerful hold that caste had both on social practice and legal doctrine. Even passing references in case reports to racial attitudes and etiquette spoke volumes about the long tradition of oppression by whites against blacks. The prosecution of a man named Evans in 1796 resulted from his quarrel with one Nicolson, and the court record succinctly explained the aggravating circumstance of the altercation. "Nicolson said, I will not fight you myself, but I have a negro fellow shall fight you. This exasperated Evans to a great degree." Like other white North Carolinians, Evans regarded the suggestion that he was, in any way, on a level of equality with a Negro insulting in the extreme. Similarly, in 1821 one man challenged another to a duel over these words, preserved in the record of *State v. Farrier*: "I would as soon vote for Jim, the [Negro] barber, as you."[3]

As events would show, there were a few whites willing to vote for blacks or put some goals above prejudice, but community mores generally demanded their chastisement. Thomas Hall, a former slave, described this reality years later near the end of his long life: "There are a few white men who are [all right], but the pressure is such from [their] white friends that [they are] compelled to talk against us and give us the cold shoulder." This rule clearly applied in 1829, when two men named Pemberton and Smith were indicted, tried, and convicted for the "crime" of playing "at cards with certain slaves." Ultimately the Supreme Court saved them from penalty on the grounds that there was no law or common law rule against what they had done, yet clearly the punishment of community opinion was already under way.[4]

As a guide for and an expression of white majority opinion, the law steadily made life more difficult for black North Carolinians during the antebellum period. Although a number of scholars have "extolled . . . the humanity shown the slave by the laws and courts" of the state, compared to the rest of the South, that humanity was far from absolute.[5] It was in North Carolina, after all, that Chief Justice Thomas Ruffin had delivered his famous dictum in 1829: "The power of the master must be absolute, to render the submission of the slave perfect." Although Ruffin's view was not always followed, there remained many areas of harshness in the law, and these increased with the reaction to David Walker's *Appeal* in 1829 and the Nat Turner rebellion two years later.[6] A law in 1830 forbade slaves to teach one another and made it an indictable offense for any white to teach a slave to read or write.[7] Slaves had always been prohibited from acting in the manner of free men (as early as 1794, for example, it was illegal for any owner to allow his slaves to hire out their own time).[8] After 1830 the legislature made it far more difficult for any slave to become free through manumission by requiring that "he, she, or they will leave the State, within ninety days . . . and never will return."[9]

The courts upheld the power of whites over both enslaved and free Negroes in social practice. White judges assumed that black people had to be kept in their place, and to assure this end the patrols were given great latitude and every white citizen was supported against the "insolence" of blacks. In an 1817 case, a master sued a patroller and several citizens for abusing his slave; even though the patroller had not acted in concert with the legally constituted patrol but had merely taken friends with him to a plantation and beaten a slave after ignoring a pass written by the slave's mistress, the jury returned a verdict of "Not Guilty, as to all."[10] In 1821 the North Carolina Supreme Court affirmed the innocence of patrollers who had been charged with beating a slave out of malice toward his owner. In its opinion the Supreme Court declared that juries were not to "examine with the most scrupulous exactness into the size of the instrument, or the force with which it was used, as some discretion must necessarily be allowed patrols"; they were free to use any punishments "commonly" employed by masters.[11]

Violence toward slaves and free blacks received a sympathetic hearing by the Supreme Court in two cases. *State v. Tackett*, 1820, concerned the murder of a slave by a white man who was not his master. The court ordered a new trial for the convicted defendant on the grounds that the trial judge had erred in not allowing testimony concerning the victim's demeanor toward other whites generally. "Where slavery prevails," held the Supreme Court, "the relation between a white man and a slave differs from that, which subsists between free persons; and every individual in the community feels and understands, that the homicide of a slave may be extenuated by acts, which would not produce a legal provocation if done by a white person."[12]

No Negro should be allowed to be provoking, as the Supreme Court made clear in *State v. Jowers*, 1850, a case in which a white man was indicted for an affray with a free black. Chief Justice Richmond Pearson declared that black "insolence" to a white man "would be insufferable." Regretting that free blacks remained in the state, Pearson wrote, "It is unfortunate, that *this third class* exists in our society. . . . A free negro has no master to correct him . . . and unless a white man, to whom insolence is given, has a right to put a stop to it, in an extra judicial way, there is no remedy for it. . . . Hence we infer from the principles of the common law, that this extra judicial remedy is excusable."[13]

These rulings reflected the reality of a social system that took the oppression of black people as a given. This assumption had not disappeared with the war. Tar Heel whites had grown up within the system and been socialized to adopt its beliefs. Though some individuals may have escaped its teachings or deviated from its practices, the great majority had not, and for every exception there were several people ready to enforce traditional rules. The victorious North may have imposed emancipation, but it had not removed the national blight of racism, and caste prejudice remained very much alive in the South.

Nothing was more obvious to the travelers and observers who visited North Carolina immediately after the war. The ubiquity and strength of racism struck them as one of the most salient facts about the state. Sidney Andrews was amazed that everyone in the white community opposed Negro suffrage and assumed little would change, ignoring "the fact that there has been a deluge." John Richard Dennett met a farmer near Greensboro who had gotten "some o' the boys" to help him "run out" a Negro because the man had briefly worked for him, then left. "We a'n't agoin' to let niggers walk over us," said the man in explanation of his action. "We can take care o' our black ones as soon as the Yankees is gone." This man preferred candidates "that'll keep the niggers in their place," and Dennett found his sentiments to be general. "So far as I have seen," he concluded, "all native [white] Southerners . . . people of the most undoubted Unionism as well as secessionists, unaffectedly and heartily despise the Negroes. Truly they are a despised race." All the system's traditional stereotypes of the Negro—as lazy, thieving, sassy, and impudent—were current, as was another assumption described by Whitelaw Reid. "Nothing could overcome," said Reid, "this rooted idea that the negro was worthless, except under the lash." Dennett likewise noted a newspaper's call for "a compulsory code of enforced labor."[14]

These travelers agreed too that prejudice abounded in all classes of white citizens, rich or poor. Of "the common inhabitant of the country," Sidney Andrews said, "his conversation runs in an everlasting circle round the negro," and the vigorous racism of prominent men appalled him even more. "The curse of North Carolina," Andrews wrote, was that "the best men in the Convention stand unblushingly in their places and repeat, one after another, . . . 'I believe in the white man only. I believe that this country was made for white men only. I believe this is the white man's government, and no negro should have any part in it.'" John T. Trowbridge observed the legislature "battling over the question of Negro testimony in the civil courts," a subject which Trowbridge, as a Northerner, knew "could be settled in only one way. One member remarked outside: 'I'll never vote for that bill unless driven to it by the bayonet.' Another said: 'I'm opposed to giving niggers *any* privileges.'" Another delegate to the convention told John Richard Dennett there was no possibility that blacks would be allowed to give testimony. "Oh no, Oh no," he said, "that won't do. The people won't have niggers giving evidence. They'll never get that. The people won't have it." And Beaufort residents informed Whitelaw Reid that Negro suffrage would be "very obnoxious to the prejudices of nearly the whole population."[15]

Sidney Andrews reported that in Concord on voting day "a gang of rowdies from the country made a wholly unprovoked attack on the negroes with clubs and stones, and the militia was . . . worthless . . . some of its members actually joined in the brutal assault." And the Freedmen's

Bureau superintendent in Greensboro told John Richard Dennett of several shootings of Negroes there and in Salisbury and mentioned an order he had provided to a freedwoman who needed to pick up some clothes from her former master. "She took it out to him, he read it and it didn't please him, so he knocked the woman down."[16]

Dennett offered the fullest accounts by any visitor of conversations with yeomen or poorer whites, and their comments revealed a primary concern for their own position. Some expressed a resentment toward those below them in the social order that could be as strong as their class resentment of the former slaveholders. In Guilford or Davidson County the widow of a Unionist who "lay out many a night" to avoid the war pronounced that she did not "want nothin' to do with black ones." Her husband had hired a few slaves once, and the slaves' natural resistance to forced work and theft of what they were never given convinced her that blacks were not "much use." An "old lady . . . of the same class" reemphasized to Dennett that slaves had been lazy. Because she had always found it necessary to work hard, she resented seeing slaves "on the broad o'their backs" in the afternoon. A farmer near Fayetteville stressed that blacks lied and could not be trusted, even under oath. A woman in Chatham County who "seemed the poorest of whites" revealed anxiety about her powerlessness and fear that she would lose status to the freedmen. "We poor folks was about ekil [equal] to the niggers, about bein' hard put to it to live, I mean, and now they's free they don't do nothin' but steal, and how we'll live I don't know. . . . I wish you'd tell me how poor folk is to live among these niggers." Without a husband or a male protector, she admitted that "me and my children's afraid to go out when we hear' em in the corn-field."[17]

A widow who lived with several children in "one of the poorest houses on the road" near Lumberton expressed some sympathy for the former slaves. "The Government is agwine to give 'em land," she stated, and when Dennett contradicted her she quickly asked, "Well, how'll they live then? The rich people won't sell 'em land, nor yit they won't hire 'em." Yet she and her son disliked the idea of blacks voting or testifying in court; "Don't it seem kind o'hard," asked the woman, "to hev a nigger come an' make oath agin ye—a right coal-black nigger? How is that? Is it right or a'n't it?"[18]

These people had been raised in the prejudices of the dominant society, so they shared common racial views, and they were in no position to be generous toward blacks who were gaining status. However much they resented aristocrats or had resisted secessionists, the war had made their difficult lives harder, and they did not want the slaves to be the only beneficiaries or to benefit at their expense. Moreover their experience in slavery times had not helped their image of black people. Either the slave codes had kept them apart from slaves, who thus were strange or frightening, or they had observed and condemned the behavior that slaves adopted to avoid overwork or get back at exploitation. Thus for both general reasons and reasons specific to the circumstances of their class, racism was a potent force among the ordinary white population.

Blacks generally experienced racism's effects first, however, at the hands of the upper class. Socially more powerful, the former slaveholders also had an enormous influence over the immediate future of their former slaves. What would become of them? Where would they work? Strange as it seems today, many North Carolina whites shared an expectation that was widespread throughout the South, namely that the former slaves had no future there or anywhere.[19]

"The law of natural destruction to inferior races," wrote attorney David Schenck, would bring an "alarming decrease in the race" within ten years. "They are dying rapidly . . . there is no remedy for this great calamity," declared a correspondent of Samuel Finley Patterson. The abolitionists bore the responsibility for "thus destroying an innocent helpless race." Using almost the same words as Schenck, Jonathan Worth instructed an abolitionist relative on the fact that black people, "by an irresistible law of nature, will soon perish out in contact with a superior race—and in the mean time will be the curse of the country."[20]

Worth sounded a popular theme, too, in denying that Negroes, on whom the Cotton Kingdom was built, had anything to contribute to the postwar South. "Indolence [is] a feature in the character of the African for which he should no more be held responsible than the leopard is for his spots. It is his nature," said Worth. "The race never did work voluntarily—and never will," he believed. "With free negro labor we shall never prosper." William Waightstill Lenoir likewise believed it was necessary to plan for an economy that was not dependent upon black labor. "We cannot get along for the present at least with colored labor," he wrote; it was necessary to reduce expenditures and "change our system of farming as rapidly as possible to stock raising, or such other plan as will enable" a small work force to use the land productively. He urged hiring immigrant labor as quickly as possible, preferably the Scotch, Irish, or English, and G. W. Harper, a friend of the family, reported, "we want to get a smart Irish 'biddy' and be rid of the whole colored tribe."[21]

Paul Cameron congratulated Thomas Ruffin upon the judge's obtaining some "imported labourers" in 1865. "That seems to me to be the *best step* that can be taken if we propose to hold and cultivate our lands." Even the *Raleigh Daily Sentinel*, which took a notably sympathetic stance toward blacks in August 1865, agreed that colonization might be the best thing for the race; if black suffrage was to be required, the paper added, "the sooner they are colonized in one State, the better." Leading postwar Unionists like Alfred Dockery and Thomas Settle also favored colonization. One index of the interest in foreign laborers was the prompt establishment by Kemp P. Battle and others of the North Carolina Land Agency. "I've been trying to sell the lands of our people so desiring and to induce immigration here," Battle wrote to Zeb Vance. "It struck me as being a good plan to . . . supply men who can be employed as laborers by those disliking the colored."[22]

The number of those "disliking the colored" was large, even among individuals who had always spoken of their slaves in the warmest paternalistic accents. The death of benevolent paternalism was shockingly swift, occurring as soon as the war's outcome began to destroy old patterns of the master's absolute control. For paternalism had always been a style of exploitation rather than an exacting moral code that forced the slaveowner to sacrifice for the benefit of his slaves. Slaveowners found it comforting to discuss their "duty" and "responsibility" toward their slaves, but they never forgot that slavery was supposed to benefit the master. Slavery assumed that their power would be unchallenged, their commands law, their profit the primary goal; paternalism interfered with these prerogatives very little. As soon as the power and control of the slaveowner began to crumble, the facade of benevolent paternalism began to disappear.[23]

Nowhere was this more apparent than on the lands of Paul Cameron, the state's largest, apparently most paternalistic slaveowner. His correspondence in the spring and summer of 1865 was a litany of complaint about his former slaves. "All," he said in May, were "idle and indisposed to work or return to their former duties." By August there was still "a sort of Carnival" underway—"not *one* is at work." "Will you believe it?" he asked Tod Caldwell; in six days he "did not see but a single *one* at any sort of work." To Cameron such behavior showed the worst form of ingratitude; it tried his patience and no doubt hurt his feelings. More disturbing was the fact that the freedmen's attitude and the presence of federal power threatened to upset the old distribution of power. "My old slaves seem resolved to hold on to *me* or to my *land*," he observed, "and it is very plain to me that it is the purpose of the authorities to make us take care of the old and infirm."[24] Cameron did not intend to be saddled with an unprofitable arrangement under the new regime.

What he had in mind, and why his former slaves were uncooperative, is clear in a standard contract that he drew up in April 1865. Promising laborers a one-third share of corn and molasses and one-quarter of the wheat, sweet potatoes, and peas, this contract proposed a division that was not generous but not unusual compared to practice at that time. Its objectional features related to the method of labor and the controls over the workers. Cameron wanted a common depot for all farm tools and insisted that direction of the "whole business of the farm" be in the hands of "the proprietor" or his agent. Thus the gang system of supervised labor would have to continue. Moreover, every laborer was to "promise to be perfectly respectable in language and deportment to the proprietor"; the proprietor could approve or reject any preacher for the workers and would have the power to regulate all sales "of any species of property, by the Negroes"; visitors to Cameron's plantation were prohibited; and no nonreligious assembly on Sunday could be held.[25] Despite emancipation, Cameron was determined to maintain the control that he had enjoyed over slaves.

The former slaves were determined to gain more than that from freedom, and all over the South their resistance to gang labor caused the breakup of the old slave quarters and the relocation of families into small, separate farming units. Sharecropping, though inferior to owning land or renting, at least freed blacks from the constant supervision of former masters. But Cameron did not change his expectations. He hoped that the legislature would provide that blacks "be kept at home especially at night and restricted in their *sales* of property. . . . It seems to be impossible to contract with them—they do not know *when* a good contract is offered to them." Vowing that "they must go to work or they must leave the places," he hired a butcher and began to "sell all the sheep and cattle to get them out of the way of the negroes." A "Yankee officer" helped him by reducing the freedmen's wages on account of bad conduct, but Cameron's irritation only grew. He considered stronger action, seconded by his wife who urged him to "drive [them] all off—get white tenants on any terms."[26]

On Christmas Day 1865, he wrote Samuel Finley Patterson of his decision to force his former slaves—nearly a thousand of them—off his land. "I very much hope that the prices paid for negro labour in this timber—transportation and good Cotton districts will free us of the negro," he wrote; in any event he was going to free himself. "I am convinced that the people who gets rid of the free negro first will be the first to advance in improved agriculture. Have made no effort to retain any of mine." Cheered that two hundred had already left, Cameron declared, "I do not think any of our large plantations can be conducted under the new order of things. . . . We will not attempt a crop beyond the capacity of 30 hands." Thus he jettisoned his black "family" and leased his land to a small number of white farmers, presumably to work with "improved" methods.[27]

Not all slaveowners reacted in this manner, of course—former slaves testified that some invited the freedmen to build cabins and stay, or even aided them with building materials and "cows to milk."[28] But the elite's hostile rejection of the freedmen was surprisingly general, considering landowners' need for agricultural laborers. John M. Morehead thought it "best" that all former slaves leave their plantations, "for they will be no account to their former owners." Thomas J. Lenoir, who shared Cameron's desire to keep wide powers over his laborers, regretted that Negroes who had left Caldwell County were said to be coming back. Edward Conigland (who was a member of the 1865 Convention) had opposed colonization "on principles of political economy, that to deprive the State of so many able bodied labourers would be the depletion of her wealth." But by December 1865, he declared, "I wish we could get rid of them, and I wish we could supply their place with white labour." Thomas Ruffin kept some of his black laborers but imposed such harsh controls on them that the Freedmen's Bureau eventually objected both to their wages (only $3.50 per month in 1868) and their lack of freedom. The spirit of Ruffin's management was revealed in a report from his overseer, who said, "I have driven off 2 since Christmas for neglect of duty and what is left no very well that have got to work and act slave fashion or they can't stay."[29]

One of the few dissenting voices was that of Rufus Lenoir Patterson, who urged his father to try a more liberal policy of dealing with the freedmen. The younger Patterson was no bleeding heart—he wanted county courts to "punish with promptness and severity *vagrancy and theft*"—but he believed the freedmen and free labor deserved a chance. "We ought to educate the negro," Patterson wrote, "and endeavor to train him to be a faithful and steady worker." Showing that his sense of hierarchy was intact, he summed up his expectations in these words: "We can do as much with the negro as with Irish and Germans."[30]

Obviously no egalitarian, Rufus Lenoir Patterson nevertheless was rare in his ability to imagine, from an early date, that black people could become "steady workers" and fill roles somewhat different from those of slavery. He was even able, within a few years, to encourage and praise Negro education.[31] But he was not typical. Outraged protests over new roles assumed by the freedmen showed that the "institution" of caste prejudice was still very much alive.

A particular complaint, almost a cause célèbre, for white North Carolinians was the stationing of some black federal troops at Wilmington. One resident of the city wrote his brother that he could bear the sickly season, "typhoid fever and small pox . . . with some degree of patience, not so the negro soldiery that it has pleased our very good masters to place over us to insult, abuse, and annoy our citizens." He could imagine no reason for placing Negro troops over white citizens except to "humble us." Quickly, protests from the citizens of Wilmington reached Provisional Governor Holden, including one from Alfred Moore Waddell who would subsequently be prominent in that city's race relations. Waddell charged that "daily outrages" had created "fears for the safety of our unarmed and defenceless people" and that the situation would "inevitably result in *massacre.*" Holden stoutly took the white citizens' side and pressed their request despite the issuance of "stringent orders" by U.S. General Cox. Holden soon requested that the government arm the Police Guard and leading citizens of New Hanover County against the black threat. The carrying of firearms by blacks or any kind of "insolent" behavior continued to cause great excitement among whites because it contravened the traditional racial roles.[32]

Indeed, black North Carolinians and Freedmen's Bureau officials agreed that the traditional role of slavery itself was still alive in many people's minds and in practice. Blacks and some whites in Wilmington told Whitelaw Reid that "in the country slavery still practically exists. The masters tell them that slavery is to be restored as soon as the army is removed." John Richard Dennett learned that twenty or thirty miles away from a city and its federal officers it was "still usual on some of the plantations to beat the Negroes for any offence . . . especially is this the case in the country districts." In Randolph County James A. Leach, newly appointed as a Freedmen's Bureau agent, made a thorough inspection and concluded that "there is a tendency on the part of *Some of* the citizens to keep every thing they can from the knowledge of the Freedmen that pertains to their welfare."[33]

Another means of controlling the freedmen was to control their wives or children, as had occurred in the case of Benjamin Harrington. By apprenticing a child, a landowner gained that child's labor and leverage with which to hire his parents, if the landowner desired. Early in 1866 the assistant commissioner of the Freedmen's Bureau for North Carolina reported that, "Complaints often reach [us] . . . that the Apprentice system is abused." He issued orders against abuses, but later that year one of his agents wrote that,

> The County Courts of . . . New Hanover, Brunswick and Robeson . . . pursued the plan of taking colored children away from their parents, and binding them as apprentices to their former Masters. In many cases the children bound were over fourteen years of age, and capable of earning good wages. . . . As the matter now stands, no Freedman is safe in the possession of his children as they are liable to be taken away from their parents at any time, and apprenticed by the County Courts, and this without regard to whether the parents can support the children or not.[34]

The North Carolina Supreme Court overturned some egregiously unfair indentures, but one year later, in September 1867, an agent in Plymouth still reported "quite a number" of illegal apprenticeships. "There appears to be a great desire on the part of many to obtain possession . . . of colored children and every pretext is" used for that end. Substantial numbers of parents may have found themselves in the position of "Friday Williams[,] Freedman," who wrote to the governor to protest his son's apprenticeship "against the consent of the child or myself. . . . I want you to give me advise how to get him . . . I am able to raise the child."[35]

Faced with these types of conditions present almost from the end of the war, North Carolina's freedmen initially chose to chart a moderate, cautious public course in 1865. In Raleigh marchers in a Fourth of July parade, which would have been off-limits to them in slavery, were well dressed and carried a banner reading, "With malice toward none, with charity for all." A mass meeting of black people in New Bern resolved, "that we disclaim any intention of stirring up strife." And the state's A.M.E. Zion Church resolved before the year was out that "it . . . [is] our duty to avoid all irritative expressions both in our private and public discourse."[36]

From a meeting of blacks in Wilmington came the call for a convention to meet in Raleigh in September "to express the sentiments of the Freedmen . . . let each county send as many delegates as it has representatives in the Legislature." Approximately half of the counties were represented by 117 delegates, mostly former slaves rather than antebellum free negroes. Their leaders included James H. Harris of Raleigh, an impressive, self-educated man who had been a free black in Granville County before the war; A. H. Galloway of Fayetteville, a veteran of the federal army; John P. Sampson of Wilmington, northern educated; Isham Swett of Fayetteville, a barber; and John Randolph, Jr. of Greensboro, a carpenter and teacher, "radical in desire, but conservative in action."[37]

The convention drew up an address to the state constitutional convention that was soon to assemble under President Johnson's reconstruction plan. Though respectful and tactful, the address was far from groveling. Taking no notice of the claim that slaves were happy in bondage, the convention noted that "it was impossible for us to be indifferent spectators" of the Civil War. Forced at times to help the Confederacy while "our brethren," northern blacks, fought for the Union, the delegates asked, "Do you blame us that we have, meantime, prayed for the freedom of our race?" Disarmingly the convention used the language of paternalism to bolster its appeals for justice. Referring to "the kindly ties which have so long united us" and to "attachments . . . which must be as enduring as life," the address juxtaposed the current denials of freedom, the reluctance to give fair wages, and the expulsion from plantations that were occurring and asked, "Is it just or Christian?"[38]

Looking to their future status, the freedmen appealed for "mutual co-operation" and asked for aid in securing "adequate compensation for our labor. . . . We desire education for our children," the removal of "the disabilities under which we formerly labored . . . and to have all the oppressive laws which make unjust discriminations on account of race or color wiped from the statutes of the State." This language seemed sweeping but did not specifically include the right of suffrage. Though black leaders did not underestimate its importance, they knew how difficult it would be to obtain immediately; one of them told John Richard Dennett that the ballot was important but that the right to testify in court was absolutely necessary. Still, probably all would have agreed with the Wilmington man who explained why suffrage was ultimately essential: "We ain't noways safe, 'long as dem people makes de laws we's got to be governed by. We's got to hab a voice in de 'pintin' [appointing] of de law-makers."[39]

Experience with whites made black North Carolinians both determined to gain their rights and prone to rely on themselves for assistance, encouragement, and friendship. The marchers in Raleigh's Fourth of July parade, though respectful and without malice, also raised banners that proclaimed, "No Slave lives beneath this flag!" and "Equal Rights before the law: the only equality we ask." Even before the delegates were chosen for the Freedmen's Convention, blacks in Wilmington and Beaufort had organized Equal Rights Leagues to press for full rights, which they knew they would need to protect themselves. Frank W. Gibble, a delegate to the Freedmen's Convention from Carteret County, expressed both the well-founded expectations of hostility from whites and the determination shared by blacks: "We don't ask for social equality, but merely to be recognized as citizens, and entitled to our *political* rights in common with others." And upon adjournment the Freedmen's Convention resolved itself into the North Carolina Equal Rights League to secure "repeal of all laws . . . that make distinctions on account of color."[40]

The constitutional convention that President Johnson had called into being soon showed that it had no intention of granting any of the freedmen's requests. The sentiment of white leaders was virtually unanimous, from Provisional Governor Holden through the most defiant Confederate, against any significant improvement in the status of black North Carolinians. Though the convention put off substantive action and left action on race relations to the legislature of 1866, it did adopt a reply to the address sent by the freedmen. Sternly this document reminded blacks that "more is to be hoped for" from the "bonds of attachment" formed under slavery than "from the assertion of impracticable claims for social and political rights." The convention "deplore[d] the premature introduction of . . . schemes that may disturb . . . these kindly feelings or inflame the inherent social prejudice that exists against the colored race." Future legislation "should be conceived in a spirit of perfect fairness and justice," but should not aim at "any theoretical scheme of social and political equality."[41]

If any further indication of whites' refusal to consider meaningful change in race relations was needed, it was evident in the position of B. F. Moore, perhaps the most prominent Unionist in the convention. Even before the convention met Moore had staked out a position that allowed no racial improvement. "The most unscrupulous despotism can do nothing worse," wrote Moore, than to require "negro suffrage [as] a condition to our re-entry into Congress." Instead of such a "destructive" course, Moore urged a different approach. "It is obvious from experience that the two races cannot harmonize, socially or politically, upon a basis of equality; . . . It is the unquestioned interest of both that they should be

separated into distinct communities. Gov. Brownlow [of Tennessee] . . .
spoke wisely . . . [on] colonization. Enlightened humanity demands it.
The negro race can now be removed, as the Indians were."[42]

Rarely did any North Carolinian dare to suggest that Civil War and
defeat had rendered racial change inevitable. Victor Barringer, who was
better informed than most about northern opinion, declared in an un-
signed article that, "Our business is . . . to recognize . . . change." Noting
that Negro suffrage had become a national issue, he said, "that man is
deluded with a delusion fit only for a fool, who dreams that he can
intrench it safe from attack behind State institutions. . . . We are not only
the weaker section of a consolidated republic. We are subjugated also. We
are held to have forfeited all rights, whether as States or as individuals, by
foul revolt." In two subsequent articles Barringer recommended the use of
property qualifications to restrict suffrage and pointed out that political
equality had not created social equality among whites—"all of our lives
[we] voted along side of men with white skins, whom we would scorn to
take to our bosoms or receive in our families!" But the *Raleigh Daily
Sentinel* printed his articles only to denounce them and to orchestrate the
attack upon them, and Barringer's realism and insight made absolutely no
mark.[43]

In this atmosphere the white people of North Carolina acted to keep
black people, supposedly free, in their place. When the Freedmen's Bureau extended its operations across the state after the close of the war, it
quickly encountered "a large number of cases of injustice" to black laborers. Wages were being withheld and "more than one hundred cases" had
been reported of black workers being dismissed "after the crops had been
'laid by.'" An officer in Raleigh noted in September 1865 that "the incli-
nation to deprive them of their just wages" seemed especially common in
Chatham and Northampton counties. "A great many difficulties . . . between employers and employees" continued to arise, and during the next
two years such matters occupied much of the Freedmen's Bureau's time.
In the fall of 1866, for example, the Raleigh subdistrict reported that the
majority of 997 complaints handled was "for wages due" and that "investigation exhibited a great disinclination on the part of the Whites to pay the
Freedmen for their labor." A year later these problems and "complaints . . .
for unfairness in the Division of the Crops" (only one of the sources
of injustice in sharecropping) persisted, including two dozen cases even
in the Quaker Belt counties of Randolph, Forsyth, Davidson, and
Guilford.[44]

Crimes by blacks were mentioned in bureau reports, but from the start of the postwar period these records revealed far more assaults by whites against blacks than vice versa. In the summer of 1866, for example, the Raleigh subdistrict reported seventy-seven "outrages" by whites upon blacks and only eight by blacks upon whites. In October 1866, the head of the state bureau wrote to his superior, General O. O. Howard, that there had been fifteen murders by whites of freedmen compared to only one case in reverse.[45] But the ratio was not as important as the pattern. Although some violence against freedmen was committed by roving bands of outlaws who defied the law in numerous ways, it also was clear that violence was embedded in the social structure and engaged in by local political leaders.

The violence of outlaw bands apparently grew out of the wartime disorder and robbery that had been so widespread. Early in 1866 the head of the North Carolina Bureau stated that "a band of men in Pitt County, calling themselves Regulators" were "committing depredations and keeping the citizens, *both white and blacks*, in a state of excitement and terror." The bureau referred to lawless bands in Sampson County as "Regulators or Horse-thieves," and Regulators in Johnston County attacked a tax collector, who certainly was a symbol of white governmental authority. But as time went on such organized violence aimed more exclusively at blacks, perhaps because local authorities tolerated crimes against the freedmen and took no effective steps to stop them. The Freedmen's Bureau declared that in Pender County in 1867 black people had to submit to Regulators or leave because no redress was available.[46]

Far more common was direct, personal violence against black people who failed to maintain the subservient demeanor required in slavery days. In Plymouth, N.C., three black women got into an argument with white women in the Clayton Moore family. Apparently the black women were angry and purposely "impudent," but the reaction to this incident showed white sensitivity to any presumption by their race: "Clayton Moore, Stephen Moore and James E. Moore went to the[ir] house . . . with pistols and whips and inflicted a severe castigation upon the women." Nearby a justice of the peace assisted the "legal" whipping of a black girl who had aroused white anger by resisting a beating from a white woman. "This unlooked for reversal of a long accustomed relation [of dominance and oppression] filled the neighborhood with consternation and rage. Couriers passed to and fro from farm to farm, inflaming the temper of the people and concerting measures to produce terror among the negroes."

Whites assembled, dragged the woman before magistrate Abram Jenkins, who quickly arranged a new indenture, and the woman's new master then sanctioned a severe whipping and beating.[47]

Jenkins was not the only local official who showed by example that black freedom should be brutally suppressed. In late 1865 the names of some members of the New Hanover County Court appeared in Freedmen's Bureau records when these men applied for and received their pardons, with restoration of their property. Several months later the Bureau's Reports of Outrages noted the arrest of William Peden and William A. Wright for beating, shooting, and whipping "Joseph Hall (free)." Both Peden and Wright were magistrates of long standing and considerable influence; Wright was in his fourth term as chairman of the county court. Before a year had passed another New Hanover magistrate, John D. Walker, was arrested and indicted by a grand jury. The bureau's records recorded that Walker had given Lucy Smith a "severe and outrageous beating. Knocked her down and kicked her. Drove her off and would not let her take her children, numbering five, which he retained."[48]

In Charlotte a magistrate clubbed a Negro in public on the street, and the Freedmen's Bureau was convinced that hostility to any change in the black man's status was strong in the county courts. In August 1865, General Thomas H. Ruger wrote to Provisional Governor Holden and pointed out that, although Holden had appointed new magistrates, "in no instance have I heard or known of official notice having been taken by any of them of acts of unlawful violence towards freedmen," despite the fact that "such acts have been by no means infrequent." Ruger knew personally of "several cases of homicide of freedmen by whites . . . but in no case . . . was any arrest made by the magistrates or civil officers, and no . . . investigation." Holden disagreed at first and appealed to the president, but only one week later he had to admit that "the local police of Sampson and many other counties . . . are not disposed . . . to do justice to the freedmen." He blamed this on the ascendency of secessionists and asked Ruger's aid in putting the local police "under the control of Union men."[49]

The bureau was probably right in viewing the problem as more general in nature, for even in Guilford County magistrates were punishing blacks for violation of the old slave codes. But the problem certainly did not go away after Jonathan Worth became governor. In 1866 the bureau's state chief reported, "the negro has very little chance of getting his due before the Civil Courts of N.C. at present." An agent observed that "in civil cases within the jurisdiction of a Magistrate, there appears to be frequently an unwillingness to adjudicate cases where Plaintiff is a Freedman and the Defendant a Whiteman." One year later an agent working in the east wrote that "nearly half the magistrates are unfit to hold their office on account of their deep rooted prejudices. . . . I sincerely believe . . . if the U.S. troops should be withdrawn from this State . . . leaving the great body of magistrates unchanged and the County Courts not reconstructured, the future of the Freedmen would be *dark* indeed."[50]

It was not very bright when the first postwar legislature, elected under President Johnson's plan of reconstruction, assembled. Prominent men who had been wartime Conservatives, like Jonathan Worth and William A. Graham, were discussing ways to tighten control over black people. Worth was adamant against Negro suffrage, of course, and he was working on tactics to forestall federal intervention in favor of the freedmen. "I think the Com[mon] School fund had better be discouraged," he advised Graham, "and thus avoid the question as to educating negroes." (Thus the education of poor whites also was to be sacrificed.) Much more defiant and outraged at changes in black status, Graham wanted the legislature to "change the law of homicide, so as to excuse [a killing] whenever there is a trespass on the curtilage [yard] in the night time with intent to steal."[51]

Even strong Unionists were aroused against any improvement in black status. B. F. Moore muttered darkly about the spectre of an "*attempted* check [by the North] on free legislation of the State in regard to the blacks." A. C. Cowles from his seat in the state senate described the agenda bluntly: "We will have no hesitation in framing a Code of laws for 'free negroes' (freedmen) that will fix their status permanently and Compel them to labor." The only difficulty lay in avoiding Radical criticism of any law that was "efficient, as you know it should be. . . . Several prominent men [thought] it best to remain quiet for the present until we get back into the Union." And again, as it had during the Civil War, the fear of cooperation by lower-class whites with blacks lurked in the background: Moore described the enemy as "a parcel of lowbred fanatics, abroad and *among* us."[52]

The legislature did the minimum that it felt would be required by the North. The basic principle of its "Act concerning negroes and persons of color" was that blacks "shall be entitled to the same privileges and subject to the same . . . disabilities as . . . were conferred on . . . free persons of color prior to the ordinance of emancipation," no more. This meant that the freedmen could not testify against whites, serve on juries, intermarry with whites, or execute a contract concerning ten dollars or more unless it was "witnessed by a white person who can read and write." In addition the penalty for rape of a white woman, which for a white man was death for commission of the crime, was set at death in the case of "assault with intent to commit rape" by a black upon a white woman. Six sections of the 1854 Revised Code were retained by substituting "persons of color" for "slaves and free negroes"; these sections prohibited black people from migrating into the state, reentering it after an absence of ninety days, or wearing or keeping a gun, bowie knife, or other weapon without a special license. In addition the courts had considerable powers in punishing vagrancy and apprenticing blacks. Former masters received preference in taking on any freedmen apprenticed by the courts.[53]

These provisions, which Cowles indicated were a first step, maintained a markedly inferior status for black people and testified to the utter inability of most North Carolinians to imagine legal equality between the races. The only Tar Heels who accomplished this mental feat were those who left the state and sojourned in the North for a considerable period. (A short visit north seemed only to heighten the revulsion from what many called Yankee equality.) One of Jonathan Worth's friends who went to Kansas before the war out of antislavery feeling wrote the governor a letter full of sentiments as radical as any in Washington. More representative was Frederick Lynn Childs, who tried a number of different places in hope of finding a promising occupation. While he was in South Carolina his views remained unchanged, but after several months in New York he had accepted precisely the democratic principles that North Carolina's elite was fighting against: "The tendency of the world is toward extending to the lower classes the right of a voice in the government of the Country and sooner or later the negro will vote." His racial views had evolved too, although not beyond the prejudice common among northerners. "I do not believe the negro can ever become nearly the equal of the white man," Childs wrote, "yet I think he can be vastly improved and approximate . . . [the lower] class of whites . . . [whom] we do not feel . . . are by any means our equals."[54]

To whites within North Carolina, however, the evolving egalitarian views of the North only provoked bitter resentment and hardened the intense determination to resist change. Edward Conigland, a member of the convention, felt that northern Radicals were bent on "subjugat[ing] the Southern people after the manner of Poland . . . and to effect this purpose . . . they will not scruple to call in the aid of the blacks in our midst. We have men in this State who are ready to sustain such a purpose." The Fourteenth Amendment was a compromise among northern Republicans, but to North Carolinians it was an extreme measure designed to embarrass the white race. "It is truly humiliating," wrote Jonathan Worth, "that there should be any white man in the State in favor of placing a negro and a white man side by side in a jury box, and making ineligible to office nearly all her representative men." A man from High Point told the governor that he could understand the "idea of Christian philanthropy which takes in all created human beings. But this new fangled idea of worshipping the negro, and denouncing and prosecuting native born straight haired citizens I cannot exactly understand." Perhaps Weldon Edwards summed up the feeling of many when he described emancipation as a "crime committed against humanity."[55]

Tar Heel whites were keenly aware, too, that northern whites were hypocritical about black equality. The convention took notice when Connecticut became the first of three northern states to reject black suffrage in 1865. Jonathan Worth pointed out that "every Northern state is averse to negroes settling among them" and argued cogently that northern actions belied the claim that "they *really* believed him an equal and oppressed brother." This realization magnified white North Carolinians' resentment and confirmed their traditional sense that blacks should be kept in their place. One of the frankest expressions of this feeling came from Worth, who interceded with federal officers on behalf of men who had murdered a Negro accused of rape. The governor argued that they should be released because theirs was "a crime springing from a noble rather than a depraved heart."[56]

Obviously presidential reconstruction had not created the conditions that would permit real freedom for black people in North Carolina. Yet federal power was a presence signifying that some change would be required. Whereas whites prepared resistance, blacks sought whatever improvements were possible in the new situation. The most important gains for them before 1868 were necessarily in the private areas of life and in putting small but significant distances between themselves and white control.

Owners admitted that individual slaves were "jubilant to be free" or "loud in their welcome [of U.S. forces] particularly to the negro troops among whom they found some old acquaintances." Long-owned servants began to speak up and bargain for their pay—behavior which of course struck many whites as "very independent, demanding exorbitant wages and exhibiting pleasure at the perplexities of their former owners." "Insubordination and insolence" in work were reported by whites, and blacks began to pare down the maximum hours that they had been kept at work in slavery. "Freedom with Sue was laziness," concluded one former owner, but it was also a matter of allowing women and children to leave the fields and providing great protection and enjoyment of life for one's family. Throughout the South freedmen cut back on their labor to claim a benefit from freedom and to treat their dependents in the same manner as white people. They also rejected certain work: "you know they never liked to live on a Rice Plantation," wrote a resident of Wilmington, "and now 'tis with the utmost difficulty that any labor can be procured in that field."[57]

Sometimes their actions simply showed that they valued certain ties and obligations more highly than earning a day's wage. Amy was supposed to be "in the kitchen," complained one white woman, "but her husband has been very sick for a week, and because she is free she thinks she must stand by his bed side the whole-time keeping flies off him." "Yesterday Zillah," wrote another man, "without asking told me she was going to church at Cool Spring. She did what work she had to do ahead, left at daylight, and did not return till after supper," much to her employers' disgust.[58]

Black people also used their new right to move about. "Every fool negro thinks freedom consists in leaving his master," lamented David Schenck; but he overlooked the fact that mobility was a basic personal freedom, proscribed under slavery, and he overlooked too the fact that former slaves promptly left harsh masters but tended to stay with those who were likely to offer relatively favorable treatment. There were powerful, personal motives for movement as well. "Annie . . . went to Hillsboro to be with her family," and there were many like her—tens of thousands hurried to reunite with children or spouses and to register their marriages before local authorities. Many migrated to parts of the state, especially cities, where they could be close to other blacks and to the U.S. army units and agencies that "destroy[ed] the influence or power of the former masters." With food short and society disrupted, this concentration of people spawned infectious diseases in New Bern, Wilmington, and elsewhere, but as better conditions returned many migrants stayed. In 1870 the black population of Wilmington's New Hanover County remained 46 percent higher than it had been in 1860.[59]

There is no doubt that freedmen hoped for much more. Whites began to worry that the former slaves believed "that they are entitled to a share of their masters lands and goods & c, and in various parts of the state they have expressed such a determination to have it as to lead to serious fears of a general uprising." Indeed, at the close of 1865 there were "apprehensions of negro insurrection" across the state, and the Freedmen's Bureau issued a special circular to counteract the belief among freedmen "that farms will be given to them by the U.S. Government."[60] But for the present they had to resign themselves to less.

With fervor they threw themselves into desirable things that were possible. One of these, as Zillah's behavior suggested, was the formation of their own churches. Discriminated against in white churches, black North Carolinians quickly moved into congregations in which they could enjoy self-direction and black preaching. In Wilmington in 1865, when the white minister of a mixed-race congregation criticized the views of a black U.S. army chaplain, his black parishioners promptly petitioned General Schofield for permission to gain "possession of our church property" and change their church's affiliation. Similarly, in Raleigh a group of black worshipers abandoned the Methodist Episcopal Church of the South, explaining that it had come into being through a prewar schism "for the purpose of perpetuating Slavery" and had "taught rebelion." "Compelled to liston to her ministers till the coming of the Fedaral Army, now we Desiar . . . to worship God according to the dictates of our consciences."[61]

Another of life's good things that black people pursued was education. Wherever schools were organized—and the Freedmen's Bureau and private philanthropy organized many—they quickly filled. David Schenck commented on "a flourishing school of 108 scholars taught by a Quaker Yankee" that was as popular as the new "colored Methodist church." One teacher found three hundred assembled for a lesson and exclaimed, "I never knew anything like the craving the[y] . . . have to learn." And the Freedmen's Bureau noted that adult night schools were greeted with "eagerness and youthful enthusiasm." In a regular bureau school "*representatives of four generations* in a direct line were to be found—a child of six years, her mother, grandmother, and great grandmother, the latter being more than seventy-five years of age."[62] Black people also paid hard-earned money to support subscription schools and were delighted to have black teachers.

These were hopeful experiences for black North Carolinians, but they knew that political rights remained necessary. In October 1866, they sent 111 delegates from 61 counties to the convention of the State Equal Rights League of Freedmen. (White newspapers referred to this gathering as the Colored Education Convention.) Under the leadership of James H.

Harris this body ignored the injunctions of white leaders such as Holden to "keep out of politics," demanded the right to vote, and condemned taxation without representation. A petition to Congress called for "the right of suffrage, in common with other citizens of the United States, in consideration of our loyalty, citizenship and merit" and added the eloquent comment that whites "have taught us one good thing: . . . 'That all men are born free and equal, and that they are endowed by their Creator with inalienable rights.'"[63]

This did not fall on deaf ears, for in the nation the stage was set for conflict over the federal government's reconstruction program. By late 1866 or early 1867 it was clear that Congress was going to require more change in the South than President Johnson had. Yet for white Tar Heels that which had occurred was nearly intolerable. There was no way to get around the fact that what northerners viewed as equality before the law, southern whites saw as their receiving "no more dignity or respect than is shown the negro." Some felt that change was "literally turning the slave master, and the master, slave." Whites who cooperated with the new regime earned widespread hostility; a woman in Morganton who agreed to teach school for blacks met with "a general feeling of indignation . . . particularly in her own family."[64]

In 1867 Congress decided to require Negro suffrage, "the most appalling of all alternatives," and seemed therefore to elite North Carolinians to be "incarnate fiends." But some joined with William Holden in organizing a state Republican party. Once again the threat of unified pressure from the lower classes became a frightening possibility. David Schenck denounced those who cooperated as "the very low and ignorant whites . . . who formerly worked as slaves." More than one person, including Governor Worth, predicted "a 'war of races.'"[65] The violent response to democratic change soon came. And when it came not only did it confirm that racism was widespread, it also revealed that class purposes underlay racism and used it to restore the hierarchy that denied all forms of equality in society.

CHANGE AND REPRESSION,
1868–1878

Radical Reconstruction posed the gravest threat yet encountered to North Carolina's rigid social hierarchy. Would it be enough to pull down the structures of aristocratic control and racial oppression? Could it uproot the customs and emotions that accompanied these? Many who brought democratic pressure to bear from outside believed so.

Amy Morris Bradley readily offered the energy and discipline of her life to the cause of educating North Carolina's common people. No one represented the spirit of Yankee reform and democratic ideals better than this forty-four-year-old schoolteacher from Maine, who arrived in Wilmington in December 1866. Plain but determined in appearance, she immediately set out to do God's work by opening a free school for poor white children under the auspices of the American Unitarian Association. When people asked what her business was in Wilmington, she answered, "I come here to establish Free Schools, to educate your children, this is my business here and I mean to do it and succeed."[1]

She opened school on 9 January 1867, and almost immediately she had sixty scholars. Within two weeks she had induced nineteen girls to form a Young Ladies Union Benevolent Society for the purposes of mutual improvement and aid of the poor. On 10 February she started Sunday school services with eighteen children present, and on 2 March she began visiting the homes of her students. She found many "very poor" white families with parents sick or unemployed due to hard times. Some subsisted on Freedmen's Bureau rations, and many widows who "take in sewing" had lost their husbands in the war. One declared bitterly that "the first man that started the War ought to be tarred and feathered, and [I] would like to set fire to him." These poor whites told her that "if the Northern people did not help the poor, they would never be educated," for the rich did not care. "Some said that the education of their children was their greatest wish," and Amy Bradley believed that, "If I can teach them how to be good citizens, and good Christians, followers of the Savior, then I shall know that the angels of our Father have guarded and guided me aright!" In a few years she had more than three hundred pupils in three different schoolhouses.[2]

Two idealistic male teachers from the North ended up in Alamance County. One of them, Alonzo Corliss, was a crippled white man from New Jersey who taught a colored school in the neighborhood of Company Shops. Another was a man named Meder who presided over a white school but "taught negro children at night."[3] Both wanted to aid, uplift, and democratize. With scores of idealistic men and women across the state, aided by the Freedmen's Bureau and by northern churches and reform societies, these individuals set out to change society and improve the lot of the lower classes in North Carolina.

Their zeal and numbers were impressive, and behind them lay the power of the federal government, victorious in war and stiffened by the northern electorate's rejection of Andrew Johnson's program of Reconstruction. Henceforth Tar Heels had to worry about satisfying a northern master. Congress had demanded that property and racial restrictions on voting be swept away so that government was formally democratic for male citizens. A new constitutional convention had to be held and a new state government formed. North Carolina's reconstructed government could struggle to make democracy a social reality, if there were democratic forces within to carry the fight forward.

As this new phase of Reconstruction began, it was clear that there *were* determined groups seeking change within the State. Violent Tory or outlier bands continued to defy the government in some parts of the state, occasionally with whites and blacks riding and robbing together. Even Tories and Unionists who abided by the law remained openly hostile to secessionists and aristocrats. William K. Ruffin said that he moved to Hillsboro because in Alamance County his family had been "surrounded . . . by a large number of free niggers instigated to study of Deviltry by the malice and vengeful spite of a large Tory district." Jonathan Worth warned conservative leaders of the state that nomination of Zebulon Vance to high office would be fatal to their cause, for "we must carry . . . a large portion of our people such as are to be found in Alamance, Guilford, and elsewhere who will not vote for him." Nominating men with pro-Confed-

Amy Morris Bradley

erate war records, Worth knew, would "drive [Daniel R.] Goodloe, [Hinton R. or Hardie H.] Helper, the Quakers etc. into the support of the Radicals."[4]

Wartime opponents of the Confederate government had reorganized after the peace. The Red Strings or Heroes of America emerged as a force in Randolph County and other parts of the piedmont in 1866. Some members of the elite believed that their purpose was "to elect Union men to office," others feared that it was "to confiscate and divide the lands and indulge in a carnival of agrarianism." But undeniably they were growing, and their efforts fed the new, southern wing of the Republican party. Braxton Craven, president of Trinity College, exclaimed, "They are moving heaven and earth in this [Randolph] County." Chapters of the Heroes prepared slates of candidates and drew up lists of trustworthy allies for appointive office. And they were determined. A man in Alamance County wrote William Holden that he would fight before he let "unhung rebels" take over the government again: "I do not want such men to dictate and domineer over me and my friend[s] as has [been the case] for the last 8 or 10 years. . . . Death is more preferable than such rule again. In my own County there has not been one instant as yet that the peoples wishes has been granted, both in the Convention and the legisla[ture]."[5]

Encouraged by Congress's action, black people were speaking out more boldly. At political meetings some were claiming the right to be the state's agricultural workers, instead of immigrants; others were talking about gaining power. The "*secret societies*, now forming by the free blacks in *every section of this* [Richmond] *County*" which so alarmed Walter F. Leak were councils (or chapters) of the Union League. "You have to effect a great moral and political reform," wrote the League's Grand President in recruiting James H. Harris as an organizer; "There is no time to be lost," he admonished, for "the first steps in their political education should be sedulously taught." Blacks invoked community pressure against those who voted for the Republicans' opponent, the Conservative party, and the leagues promised to be a potent political instrument. Moreover, "Many demagogues and unprincipled aspirants," lamented David Schenck, "are joining them from among the white population."[6]

Prominent men of the old elite saw their worst nightmare—an alliance among the lower classes of both races—materializing under the protection of the federal government. Even though Congress seemed unready to confiscate land late in 1867, Governor Jonathan Worth worried about whites such as those "in Montgomery and Randolph, who are expecting to attain political ascendency through the negro. . . . The mean whites, cooperating with the negroes, may appropriate all the land." To Worth it was axiomatic that "the cupidity of the propertyless, the majority in all Counties, will demand and enforce distribution of property." "If non-property holders are the ruling power in both branches of the Legislature, land and property will be in much more danger of virtual confiscation from taxation than they are from the present Congress."[7]

Too late Worth had considered allowing property-owning blacks to vote or devising a compromise plan for Reconstruction in order to satisfy northern public opinion. As northern views of democracy raced beyond his, he took refuge in angry resistance, condemning Congress for impos-ing "absolute despotism" and secretly advising whites not to vote for or against the new constitutional convention required by law. Because a ma-jority of registered voters was needed for approval, he hoped that nonvot-ing could block Congress's plan. But his scheme failed, and Worth la-mented that "taxation will very soon swallow up the landholders of this State." "I regard the proposed new constitution as virtual confiscation," he wrote.[8]

Ordinary Tar Heels did not see the issue in this aggressive light, though they were conscious of class motives. Many yeomen who had suffered during the war wanted to reestablish their independence and live free of unfair laws and oppression. They hoped to "Beat the Oligarks in White voters by next election," if they could defend themselves from verbal at-tacks—"we are called Flounders or white Sided Negroes, in fact there is no language mean enough to be applied." In regard to property, poor men were fearing the loss of their own modest holdings to creditors rather than salivating over lands they could steal. Stay laws, quickly repealed during the Civil War but later renewed by the federal military commander and the Convention of 1868, had suspended the collection of debts, but many ordinary Republicans now feared that they might be driven to the wall.[9]

A Guilford County man anxiously wrote Holden that "certain lawyers [and] red hot Seseshionist[s] are making arrangements" to execute their judgments against debtors "just as quick as the [1868] legislature meats . . . [when] General Canbys order . . . will be void and before the legisla-ture will have time to pass an eximption law." Others feared they might lose the homestead exemption that freed five hundred dollars worth of property from taxation, and a Burke County man wrote Tod R. Caldwell that "more than Two Thirds of the People air opposed" to repeal of the stay law. Because the economy was prostrate and land almost worthless,

William J. Clarke

resumption of debt collections would "ruin the country. All the men of wealth have taken the benefit of the Law and poore men will have to sell the Hat off of thare head to pay thare Debts. . . . I hope to God that the authoritys of N.C. will look to the intrest of the majority of the People . . . hoo air the Poore people of the State."[10]

Such men had a strong incentive to be zealous Republicans, and they were joined by some wealthier figures. Some of these were men who finally had acquired too realistic a perception of national politics to see any wisdom in southern intransigence. Some had held power before in their communities and probably preferred to adjust rather than lose their place. In Edgecombe County, for example, where black voters predominated, a number of wealthy and politically experienced planters became Republicans and succeeded in sharing office with new black officials. Others like Judge E. G. Reade had been Whigs who blamed secessionists for ruining them as well as the South and could not bring themselves to cooperate with their old enemies.[11]

William J. Clarke exemplified the prominent whites who followed a more complex path into the Republican party. A lawyer and Confederate veteran, Clarke had been highly critical in private of those who brought on and conducted the war. During Reconstruction he found himself struggling to make a bare living in New Bern amid the depressed economy. He attended Conservative meetings, occasionally making a "rousing speech," but felt blocked by others in the unsuccessful organization and soon regretted "that I had anything to do with a party, with whom I had so little in common." As he met some Yankees and Republicans, his opinion of them improved, and criticism by Democrats of his tolerant opinion of Ulysses S. Grant drove him toward a break. Republican overtures and employment then completed his conversion into a Republican who could orate with feeling against "the anti-republican aristocratic party" bent on "continuing Conf[ederate] war."[12]

From these various sources the Republican party assembled, gained power, and began to change the face of society in North Carolina. The 1868 Constitutional Convention had an overwhelming Republican majority of 107 to 13 and included 15 Negro delegates. It wrote a constitution that guaranteed manhood suffrage, even for Confederate leaders, abolished property qualifications for the governor and legislators, and provided for the election of judges by the people for terms of eight years. Even more significant, in terms of the daily lives of most North Carolinians, was the fact that the new constitution abolished the old county

James Hood

courts and their lifetime "squirarchy," replacing them with five commissioners in each county elected by the people. The traditional aristocratic structure of local government was destroyed, and the opportunity for full, local democracy rose in its place.[13]

Provisions for a public school system promised to make these democratic opportunities more meaningful. The convention committed the state to a modern school system, though black and white Republicans recognized the depth of racial prejudice and agreed that its classrooms would be segregated. James Hood, a black leader from Cumberland County, fought against any reference to separate schools but made it clear why he favored "colored teachers for colored schools." "I do not believe that it is good for our children," Hood said, "to eat and drink daily the sentiment that they are naturally inferior to the whites, which they do in three-fourths of all the schools where they have white teachers." Hood added, "with all due respect to the noble self-sacrificing devotion" of white northern teachers, that "it is impossible for white teachers, educated as they necessarily are in this country, to enter into the feelings of colored pupils as the colored teacher does."[14] Black or white, North Carolina's children would have schools.

Under this new constitution William Holden won the governor's chair, and Republicans won all but one seat in Congress and more than two-thirds of the seats in the legislature. Sweeping change took place at the county level, also, as new types of men came into office instead of the wealthy local notables who had dominated the county courts. The results in New Hanover County illustrated the change. Conservatives nominated five candidates for the County Commission who long had served as justices of the peace, including William A. Wright, their past chairman. These men represented the economic elite, holding real estate worth $12,171 on the average and paying taxes on an average of eleven black polls each. One owned an exceptionally fine carriage; all were accustomed to power and influence. Yet all five lost, and in their place appeared five new men, including one black. Together their wealth averaged about half that of their predecessors (using peak figures during Reconstruction). In 1869 it was only $1,511; the new chairman owned no land and only $215 worth of tools and books.[15]

Elsewhere the results were similar and striking. Two of the first five commissioners in Edgecombe County were black and in many of the eastern, plantation counties blacks won office. Ordinary farmers and artisans, black and white, came to power, and the levels of wealth among officeholders dropped precipitously. Compared to the 1866–67 period, the average value of local officials' real estate in Edgecombe fell from $23,333 to $10,600 and their personal property from $24,300 to $6,800. In Alamance the drop was from $10,523 to $4,188 in real estate and from $26,388 to $1,400 in personal estate. For poorer Caldwell County the average value of officials' real estate holdings dropped from $8,127 to $4,625 whereas personal property plunged from $7,724 to $1,500. The value of officials' real estate holdings rose slightly in Randolph County, from $3,293 to $4,436, but their personal property's value declined steeply from $4,989 to $1,639.[16]

As the change in personnel indicated, a political revolution had truly begun. Thousands of ordinary white North Carolinians were voting Republican, and the cooperation of these whites with black voters was having potent effects. In the mountains most Republicans were white, and in the east most Republicans were black, but in the piedmont white and black voters together were producing a viable, competitive, victorious Republican party.[17] To men who for generations had been shut out of political decision making, the Republican party offered a new and vibrant democracy. It seemed inspired with a mission: to open up North Carolina's aristocratic politics and social system. Ordinary citizens now elected the local officials who made the most important decisions that affected them. And these men showed determination to act for the good of the people, not the elite.

In Randolph County, for example, the new commissioners promptly set out to revive and improve the public schools. Their task was a large one. The rudimentary, antebellum school system, dominated by squires from the county court, had withered away for lack of funds during the war and after. The county commissioners first ordered a full report and accounting from the old officials. Then they selected 114 men from every town and district to take a census of the entire school-age population, from six to twenty-one years old, and of the facilities and needs of the schools. Within two months the census was complete, and seven months later eleven popularly chosen school committees were working with county leaders to improve the schools.[18]

Randolph's commissioners found that there were 4,056 potential students in the county and only fifty-four schools to serve them. Moreover, fourteen of these schoolhouses were in "bad" or "not very good" condition. Despite hard times, the county commission immediately resolved that "the number of school houses to be supplied" should be increased to eighty and that each schoolhouse should accommodate at least thirty pupils. Thus, the commissioners pledged themselves to provide schooling for almost 60 percent of the potential school population, a major expansion from prewar days. Their plans included black children as well as white children, and they apportioned school funds strictly "in proportion to the number of children in each township." Another measure of the commission's dedication to helping poorer citizens came within a year, as the officials asked the legislature for permission to levy a special tax to support the poor and defray the county debt. Where the commissioners saw a need, they acted.[19]

This kind of innovative and democratic government made Republicans popular with many humble Tar Heels. It also dismayed the old elite. Aside from the content of new programs, the large-scale replacement of upper-class officeholders alarmed Conservatives deeply. They made it plain, in private and public comments, that the assault on hierarchy was deeply disturbing and objectionable in itself, regardless of black participation in politics. Ordinary men were not supposed to rule their betters. For example, David Schenck confided to his diary that Rutherfordton was a "dilapidated town" because "the old wealth and aristocracy which once gave life and animation to the place has been broken down. It is very sad to see the 'dirty, unwashed scum of society' like maggots revelling in the decaying remains of better days." Such reversal of the proper order of things could only have occurred, Schenck believed, under the domination of the North, itself a disordered community prey to "every device of the devil," to reform movements like "Women's rights! Labor Reform! International Societies! Free Love! Polygamy and the various fungus growths of putrid society."[20]

Interestingly, Schenck was not alone in his diagnosis; he merely expressed in colorful terminology what was conventional wisdom among the conservative elite. Weldon Edwards also believed that such a perversion of hierarchy could not have happened unless there were a social sickness affecting the North. He laid the blame on unrestrained immigration which had caused "the Ballot Box . . . [to be] controlled by the miserable Hirelings of foreign Birth to be found North of Mason's and Dixon's line." He predicted that this unnatural situation would soon result in "a terrible outbreak that will convulse the whole North." The *Wilmington Journal* saw the 1868 Convention as "a mongrel mob" that owed its existence to "negro suffrage and social disorder." It contrasted carpetbaggers—"that miserable scum of creation"—to Conservatives who comprised "the Intelligence and Wealth of New Hanover."[21]

When the Paris Commune gained international attention in 1871, the *Tarboro Enquirer* quickly drew the parallel to North Carolina. Both Radicalism and the Commune were disorders springing from "universal equality" and "false humanitarianism" which aimed at

> breaking down every vistige [*sic*] of honorable distinction and attempting to plant upon its ruin the unwise . . . doctrine of universal equality. Especially is the effort made in the South. The wise and good have been deprived of all chance of emolument, and offices of honor and trust debased by conferring them upon ignorance and vice. . . . The places once occupied by the best of our sons, whom our State and nation delighted to honor, are now . . . filled by men who can scarcely read plain english, or scrawl a mutilated cross for their signatures.[22]

The fact that racial change was involved added a major inflammatory element to the reaction against Radical Reconstruction. Most white North Carolinians were thoroughly accustomed to regarding black people as inferior, subordinate beings, in fact as creatures beyond their consideration. Caldwell County's Sarah J. Lenoir revealed how wide the chasm was in the white mind between blacks and other human beings when she commented on an accident she had witnessed. George, a black worker, had caught his arm in a cane mill, and as she watched in horror the arm had to be amputated. The blood and bone, the pain and mental agony of George and his family momentarily shocked her out of normal patterns of thought. "I never expected to feel for Negroes as I felt for him and his wife," she said. In amazement she added, "We feel as if our *friends* were in distress."[23]

In this atmosphere whites found shocking any attempt by blacks to assume the new political roles. A torchlight political parade by black people alarmed David Schenck, who came away convinced that they were "more like cannibals than human beings." Congress's clear insistence on black suffrage provoked "some gentlemen" to tell Richmond Pearson, chief justice of the Supreme Court, that "rather than permit free nigirs to vote and hold office, we are ready for another war." Blacks needed to avoid even the appearance of equality in some communities, as a petition to the Probate Court of Rowan County shows. A man asked to be appointed guardian of his five nieces and nephews, who had stayed on the family farm after the deaths of their parents. There was "no other white person living with them—but there is a negro man who works for them and as your Petitioner is informed and believes, is associating with them on terms of equality, eating with them at the same table and working with them in the farm or other work they do." Despite the lack of any evidence showing that the children cherished friendly feelings toward the farm-hand, their uncle found the situation scandalous and was determined to put a stop to it. Others felt the same way. David Schenck believed that "respectable whites" were ending "all association with the negro" and that "the deepest hate now exists between the two [races]."[24]

To the elite the fact that Congress had briefly taken away prominent Confederates' right to vote deepened the insult perceived from the enfranchisement of blacks. "Our people are considerably exercised," wrote one Tar Heel white; W. F. Leak called it *"galling"*; and a Caldwell County merchant described himself as "hav[ing] the honor to belong to the disfranchised class." The hypocrisy of northern whites, who rejected Negro suffrage in their own states, aroused indignant comment and infuriated people more. Black suffrage struck the elite as the last excess in the attack on hierarchy—the most outrageous, gratuitous insult in the elevation of "ignorant asses" to power and office.[25]

Not surprisingly, this angry and beleaguered elite determined to regain its privileges by attacking racial equality as the weakest point in the Republican program of social reform. Instead of letting Republicans define the issue as democracy—universal manhood suffrage, local democracy, free public schools for all, and expanded economic opportunities—Conservatives set out to make white supremacy the central question. They let no opportunity pass to stress the color line above all other issues. One county court had denounced the disruption of racial hierarchy as "contrary to the laws of God," and prominent Conservatives everywhere vilified white Republicans as traitors to their race. Any white voter who supported the Republicans was likely to suffer "the most denunciatory and vindictive" criticisms—"All decencies of debate were discarded, and social relations are broken up."[26]

Conservatives also began to appeal to the social self-interest of the ordinary white. They stressed that all white people had an interest in the continued debasement of the Negro. His subjection had been the fundamental fact in the discriminatory social order of the Old South, and power over blacks had constituted one of the rights that white people enjoyed.

The equality of Reconstruction, Conservatives argued, thus threatened a privilege and damaged the status enjoyed by lower-class whites. Through racist arguments like these the elite hoped to detach white voters from the Republican party.

Both the traditions of a racist society and the character of the yeoman class made the Conservatives' strategy plausible. The traditional social order had defined white supremacy as one of society's greatest goods, and yeomen customarily asserted themselves against change that harmed their interests. Economic conditions increased the vulnerability of their social position. Common people were poor, angry, frustrated, and tired of the suffering that they had endured for years, beginning with the war. They were not willing to accept any further deterioration of their position. Nor would they tolerate anything that could be made to resemble favoritism to another group.

The character of the yeomen class disposed it to resistance in threatened circumstances. White yeomen had never been submissive or docile, and during the Civil War they had defended their rights violently and extra-legally. Motivated by their own concepts of what was just and fair, they had frequently opposed Confederate laws and battled Confederate authorities. After the war, with a personalism that often set the law aside, some had taken strong action in their local districts to protect their vital interests. Obviously there was potential for lower-class whites to take the offensive against blacks, if Conservatives could convince them that the freedmen were their enemy.

Long distrustful of government, yeomen had also been suspicious of powerful elites or governmental intrusions from outside their locality. They valued their independence above all else and struggled to maintain a large degree of autonomy as the core of their social identity; they were not accustomed to being told what to do.[27] Suspicion of elites had often worked against the Conservatives, yet now the Congress was telling yeomen and other white North Carolinians what they *had* to do. The Conservatives seized on this as evidence of dictation to favor blacks. They urged North Carolina's common whites to resist anyone who tried to compel their obedience.

Thus racism was the obvious tool to split a lower-class democratic revolution, and even at the birth of the new political order, ambitious Republicans feared the effects of a racial backlash. "Many Republicans" of Davidson County warned Governor Holden that if he appointed a black man as magistrate "it will certainly be a great injury to the Republican party in this section of N.C." Rufus Lenoir Patterson admitted that "some of the darkies [at the Constitutional Convention] are intelligent in a surprising degree," but he himself objected that "oftener than is proper the voice of the African is heard where none but anglo saxon voices have been heard before." "It is fortunate for us," wrote a Caldwell County Republican, "that all the [white] people of the State can't witness it."[28]

Influential former Senator William A. Graham had taken the lead in defining the opposition's issue as "whether the negro or the white man is to be dominant," with "no middle ground," and Conservative newspapers began to describe each party meeting as a "Grand Rally of White Men," seeking to build excitement about "White Men Moving." The issue was potent. "I met those [illegible] Aristocrats on the stump," lamented a Mecklenburg County Republican, "and tryed to make the people believe that the[y] would not be drilled in the same Co's and Reigments with Coulered men and that white and Colored Children would not be taught in the same Schools, but I might as well have sung psalms to a horse." A Caldwell County Republican leader estimated that former Governor Vance's appeal "to the white people to stand up for their race" was cutting sharply into the party's white support in the mountains.[29]

The general strategy of the Democrats or Conservatives (the latter name gave way to the former in the 1870s) was the same throughout the state. "The lines of society are being rigidly drawn," as David Schenck put it, "all the Intelligence and Virtue . . . are with the Conservative party and they treat with contempt and scorn the miserable wretches who have deserted their race" by voting Republican. A Greensboro banker blasted "the *native* radical called a 'scalawag'" and explained, "scalawags are the ticky-scurry-scaly-mangy portion of a drove of cattle."[30] Through social pressure, appeals to racial unity, and violence, Conservatives hoped to drive these supposedly apostate Tar Heels back into the political fold. Negroes they hoped to drive out of politics. Yet the tactics appropriate to this strategy varied in different parts of the state, according to population ratios.

The east was a stronghold of anti-Republican rhetoric, for the black population was the largest there and to many whites seemed most menacing. Yet for the same reason systematic violence against blacks was dangerous and impractical. Newspapers pressured whites to stand together against dire calamities, and explicit racial threats sought to separate lower-class whites from blacks. But the political power of the large black population was undeniable—"I expect we are to be completely snowed under," commented a realist white in Wilmington.[31]

Eastern papers raised alarmist cries about the Republicans' alleged confiscation plans—"a wicked, shameless, lawless, revolutionary scheme"—or about "Radicals . . . Stimulating the Negroes to Apply the Torch to our Homes and to take our Property by Force and Violence." Poor men had the most to fear, trumpeted the *Wilmington Journal*. "Miscegenation" and integration of juries, militia companies, and schools would force the "poor men" and "their children . . . to be demeaned, debased, demoralized, and degraded" by a "ruinous social equality so much to be shunned and dreaded." The *"money, position and influence* [of the rich] *will keep the negro out of their houses,"* declared the *Journal*, but

IT IS IN THE POOR MAN'S HOUSE THAT THE NEGRO WILL ATTEMPT TO ENFORCE HIS EQUALITY.[32]

When the Republicans triumphed anyway, Conservatives and Democrats tried to lessen the effectiveness of black leaders through sporadic violence and intimidation. In a typical incident a Union League group from the Henry K. Burgwyn plantation near Halifax was returning from a meeting when "the Democratic Conservative party form[ed] a line a cross [the] public Road with gun and pistle to prevent us from going home. . . . George P. Burgwyn was the head commander of that Democratic Company," which interfered but did not injure. The masses of black voters in the east were not economically independent, so Conservatives tried to control them through coordinated pressure. Republicans had charged that their opponents were boasting, "We have the land and the houses and the meat and we will make the poor vote as we please." And indeed, Conservatives were open about it. "Discharge Them All," urged the *Wilmington Journal*, assuring whites that it was "perfectly proper" to fire any black who voted Republican. A black Republican in Hertford County lamented that "Every Sence the Elections . . . the Rebls will not let the Colard People have [bread and meat]," and John Pool believed that "turning [blacks] out of employment" had swung one election in Camden County.[33]

But by and large eastern whites had to live with their black majorities. Though they might desire immigrant white workers, landowners remained dependent on black labor. Sporadic demonstrations by whites could render blacks more circumspect, but there were too many to keep from the polls, and too many to provoke, with safety, an outright war between the races. Eastern whites had to study subtlety and patience, and the Ku Klux Klan did not play a major role in their struggle against democracy.[34]

Nor did it in the mountains, for different but obvious reasons. There were so few black people in mountain counties that they rarely had an impact upon elections, and mountain Republicanism was a movement primarily of whites. It had its roots in prewar unionism, wartime resistance to the Confederacy, and continuing contests between stubborn whites who focused first upon what was going on in their locale. Racial issues always had less salience in the mountains because racial variety was slight, and the Ku Klux Klan seemed irrelevant to conditions there.[35]

The piedmont was a different story. All the common forms of resistance to Republican rule appeared there. Democratic officeholders delayed turning over their responsibilities to victorious Republicans. Party leaders like Caswell's John W. Stephens found that they could no longer get money, friends, or credit and that old creditors were pushing them hard. "The truth is," admitted Stephens, "I have not means to buy what I actually kneed for the support of my family." Black candidates were urged, with "the most *tempting* considerations, . . . to come out and curse the party"; one man who refused to cooperate then reported, "My life has been freely threatened, and once attempted. . . . [There is] a general conspiracy among the landowners of this section to starve me and my family out and to kill or drive me from the country." In Alamance County a black leader of the Union League assured William Holden that "we the colard peopl are your true friends in . . . Company Shops," yet black workers there were suffering wage discrimination, and the writer had lost his job.[36]

Beyond these elements, however, there was something more: a large-scale, systematic reign of terror against black and white Republicans. William Holden learned directly of the danger from the Klan through a letter signed "More than one." "Let a word of warning suffice," read the note. "Your life is in danger. Brave men live. Thousands have sworn *traiters* death. Beware lest *you* are included, and ere long fill an unknown grave. To prevent—change and too, quickly."[37]

Essie Harris, a black man in Chatham County, saw just how serious the danger from the Klan was one night. Harris lived with his wife and six children on land owned by two elderly whites, Mr. Ned Finch, aged sixty-one, and his sister, "Miss Sallie," who was more than seventy. Suddenly Klansmen shattered the quiet of darkness by breaking in his cabin window and starting to shoot at him. For almost an hour and a half the forty or fifty night riders poured bullets into Harris's home; "The shot just rained like rain," he said. Courageously, Ned Finch "came out among them" and pleaded, "Gentlemen, . . . let this nigger alone. He is a nigger that I have here to work my land. He is a hard-working nigger, and don't bother anybody." After the Klansmen "ran him back into his own house," Miss Sallie appeared and "begged them not to bother me . . . she came out among them and walked among them till they left." Harris survived along with his family and even wounded one of his attackers, but he was shot "almost to pieces" and badly frightened. "I thought my wife and children were all dead; I did not expect anything else."[38]

Alonzo Corliss, the white man from New Jersey who came to Alamance County to teach school for freedmen, also suffered from the Klan. Crippled and unable to defend himself well, Corliss was dragged out one night and whipped. Then his attackers shaved half of Corliss's head and painted it black. His idealistic efforts to aid former slaves were obnoxious to the Klan, whose members also believed he had urged blacks to attend a white church in Company Shops.[39]

Corliss's fellow educator from the North, Meder, also experienced the Klan offensive against schools and schoolmasters. Meder taught in a frame schoolhouse near Company Shops, and "an order from the High Chief of the county," Jacob Long, went out to put a stop to the "nigger school." The camp chief, John Trollinger, ordered John W. Long, Thomas Gray, and William Kirkpatrick to come to his barroom one night to prepare for the deed. Long was barely twenty; when his wife told him not to go, and Kirkpatrick refused to accompany him, Long went on to Trollinger's tavern, but with misgivings. There around 10:30 he met Gray, who took kerosene and a syringe and led the way to the school. Sitting on a fence, Long and Gray talked the matter over for almost an hour, with Long offering reasons to leave. But Gray said, "I will burn it in defiance of the devil," took the kerosene and "squirt[ed] it up each way on the gallery, in the cellar, under the clapboards, and under the doors and windows. Then he t[ook] the rest and pour[ed] it on [a hemp] bag and la[id] it on the piazza. . . . The second match it was lit," and with a roar fire consumed the schoolhouse.[40]

Perhaps Daniel Jordan, a black man in Alamance County, suffered the most common type of Klan violence. Under cover of darkness ten Klansmen suddenly broke into Jordan's house, frightened his child, and chased Jordan into the surrounding woods where they caught him and gave him forty to fifty licks with switches. Undoubtedly Nathan Trollinger, another black man in the county, felt Jordan had been lucky. The Klan whipped Trollinger with hickories and then "made him take out his penis and stab it with a knife."[41]

Between 1868 and 1872 the Klan's reign of terror accounted for at least one to two hundred whippings in Rutherford County alone, and far more across piedmont counties such as Alamance, Caswell, Lincoln, Gaston, Cleveland, Mecklenburg, Guilford, Orange, Randolph, Chatham, Montgomery, and Moore. Innumerable schoolhouses were burned and scores of black and white Republicans were murdered. To avoid assault "quite a large number of respectable farmers . . . [did] not sle[ep] in their houses any time" during months of KKK nightriding. In Alamance the Klan hung Wyatt Outlaw, the county's foremost black Republican, from a tree only thirty yards from the door of the courthouse in Graham. In Caswell County during the local Democratic convention, a Klan deception lured Senator John W. Stephens into a backroom of the courthouse where one man choked him with a rope while another stabbed him fatally in the throat with a new barlow knife.[42]

The old, formerly established elite organized the Klan and directed its violence to accomplish one central purpose: to reestablish the hierarchy and control to which they were accustomed. The immediate and primary goal of the Klan was to wrest political power away from Republicans. There were also a number of secondary reasons for Klan persecutions. Naturally, amid so many acts of lawless violence, a variety of other motives came into play. Punishing of *whites* who aided the freedmen, for example, was a potent way to shore up white unity and weaken the lower-class threat. Elias Bryan of Chatham County saw his barn go up in flames after he had helped black victims of the Klan; Bryan also was guilty of assisting his former slaves and erecting two churches or schoolhouses for blacks. The attackers of James M. Justice, a white Republican legislator in Rutherford County, emotionally spoke of race: "Damn such an infamous Government, that would put ignorant negroes to rule over and control white men." Cleveland County's Aaron Biggerstaff suffered at the hands of the Klan because he had been an outspoken Unionist and foe of the Confederacy and was "very talkative" and "fussy" about his views. A few whites were whipped for their "low character" or involvement in legal disputes with members of the Klan.[43]

Punishment of blacks for abandoning their traditional subordinate place was a frequent subtheme in Klan violence. An old man approved of the Klan as a tool to keep blacks from edging out whites before a morning's fire. Blacks who had prospered enough to buy buggies were whipped for their success near the corner of Moore, Harnett, and Chatham Counties, and any black who was "bold and aggressive" in the eyes of whites was in danger. When Sandy Sellers in Alamance County conveyed to a white woman the order of a white landowner that she get her livestock out of the crops, he was soon whipped and accused of impudence and propositioning the woman. Klansman John W. Long admitted that they "punish[ed] anyone that had a difficulty with their members," as for instance over "dividing some corn." Those who savagely beat Alonzo Corliss announced to him that "they mean to rule the country . . . if they could not rule by a political majority, they would rule anyhow."[44]

A political majority was the goal, however. A Rutherford Democrat testified that he was told upon induction that the purpose of the organization was to show the strength of the Conservative party, and another Rutherford man flatly declared that the Klan "is a political organization of the Conservative party, in the interest of the conservative party." Alamance County's John W. Long admitted that the initiate's oath bound him to overthrow the Republicans and frankly said that whippings were "for the object of overthrowing the Republican party." Dr. John A. Moore recalled his understanding that the purpose was "to strengthen the Conservative party"; William Tickel said the aim was "to keep down the style of the niggers and to increase the Conservative party." James E. Boyd swore at initiation "never to vote for any man . . . who was in favor of the civil or political advancement of the negro race." "It was understood," he added, "that on the night before election the Ku Kluks would turn out *enmasse*, and visit the houses of the colored people" with a message—"if [Negroes] went to election they would meet them on the way."[45]

The succession of white terrorist organizations in the state—the Constitutional Union Guard, the Ku Klux Klan, the Invisible Empire, and the White Brotherhood—served the purpose of safeguarding this political goal. Knowing that federal power would oppose them, Klansmen needed to accomplish their purpose without getting caught. Exposure and punishment could spell ruin. Therefore members had to swear secrecy and loyalty to the terrorist organization before any other oath. The penalty for informing "would have been death," said John W. Long. To cover the trail further and elude investigators, one organization succeeded the other. As

James E. Boyd put it, the Invisible Empire was set up "to supersede the Ku Kluks," and the White Brotherhood likewise provided a new name useful in denying any knowledge of the Klan.[46]

Even more indicative of the Klan's political purpose were the political facts in the counties where it was most active. Alamance County gave Republican Ulysses S. Grant a 47 vote majority in 1868, but after the Klan recruited 700 members it had "a majority of the white voters" and had successfully intimidated some of the black.[47] Alamance and Caswell counties, the two areas in which Klan violence was greatest during 1869 and 1870, were "the only two counties that were gained by the Republicans" one year earlier, in the fall elections of 1868. Ten of fifteen counties that moved from the Republican to the Democratic column in 1870 had seen considerable Klan violence. In Rutherford County the Klan broke up the effective alliance of black and white Republicans. Formerly Whig and opposed to secession, Rutherford had been barren ground for Democrats; before the Klan, Republicans had enjoyed a 590 vote majority from an electorate of 460 blacks and 1,800 whites. Afterwards some whites were intimidated and an observer doubted that "the colored men would dare to vote at this time." Likewise in Cleveland County it was doubtful that of "three or four hundred colored voters, twenty-five of them would dare to vote the Republican ticket." As Essie Harris put it, "It is not worth while for a man to vote and run the risk of his life."[48]

The social status of members of the Klan demonstrates two important facts. The first of these is that prominent men—gentry and middle-class figures who were accustomed to holding office and wielding power—led the Klan. In counties that had voted Republican, the displaced officers of the old county court plus Democrats who had held higher county offices organized and ran the Klan. It served as a kind of shadow government for men intent on regaining their positions and control. It was the elite's instrument to divide and weaken the lower-class threat manifested in Republicanism, and it used terror to seize actual power from the legally constituted government.

Across the piedmont evidence indicates that traditionally powerful men directed the Klan. In Cleveland County a Democratic candidate for the legislature organized the Klan, a state legislator belonged to it, and the sheriff participated in its raids. In Rutherford County one leading member was a merchant and the son of a physician and state legislator; others included "a very extensive farmer," a store owner, "a son of one of the wealthy farmers," "a farmer . . . of some property," a man connected with the Conservative newspaper, and "a very respectable man, a merchant." In nearby counties rising attorney David Schenck promptly joined, his friend attorney Calvin E. Grier headed up the Gaston County Klan, and Alamance's Dr. John A. Moore joined while he was in the legislature and told others "that nearly all the members of the Legislature were members." Historian Otto Olson identified the head of Caswell County's Klan as a planter and gave this description of the Klansmen who arranged Senator Stephens's murder:

> One of the most prominent landowners in the county had engineered the plot and helped carry it through. Another planter, who was the son of the chairman of the board of county commissioners, a State university graduate, and one of the most cultured men in the community, had played a prominent part. So also had a Conservative candidate for office, a respected coachmaker and merchant, an ex-Confederate captain, and one gentleman with the name of a prominent planter family. Four, perhaps five, of the men participating . . . were Conservative political leaders.

Moreover, the former sheriff who lured Stephens to his death was "'a large and successful farmer.'"[49]

In Alamance County "the sheriff and all his deputies" belonged to the Klan, as did the representative in the North Carolina House. James E. Boyd, who was one of the first to submit to legal authorities and confess his Klan activities, was the son of a powerful magistrate and legislator. His father, Archibald H. Boyd, had chaired the county court and also belonged to the Klan. James Boyd's law partner, G. F. Bason, was chief of one of the ten local units of the Klan, called camps, and lieutenant to the county chief, Jacob A. Long, who held the position of assistant clerk of Superior Court. William Stockard, chief of Camp #7, had been a magistrate in 1866. John Trollinger was both a camp chief and former chairman of county schools. Four other camp chiefs bore the family names of former magistrates and were probably their sons. Testimony about the Klan's reign of terror named Dr. J. A. J. Patterson, Daniel Foust, Dr. W. C. Tarpley, Henry J. Albright, and Patterson Thompson as active, and in a letter to William Holden, John R. Stockard, John G. Albright, and Chris C. Curtis admitted their membership. All these men had been magistrates and possessed considerable wealth. In short, the old power structure of the county was deeply enmeshed in the leadership of the Klan.[50]

The second fact about Klan membership was that it partially succeeded in bridging class divisions among whites and involving substantial numbers of white yeomen. The organization claimed forty to fifty thousand members statewide, less than 10 percent of the white population but nearly one-third of the adult white males. These numbers may have been exaggerated, but Klansmen from Alamance agreed that there were five to seven hundred members in their county, a similar proportion of the county's adult white male population.[51] Many whites continued to vote Republican, but the Klan, and the coercive influence and fear that it generated, split off an important segment of the yeomen class.

Manuscript census records show that many rank and file Klansmen in Alamance were farmers or laborers who owned no more than a few hundred dollars in property. Social pressure from the Klan's powerful leaders or from friends and acquaintances, as well as prejudice, helped to enlist them in the organization. Recruitment brought many neighbors whose farms adjoined each other into the Klan, and family relations were another channel through which membership spread. For example, three brothers and one cousin named Tickel were all Klansmen in Alamance.[52]

The Klan's success was thorough enough to alter election results but less than complete in men's minds. Klan terror supplanted a legal order, ordained by Congress and officially instituted in North Carolina, with the reality of vigilante rule. But close examination of the Klan phenomenon reveals that the Klan did not unify all whites on the common ground of racism. In Randolph County, for example, where the vast majority of ordinary folk had signaled their support for wartime "bushwackers" when they refused to muster with the Home Guard, most whites did not ride with the Klan. White support for the Republican party persisted stubbornly there and in many other piedmont counties. Moreover, violent persecution of black people failed to achieve general acceptance as morally right, though it seemed so to some individuals.

Democratic newspapers denied all wrongdoing by the Klan or excused it by fabricating charges against Republicans or the Union League. Nevertheless, many Klansmen were morally uneasy about their acts. Far from seeming moral and right, racial violence was emotionally complex for many North Carolina night riders, who admitted to feelings of guilt during state and federal investigations. "Well, we knew we were violating the laws," acknowledged William R. Tickel, a camp chief, and John W. Long declared, "We all knew that [it was wrong]." After participating in a whipping, Long said, "I didn't think it right," but on the other hand he "didn't feel mean about it." Long's doubt and ambivalence arose from two sources.[53]

Like other Klansmen he was nervously aware of the illegal nature of Klan violence and its defiance of government and law; Klansmen naturally feared punishment. Yet brutality toward other human beings often remained distasteful in itself, and inevitably the beatings, whippings, and murders seemed excessive, cruel, and hard to justify in regard to particular black individuals. The easiest justification was the recourse to other people's example. "Pretty much all the [white] people in the County belonged to [the Klan]" and supported it, John Long said. The authority of tradition did support white supremacy; prominent people engineered and defended the violence of the Klan. Thus, to men like Long, the abuse of black people had worrisome aspects but did not seem positively wrong because they felt the white population generally wanted to keep blacks down. Virtually no one would dare to question the subjection of blacks.

In the long run Klan violence undermined some vital interests of the elite, for it demonstrated (and thus taught) certain lessons about legality and government. One important lesson was that extralegal violence was not only an effective but also a valid means of nullifying government policy and law. After all, the lawlessness of wartime bushwackers, robbers, and resisters, which the elite had deplored, now was continuing in another setting. Yet this time it was receiving praise and support from the highest levels of the social structure. A second message was even more subversive in the long run. For decades common white folk had suspected government of serving the few at the expense of the many; only the gentry had believed wholly in the rightness and moral authority of government. Now the gentry itself had led an assault on government, seeking to overturn and manipulate it for their purposes. The very men who had stood for law attacked and subverted it. Plainly government for them had been a tool for the protection of their interests. Distrust of government deepened as people saw that social processes boiled down to the question of who had the most power.

In the short run, however, the upper class's appeal to racism was working. A Republican county commissioner in Alamance warned Governor Holden that the situation was far out of hand, and another man wrote from the county that after two Republican magistrates arrested Klansmen, "not one of them was ever punished" but the magistrates "are now threatened with their lives." Friends provided alibis for Klan members, and one of their leaders "boldly proclaim[ed] that the men who reported the actions of the Klan to Gov. Holden will be summarily dealt with." Even in Randolph County a Republican wrote to Holden, "I am sorry to have to inform you that Randolph County is almost entirely governed by the Ku Klux. . . . I know a great many men who laid out during the war, who were whipped, kicked, and handcuffed by the rebels during the war, who are now among the Ku Klux, and voted for the men that abused them so badly."[54]

Other issues were working against the Republicans as well. Corruption was a powerful charge for Democrats to use against them, because its truth was apparent. Among the Republicans were some greedy opportunists like General Milton S. Littlefield. A fellow Republican had recognized as early as 1864 that this man, later dubbed the "Prince of Carpetbaggers," "will look after Mr. Littlefield's interest, always first." With the aid of North Carolina businessman George W. Swepson, Littlefield began buying votes to support grandiose and fraudulent railroad schemes. Though Tar Heels of all parties were hungry for railroads, and though some Democrats were involved, Republicans bore the main responsibility for the issue of $28 million in state bonds for railroads and the accompanying corruption. This sum, enormous for the time, aroused great concern. Democrats condemned the legislature's "depraved villains, who take bribes every day," and wiser Republican officeholders corresponded in sober tones such as these: "I deeply regret the course of some of our friends in the Legislature as well as out of it in regard to financial matters, it is very embarrassing indeed."[55]

Extravagance and corruption were inflating taxes and the costs of government in a state that had always favored low expenditure. Some money went to very worthy causes—the 1869 legislature, for example, passed a school law that began the rebuilding and expansion of the state's public schools. But far too much was wrongly or unwisely spent to aid a party that was already challenging the prejudice against Negroes. W. A. Patterson, a Republican county commissioner in Alamance, eloquently denounced the situation: "Men are placed in power who instead of carrying out their duties . . . [form] a kind of school for to graduate Rascals. Yes if you will give them a few Dollars they will liern you for an accomplished Rascal. This is in refference to the taxes that are rung from the labouring class of people. With out a speedy refformation I will have to resign my post."[56]

Democratic papers were less restrained. The *Charlotte Democrat*, for example, declared that "extravagant appropriations and an increase of State expenses" had made repudiation "the only means left the people to protect themselves against being plundered." The *Salisbury Examiner* printed columns with headings such as "I Am Trying to Raise Money to Pay My Taxes" and quoted an "honest, hard-working old farmer" as saying his taxes were "way up yonder." The *Examiner* gloated that "Tax Collector, Esq. [is] a most eloquent orator, and the most effective stump speaker we have." The issue of high taxes, it realized, could even be turned against the Republicans' class-based appeal by arguments that the poor were "the greatest sufferers in consequence of the high taxes." Republican policies were forcing "the poor laboring men of the country" to sell "everything they can spare, even bread out of their children's mouths."[57]

In fact, taxes rose substantially compared to prewar and postwar levels. In 1859 the state had levied a tax of 20¢ on every $100 valuation of land and 80¢ on every poll. Though the Civil War was responsible for multiplying the tax on land five times, rates dropped back to 10¢ on $100 of land and $1 per poll in 1865. The 1867 legislature had assessed a 50¢ poll tax and 10¢ on each $100 of land, with a family's agricultural supplies and $100 of personal property exempt from taxation. The Republican legislature in 1868–69 provided that families could lay off a homestead that was exempt and increased other exemptions to $500 of personal property and $1,000 of real property. But rates rose to 35¢ on $100 of land and $1.05 on each poll. The problem was that Republicans could not be as hostile to new taxes as Democrats were, because they needed to pay for their schools and other programs. In 1870 the period of exposure to the poll tax requirement was lengthened by five years for everyone, and a special school tax was enacted along with taxes on certain kinds of property such as corporate stock and dividends. That year the Republicans tried to freeze total state plus county taxation at 66¢ on $100 valuation of land.[58]

County taxes had been substantial under the Republicans as well. The 1869–70 rates on every $100 of land were 31¢ in Alamance, 30¢ in Edgecombe, and 30¢ in Caldwell. In Randolph County they remained at 50¢ in 1874. (No records for New Hanover County have survived.) Although poor people should have been exempt from much of this taxation, increases in tax rates are always disturbing. They were more so due to hard times, which were responsible for "utter stagnation in every department of trade" and "much depression about the suffering . . . among the poorer classes of whites and blacks." Too late Republicans recognized that their foes were "scaring people on the tax question, making them believe that their taxes would [be] multiplied by 5 or 6 or even more."[59]

The Republican party faced internal difficulties as well. Some Tar Heel Unionists thought they saw, and resented, an "evident design of a few northern men, but a short time resident here, *to take charge of the State*." More important as time went on was the restiveness of black Republicans under control of their white allies. One freedman called on Governor Holden to do more for blacks in these words: "We the colored people of north carolina are very much dissatisfied with the laws we are working under. The white man has got every advantage over us, and they did not put you in the office and you are doing Everything for them in you[r] power and not for us."[60]

For all these reasons Governor Holden knew that his party's fortunes were slipping in 1870. Moreover, the situation was particularly disturbing in counties such as Alamance and Caswell where Ku Klux Klan terror was rife. Republicans in these counties were in mortal danger—as one man reminded Holden, "it [politics] may be sport to you but it is death to us." Death came to two Republican leaders in those counties in 1870, and no one was punished. An Orange County black wrote that "the Ku Klux [is] threatening to kill me. . . . I wood be glad if you sir could do something for me. . . . The Powder is thyne and let me feel it as I have feelt it [from the Klan]."[61]

Holden decided that he had to do something. To give the Republican party a chance, to protect threatened Republicans, and to restore law and safety, he accepted advice to act strongly.[62] Under authority of an 1869 law, he declared martial law in Alamance and Caswell and dispatched state troops there under the command of federal veteran George W. Kirk. Quickly these forces arrested 101 prominent Klansmen, taking some into custody during public political meetings. This marshaling of governmental power caused the Klan's terror to cease, at least momentarily. White and black Republicans who had lived in fear breathed more easily with the military on the scene. One Republican candidate, William L. Scott, felt hopeful that he now could have the benefit of a fair election. "The colored people say," he wrote, "that white men who were afraid to speak before say they will vote for me."[63]

But Scott and his supporters were wrong—Holden's use of troops had precisely the opposite effect. He had tried to coerce independent-minded North Carolinians by sending troops into their home districts, and he had done it, arguably, to defend a despised race and unpopular carpetbaggers. Seeing their chance, "the Ku Klux and their friends" immediately "rais[ed] a fierce howl." "The feeling is intense," wrote a Democrat, and William Scott began to worry that "this may lose me votes and may defeat me."[64]

William J. Clarke was one Republican who served with Kirk's troops. For that he received much "brow-beating and villification" and learned that his actions ran "counter to the prejudices of a large portion of our people. It amazes me," Clarke wrote his son, "to see gentlemen, held in reputation for wisdom and honor, defending and making common cause with murderers." He believed that "the root of the whole matter lies in the deep hatred to the U.S. government, and prejudice against the negro." But there was more to it than that. With their propensity for settling matters directly, personally, and without recourse to the law, many North Carolinians felt "indignation" at the "lawless usurpation of that infernal despot W. W. Holden." Conservative John K. Ruffin in Alamance County wrote, "I do not regret Holden's military movement, on the contrary, I rejoice at it as having . . . effectually broken up radical rule." Thomas M. Holt, whose father, Alamance textile manufacturer E. M. Holt, apologized for Klan violence before a committee of the U.S. Senate, was elated over the popular reaction. "Tongue cannot describe," he declared, "the indignation of our *whole* people."[65]

Holden had taken a great risk, one against which Republicans had warned him on earlier occasions. In 1868 a Granville County Republican named Silas Curtis had appealed, desperately, for help against the Klan. "God in heaven knows we must have something otherwise we will have to give up Gen. Grant and take [Democrat] Seymour," stated Curtis, who added with determination, "and if I have to do that I am going to take me a Rope and go to the woods." But even Curtis had said, "We dont want a malissia [militia] here among us." And mountain Republicans had reacted with great anger to an intrusion of government power in the form of the arrest of distillers who failed to get permits in 1868. "It would be impossible to elect a Republican," advised one party member, "in the present state of feeling."[66]

Thus in 1870 the Democrats swept to victory. It was not quite the "Political Revolution" that David Schenck had ecstatically heralded, but it did give the Democrats large majorities in both chambers of the legislature. Promptly they moved to impeach William Holden, succeeding on 22 March 1871. In the words of pro-Klan historian J. G. de Roulhac

Hamilton, "The second step in the overthrow of Reconstruction was complete."[67]

Almost immediately Conservatives began to plan changes in the constitution to cripple the chances of democracy getting out of hand again in the future. Prominent among their goals was "a return to the old system of county government," and to this end they scheduled an election at which the people would decide for or against holding a constitutional convention. Newspapers were mostly Conservative and "overwhelmingly favorable" to a convention, and Conservative leaders campaigned hard. But Republicans countered with warnings about repeal of the homestead exemption, removal of black rights, and the possibility of renewed congressional interference. These concerns produced a majority against the convention. The desire for democracy was not dead in North Carolina.[68]

Conservatives ran into another obstacle when Congress refused to waive Zebulon Vance's federal disabilities and accept him into the U.S. Senate. Renewed Klan violence in Cleveland, Rutherford, and western counties resulted in the arrival of federal troops and numerous arrests. Clearly Conservatives did not have a free hand yet to restore aristocratic control in the state, and the 1872 elections drove that point home when Republicans carried the state for president and governor, even while they lost in the legislature.[69] Although they were gaining power, Conservatives had to be patient.

They revealed their attitudes, and their ultimate intentions, plainly in the newspapers. The *Tarboro Weekly Enquirer* observed in 1871 "that negro enfranchisement is not *now* a *living* issue," signaling through its use of emphasis that eradication of black political power was an ultimate goal. Similarly, the *Wilmington Journal* declared that each black person "must be made to understand that social equality cannot be, and will not be, tolerated, and that he will not be permitted to control the Government." Nevertheless all these things could not be achieved at once, so the *Journal* pledged to respect the legal "privileges" of blacks, while Democratic leaders in Wilmington negotiated a sharing of power between black and white in the government of the city.[70]

The most serious problem remaining for Democrats was that poorer voters of both races were still uniting to support Republicans. David Schenck admitted that twenty thousand scalawags (including a few prominent men) cooperated with black Republicans, and in 1872 he feared that whites were joining the Republican party in increased numbers.[71] To overthrow Reconstruction thoroughly, Democrats had to break the alliance between poorer whites who wanted more democracy and opportunity and Negroes who were reliable Republican voters.

Appeals to racism remained one means to achieve this, of course, and Democrats used any opportunity that presented itself. Senator Charles Sumner's Civil Rights Bill gave them a welcome target for attack; Tar Heel Republicans speedily distanced themselves from the bill and even black leader and educator Charles N. Hunter acknowledged that the bill cost votes in the state.[72] But Democrats also had to make some headway against the appeal of democracy. The attractiveness of this issue was giving the Republicans a steady infusion of strength. Thus Democrats struggled to find ways to present themselves as champions, not of the aristocrats, but of the common people.

It was a difficult task—when the Democratic legislature passed a usury law it alienated many wealthy merchants and businessmen.[73] Inevitably it was hard to be the party of the gentry and the yeomen simultaneously. But rhetoric was very malleable, so party spokesmen began to construct arguments to picture themselves, not the Republicans, as the bulwarks of democracy. These arguments became very frequent in 1875 in relation to a new proposal to call a constitutional convention. Though tortured, Democratic efforts to picture themselves as the bulwark of lower-class democracy were often ingenious, and they testified to the importance of this issue among the common people. Statewide, Josiah Turner's *Sentinel* and W. L. Saunders's *Wilmington Journal* led the campaign, but a glimpse at the grass-roots struggle over the appeal of democracy is afforded by the *Gleaner* in Alamance County.[74]

The *Gleaner*'s Democratic editor first had to labor to reduce fears that a convention would restore the appointed county courts and repeal the homestead exemption. Little could be said to obscure the vulnerability of elected local government, for although the legislature had placed restrictions on the proposed convention, none of these safeguarded local democracy; the *Gleaner* lamely joked that the legislators' restrictions did nothing to prevent sex or childbirth either. But the paper pointed out that removal of the homestead exemption was prohibited and claimed, "The homestead is a [D]emocratic measure." Because the 1867 legislature had exempted $100 of personal property from taxation, the *Gleaner* proclaimed that "The [D]emocratic party introduced it into our law. No [D]emocratic newspaper or [D]emocratic speaker has ever opposed it."

Subtly tying this issue to race, the paper argued that many Democrats were "personally interested in the homestead being good, now and for-

ever," whereas "four-fifths of the radical party, the negroes, have no personal interest in this . . . provision . . . and never will have." Democrats
knew that yeomen had a jaundiced view of government because it was
manipulated by the elite. Playing to that distrust, Democrats now charged
that Republicans were using the Negro vote to seize government for
selfish purposes.[75]

To hear the *Gleaner* describe politics, Republicans were oppressing the
poor. An article entitled "The Poor Man" blamed radicals for trying "to
array . . . one class . . . against another" and charged that the existing
constitution brought "great oppression to the poor man." His "law suits
involving a few dollars" were as important "to him as the rich man's law
suit involving hundreds or thousands"; but the law allowed no appeal
from the decision of the elected magistrate in cases worth twenty-five
dollars or less. And should a railroad train "kill a poor man's cow," he
would have to suffer the expense of going to Superior Court because
contracts had to be involved for cases heard before the magistrate. Moreover, state government had been far more expensive under Republicans
from 1869–70 than under Democrats from 1871–74. Radicals will "make
it worse for the tax-payers." "The people want an organic law that will be
less expensive," declared the editor, "and will give to the poor man with
his small matters the same rights that is [*sic*] given to the rich man with his
large ones." Republicans, he warned, would use their Negro minions to
force payment by the state on fraudulent bonds.[76]

In addition to these arguments, Democrats stressed race. "The Issue"
was simple—"Shall the [Convention] . . . be controlled by white men or
by the negroes of the State?" An editorial entitled "Negro Equality" argued that national Republicans had "passed a law to compel your children
to go to school with negro children, and you to sit with negroes at
church. . . . You are not in favor of negro equality. Then leave the party
that advocates it. You owe it to yourself, and your children, . . . to your
race, and your country." These arguments failed to produce a Democratic
majority in Alamance, or in Randolph, and eastern counties with large
black populations such as Edgecombe and New Hanover also went heavily Republican. In fact, the Republican party won the most votes statewide, but because those were grouped in fewer counties, the Democrats
won the campaign for a convention and narrowly controlled its membership.[77]

The 1875 Convention predictably drew up amendments to restrict democracy in North Carolina and make Democratic control more secure.

The most important of these gave the general assembly "full power by statute to modify, change, or abrogate" the existing rules of county government, including the selection of commissioners and justices of the peace. To emphasize white solidarity the convention also proposed a prohibition on intermarriage and integrated schools.[78]

It is easy to see why the Democratic offensive was aimed so directly at local government. Control of county affairs had been the foundation of North Carolina's aristocratic social order; local gentry who made the decisions about roads, schools, and tax rates and who adjudicated most ordinary civil and criminal cases had easily dominated politics at higher levels. Reconstruction had threatened the whole system, however, and had substantially revolutionized its foundation in the counties. Between 1868 and 1877 new men had come into office as county commissioners, pushing aside the familiar faces that long had appeared on county courts. Despite Democratic gains after 1872, the figures for new men in office during the whole period were twelve out of sixteen officials in Randolph County, twenty-three of twenty-five in Edgecombe, twelve of thirteen in New Hanover, seven of sixteen in Alamance, and eleven of eighteen in Caldwell.[79]

In the east some of these new officeholders were black; for example, two of Edgecombe's first five commissioners were black, and they were followed by four more victorious black candidates. The desire to restrict black influence led to the legislature's decision in 1875 to carve a new county, Pender, out of New Hanover. But everywhere the social position of county officials changed markedly. Whereas wealthy "farmers" had dominated the county courts, the elected commissions included humbler men who had the respect of their peers or whose modest occupations brought them into contact with large numbers of voters. The "merchant," "wagonmaker," "farmer and mkanic," "farmer and minister," "farmer and miller," or "brickmason" appeared much more frequently in government councils. The "farmers" were usually small farmers with modest landholdings rather than large planters, and even a "boot and shoe maker" could win local office.[80] The wealth of county officials of 1868–76 changed notably compared to Jonathan Worth's appointed county courts (see table 13).

To uproot this system, the proposed constitutional amendments first had to be adopted, so in the campaign of 1876 the few Republican newspapers assailed the attempt to restore aristocratic control to county government. The *Raleigh Constitution* and the *Lexington Central* praised the

TABLE 13

Changes in Average Wealth of County Officials, 1866–1876

County	Years	Real Estate	Personal Estate	Years	Real Estate	Personal Estate
Caldwell	1866–67	$ 8,127	$ 7,724	1868–76	$2,612	$1,162
Randolph	1866–67	3,293	5,989	1868–76	3,323	2,675
Alamance	1866–67	10,523	26,388	1868–76	6,604	3,825
Edgecombe	1866–67	23,333	24,300	1868–76	7,278	4,861
New Hanover	1866–67	$13,050		1868–76	$3,761	

Source: U.S. Census of 1860 and 1870, manuscript census returns, and for New Hanover County tax lists, 1869, 1871, and 1877.

Note: Data were located on 12 of 16 commissioners holding office from 1868 to 1876 in Alamance County; 9 of 25 in Edgecombe County; 15 of 18 in Caldwell County; 15 of 16 in Randolph County; and 12 of 13 in New Hanover County. For the years 1873–76 in Alamance, when Democrats regained control, the figures were $10,917 and $4,867.

No data for 1877–80 were available for New Hanover County, but in the other counties it appears that the Democrats began, somewhat cautiously, to place more affluent men in charge of local government. During those years the average holdings of real estate and personal estate by local government officials were $2,650 and $4,433 in Alamance (data on 6 of 8 individuals); $7,108 and $17,108 in Edgecombe (data on 6 of 10); $3,889 and $1,511 in Caldwell County (data on 9 of 10); and $3,029 and $6,643 in Randolph County (data on 7 of 9).

Republican party for abolishing the former "abominable system" under which "county squires were made by their particular friends in the Legislature." "It is right in itself," they declared, "that the people of each township should choose their own local officers." Denouncing "the infamous proposition to strip you of your local rights," this editorial charged that in the eyes of Democrats ordinary citizens who supported democracy had "committed a terrible sin, for which you are not to be pardoned by the aristocracy and nabobs of the State." In similar tones the *Roan Mountain Republican* blasted Democrats for their attempt "to take the voting power out of the people's hands and turn back the dial of liberty and progress in North Carolina fifteen years."[81]

Democratic papers made some feeble attempts to answer these charges —a Stanly County organ proposed that rules of county government should be changeable by law "as they ever have been" and illogically asserted, "If the people of North Carolina are capable of self-government, then these matters ought to be entirely under their [the Legislators'] control." But on the whole other issues were much more promising. The *Raleigh Sentinel* deplored "Taxes! Taxes! Taxes! Nothing But Taxes!" and other journals took up the cry. "If you would see prosperity again restored to North Carolina, vote for the amendments, and save $200,000 in taxes annually," urged the *Randolph Regulator*. "Poor men," declared the *Sentinel*, "ask [Republicans] . . . why it is that the poor are every day becoming poorer and the rich richer."[82]

But the dominant theme of the Democrats' campaign was white supremacy. Much was made of an allegation that in the east some white paupers had been auctioned off by black officials and their labor purchased by black farmers. If such had occurred, the method of poor relief was traditional, but with the races of those involved reversed, the story served Democratic purposes. Eastern papers appealed to whites in the piedmont and mountains to defeat the Republicans, who "brought such shame upon us. If you are a white man, and the blood of a freeman runs through your veins, then vote this party out of power." A broadside distributed by Democratic campaigners focused on this allegation with a drawing and headlines that screamed, "White Slavery in North Carolina— Degradation Worse Than Death." The message was plain: "White Men of North Carolina Help Your Eastern Brethren By Voting For the Constitutional Amendments." For white supremacy, piedmont and mountain whites should surrender local democracy. To reinforce the point, other papers raised new specters: "Do you think negro children and white children ought to sit side by side in the school house, and do you think negroes and whites ought to intermarry?"[83]

This campaign, which also featured Democrat Zebulon Vance against Republican Thomas Settle in the gubernatorial race, was "the most heated and exciting" in many people's memory. It was also the most racist. David Schenck felt that "the negroes were despondent and many stayed away from the polls" in his precinct. But overall the turnout was larger than in 1872, and Democrats won both the governorship and the legislature and carried the state for Samuel Tilden, their party's nominee for president.[84]

Reconstruction had been overthrown. The brief period of change that had begun to modify a conservative social structure was over. Democrats had resorted to lawlessness, brutality, and murder to weaken the Republican party, and their appeals to white supremacy, added to the Republicans' mistakes, had eventually prevailed. North Carolina had been returned to aristocratic control, and it was not surprising that the democratic forms of government initiated by Reconstruction lived on in full vigor only briefly.

In February 1877, the legislature abolished elected county government and put local power back into the hands of appointed officials.[85] It could not immediately challenge the right to vote itself, but overall the forces that opposed democracy seemed securely in control once more. A protracted propaganda campaign and massive use of physical intimidation had enabled the conservative elite to regain the political and social control which they believed was rightfully theirs. Appropriating an appealing religious and financial image, they claimed to have "redeemed" the state from the evils of Reconstruction.

UNSTABLE DOMINANCE
IN A "NEW" SOUTH

Security is elusive in life, because life is change. Between the overthrow of Reconstruction and the 1890s, Democrats in North Carolina encountered this disturbing reality. They tried to secure their control over a conservative political and social order; they even attempted to take advantage of change and make it work for them. But bit by bit their dominance became more unstable, their control more imperfect, the challenges from below more threatening.

To consolidate past victories, the Democrats built shibboleths of party, defining themselves as the agents of reform, white unity, and deliverance from the "horrors" of black rule. To strengthen themselves in the future, they supported visions of a New South of progress, improvement, and prosperity. But always some Tar Heels stubbornly refused to accept the Democratic version of history, and the New South vision failed, in practice, to include many more citizens. Farmers followed hope but sank into debt, tenancy, and discontent. Blacks pressed for betterment and grew restive under retrogression. Republicans refused to fade away as a viable party, and those whom progress harmed prepared to fight back. During years of apparent dominance the foundation was being laid for a democratic challenge of unprecedented breadth.

Through rhetoric the Democrats sought to wring every possible benefit from their triumphs of 1876–77. A special vocabulary served, in the 1870s and thereafter, to interpret the reality of Reconstruction in a particular way that enshrined the party. In this lexicon Republican measures without exception were a species of sin, Republican rule a nightmare of degradation. This same rhetoric sanctified the Democratic party for "redeeming" North Carolina and made veneration of the party a moral obligation.

Never again should North Carolina suffer "the evils of negro rule." Reconstruction had been a period of "perpetual negro thraldom" with native whites "abandoned to the [Republican] vandals who are plundering and destroying them." "Radical Extravagance" was always stressed to hard-pressed taxpayers, along with Republican "fraud . . . corruption . . . [and] iniquity."[1] Reconstruction was "military dictation" aimed at "humiliating" a free people, and the Democratic party deserved the credit for ending these "outrages."[2] Through such rhetoric the Democrats attempted to pile up ideological treasure and create social pressure for white supremacy and their party's cause. The Democrats' legacy from the past in this way served their dominance.

There was something new in the air besides, something so compelling to business people that Democrats tried to align themselves with it. After long years of war, destruction, defeat, and impoverishment, people across the South were yearning for tangible change and improvement. Their suffering required a new day, and it was painfully obvious that the region required rebuilding and invigoration. The energy for this task came from the generation born essentially in the 1840s and 1850s. Men whose youthful powers were wasted in defeat and boys who came to maturity amid the South's collapse supplied the leadership for change and preached the gospel of a New South. Challenging their region to learn from the bitter lesson of defeat, they pointed the way to a new path of progress.[3]

Salvation for the New South, they prophesied, lay in industrialization, improved or "scientific" agriculture, education, and reconciliation with the North.[4] The stirring editorials of Henry Grady have made the industrial portion of the New South Creed famous, and there was much excitement about industrialization in North Carolina. "Everything about Charlotte seems to be on a big boom," wrote a visitor in the 1880s, "and everybody seems to be in good spirits at the prospects." The reason for the town's anticipation was simple: three new "Cotton Factories" were forming. "Everything is going ahead and there is more evidence of push and enterprise than I have ever seen. . . . Business men are up and doing."[5]

Much more will have to be said about industry (see chapters 8 and 9), but it is important to note that industrialization was neither the sole nor the dominant portion of the New South idea. North Carolina had a prominent exponent of the vision, Walter Hines Page, who placed greater emphasis upon education and reformed agriculture. He organized the

Watauga Club in Raleigh to lobby for the establishment of a state agricultural and mechanical college and argued that the key to genuine progress was "agricultural improvement." Though Page was a Democratic editor, his views on education were hostile to the aristocratic forces so powerful within the party. He denounced the influence of "aristocratic shackles" on society and wrote that North Carolina discouraged "intellectual aspiration . . . independent thought and . . . mental growth. . . . There is absolutely no chance for the ambitious men of ability, proportionate to their ability." North Carolina was falling behind because it refused to give "every man a chance in making intellectual and social progress."[6]

Richmond Pearson, son of the Civil War and Reconstruction jurist, deplored in public speeches the fact that the North State was "far behind, in commerce, in manufactures, in agriculture, in internal improvements, and above all . . . as the cause of all, behind in Education." He stressed the 1880 census's "dishonoring fact: that North Carolina has a larger proportion of illiterate whites than any other State." Even Democratic leader W. M. Robbins declared that the South needed centers of learning and "improved agriculture" to go with industry.[7]

Across the state newspapers took up the cry for improvement in the agricultural economy. Progress and prosperity could come—had to come, they argued—to the rural countryside as well as the smoky factory. The *Lenoir Topic* applauded the arrival of Caldwell County's first railroad line, which would open up markets for the area's products, and praised the prospects for growing tobacco locally. Rural papers shared the *Caldwell Messenger*'s dedication to aid "in developing the resources of this and adjacent counties," or like the *Littleton Courier* were "Devoted to the Upbuilding" of their town "and Surrounding County." Even small market towns like Monroe, in Union County, hoped to prosper through commerce; Monroe heralded the era of progress by making it a crime to ride a horse fast through town or let hogs run about in the streets.[8]

For farmers there were barrages of hopeful advice, all suggesting cash crops and the market as keys to prosperity. The *Pittsboro Home* excitedly asserted that Chatham County farmers were "all pleased with the success they have met" in growing tobacco, and the *Alamance Gleaner* printed practical articles such as "Tobacco[:] How to Grow and Cure it." Tobacco, the journal said, "is becoming the cry throughout the length and breadth of the old North State. They raise it on the mountain tops and among the sand hills. It brings money more readily . . . than any other crop." Warehouse advertisements trumpeted "Big Sales and Big Prices," and the

Gleaner rejoiced that "Alamance will set more tobacco this year than ever before . . . it is almost an entirely new departure in farming."[9]

Along with innovations in crops there were to be significant improvements in methods. The *Randolph Regulator* preached repeatedly about the basic elements of scientific farming. Articles on "Thorough Culture," "Raising Hogs," and "A Change in the System of Farming—A Necessity" showed the way. Other papers echoed these prescriptions, providing the state's farmers with steady advice on the wisdom of smaller farms, better culture (deeper plowing and more intensive, varied cultivation), and improved breeds of livestock.[10] The New South was going to elevate the life and enrich the purse of North Carolina's suffering farmer.

Beyond a doubt Tar Heel agriculturalists hungered for improvement. Starting in Guilford, one of many piedmont counties where small farmers were struggling to avoid debt and depression, the Grange had quickly attracted attention in the mid-1870s. By 1876 it boasted more than five hundred organizations in the state and fifteen thousand members. Predictably, this organizing disturbed some conservatives—David Schenck saw an "evil and dangerous" tendency to promote class division and white disunity. They worried prematurely, for the Grange did not increase its power.[11] But as farmers entered the 1880s their problems continued to mount.

Across the South agriculturalists faced a number of large-scale dilemmas. Until about 1880 southern cotton growers were fighting to regain shares of the market that Brazil, Egypt, and India had captured during the Civil War. Thereafter, although few people realized it at the time, a marked decline in the growth of British demand for cotton doomed southern growers' prospects. Increasing supplies went hand in hand with steadily decreasing prices for the white fiber that had yielded gold to large landholders and slaveholders through the antebellum decades. Moreover, the nation was entering upon more than two decades of deflation, which lowered all farmers' prices at sale but raised the value of any debts they owed—and farmers customarily were debtors. In a general way too, with specific variants in different localities, manipulated railroad prices and "the iniquities of high finance" and manufacturers injured farmers' interests. The near absence of banks and the weighty presence of the crop-lien made these conditions more severe in all parts of the South.[12]

North Carolinians, unfortunately, had some special reasons to suffer, in addition to these general factors. The decade of the 1870s marked a great divide in the practices of large numbers of Tar Heel farmers. Prior to that

TABLE 14

Production of Selected Crops and Livestock, 1860 and 1880

Crop	1860	1880	% Change
Tobacco	32,853,250 lbs.	26,986,213 lbs.	− 17.86
Cotton	145,514 bales	389,598 bales	+ 167.74
Corn	30,078,564 bushels	28,019,839 bushels	− 6.84
Sweet potatoes	6,146,039 bushels	4,576,148 bushels	− 25.54
Wheat	4,743,706 bushels	3,397,393 bushels*	− 28.38
Milch cows	228,623	232,133	+ 1.53
Swine	1,883,214	1,453,541	− 22.82

Source: U.S. Census, Census of Agriculture, 1860 and 1880.
*1879 harvest.

time the yeoman had characteristically placed his emphasis upon subsistence farming and providing for himself; odd jobs or a small cash crop raised in one's spare time generated money for a few store-bought goods, but these were few. The typical "one-horse farmer" took care of his own needs first, protecting his treasured independence.

This had remained true in the hard decade of the 1860s, when the ravages of war, weather, and a dislocated economy resulted in grinding poverty. Between 1860 and 1870 the production of virtually all crops had fallen substantially. Only cotton planters managed to maintain their pre-war level of production, and there was no increase in harvests of other commodities or general shift toward cash crops.

A momentous shift occurred before 1880, however. Saddled with poverty or with wartime debts that they had never been able to throw off, thousands of small farmers in North Carolina finally succumbed to the lure of producing for the market. They suppressed their misgivings and made the plunge, investing their energy in risky but potentially remunerative market crops. The yeomen in large numbers abandoned their traditional way of farming in hopes of finally reaching better times.

By 1880, North Carolinians were growing less food and beginning to concentrate their efforts on cash crops (see table 14). Tobacco had nearly recovered from the catastrophic 66 percent decline it had registered in 1870, and cotton production had taken off, climbing to 268 percent of the 1860/1870 level of output. Meanwhile, although the state's popula-

TABLE 15

Production of Selected Crops and Livestock, 1860 and 1890

Crop	1860	1890	% Change
Tobacco	32,853,250 lbs.	36,375,258 lbs.	+10.72
Cotton	145,514 bales	336,261 bales	+131.08
Corn	30,078,564 bushels	25,783,623 bushels	−14.28
Sweet potatoes	6,146,039 bushels	5,665,391 bushels	−7.82
Wheat	4,743,706 bushels	4,292,035 bushels	−9.52
Milch cows	228,623	223,416	−2.28
Swine	1,883,214	1,251,006	−33.52

Source: U.S. Census, Census of Agriculture, 1860 and 1890.

tion had increased by 41 percent, its harvests of corn, sweet potatoes, and wheat decreased by 7, 25, and 28 percent respectively.[13]

The trend away from self-sufficiency continued during the 1880s. In that decade North Carolina's farmers committed themselves fully to the market and to its vicissitudes, for good or for ill. As the state's population continued to rise steeply, from 1.4 million to 1,618,000—an increase of 15.6 percent—its farmers put 20.8 percent more acreage into production on 13.2 percent more farms. But this increase in cultivation was not primarily to feed families; it was to earn money from sales in commodity markets that were national and international in scope. The number of swine, milch cows, and bushels of corn raised declined absolutely. Cotton production remained high, but tobacco boomed as the cash crop of the 1880s. A line of counties running across the state just below the Virginia border led this change, with tobacco production jumping almost 35 percent in one decade.[14] The dimensions of change were significant during the thirty years from 1860, a period in which population increased 62.9 percent (see table 15).

It is clear also that this shift in agriculture was a general phenomenon, not a misleading statistic arising from change in some plantation districts while the pattern in small-farming areas remained stable. Four of the five counties singled out through this study harvested less corn and fed fewer milch cows and swine. All five started growing substantially more tobacco. Perhaps the change was most profound in a piedmont county like Alamance where, between 1880 and 1890, tobacco production rose from

TABLE 16
Leading Counties, Cotton Production, 1860 and 1890

	1860			1890	
County	Cotton Bales	Location	County	Cotton Bales	Location
Edgecombe	19,138	east	Mecklenburg	22,709	piedmont
Halifax	10,432	east	Richmond	17,944	piedmont
Anson	9,378	piedmont	Robeson	16,207	east
Pitt	7,634	east	Johnston	13,965	east
Rowan	6,957	piedmont	Edgecombe	13,483	east
Bertie	6,672	east	Pitt	12,493	east
Northampton	6,632	east	Anson	10,822	piedmont
Mecklenburg	6,112	piedmont	Cleveland	10,225	piedmont

Source: U.S. Census, Census of Agriculture, 1860 and 1890.

695,013 pounds to 901,922 pounds whereas the number of swine dropped from 11,796 to 8,707, milch cows from 2,891 to 2,639, and corn from 305,874 bushels to 286,050 bushels. But even Caldwell County in the west followed the same pattern.[15]

The boom in cotton production centered around Mecklenburg County and included numerous other piedmont counties. In 1890 the highest yields of cotton per acre or square mile were in the vicinity of Mecklenburg and in an arc below Raleigh. Similarly the tobacco boom of the 1880s, affecting several counties all along the Virginia border, was primarily a piedmont phenomenon and not something limited to eastern plantation districts.[16] During the period from 1860 to 1890, the piedmont gained in cotton and was dominant in tobacco (with two mountain counties even achieving prominence—see tables 16 and 17).

Cash crops tended to reduce food crops because the farmer who sought large profits from the market simply did not have time or energy left to grow food. Nine counties in tables 16 and 17 had been leading producers in 1860 and managed to remain among the leaders thirty years later. All but one of these counties were growing less corn at the end of the period. A few recorded only a modest absolute decline, but in most cases the reduction was large. Edgecombe County raised 725,487 bushels of corn

TABLE 17

Leading Counties, Tobacco Production, 1860 and 1890

1860			1890		
County	Tobacco	Location	County	Tobacco	Location
Warren	6,148,321 lbs.	piedmont	Rockingham	4,189,416 lbs.	piedmont
Granville	6,025,574	piedmont	Granville	4,170,071	piedmont
Caswell	4,605,558	piedmont	Stokes	3,119,289	piedmont
Rockingham	3,158,333	piedmont	Caswell	2,510,699	piedmont
Person	2,729,709	piedmont	Person	2,327,201	piedmont
Franklin	1,732,883	piedmont	Madison	2,168,823	mountains
Stokes	1,513,040	piedmont	Vance	1,979,070	piedmont
Orange	1,159,764	piedmont	Forsyth	1,607,323	piedmont
Halifax	845,200	east	Buncombe	1,482,688	mountains
Guilford	724,348	piedmont	Surry	1,429,025	piedmont

Source: U.S. Census, Census of Agriculture, 1860 and 1890.

in 1860 and only 266,855 in 1890; corn production for Pitt County dropped from 707,703 bushels to 419,097 bushels; and the figures were 303,921 and 214,309 for Anson, 549,777 and 336,367 for Granville, and 403,288 and 233,116 for Caswell.[17] By 1885 the Wilmington and Weldon Railroad, which served many cotton areas in the east, was carrying twenty-one times as much imported bacon, six times as much imported flour, and twice as much imported grain as it was quantities of these products grown within North Carolina.[18]

This enormous change in agricultural activity occurred at precisely the wrong time for small farmers. Cotton prices fell "from twenty-five cents a pound in 1868 to twelve cents in the 1870s, to nine cents in the 1880s, and to seven cents in the early nineties." Costs to producers—for fertilizer, bagging, machinery, and other supplies—fell much less, and railroad rates discriminated against small farmers. The tax system, because it was based upon land, continued to weigh more heavily upon them than it did upon businessmen and corporations, especially the railroads, which enjoyed many exemptions. Deficiencies of the inadequate credit system became more painful due to deflation and falling crop prices, which raised the real value of farmers' debts 16 percent "during each five-year period for the twenty years after 1875."[19] Farmers were falling behind, yet the only way to climb out of significant cash-crop debts was to gamble still more heavily on cash crops.

The gamble was not working. Between 1880 and 1900 the number of tenants increased from 53,000 to 93,000, and the percentage of farms operated by tenants rose from 33.5 to 41.4.[20] Farmers' debts—and worries—were getting out of control; everything seemed against them. As John F. Flintoff put it, "the towns and cities are building and prospering fast all over the country while the farmers are getting poorer. . . . Trusts and monopolies are all against the farmer's interest."[21] This depressing situation multiplied the dissatisfaction of thousands of yeomen who had surrendered their precious independence or, as many felt, seen their proud heritage stolen. Obviously, in the affairs of farmers, enormous discontent was building, discontent that would compel action.

There was discontent too among black North Carolinians, discontent that grew steadily as time went on. A white man in Bladen County admitted, "Most farmers work so as to keep their tenants poor, for they say, 'give a laboring man money and he will not work.'" Yet, despite the dismaying collapse of Reconstruction, blacks had kept striving to progress in any way that was open to them. In 1879 they organized the first Negro State Fair, at which J. E. O'Hara chronicled some of the reasons why the future offered hope to freedmen compared to the closed doors that had confronted slaves. Praising blacks' "accumulation of wealth," O'Hara asserted that black North Carolinians owned "in the county of Halifax over 13,000 acres of land; in the county of Warren over 8,000 acres of land, and in each of the counties of Nash, Wilson, Edgecombe, Wake, Franklin, Granville, Craven, Northampton and Wayne, thousands of acres."[22] Although most black farmers worked for others and total landholdings were small, every landowner represented a substantial advance over what had been allowed in the recent past.

Eager to share the benefits of the progress that whites so avidly sought, black people entered every field of endeavor and organized to promote their interests. *The Monthly Elevator* in 1876 praised the achievements of five licensed black lawyers—George L. Mabson of New Hanover, Charles B. Warrick, Jno. Sinclair Leary, J. E. O'Hara, and J. H. Smyth. In the east black businessmen tried to develop the Wilmington, Wrightsville, and Onslow Railroad, and W. C. Coleman of Concord (who would eventually establish a black-run textile factory) built up a very successful mercantile business as a wholesaler and retailer of "groceries, provisions, confectionaries, notions, hay, lumber, etc." Negro businesses increased from 80 in 1880 to 175 in 1890, worth $129,000 altogether. In 1888 black businessmen formed themselves into a North Carolina Industrial Association, thus showing a determination to aid each other and to push forward in the supposed age of progress that Americans were discussing widely.[23]

The most vital centers of group activity remained the churches and educational institutions. Black churches were very active—counting "their converts by the hundred" in Raleigh and baptizing sixty-four in Charlotte "in the presence of 2,500 spectators or more"—and their pastors often rose to positions of leadership in their communities. Reverend J. C. Price became president of Zion Wesley College (later Livingstone College) in Salisbury and quickly distinguished himself as one of the most able black leaders in the whole South.[24] In regard to education, whites admitted that blacks "will deny themselves of any comfort to send their children to school," an attitude that helped bring their illiteracy rate down from 77.4 percent in 1880 to 47.6 percent in 1900. Although the Democrats discouraged public schools by various enactments after 1870, blacks took advantage of the opportunities that were available, including Fayetteville Colored Normal School, established in 1877 to train Negro teachers. Allied to formal educational institutions were a variety of voluntary organizations such as the Colored Masons, the Good Templars, and various clubs, all of which emphasized moral improvement, temperance, education, or other forms of uplift.[25]

Perhaps the most important black voluntary organization outside the churches was the North Carolina State Teachers' Educational Association. From the beginning, meetings of the state's black educational leaders attracted a constellation of outstanding men in politics and other fields as well. The State Colored Educational Convention, which met in Raleigh in 1877 and attracted 140 delegates from forty counties, elected former legislator James H. Harris as president. Other political leaders took prominent parts, such as former state senator and representative G. W. Price of New Hanover and his colleague G. L. Mabson, who was chosen a vice-president of the convention. When the fourth annual meeting of the State Teachers' Educational Association took place in 1885, its Executive Educational Committee included two future congressmen, Henry Plummer Cheatham of Plymouth and George Henry White of New Bern.[26] Obviously black leaders viewed education, like politics, as an area that was crucial to their success in the secular world.

Black leaders had not abandoned politics, nor had black people stopped voting after the overthrow of Reconstruction. The Ku Klux Klan, the white supremacy campaigns, and the Democrats' return to office had made it clear that those in control were not going to tolerate substantial black political power. Blacks lived under an implicit but well-understood threat that effective use of their rights would bring prompt, severe repression ("being annihilated by the whites" was the way David Schenck put it in his diary). But the federal government remained a force that southern whites had to reckon with, and although federal concern for black rights in the South continued to weaken, the Democratic "Redeemers" were not yet free to eradicate black political activity. Thus the immediate threat of white violence hung over black people, but a more distant possibility of federal intervention inhibited white Democrats.

Within this situation black Tar Heels continued to vote, with surprising strength. Although some were intimidated, most blacks continued to go to the polls and formed the backbone of a Republican party that was far from moribund. In the first twelve years after the Democrats regained power, their margin of victory ranged only from six thousand to twenty thousand votes in gubernatorial elections and from nine thousand to eighteen thousand votes in presidential elections. As historian Jeffrey Crow has pointed out, "North Carolina had the most competitive two-party system in the South prior to 1900. Between 1880 and 1896 the Democrats never won more than 54 percent of the gubernatorial vote."[27]

A considerable number of black politicians won office, particularly in eastern counties with large Negro majorities. The legislature restricted appointed positions to whites, but occasionally black candidates won elective offices such as register of deeds or solicitor. Moreover, from 1877 through 1890 Edgecombe County elected eleven black men to the state legislature to serve a total of fifteen terms; New Hanover County sent six men to the legislature for a total of twelve terms. In the same period, statewide, forty-three blacks went to the state house and eleven to the state senate to serve sixty-five and sixteen terms respectively. James E. O'Hara of New Bern won a seat in the 48th and 49th sessions of the United States Congress, 1883–87, and Henry Plummer Cheatham went to Congress from 1889 through 1893.[28]

Clearly, black people were still exercising their rights and seeking full citizenship, but under great difficulties. The insecurity of their position and the threats under which they labored put stress on black people's political outlook. Inevitably there were disagreements about how to proceed, and two alternate stances emerged—one outspoken and challenging, the other protective and cautious.

These differing styles were inherent in the Negroes' minority position and had emerged even before the defeat of Reconstruction. In 1874 educator Charles N. Hunter had printed a complimentary report of the goodwill shown by whites toward black students; arguing that the "identical" interests of white and black North Carolinians required close harmony, Hunter went so far as to praise the whites of the state as the "best people in the world" and comment that the Civil Rights Bill would be unnecessary if other people followed the Tar Heels' example. Such words played to the paternalistic overtones that returned to white rhetoric as the Democrats regained power. On the other hand, James O'Hara immediately claimed his rights when the Civil Rights Bill passed in 1875, personally desegregating the main saloon of the *Cotton Plant*, a Tar River steamer. Similar action by blacks in Wilmington spurred G. L. Mabson, a leader among "diplomatic" blacks, and twenty-seven others to publish "A Card to the Public" expressing their "disapprobation and condemnation. . . . While we rejoice in the passage of that bill by Congress," the careful group declared that the purpose of the law was to protect "legitimate rights" of black people, not to be "an engine of oppression to any class of our fellow citizens."[29] Although logically unclear, their "Card" unquestionably conveyed a desire to go slowly and avoid strife.

The same difference about tactics or strategy appeared in regard to other issues—whether to praise the legislature for its support of education, for example, or how to counter retreats from that support. But such differences did not obscure the fact that the overall aim of black North Carolinians was the same: full rights and equality. In a trying and dangerous social situation, few could blend assertion and blandishment as ably as Dr. J. C. Price, who charmed the *Charleston News and Courier* with a speech in 1887 on "The American Negro, his Future and his Work." Price defined the Negro's goals as intellectual development, moral culture, material possessions, and social refinement, and he sounded a few themes complimentary to whites. His praise of "mind power" as the secret of Anglo-Saxon success was certainly not controversial, yet he deftly linked it to the argument that able Negro leaders proved the equality of black "mind power." Politely he used facts to ridicule the belief that Negroes were dying out, and he parried white desires for colonization of blacks by noting that Africans had been in this country longer than some of the

J. C. Price

early colonists. "Why not . . . send back home the Pilgrims' descendants?" he asked. Price's fellow-educators shared a belief in "the importance of . . . *self-help*" and felt the same race pride—one spoke of "the importance of teaching *color* in the [black] schools" as a tool of improvement.[30]

Variety and ingenuity of tactics could not offset, however, the discouragement blacks felt about trends in the 1880s and the dissatisfaction that was growing within them about their position. Some of their discouragement arose from the continuing federal retreat from equality, a retreat clearly marked in the Civil Rights Cases of 1883, which carried still further the Supreme Court's narrowing and gutting of the Fourteenth Amendment.[31] But even more stemmed from a series of battles within the state. These included an insidious change in the mechanism of funding public schools, a veiled attack on black suffrage, and the increasing virulence of white racism that lay behind all issues.

After their victory in the 1876 election, Democrats had claimed that they would guard and protect the rights of black citizens, and Governor Vance had urged the legislature to "make no discrimination in the matter of public education." Black people had reason to be skeptical—one of their educators described the South as "a land whose upper class had always been implacable foes to popular education," and many whites believed, "Educate our colored laborers and you spoil them." Yet surely they wanted to hope, for public schools were a vital right of citizenship for their people. In 1880 the Democratic-controlled legislature began to undercut that right. Twice the lawmakers authorized the town of Goldsboro to fund its separate schools from separated tax revenues, using taxes paid by whites to support white schools exclusively and forcing black schools to rely on the smaller revenues derived from the poorer black population. Obviously this method of financing would cripple black education, and in 1883 the legislature authorized "any school district in the state to vote local taxes on that basis." Under the new law only ten white petitioners were needed to force a vote on the issue.[32]

Representative James H. Harris called this law "wrong and unjust," and his colleague Noah R. Newby threatened that many blacks would emigrate "when such an injustice was done them." The *Salisbury Star of Zion* blasted the new law as a "monstrous enactment—a disgrace to the State," and Negro voters opposed local changes in funding, with some success. The predominantly black voters of Tarboro, for example, defeated a shift to racially based funding and angered the white *Tarboro Southerner*, which denounced their "ingratitude." Perhaps to overcome these obstacles, the

1885 legislature made county boards of education appointive, thus elimi-
nating most black members, and gave these boards discretionary power
over one-third of their school fund. Spending out of this third did not
have to be in proportion to the number of schoolchildren in each school;
instead it could be used to "equalize school facilities" in a variety of ways
defined by the imagination of the white board members.[33]

The future of black schoolchildren won a reprieve in 1886 when the
North Carolina Supreme Court ruled the legislature's changes unconstitutional. It was a triumph of color-blind justice when the court declared that
under the state's constitution "there shall be no discrimination in favor of
or to the prejudice of either race." But the trend was unmistakable, and
efforts against blacks quickly sought new channels. The *New Bern Daily
Journal* proposed a new layer of supplementary school funds that could be
distributed primarily to whites, and several towns briefly "abandoned
their white graded school system rather than support schools for their
Negro children." Noah Newby's prediction began to prove itself, as a
Charlotte business leader reported that, "Labor is somewhat demoralized
here by a desire to emigrate to Liberia."[34]

Deeply disturbing also to blacks was an 1889 statute that affected suffrage by giving local registrars considerable latitude to judge the qualifications of voters. Negro voters knew how white registrars would use this
law, and coming as it did on top of other discouragements, it sparked a
sizable migration out of the state. Black North Carolinians had joined the
Exodusters of 1878–80, who left the South out of despair over the defeat
of Reconstruction—several thousand from eastern counties moved then
to Kansas and Indiana. But after 1889 as many as fifty thousand departed
for Kansas, Arkansas, Texas, or Oklahoma, and worried white landowners
began to discuss the danger of a labor shortage. The postemancipation
desire to drive blacks out was gone; as one "Colored Mechanic" put it in a
letter to the *Wilmington Post*, "you Bourbon gentlemen" condemn black
laborers as "'worthless, no account,' etc., etc., but when they do attempt
to go . . . you discourage them and do your utmost to retain them here."[35]
Economic reality had impressed upon white landlords a stronger appreciation of black labor.

In no other way could one speak of white appreciation for black people
during these years. The tone of white racism was changing, taking on a far
more menacing and ugly aspect. Overt and vicious racism became a highly
visible feature of daily life, often a source of amusement for whites. Although racism had been deeply ingrained in North Carolina and the na-

tion for centuries, it now presented a noticeably more hostile, threatening face.

Newspapers both promoted this shift and reflected it, for the new tone of racism arose from deepening crisis within the state and external changes. As farmers' problems mounted, the Democratic party merely repeated propaganda about "black domination" and invoked white supremacy as a sacred cause. Meanwhile the federal government steadily retreated from the protection of civil rights, and the northern public soured in its attitude toward the freedmen—both of which gave more scope to racism and encouraged voluble racists. In the nation as a whole, Social Darwinism prompted invidious comparisons between Anglo-Saxons and either newly arrived immigrants or native-born blacks. An "unsentimental" assumption that superior and inferior races were pitted against each other in the "struggle for existence" gained adherents in major white institutions. Even in the formal, cultivated atmosphere of an educators' convention the state superintendent of public instruction considered it appropriate to tell black teachers that their African ancestry had been "of most barbarous kind."[36]

The newspapers were an easy place both to fan these flames and to see the effects of the expanding fire. Virulent hatred and unvarnished racial hostility appeared frequently in reports of lynchings or in more casual items. The latter were often meant to be humorous. The *Monroe Enquirer*, for example, quoted another paper on the remarkable fact that "a white man . . . [recently] succeeded in breaking a negro's head with so feeble an instrument as a hoe-handle . . . surely this is the age of miracles." A more grisly version of racist humor appeared in the *Alamance Gleaner*'s report that a "big buck darkey" had attempted to purchase a meal in Polkton, Anson County. Meeting with denial, the man objected. Without further explanation the article continued, "Several experienced physicians . . . think that he will certainly get well in a few weeks. The ball entered the left breast and took off the edge of that darkeys appetite." With such attitudes prevalent, and with agricultural wages at 20¢ to 50¢ per day for black laborers, it was little wonder that black people were dissatisfied and discontented.[37]

One message of the new, virulent racism was that white paternalism would return only under conditions of strict white supremacy. Mirroring the political themes that helped engender racism, private attitudes revealed that only when blacks were prostrate were friendly relations possible. The *Asheville Citizen*, for example, declared "that this is the white man's country and this, the white man's government" in which Negroes must have no role. Yet, in its next paragraph, the *Citizen* could proclaim, "We have the kindliest feelings for the negro."[38] An insistence that harmony would prevail only if blacks were in their place had been an unspoken element of antebellum paternalism, but now, due to Reconstruction, the emphasis fell upon threats about the necessary precondition.

This occasioned some incongruous actions and sentiments on the part of whites. In a "Home Sketch" in his diary David Schenck fondly described "'Uncle Lee'... my colored man servant" and "Aunt Cheney" the cook. "Uncle Lee" was "a most faithful and trusty servant... an institution... contributing to our happiness." Always ready with "a kind word or a little joke," "Uncle Lee" gave the Schenck children rides "on the waggon or in the wheelbarrow," and Schenck himself entertained "warm feelings of attachment" for both servants. Yet Schenck showed the other side of race relations when another servant, Bob Burton, got drunk, used "abusive... language to me, said he was not afraid of a white man, didn't care if I was a Judge." Schenck tried to walk Burton off his property, but at the gate, when Schenck threatened Burton with a stone, the latter drew a knife. Schenck threw his stone "immediately," Burton cut Schenck on the left elbow, and Ned, another servant, then grabbed Burton. Schenck called for his double-barrelled shotgun, and "when Bob saw the gun he let Ned go and walked off and was about 35 steps distant when I got my gun." The judge "immediately" fired on the retreating Burton, wounded him, and had him arrested. "The white men of the community," concluded Schenck, "except a few radicals, unanimously approve my course.... My conscience approves all I did. We cannot permit these wretched negroes to trample on us with impunity."[39]

Upon any provocation whites were ready to inflict summary violence on blacks. The immediate resort to violence was the background threat that kept race relations running on a "proper" course. In similar fashion whites continued to resort to violence among themselves to settle disputes and to assert or maintain social status. Judge Schenck, before he ascended to the bench, had grappled with other attorneys in fistfights during open court and had defended respectable men who shot, slashed, or beat each other. The younger Richmond Pearson, embroiled in a controversy with Representative Johnstone Jones over the stock law, challenged Jones to a duel in 1886. Jones declined out of distaste for dueling and won some newspaper support, but before the quarrel subsided Pearson had challenged businessman Rufus Y. McAden, who also refused. Though some gentlemen "no longer recognized" dueling, others like Pearson were eager to defend their reputation at twenty paces. Moreover, the governors' papers of the 1880s reveal that the less formal violence of outlaw bands remained a problem in some localities, especially the mountains.[40]

The stock law, which triggered the conflict between Pearson and Jones, caused much wider political conflict throughout the state during the 1870s and 1880s. The stock law uprooted a legal tradition that was older than the state and threatened the rights and interests of poor rural folk, both white and black, throughout North Carolina. Nothing else generated so much legislation during the 1870s and 1880s, and the pages of stock law ordinances that swelled each legislature's statute books bore witness to the intensity of the battle over this issue. Eventually the interests of commercial farmers prevailed, but not without embittering many poorer whites and blacks and stoking their resentment against the dominant regime.

The stock laws involved a proposed change in the age-old tradition of the open range. In North Carolina and the rest of the South custom and law had decreed that farmers had a responsibility to fence their crops; livestock, on the other hand, were free to roam over the landscape, foraging for food and watering themselves from creeks and streams on land possessed by people who were not their owners. Over the generations many southerners had supported themselves in large part from slaughtering pigs that fed on the open range. Many yeomen and landless whites had hunted, as well, on others' land. The stock laws (or "no fence" laws as described by agriculturalists) proposed to reverse tradition, close the open range, and require the owners of livestock to fence in their animals. Crops no longer would need a fence's protection.[41]

Proponents of the change argued that "timber is becoming scarce," especially where wood was burned to flue-cure tobacco, and that "the great scarcity of timber" argued for "the necessity for the preservation of what remains." In addition, they claimed, "laboring hands are diminishing in numbers so that it is almost impossible to 'keep up' lawful fences." Moreover, in the eyes of the commercial farmer, the old rule of fencing crops was "oppressive, burdensome and ruinous to the future prospects of our State, from the fact that it require[d] many acres of land to be fenced, to secure our crops from the depredations of stock, while but few acres, comparatively, would suffice to confine the stock."[42] Clearly the stock law represented a convenience for commercial farmers, and for that reason its promotion coincided with the shift toward cash-crop agriculture.

So radical a change, however, was too much for a conservative rural population, and even for some of its commercial farmers, to swallow quickly. Thus stock-law legislation followed a pattern: year after year the legislature authorized more counties or townships to vote on the stock law. Each locality could try the new system by fencing in its boundaries, thus taking itself out of the open range, even if surrounding areas refused to change. Considerable debate and ambivalence accompanied local consideration, but gradually, steadily, more of North Carolina adopted "no-fence" rules for the farmers. Supporters of the law, such as H. A. Foote in Warren County, frequently enjoyed the financial support of merchants and railroads, which stood to benefit from an expanding commercial agriculture. These were the forces behind the movement. And proponents were confident, as Foote put it, that if the law prevailed for only a year or two "you would [thereafter] find no serious opposition to it."[43] The constant advance of no-fence rules, in fact, showed that they did serve the interests of the majority of farmers, who were shifting to cash crops.

As stock laws were adopted, however, changes took place that some may not have foreseen. Shortly before Union County adopted the stock law, for example, advertisments began to appear frequently in the *Monroe Enquirer*. They typically read "Notice" or "Lands Posted," or—more aggressively—"A Warning!" and stated: "The undersigned forbid all persons hunting or fishing, either with or without dogs, or in any way trespassing on our lands. The law will be strictly enforced against any person found so doing."[44] The new system made "Every owner of real estate . . . lawfully entitled to the entire and exclusive use of his own soil, and every entry upon lands unless by leave of the owner thereof [was] unlawful." Thus landowners could and did prohibit "cutting timber, moving the same . . . firing the woods" and trespassing or "depredat[ing]" in any way. The stock law had changed the relationship between people, not just the relationship between animals and crops.[45]

The burden of this change fell disproportionately upon the poor. Landless whites and blacks depended on the open range to support their pigs or other animals; under the new law that range became other peoples' land, inaccessible. Many small farmers who owned land still needed the water courses or decent pasture that lay on neighbors' property; now that was foreclosed. By closing the open range, the stock law deprived many poor farmers of valuable resources that had always been available to them, and the loss was serious.

In petitions to the legislature some of those who were injured spoke out strongly. "The so called stock or fence law . . . will only benefit a few," declared several dozen residents of Gaston County, and will "prove injurious to the masses of the people." Residents of Alexander County, who asked for "protection of the poor people—the backbone and sinew of the country" charged that their land was hilly and mountainous and well-suited for grazing, but the stock law forced many on "small farms" and "elevated ri[d]ges" to water "their stock from *wells*." Seventy-eight citizens in Rowan County objected out of a similar concern over "the scarcity of water and good range in the summer season." And four to five dozen from Pasquotank County in the east protested that "there is a very large amount of swamp land . . . unfit for cultivation and . . . only valuable for timber and for a range for stock."[46]

These and other protests revealed considerable class consciousness. The fence law, they charged, would "utterly ruin the stock raising interest of the labouring classes and work great injury to the poor people of this County." "Look to the intrest of the Poor People," demanded a petition from Caswell County, "for the in actment of Such as fence Law would be the Richmans Kingdom and the Poor mans Destru[c]tions." Another petition from Gaston County denounced the law as "oppressive on the poor Class of people" and warned, "God in his holy word tells us the doom of the man who oppresses the poor, the widow the orphant etc. Will it not apply to a county stait or nation?" Two sizable petitions from Edgecombe County declared that "only a few large land owners" or "only a *very very* few of the largest land owners . . . are praying for this law. If you will grant it the people will suffer." Of forty-four names on one of these petitions, twenty-nine signed with their mark.[47]

Even more significantly, many of these poor people spoke angrily about their *rights*. To them more than justice was involved—their rights as citizens and free men were being abridged. Some spoke of "our rights and liberties, which Nature's God hath given us." Others denounced proponents' efforts as "gotten up by a class in our County to trouble our rights." One petition demanded the opportunity to "vote on the stock law separ[a]t[e] and apart from . . . other townships . . . and Be a Free People." Few were as eloquent as approximately eighty citizens of Nash County, who linked their complaint to other grievances that they held against the Democratic regime. "We the undersign[ed] Sidersons of This Township ask . . . that the no fenc Law will not Be . . . Pass[ed]," they began, pleading for "Co[m]pas[s]ion on the Needy People." But they also complained that "We [Feel] that our Rights Have Been Taken Away from us

By unfriendly Representatives and we are Paying as much Taxes as ever do. [We] ask General Assembly of North Carolina to Allow us [to] Ellect Some of our Magistrates if not all."[48]

These people, injured by the kind of "progress" embodied in the stock law, added their anger to the growing discontent with the Democrats' domination. And their complaint about the stifling of democracy touched another source of popular unrest. Many ordinary Tar Heels had never appreciated the closed, hierarchical society that existed before Reconstruction and returned with the Democrats' triumph. To find more opportunity, some had moved away, like J. W. Hinshaw of Randolph County. Writing from Prairie Center, Kansas, Hinshaw encouraged his relatives to join him and gave "several reasons why I had rather live here in preferece to North Carolina. One is the society is better among the common people. Have good schools for at least seven months in the year. Theachers get from forty to fifty dollars per mo. . . . It being a farming county capital is more equally divided hence you see people are on more of equality—not like it is in N.C. all the money in the hands of a few monopolies."[49]

Many who stayed behind felt just as strongly as Hinshaw. The *Randolph Sun* remembered 1868 as the year when "for the first time in the history of the State . . . the people [gained] the right of electing their township officers." The Democratic party, by contrast, "destroyed local government, [and has] taken from the people the right of self government." Asking "Do the people elect the County Commissioners," justices of the peace, school board members or other officers, the *Sun* answered, time after time, "No. The Democratic office holders took that right away from the people." The principle at stake was democracy, argued the *Sun*. Democrats "say the ignorant people are not fit to choose their own officers. Is that right? No, it involves a principle of tyranny and oppression."[50]

The homestead exemption was another cause of grievance. Accurately pointing out that Republicans had passed it in 1868, the *Sun* estimated that it saved one-half of those eligible by giving them ten years in which to clear up their debts. Although the North Carolina Supreme Court, staffed largely by Republicans, upheld the exemption many times, the United States Supreme Court ultimately invalidated it as unconstitutional. The suit against it, stated the *Sun*, had been brought by Col. L. C. Edwards, a member of the Democratic State Executive Committee.[51]

During the 1880s this discontent surfaced occasionally in attempts to form stronger electoral coalitions against the Democrats. The *Lenoir Topic*, a Democratic journal, worried in 1882 that anger over the no-fence law might encourage "embryo Mahones and Riddlebergers" to challenge the party, as they had in Virginia. When Caldwell County's Walter W. Lenoir expressed the wish that western Democrats could elect their own officials, the *Topic* and other Democratic papers promptly assailed him with horror stories about black rule in the east. Yet independent Democrats occasionally allied with Republicans and "agrarians" to challenge the stock law, or, in Buncombe County in 1888, to support the Blair Educational Bill (to provide federal aid to schools) and "to declare uncompromising war against the undemocratic and unrepublican system of County Government." Democrats admitted among themselves that these issues cost them some votes and kept alive the possibility that "the poor classes of the whites and negroes . . . [would] combine."[52]

The real question facing the Democratic party was whether it could respond to social discontent, whether it would make an effort to alleviate the problems of the lower classes. Only in Thomas Jarvis did the Democratic party find substantial progressive tendencies. Jarvis, who was governor from 1879 to 1885, had a sense of the difficulties facing ordinary North Carolinians and held a few mildly reformist ideas. His career illustrated, however, the stifling effects of orthodoxy in a party that required all to do homage to white supremacy. If Democratic unity was the means of white control, every man had to fall in line.

Toward blacks Jarvis professed to be a benevolent paternalist (if these contradictory terms have meaning). Black people had to stay in their place, and Jarvis told them flatly at the Negro State Fair in 1879 that their place was on the farm. "You are peculiarly an agricultural people," he declared, and "when you have secured homes for yourselves and identified yourselves with the soil you will all be happier." Yet he announced at the 1880 fair that black North Carolinians were "entitled to the same privileges as the Governor himself enjoys." And he claimed that since the advent of black suffrage it had become "wise to educate them." Jarvis did not distinguish himself in defense of black education, but he also passed up several opportunities to use state troops against black strikers or accused criminals.[53] If not the Negroes' friend, Jarvis was not their worst enemy.

Jarvis supported the New South's visions of economic improvement. Accepting an invitation to speak to the New England Manufacturers' and Mechanics' Fair in 1883, the governor promoted sectional reconciliation and urged cooperation "for the material interest of our common country." He invited northern investment in southern industry and boasted of

Thomas J. Jarvis

North Carolina's new textile factories. During his years in office he also labored to promote development of the state's mineral resources.[54]

But Jarvis was not an uncritical booster—he had a critical perspective on New South industries and was aware of the people's problems. His progressive views came out most clearly in regard to safeguarding the public from the misdeeds of private corporations. In a region that was courting corporations with generous tax breaks, in a nation that was witnessing enormous growth in corporate power, Jarvis dissented. As governor he urged the legislature to establish a railroad commission, and in 1886 he wrote that a marked change of course was necessary. Condemning the venerable Dartmouth College Case and its protection of corporate charters as a judicial error that offered private entities too much power, Jarvis argued that government had to reassert control. The great corporations were often in the wrong. By numerous "outrages and wrongs," he felt, they had brought ill feeling against themselves; strikes and labor violence would grow worse unless government made the corporations subject to legislative control. Jarvis favored a federal department of cabinet rank to oversee labor-management relations and to prevent trouble by enforcing justice for workers.[55]

These were advanced ideas about industry, and on agriculture, too, Jarvis urged a progressive approach. Farmers were struggling against growing difficulties, and Jarvis believed that the Democratic party needed to respond to their problems, not cling to old, worn-out issues. He warned party leaders in 1888 that not even Zebulon Vance, with his great skills "as a stump speaker and his great influence with people," could "hold the party in line on a purely Tariff Campaign." Jarvis worried about the relationship between white landowners and black tenant farmers; the black man's alienation from whites, he believed, was responsible for poor work, and the cure lay with the whites. "Can it be truthfully said," asked Jarvis, "that all of our land owners have done their full duty in looking after the morals, the comfort, the habits, and the general welfare of their tenants[?] I fear not." He urged the newly emerging Farmers' Alliance, which had not yet found it necessary to leave the Democratic party, to "take hold" of the "*burning question* [of] Land and Labor." Constructive approaches to issues could guarantee the "liberal, progressive [D]emocratic party" that Jarvis favored.[56]

But Jarvis's voice was a lonely one within the Democratic leadership. As the authors of the leading history of North Carolina have recognized, the Democratic party was unresponsive to social problems and absorbed in a reflexive defense of the status quo. "The conservatively controlled Democratic party became the ally and guardian of the railroad and industrial interests." Instead of supporting the regulatory ideas that Jarvis espoused, "it adopted the policy of stimulating railroad, industrial, mercantile, and banking development by unrestrictive private enterprise protected and aided by the state government. . . . It opposed a rising demand among depressed farmers, liberals, and reformers for a regulatory railroad commission, lower freight and passenger rates, and the abolition of abuses and favoritism. It opposed also the demands for a readjustment of the discriminatory system of taxation; for social legislation to correct the evil effects of long hours and low wages upon mill workers; and for the expansion of the system of public eduction. It opposed all such measures of economic and social reform" and concentrated upon "the negative policy of maintaining . . . Democratic supremacy in politics."[57]

Loyalty to such a party carried a definite price. Yet the shibboleths of white supremacy and Democratic "redemption" from the "evils" of Reconstruction were so powerful that they coerced even Thomas Jarvis into loyal obedience. Jarvis remained ambitious for a seat in the United States Senate, which was periodically the gift of the Democratic-controlled legislature. Like other leaders, he stressed his devotion to the party's interests. "In no event will I do anything that will hurt the party," he assured its key operatives. "[I will accept] perpetual retirement if that will give unity and strength to the Party. I beg that you will not regard this as mere idle boasting for I mean every word of it as earnestly as I ever said anything in my life. . . . I put the State and party together all the time because I honestly believe they belong together."[58] This was precisely the attitude that Democrats labored to plant among white voters, and party stalwarts had learned their lessons most completely.

In the 1890s loyalty to Democratic ascendancy and white supremacy would require much of Thomas Jarvis and pose a dilemma for dissatisfied Democrats, for social problems continued to increase, building toward a profound political challenge. Meanwhile, the growth of an industrial New South reinforced traditional relationships of power while it altered traditional ways of life and stirred discontent among workers.

LEADERS OF THE
NEW SOUTH

In the closing decades of the nineteenth century, the industrial transformation of North Carolina began in earnest. Everywhere people looked they saw signs of new industry and new businesses; machines were appearing in what long had been an agrarian world. Tar Heels felt the first substantial impact of industrialization upon their lives and culture in this period.

Walter Hines Page, editor of the *State Chronicle*, reminded people of the growing importance of factories by keeping up a steady drumbeat of news about industry. In the early 1880s he described cotton mills, cotton seed oil mills, tobacco factories, foundries, iron works, and other manufacturing plants in month after month of articles. The Yadkin Falls Manufacturing Company was building a two-story factory, his paper announced in a typical story, and two weeks later he reported that Swepson Cotton Mills in Alamance County had exceeded two thousand spindles. Once he listed most of the textile mills in the state, while his columns catalogued the variety of industrial ventures: Edward Dilworth Latta employed 118 workers at his Charlotte Clothing Factory; the firm of Wainwright and Royall in Wilson manufactured one thousand to fifteen hundred plows per year; C. A. Hege's Salem Iron Works was the state's largest establishment of its kind, but both Vinton Liddell and John Wilkes had started foundries in Charlotte; Hickory had the Piedmont Wagon Works, a building material company, a foundry and machine shop, three tanneries, and six tobacco factories; by 1888 the Bonsack Cigarette Machine had been put into extensive operation by W. Duke, Sons & Co.[1]

As this litany indicated, industrial activity was spreading and with it came a growth in towns and small cities and an expansion of the ranks of merchants. Winston was now "a noisy inland metropolis, possessing every accompanying indication of city-like thrift and go-aheadativeness." The tobacco industry had sparked Winston's growth, but other shops, stores, and businesses located there to participate in the energetic business climate. Many towns were desperate to be on a rail line, the throbbing artery of commerce. To achieve their goal they offered railroad builders assurances like these: "Statesville is heart and soul with you, and prepared . . . to give you aid." One of Page's readers believed it would all continue, writing, "I am an optimist. There never was such a railroad man as Colonel [A. B.] Andrews, a manufacturer of such unanimously acknowledged success as Col. [E. M.] Holt, such a pronounced commercial and manufacturing success as the Blackwell Tobacco Company."[2] And truly, there never had been announcements such as the following during the agrarian, antebellum era:

> Wanted at Once
> Five Hundred white boys and girls from 14 to 21 years of age to learn cigarette making. The work is light and very profitable to those who are willing to apply themselves diligently.
> > Address W. Duke, Sons & Co.
> > Durham, N.C.[3]

Nevertheless, some perspective is needed. The state's rapidly growing industries were building upon a small base, and they remained small throughout the nineteenth century. Industrialization was only beginning and was far from achieving dominance. The Census of Manufactures revealed that there were 3,667 manufacturing establishments in North Carolina in 1890. These employed 36,214 people, which was not quite one-tenth of the number of workers in agriculture and only 6.7 percent of the total work force. By 1900 the number of industrial workers had more than doubled to 73,571, but this figure still accounted for only about 12 percent of the working population.[4] Industry was small, though it was noticeable and growing.

The pace of growth attracted attention because it signaled industry's future importance. From 1880 to 1900 the number of industrial workers doubled each decade, and other measures of manufacturing's importance increased just as rapidly or faster. Capital invested climbed from $13,045,639 to $32,745,995 to $76,503,894; the cost of materials used climbed from $13,090,937 past $22,789,187 to $53,072,388; and the value of the products rose from $20,095,037 in 1880 to $94,919,663 in

1900. Cotton textiles were preeminent among the other industries. By 1890 they employed the most workers, with lumber products and tobacco manufacturing ranking second and third, and in the following decade textiles surged far ahead in importance. At the turn of the century the cotton goods industry in North Carolina employed four to five times as many people as tobacco manufacturing and accounted for almost half of all industrial workers and all capital invested.[5]

It was difficult to tell from newspaper reports that industry was still small, for the booster psychology that accompanied the New South (and still characterizes its cities) flourished with little restraint. Even a county journal like the *Alamance Gleaner* featured enthusiastic articles on "The Industrial Progress of a Week in the South." In the ambitious towns and cities this tendency went further. In Charlotte the influential engineer and mill designer D. A. Tompkins decided to act directly and purchased the *Observer*, saying, "The one thing that I wanted the paper for was to preach the doctrines of industrial development." Elsewhere editors readily did the industrialists' work for them. Newspapermen promoted industrial growth as if their lives depended on it, along with their town's future. The *Salisbury Herald*, for example, regularly featured an article extolling the virtues of Salisbury as a site for manufacturing. And to keep interest up it printed a seemingly endless series on economic booms—"The Secret of Booms," "How to Make a Boom," "Our Boom," "The Boom Will Stay," and even "Who Kills the Town?—The Grumbler."[6]

These industrial developments were highly significant. Although small and limited in scope, they marked the beginning of new economic and social patterns that had the potential to transform society, changing its centers of power and the relationships among its people. It is important to ask how industrialization, particularly in cotton textiles, affected North Carolina's hierarchical social system, in which power was closely held by a conservative elite. It is important, too, to ask what kind of men led the new industry and how they saw their role in society.

Research by Professors Richard W. Griffith and J. Carlyle Sitterson has provided relevant information for the early decades of the postwar period. Griffin studied the rebuilding of the textile industry from 1865 to 1885, and Sitterson examined the backgrounds of 120 business leaders drawn from the period 1865 to 1900. Both identified important elements of continuity between pre- and post-Civil War eras.[7]

The state's antebellum textile industry had been substantial for that time, with certain counties and families playing leading roles. E. M. Holt and his sons operated several mills in Alamance County; the Worths, the Odells, and others made Randolph a textile center; the Fries family was successful in Salem; the Pattersons were prominent in Forsyth and Caldwell counties; and other families such as the Moreheads, Battles, Cannons, Schencks, Linebergers, and Leaks were active in textiles before the Civil War. These social and geographical patterns, Griffin and Sitterson demonstrate, remained influential in the postwar period.

The rebuilding and expansion of the industry centered in areas where it had previously been well established. New water-powered mills spread up and down the Deep River in Randolph County and the Haw in Alamance, and as the piedmont produced greater quantities of cotton it began to exert an even stronger attraction for factories. Prominent textile families renewed their commitment to the industry and led the revival of production. When individuals who married into textile families are considered, such as the Williamsons who were allied to the Holts, there is strong evidence for "continuity of economic development and business leadership" during the supposed break of the Civil War. Half of the postwar business leaders studied by Sitterson were upper class, with fewer than 5 percent self-made men from poor backgrounds. Many of his upper-class families had been involved in agriculture, even more in business, and considerable numbers in both.[8]

This was consistent with the nature of the antebellum elite. North Carolina had boasted some planters, of course, but it had not been marked by a distinctive planter ethos. Its wealthy and powerful men, from John M. Morehead through the Pattersons, Worths, Leaks, and others to Paul Cameron, had always invested in agriculture, industry, transportation, and commerce. (See chapter 1.) Both Morehead and Cameron, for example, served as president of the North Carolina Rail Road and ran or invested in textile mills.[9] Diversified investments were typical of the wealthy, elite men in the state. They readily sought to take advantage of any type of opportunity that presented itself.

The desire to prosper in more than one field and the willingness to combine agriculture and industry continued after the war. Rufus Lenoir Patterson, who was more optimistic than most about profiting with free Negro labor in agriculture, vigorously expanded his commercial and textile activities before his death. Thomas M. Holt, a son of E. M. Holt, aspired to distinguish himself both as a scientific farmer and an industrialist. In measuring his success, the *Raleigh State Chronicle* noted in 1883 that his profits from textile manufacturing had helped to make him

Edwin Holt

"worth over half a million dollars" and that he ran a store, a flour mill, a productive plantation, "Linwood," and had been president of the State Agricultural Society.[10] Men like Holt constituted a powerful and aristocratic elite in North Carolina, but its activities were broad and entrepreneurial rather than restricted to a narrow, plantation outlook.

Thus it was normal that men from planting families became involved in New South industry and that money from wealthy agriculturalists provided much of the capital needed to spur manufacturing in a poor state.[11] These were aspects of established tradition in North Carolina. Yet the rise of the New South created a sense of change, both in the composition of the economic elite and in the perceptions and style of its leaders.

There was substantial growth in the postwar decades—growth in population, products, the number of factories, and the industrial and business classes. This was particularly the case after 1885, for in the last fifteen years of the century the pulse of industry noticeably quickened. With literally dozens of mills being started all over the state, hundreds of investors participated and the category of industrial leaders expanded. (The backgrounds of these investors, and the significance of an enlarged business elite, will be examined below.)

The effects of growth in textile manufacturing were evident in an exchange of letters between Henry and Frank Fries and their nephew, Sam Patterson. The Fries brothers had arranged for young Sam to start his career working for J. M. Odell, who promised to "do our best to make a 'man' of him" and guard against "any disposition to disipate [sic]." This in loco parentis arrangement was typical of the close personal relations and gentlemanly code that had prevailed in the years when manufacturers were few and close-knit. But inevitably the personal relationships between manufacturers broke down as the industry expanded. Before long the Fries brothers angrily accused Sam of luring a skilled employee away from their mill "without our knowledge or consent." Sam insisted that the employee had decided on his own to leave the Fries mill, but he also explained to his mother that things had changed by 1888. *"Even if I had* . . . persuaded him . . . to leave," Sam said, "it would not have been any worse than all the rest of the Manfgs. and Supts. & c. are continually doing every where else. Mr. [James] Cannon told me just last night, that he had been writing to weavers nearly all over the state to get them to come to his factory, and Superintendents of other mills are always writing to the help here . . . so you see, nobody considers it such a gross sin, except my dear Uncles."[12]

Just as the industry was growing and changing, the self-image of some of its leaders altered. There was a self-consciousness about the efforts of younger New South industrialists. Because they had come to maturity amid the South's defeat, men of the rising generation were convinced that the South had to change. To be strong, their region had to adopt Yankee habits of thrift and hard work and develop industry. Their sense of the necessity for change was acute.[13]

Often in their crusading zeal they emphasized a break with the agrarian past. "New ideas of life have taken a firm hold of the South," declared D. A. Tompkins, "and, to succeed and prosper, we must spin cotton . . . in the light of the new order of things. . . . The people who have adapted themselves to the new conditions constitute the New South." Once-sacred southern traditions also came in for criticism. Although he defended the South's history of race relations, Tompkins, like other New South leaders, condemned the economic effects of slavery. "The loyalty with which our fathers and grandfathers supported the institution of slavery was a mistake. It drove out diversified manufactures and turned commerce away from us." Arguing for industry, he concluded that historically, "As the institution of slavery grew stronger, the South grew weaker."[14]

These men chose for themselves the role of spokesmen for progress, and in that role they sometimes spoke with new accents. Social Darwinism gained powerful adherents in Gilded Age America, so it was not surprising that the New South leaders echoed its teachings. Tompkins dismissed reformers as "sentimental" and affirmed that "the history of nations is largely a record of 'the survival of the fittest.'" Such Darwinian thinking could lead to a complete contradiction of southern paternalism, as for example in Tompkins's declaration that "It is a wise, a righteous provision of God's law that provides that the imperfect must die."[15] Yet on many occasions Tompkins and others used paternalistic rhetoric to defend industry. The ideas of Social Darwinism apparently were useful rather than fundamental, part of an arsenal of handy justifications for power.

How new was the New South in North Carolina? Did industry and its leaders represent a change in the structure of power in society? Did the New South alter social relationships or reinforce old patterns of hierarchy? To answer these questions, it is necessary to penetrate some influential but misleading ideas.

In the 1880s the *Charleston News and Courier* launched a campaign to establish a cotton mill that could invigorate that city's declining economy.

In its editorials the *News and Courier* often spoke of "poor women and children" who were suffering "great destitution" because they needed better-paying jobs. A humanitarian appeal to better their conditions alternated with arguments that industry was necessary to the city's progress. As David Carlton has shown, the historian Broadus Mitchell relied heavily on these newspaper editorials to construct a general interpretation of the origins of the New South's textile industry.[16]

In *The Rise of Cotton Mills in the South*, published in 1921, Mitchell declared that, "To give employment to the necessitous masses of poor whites, for the sake of the people themselves, was an object animating the minds of many mill builders." This was an important conclusion about investors' motives and about the social significance of the textile mills. Mitchell based his assertion on the *News and Courier*, on articles from some other journals that were eager to promote industrialization, and upon the recollections of industrialists whom he interviewed. One of these told him that cotton mills grew "out of a moral movement to help the lower classes." The most effective charity was "to furnish work," and Mitchell further insisted that "the desire for mills" was "general." Taking the promotional articles of newspaper editors as representative of the entire community, he described the cotton mill campaign as a unified folk movement.[17]

Mitchell used events in Salisbury, North Carolina, to illustrate what he thought was the general pattern.

> The town of Salisbury, North Carolina, in 1887 had done nothing to recover from the war. It was full of saloons, wretched, unkempt. It happened that an evangelistic campaign was conducted; Mr. Pearson, remembered as a lean, intense Tennessean, preached powerfully. . . . The evangelist declared that the great morality in Salisbury was to go to work, and that corruption, idleness and misery could not be dispelled until the poor people were given an opportunity to become productive.

This fiery preaching supposedly ignited a desire throughout the community to aid the poor by erecting a cotton mill.[18]

Mitchell insisted upon a unity among all classes of whites flowing from the fact that "the white population of the South is homogenous. . . . The inauguration of the industry, in point of labor and capital alike, took place within the Southern family." He asserted that there was "mutual respect prevailing between management and work people" and claimed that "the owners of cotton mills did not look down upon their employe[e]s." Approvingly, he quoted an earlier scholar, Holland Thompson, who alleged that prior to the Civil War there had been substantial "social democracy" in "the Piedmont section of North Carolina"; relations among whites had been so close that mill girls had often "married officials of the mills." With this kind of social unity and "intimacy," it was not surprising, said Mitchell, that southern mills were built not "from the capital of the rich" but "from the combined capital of many of little means."[19] Thus Mitchell completed his picture of a moral crusade for cotton mills embracing all whites rich and poor, the latter in large numbers providing investment capital for the cause.

This interpretation was taken up and repeated by journalists and politicians until it achieved a staggering degree of acceptance.[20] The respected columnist Gerald W. Johnson summed up and further propagated the myth in 1925:

> This was not a business, but a social enterprise. Any profit that might accrue to the originators of the mill was but incidental; the main thing was the salvation of the decaying community, and especially the poor whites, who were in danger of being submerged altogether. The record of those days is filled with a moral fervor that is astounding. People were urged to take stock in the mills for the town's sake, for the poor people's sake, for the South's sake, literally for God's sake.[21]

This interpretation, which should have appeared implausible on its face, served the ideology of white supremacy and achieved remarkable acceptance. Yet in every major respect it was wrong or misleading. The men who dominated the textile industry were people of established or increasing social power. They perceived a wide social distance between themselves and their workers and intended to command the enterprises they owned, not to distribute charity. They built up a major industry, a considerable achievement, but in doing so they continued the hierarchical, aristocratic patterns of power in society that had characterized antebellum North Carolina. Public enthusiasm for mills was real, but it was limited primarily to the promoters and urban business classes who expected to benefit directly from industry. Workers, as will be shown shortly, were dissatisfied with their condition but lacked an alternative.

D. A. Tompkins furnishes a good example of the industrialist's social position and self-conception. Described by the *Augusta Chronicle* as "the man that put Charlotte on the map for cotton mill machinery," Tompkins designed, equipped, and promoted dozens of textile mills and cotton seed oil mills, in addition to being a major investor in several. As a young man he left the South to study engineering at Rensselaer Polytechnic Institute in Troy, New York, and worked in New York City and Bethlehem, Pennsylvania, before returning to his native region. He was a self-conscious and untiring advocate of the New South, an apparent prophet of change.[22]

Yet Tompkins came from a wealthy, slaveowning family in Edgefield, South Carolina, and his background in a rigid social structure affected him deeply. When he started work at the Bethlehem Iron Works, his social surroundings in the polyglot North caused him much anxiety. He worried about "the possibility of becoming coarse and vulgar in my manner of thinking because of the near contact I must daily have with the workmen." He hesitated to move closer to the factory because it would put him "in the neighborhood of irish before whom I w'd have to be a model of dignity & morality in order to make them respect me." When traveling on days off he took care "to avoid . . . meeting a well paid class of men at the works, whom to meet under such circumstances w'd make familiar & whose familiarity I don't want to cultivate."[23]

Tompkins missed the patterned interchanges of the South in which social distances were automatically accounted for and the social prominence of the powerful implicitly recognized. As an outsider in the North, his status was not well known, and therefore he was obliged to carry on a long contest with his landlord, who "tried regularly at intervals of three and five days to drop the Mr. from my name and enter upon such terms of familiarity as he is used to assume with the average Bethlehem shopkeeper who happens to board with him." Tompkins could not permit "familiarity" because it "w'd be taken up by the cook and then by the servants"; accordingly he resisted until "they . . . all . . . arrived at the opinion of me I intended," a triumph that completed the "work of defining what I am to them."[24]

A friend observed that Tompkins "aim[ed] . . . at a certain social success for which we are both fitted by birth and by education." Tompkins would let nothing come in the way of that success, even the reading of novels that his fiancée urged upon him instead of "science" and "mechanical" books. For ten years he postponed marriage so that his career could be well started and eventually broke off the relationship when he located in Charlotte. In his years of success he was a stern employer, commenting

D. A. Tompkins

that "I heartily approve discipline and good order in my organization and my experience in handling my own force always con[s]trains me to support any proper efforts to maintain discipline."[25]

Other rising industrialists in North Carolina carried the Old South's assumptions about power into the New South with even more confidence and determination. Samuel L. Patterson, son of Rufus L. Patterson's second marriage to Mary Fries and connected through his father's first marriage to the Moreheads, displayed a remarkable habit of command and readiness to seize authority. Sam was treated with respect when he arrived in Concord in 1888, and J. M. Odell boarded him with his son, "Mr. Will Odell," introducing him to men from the right fraternities, and telling him to "have a man to saddle" a pony anytime he wished to ride. In addition, Sam, who had dropped out of college and was only twenty years old, was allowed "to manage four hundred hands" as superintendent of the entire factory. Sam was not frightened by his responsibility; after two weeks he reported to his mother, "I have gotten along very well with most of [the hands] thus far. I have only discharged one or two."[26]

After a month Sam wrote, "I am weeding out pretty rapidly" the hands "I *cannot* get along with," and "Mr. Odell has not taken back a single one." But the Odells probably were unprepared for the extent of Sam's readiness to assume authority. Within a year he had clashed with the owners of the mill and won. Under previous managers the Odells had been "accustomed to 'dabble' into things," but Sam wanted no interference with his direction. "I think," he wrote to his mother, "they saw that I was not going to give way one bit" or allow them "to 'dabble.' . . . When they do, I just tell them a few things." Thus Sam obtained complete authority to run the mill, where he increased production while removing fifty-five workers from the payroll and cutting wages up to 20 percent.[27]

Along with Sam's assumption of executive authority went readiness to supervise the lives of his workers. Early in 1889 he reported that some men who liked to drink had aroused his suspicions—he had seen them collecting money. Without hesitation he swung into action, organizing raids between 7 P.M. and 5 A.M. that resulted in several arrests. "Capt. [Odell] and Mr. Will [were] delighted" with Sam's initiative and success, and he resolved to "break up this whiskey selling around here." Three weeks later he staged another "Revenue Raid."[28]

A stronger test of Sam Patterson's willingness to use power came in 1891, when fifty operatives walked off their jobs. Underlying dissatisfaction found expression in an issue of health. Some workers had come to the mill from Lexington, where they had been exposed to what many believed was a case of smallpox. Sam kept them "out of the Mill for over two weeks," but those who organized the " 'bolt' . . . pretended to think that they were all going to die of Small Pox." Sam felt that "Captain [Odell] was almost scared out of his wits," but "I heard of it right away and gave them fifteen minutes to get back into the Mill, and also told the Parents that if they didn't send their children in the Mill immediately, that they would have to vacate our houses at once." The ultimatum worked: "All came back in time." Sam fired only one ringleader and confidently declared, "the hands won't try that sort of thing again."[29]

This incident confirmed Sam's commanding personality, but he may have exaggerated at his employer's expense. J. M. Odell was no stranger to having or wielding power—he had been doing it for decades and came from a class in which power and decision making were viewed as a routine privilege. What was notable about Sam Patterson was the alacrity with which a young man took to an established role, but not the role itself. Odell's ability to act manifested itself in 1884 when he called the first of several meetings of textile manufacturers through the state and beyond; "the purpose of the [initial] conference was to come to an agreement about the price of plaid goods" and stop the practice of "cut[ting] under one another's prices." Odell's consciousness of his status appeared in his interest in his distant ancestors, who supposedly "could trace their lineage to the best royal blood of European courts." Similarly, D. A. Tompkins prided himself on his genealogy, claiming that his forebears "came into England with the early advent of the Saxons and with the early Britons helped to lay the foundation of the Anglo Saxon civilization."[30]

Men who saw themselves as part of a privileged aristocratic class were not accustomed to establishing real equality or intimacy with their employees. The workers had their place in society and a limited role that, supposedly, suited them; the upper class, whom everyone knew as gentry before the war, had a far more important and influential place. Life for these two classes ran along on separate and widely separated levels. Whereas workers in the Holt family mills in Alamance County labored long hours six or seven days a week, the owners kept up a life-style characteristic of the state's elite, frequently visiting and meeting with other important North Carolinians. One of their overseers, Henderson M. Fowler, noted in his diary the Holts' construction of new homes and frequent excursions—"left for the mountains," "left here for the Spring," "left for senteniel [the nation's centennial in 1876]."[31]

Once, in July 1878, a threat arose to the separate social position and high status of the Holt family. Fowler's diary recorded that one of E. M. Holt's grandsons, "J Y Holt left here Monday morning . . . with Jin Ashworth to get married." This was unusual news, but it is important to observe that Jin Ashworth was neither a poor farm girl nor a child of unskilled mill hands. Her father held a highly responsible position in the Holt mills. Occasionally Ashworth directed workers, but primarily he was a talented mechanic on whom the Holts relied to install and adjust all their new machinery, start up new factories, and make critical repairs. His knowledge, skill, and duties made him one of the most important employees in the Holt mills, but he was not of the owner's social class.[32] His daughter's elopement with the young Holt son constituted a social calamity for the boy's family. Subsequent events in this love story revealed the tension and strain imposed by the Holts' mortification.

After a week had passed Fowler made two laconic entries in his diary: "L S Holt gone after Miss Ashworth & returned with her not married. . . . J Y Holt & Jinnie Ashworth was married by R[ev.] Thimble in her Farther's hous Sunday, July 28th 1878." One month later Mr. "Ashworth gave notice of leaving" and went to work for manufacturer George Swepson. For eighteen months Fowler heard nothing about the unfortunate couple, but then someone evidently attempted to heal the breach. Suddenly "J Y Holt & wife [appeared] here today, the first since married." About the same time Jinnie's father returned to the factory and began installing new machinery. But within four months the class barrier had proved too great to overcome. "Ashworth quit & went back to Swepson's Mill to work," his family left the town of Alamance, and Fowler never mentioned them again in the seven years of entries that followed in his diary.[33]

Obviously there was little social equality in the Holt mill, and the bonds of friendship, equality, and even intimacy that Broadus Mitchell and Holland Thompson talked about would have seemed undesirable to mill owners. They wanted no impediments to their authority over the manufacturing process. They saw themselves as prominent men running important enterprises, pioneering a new industry, and breaking into the market, and, as H. F. Schenck of Cleveland County noted, they were doing it with "perfect[ly] green M[e]n who [were] never in a mill before." Mill managers would have agreed with Schenck's son about the need for complete authority: "If a Superintendent had to argue and explain and talk over every little difference between himself and his employees . . . he wouldn't have time for any thing else, and would be worried to death. Most of my people understand me, and know that when I say anything positively I mean it."[34]

Schenck, who to this day is remembered in Cleveland County as "Major Schenck," took pains to see that his bosses had established their power firmly. To manage a new mill that he was building with financial support from J. E. Reynolds, Schenck hired a superintendent from Connecticut named Warner. Among the other problems of starting a new factory, Schenck worried about Warner's ability to take charge. "Confidentially," he wrote to Reynolds, "I . . . think Mr. Warner less capable to start than to run a mill." After some months Warner decided to leave, explaining that his wife had "always been in some village or city, also accustomed to good public schools." Again Schenck had to find a strong-willed superintendent. "I think it . . . best for me to remain at the new mill," he advised Reynolds, "til I know [that] Cline has perfectly mastered all our business there, and has propper controll of the help. He is young, and has worked through as a common hand on a level with hands and underneath the bosses—and I must be convinced that every thing will go smooth befor I will feel easy to leave the mill under his controll."[35]

The circumstances surrounding the establishment of many new mills, including Schenck's, increased the power of the owners over the workers. Even at the end of the century some entrepreneurs were locating mills in rural areas to take advantage of the water power along streams. "We are in the country," commented H. F. Schenck, who located there despite earlier laments that part of his cotton "must be hauled 12 miles on wagons"—a "heavy job" without a railroad. Often he "had to build another house . . . for a family" because there was literally no housing standing at the new mill site. "We think we have enough houses under way," he wrote on another occasion, adding, "Most of the families to move in here are farmers, and must take care of their crops before they can come."[36] Thus mill owners provided and controlled the mill village and all the houses workers lived in, as well as the jobs at which they labored.

Very often this condition held true around towns or cities as well, because factory owners often followed the advice of D. A. Tompkins and located outside an incorporated area. Tompkins believed that employees liked urban locations, but cities levied taxes, and there were other problems as well. "The proximity of lawyers . . . promotes law suits," he said, and "a mill in the country can operate its own store and thereby get back in mercantile profit much of the money paid for wages." In the country or beyond the edges of small towns, the factory frequently had to supply workers' housing if it were to be available. To help owners meet this need Tompkins drew up and published plans for inexpensive mill houses. He advised management to follow the "rough rule that the house ought to furnish one operative for each room in the house."[37]

This situation led W. J. Cash to contend that "the Southern factory... was a plantation, essentially indistinguishable in organization from the familiar pattern of the cotton fields." More recently sociologist Dwight Billings has argued that "mill village paternalism" was an aspect of a Prussian, Junker-style "revolution from above" engineered by "planter-industrialists." Yet, as Billings himself admits, southern textile manufacturers were not the first in their industry to build housing for workers, and its construction was often a necessity.[38] Furthermore, North Carolina's elite was not an exclusively planter group tied to the plantation or to plantation paternalism. But the assumptions of upper-class dominance were strong and enduring, and there is no question that ownership of the entire factory complex increased the power of owners and managers who already expected their influence to be far-reaching and nearly exempt from challenge.

Undoubtedly there were many times when owners felt they had to be free from challenge in order to cope with the other problems they faced. The building of North Carolina's textile industry was not an easy task, nor were the postwar decades entirely favorable years in which to launch corporations. Many factories closed or suspended operations during the recessions or depressions that struck the national economy each decade from the 1870s forward.

Few manufacturers were in as strong a position as E. M. Holt, whose reaction to the Panic of 1873 was, "keep running and pile up goods ... and when a reaction takes place [mills] will have the goods ready to put on the market.... I see ... a good prospect for those who have means, but those that have not, must stop in self defence." The Minutes of the John M. Worth Manufacturing Company told the story of 1884: "The continued depression, with accumulated goods in hands of commission merchants with high [priced] cotton and continued decline in price of goods, has rendered it almost impossible to keep body and soul together." Three years later the mill was finally overcoming the effects of bad times. In the severe depression of the 1890s many new factories foundered, only to be reorganized and become profitable as the economy improved.[39]

Occasionally mills burned, and far more often they lost their source of power as streams either dried up during droughts or became flooded after rains. "The water is so low we cannot run all day," wrote one superintendent, and Henderson M. Fowler's diary contained entries such as "Factory standing [still] for high water" or "Water the lowest in the Alamance ever knowne." The Holts were among the earliest owners to convert mills to steam power, but even after they did Fowler's diary testified that the mill was still vulnerable to the elements. In July 1886, he wrote, "Hardest raine ever here . . . water in the factory 2 ft deep and lots of mud."[40]

H. F. Schenck relied on water power to drive the machinery in his new mill, but the water wheel he purchased failed to perform efficiently. "Your wheel is not giving the power you claim for it," he complained to the manufacturer; eight months later it was still not fixed and he had received "no reply to two last letters." "I am *sick* of them," Schenck wrote to his partner, "I am *out of patience* long ago." He also had disputes with the D. A. Tompkins Company over billing, and especially over some "worthless" lamps that only burned fifteen, instead of the promised six hundred, hours.[41]

Drawing on experience, Schenck eventually overcame these difficulties, whereas the sons of Rufus L. Patterson relied on abundant mechanical ability to bring them success. Young Sam seemed to have no difficulty absorbing the details of nine different operations in the Odell factory and successfully coped with emergencies. One night he worked "until half past one o'clock . . . mending the main driving belt . . . but I got it all right." On another occasion the dyer, who had never trained an assistant, got sick, but Sam stepped in and reproduced the hues, saying "I am not at all afraid of any of the colors made here." He proved valuable in installing new machinery and increased both production and quality of the finished goods.[42] Before long Sam and his brothers were running family-owned mills in Ilchester, Maryland, and Roanoke Rapids, North Carolina.[43]

Sam brought his brother, Rufus, Jr., to the Odell factory in Concord as a bleacher, but soon Rufus's mechanical ability involved him with machines that manufactured cloth bags. He became president of the Automatic Packing and Labeling Company in Durham, and by 1897 developed machinery that James B. Duke called "the most ingenious Tob[acco] Mchr'y he ever saw." Rufus went to work for American Tobacco and in 1900 heard "Buck" Duke say, "Patterson, . . . your schemes for vacuumizing tob. and for making cigars is going to revolutionize the . . . Cigar business the world over, and you ought to get rich out of it."[44]

By the turn of the century the Patterson brothers had entered upon the next technological advance—the electrification of manufacturing, with twenty-four-year-old John L. Patterson supervising the conversion of a factory to electric power. Beyond a doubt, the skills and knowledge of such men, and the dissemination of information by others like Tompkins, advanced industry in the piedmont. In the later years of his career Tompkins was hoping to find time "to work up plans for the comprehensive development of Southern water power," a task eventually carried out by James B. Duke and William S. Lee.[45] Talented men built these industries.

Nevertheless, it is fatuous to attribute their actions to philanthropy or describe their motives as a desire to help the "necessitous masses." "I am ambitious to . . . make as much money as I can," wrote Sam Patterson. To him the best argument for investing in a factory was that "these mills have never paid less than 10% on the stock invested, and they declared 11% last year, which was decidedly the dullest year that Plaid men have ever had." The owners of the Worth Manufacturing Company had struggled through the 1880s not to serve mankind but so that they could earn steady dividends in the 1890s, usually of 3 or 4 percent.[46]

And that was a low rate of return; at the bottom of a depression in 1895 the Vance Cotton Mills in four months repaid previous losses and earned a 4 percent dividend. "I don't know any reason," wrote one of the owners, "why it should not make ¾ of 1% per week for the next three months." The Trenton Cotton Mills declared dividends of 10 percent in 1895, 12 in 1896, 30 in 1899, and 100 percent in 1901, and the Erwin Cotton Mills in Durham exceeded the expected profit rate of 40 percent by handsome margins. D. A. Tompkins calculated that in general cotton mills should make a profit of 10 to 30 percent depending on the skill of the management. He publicly declared, "about 15 percent is the average annual profit in clear money."[47]

Because people invested for profit, it is not surprising that the wealthy and the comfortable did most of the investing. The tale of the Salisbury cotton mill reveals much about industrialization in the piedmont, but the real story is very different from Broadus Mitchell's myth. An accurate version should begin before preacher Pearson's revival, in April 1887, when Salisbury businessmen began considering whether they wanted to establish a mill.

The editor of the *Salisbury North Carolina Herald* learned that James A. Johnston, owner of the Charlotte Marble and Granite Works, had returned from a visit to Salisbury and said, "that the question of cotton mills has been sprung in that town, and that their establishment is now considered a certainty." Always eager to promote a "boom" and boost enterprise, the *Herald* immediately praised the idea of "Cotton Mills for Salisbury." A fervid newspaper campaign to spur the businessmen's plans was underway. Finding that some stock had been subscribed and that "several of our citizens of ample means are interested in . . a factory," the paper exhorted, "Let All Pull Together and Our Factory will be Assured."[48]

To push the plan ahead, the *Herald* named ten citizens and publicly challenged them to ante up the rest of the capital. The paper also urged "every man and woman in Salisbury who can" to buy "at least one share," but it obviously set most of its hope on the ten men, whom it described as busy and prosperous and all running businesses worth far more than two or three thousand dollars. Together, the paper reasoned, they could easily finance a fifty thousand dollar mill.[49]

The ten men illustrated the expanding commercial investment in industry that was occurring. They were Samuel H. Wiley, John M. Knox, Wm. Smithdeal, Theo. F. Kluttz, J. A. Hedrick, S. W. Cole, Reuben J. Holmes, M. L. Holmes, Thomas J. Sumner, and Alex. Parker. Wiley was a partner in the mercantile firm of Davis & Wiley and an officer of the town's National Bank; Knox owned a general store; Wm. Smithdeal was a merchant and manufacturer of coaches and carriages; Theo. F. Kluttz was a lawyer who owned a drugstore and, by 1890 if not before, also operated a gold mine and served as president of the Perpetual Building and Loan Association; Hedrick ran the public ferry; Cole was president of First National Bank in 1890; Reuben Holmes ran a dry goods and grocery business in which M. L. Holmes probably was also involved; and Alex. Parker owned a grocery, bakery, and confectionery in Salisbury. The occupation of Thomas J. Sumner has not been identified, but his role as a county commissioner attests to his prominence.[50] Another county commissioner eventually invested, along with the pastor of the Episcopal church and a man who sold fertilizer and insurance.[51] Obviously these were not planters but businessmen, merchants, bankers, and professionals who were prospering from the increased activity of New South towns and looking for attractive investments.

Despite the *Herald's* public challenge, however, the cotton-mill scheme languished. The capital was not immediately raised, and by August the paper's editor was getting impatient. "How is the Cotton Mill Scheme?" he asked, and began to develop arguments showing why its success was necessary. For the first time the *Herald* mentioned aid to the poor, saying that nearly every town had a textile factory "giving work to the poorer classes of people." But the main appeal was to town pride: "Shall old substantial Salisbury fall behind her more enterprising sisters in the march of progress?"[52]

By October the booster-editor was growing desperate, for still the mill was not a reality. Again an editorial mentioned that a factory gave poor people a chance to help themselves in addition to paying investors handsome dividends, but the editor put far more emphasis upon, and devoted more space to, a racial argument. "As things are now," the *Herald* announced, "the colored population of Salisbury will soon greatly outnumber the white people." Blacks were coming to Salisbury to work in tobacco factories or seek education at the graded schools and at Reverend J. C. Price's Livingstone College. "Unless something is done to prevent it," warned the *Herald*, "the colored people will soon swamp the town."

> Now there are two ways to prevent it. One is by trying to hinder them in their battle for prosperity. The other is to awake and move fast enough to keep ahead of them. The white man who is willing to take the former course ought to be drummed out of the Anglo Saxon race. . . . Use white men's capital to draw white population to the town. Build cotton factories that will draw and employ them. . . . Race pride, if nothing better, ought to spur us up to keep ahead of the colored people.[53]

Eventually the racial argument plus the constant pressure and the investment opportunity itself worked, for six weeks later the *Herald* was able to report that the capital "for the factory has reached $30,500." A meeting to organize the company was being delayed because "a few wealthy men [who] it is hoped . . . will make up the remainder of the stock . . . desire to consult together." When they had consulted, these few produced large amounts of new capital, "headed by three subscriptions of $10,000 each." The ecstatic editor announced "Our Two Factories," one with $63,000 in capital and the second with more than $38,000. Of the ten businessmen originally challenged, at least seven invested money and served as officers of the two companies.[54]

The Salisbury experience can serve as an example of what was happening elsewhere in the piedmont between 1885 and 1900, but it exemplifies phenomena different from those described by Broadus Mitchell. The campaign to start the factory was a crusade, but it had less in common with a "moral movement" than a modern-day chamber of commerce offensive. The object was to spur business and stimulate growth; helping the poor, when that was mentioned at all, was merely one among many arguments pulled out to try to convince people to give their support. There was no evidence of fervent popular belief that mills represented salvation, no folk movement motivated by "desire for mills."[55] Beyond question the people of the South wanted economic improvement, but real enthusiasm for cotton factories was a town phenomenon pushed by newspapers and "go-ahead" businessmen; as the next chapter will show, ordinary white farmers who had experience with mills had reason to be less than enthusiastic.

As for building an industry "from the combined capital of many of little means," the truth in Mitchell's statement is very modest in size. D. A. Tompkins stated in 1898 that he had started more than four mills on the cooperative subscription plan, and he thought that this method had been "utilized for building 15 or 20 cotton mills in the South." This would account for a small fraction of the new factories, and even Mitchell admitted that once "community spirit" had launched "initial mills, stock after a few years tended to come into the hands of the larger investors who had been central in the subscription."[56]

When the Odells started a new mill capitalized at one million dollars in Concord, they invited Sam Patterson to invest but warned him within a month that most stock had been taken, even before they left the state and journeyed to Philadelphia to interest investors there.[57] When Caesar Cone and others started the Proximity and Revolution Mills in Greensboro, they had Ben Duke and George Watts, a partner of the Dukes, as investors of ten thousand dollars each and could tell an associate "to consider the stock as all taken and the money forthcoming as needed."[58] There was a good number of "larger investors" in the state. The Dukes, who made extensive investments in the 1890s, were probably the premier examples of men who had risen to command immense wealth.[59]

But there was broad participation by smaller businessmen also. Typically they came from the piedmont and worked in towns, which were growing and emerging as new generators of wealth. These men, who would have been considered middle class in antebellum days, were rising higher in North Carolina's power structure as they prospered. They were hardly a Junker-style planter class extending its control. They were rising on town-based marketing, manufacturing, and financial and legal services. They represented smaller businessmen who were increasing the size of the wealth-holding elite. The pattern of elite dominance continued unchanged, as did the elite's emphasis on wealth rather than family background as its primary criterion for membership. But there was inevitably a broadening of membership as new faces took advantage of new opportunities. Successful businessmen were rising not to become a counterforce to planters but to assume more prominent places in a system that had always restricted influence to substantial citizens.

Between 1885 and 1900 the piedmont counties of Alamance, Randolph, Guilford, Cabarrus, Gaston, and Mecklenburg, plus Caldwell County saw seventy new mills founded. According to the records of incorporation, a total of 480 individuals were original investors in these new corporations. Through a search of business directories and some census materials, 238 or almost half of these investors have been identified. These represented the major elements in the launching of new textile factories and accounted for much more than half of the capital ventured. (Where the number of shares held appeared in the records, those identified owned 7,423 of 10,417 shares, or 71.3 percent.)[60] Most of those who could not be found made only token investments. What kind of people were these mill founders?

Two patterns stand out from the data. First, men who had already established themselves in the textile industry steadily reinvested. The role of several prominent textile families was immediately apparent. Of the seventy mills studied, the Holts invested in eight, the Cones in five, the Odells and the Cannons in four each, the Worths in three, D. A. Tompkins in three, the Dukes in two, and the Frieses in one. When less well-known textile men are included, fully 100 of the 238 investors were owners and/or managers of other mills. (See table 18.)

Of course, these textile figures were not all from old textile families; some of them had come to the industry through different occupations. In Caldwell County, for example, two principal investors owned general stores, a third man was partner with one of the first two in operating a steam tannery, and a fourth owned a flour and corn mill. Traditionally such businesses had provided the capital for many manufacturers. William Alexander Smith, a partner of the Cones in two mills and president of two others, ran a general store for almost twenty years to build his financial position. He eventually put some of his profits from textiles into banking, insurance, real estate, tobacco, furniture, transportation, mining, and other ventures.[61]

The second clear pattern was that significant numbers of merchants, businessmen, and professionals, large and small, were investing in the textile industry. Store owners, along with bankers and professionals, were especially important in the towns, such as Charlotte. When its boomlet

TABLE 18
Investors in Seventy Piedmont Textile Mills, 1885–1900

Occupation		No.
Textile mill owners and managers		100
Merchants		
General stores	35	
Dry-goods stores	6	
Other stores	10	
Subtotal	51	51
Others in commerce		
Craftsmen	7	
Hotel proprietors	5	
Insurance agents	4	
Subtotal	16	16
Nontextile manufacturing or mining		24
Professionals		
Attorneys	9	
Physicians	9	
Ministers	5	
Subtotal	23	23
Bankers		3
Farmers		11
Holders of political office		10
Total		238

Source: County Records of Incorporation, *Branson's* business directories for 1884 and 1896, and U.S. manuscript census for 1880 and 1900.

of 1888 produced three new cotton mills, individuals and businesses like the following made up the core of investors: J. H. McAden, president of Merchants and Farmers National Bank; Rufus Barringer, a lawyer; M. P. Pegram, a banker; S. P. Alexander, a merchant; Samuel Wittkowsky, a merchant and president of a building and loan association; F. B. McDowell, a lawyer; and two dry-goods firms, Elias & Cohen and Alexander & Harris. The growing ranks of New South businessmen provided important support for industry.[62]

Although industry remained rather small in 1900, the basis for a more diverse economy was emerging, particularly in the piedmont towns and cities. New sources of wealth, which would eventually overshadow land-ownership and agriculture, were becoming important, and some new men of wealth were gaining influence. But this development did little to democratize North Carolina's social system. For a few, new avenues to wealth promised power and privilege, but the elite continued to believe that the lower half of the population—blacks and poorer whites—was supposed to remain without influence. Farmers who became factory workers discovered this fact, and sometimes protested against it. Their grievances, too, contributed to the conflict of the 1890s.

WORKERS IN THE
NEW SOUTH

Industrialization had its strongest impact on the workers in North Carolina's factories. Few Tar Heels had lived a factory life in the Old South, but by the end of the century more than seventy thousand of the state's wage earners were in manufacturing, and the number was growing each year. These people were at the center of economic change, and many of them found that it had a wrenching effect on their habits and values. For industrialization undercut the basic values of North Carolina's yeoman farmers.

As it would for decades to come, the state's economically troubled white farm population provided a large pool of potential laborers for industry. "A large per cent. of [our] employees are from their farms," confirmed an Alamance County mill owner, who added that he had "numerous applications" for work from other farmers. A Cleveland County mill owner agreed, saying, "Our laborers here are mostly persons who were raised on farms around us. . . . They come to the mill because they can make more money . . . than on the farm."[1] But this movement from farm to factory arose less from opportunity than necessity.

"The mortgage system, which hangs like a pall of death over many an honest, hard-working man," combined with falling prices was causing many farmers to lose their lands and become tenants. Yet tenancy, which some called "the greatest evil," entailed still greater dependence on "the one-crop (cotton) system," and as one farmer ruefully testified, "Making but one thing for [a falling] market . . . ruined many." A cultivator in Alamance County lamented that "the farms in this section are generally run by tenants," and a man in Randolph County confirmed that there, too, "The outlook is gloomy in the extreme for farmers."[2]

Most agriculturalists would have agreed with the piedmont resident who in 1887 said, "Depression, to a great extent, is universal in this and adjoining counties, rendering it impossible for the ordinary farmer to run his farm without the death warrant (mortgage)." And "the common land-less laborer" (often a yeoman whose death certificate had already been issued through foreclosure) was "down very low in humility, and for the last five years very much depressed in spirits." One mill owner openly worried that the agricultural depression might lead to "revolution" because "the people of this country have tasted liberty and . . . never will submit to be enslaved by a few." Yet, "such is the condition of the country that poor men with large families cannot make their living by farming, so they go to factories." And a worker agreed with frank and simple under-statement: "We can do better here than on a farm."[3]

But the yeomen had wanted to stay on the farm, to remain independent, landowning farmers. They cherished a way of life, not just an occupation, and the core of what they valued was independence. Traditionally the yeoman farmer in North Carolina had enjoyed a feeling of control over his personal life and a large measure of economic and social safety because he provided for himself and knew that he was beholden to no one. The psychological importance of this status stands out in one farmer's comment on the anxiety that accompanied debt. "When a man mortgages his property," he said, "he can't help thinking about it, consequently he can't work *like a free man*."[4] The yeoman farmer had not been an agricultural businessman; rather, he was a tiller of the soil who lived and worked "like a free man." His independence and freedom had always formed the core of the Jeffersonian ideal.

Yeomen had fought to defend that vital measure of freedom in North Carolina's rigid, undemocratic society. In the antebellum era the non-worldly priorities of evangelical religion and the salience of family or individual aspirations had helped yeomen define independent goals, while their distance in everyday life from the power of planters and other privileged people had enabled them to tolerate society's inequities. The Civil War violated key elements of their status and revealed how deeply they valued their independence: many yeomen resisted Confederate authority, with organized violence if necessary. Their devotion to independence remained strong in the postwar years, but economic conditions and the unsuccessful shift to cash-crop agriculture steadily undermined their position.

Going to work in a mill was the final misfortune. People were glad to have a job and some way of making a living, but they did not welcome other aspects of factory labor. Going to work in a mill meant being dependent; it was "public work," a term used even today to suggest one's dependence on the outside world and vulnerability to others. At length hardship reduced many Tar Heels to this step, but it was not consistent with their traditional values and not a step they would have taken voluntarily.

W. J. Cash was badly mistaken when he declared that mill work elicited from the masses "a wide, diffuse gratefulness pouring out upon the cotton-mill baron; upon the old captains, upon all the captains and preachers of Progress; upon the ruling class as a whole for having embraced the doctrine and brought these things about."[5] That is not the way people greet tragedy or respond to the loss of a way of life. Nor was it the way ordinary Tar Heels had always regarded the ruling class. Yeomen generally turned to factory work because they had to, with pain and a sense of necessity instead of gratitude.

They discovered in the factory a way of earning a living, but not much to be grateful about. Factory work was dangerous, especially for inexperienced men and women just off the farm. Henderson Monroe Fowler's diary recorded many serious accidents in the Holts' Alamance mill. "Gaston Sharp was caught in a lapper on Saturday evening," he wrote, "and arm broken . . . Drs. Montgomery, Moore and Cobb arrived & after examination postponed untill next morning & then cut the arme of[f] above elbo." Repeatedly Fowler mentioned the arrival of a new worker and soon after was describing an injury suffered by the same person. On 5 April 1879 he noted that, "The Canada famely moved to this place"; six days later, on 11 April he wrote, "Mary Canada got her finger hurt in the factory." Similarly a girl named Em Shoffner started work as a "full hand" in 1876, the year William Holt and his wife "left for senteniel [the centennial]." The next year "Em got her finger hurt . . . badly hurt."[6]

Accidents were common in other mills as well, although owners did not often publicize them. Once H. F. Schenck, however, brought up the subject of injuries at his mill. After writing to his insurance company to correct some records, Schenck impulsively added this postscript:

> Since writing the foregoing, it has occurred to me that I should report to you that several accidents have occurred in the past 6 months, and at many places would have given . . . some trouble. Quite recently a boy broke his arm under a belt. We think under the circumstances that you ought to make our rate as low as possible, for we never have had a claim for damage . . . notwithstanding we have had some right serious accidents among our people.[7]

A state official once suggested that the rate of injuries was far higher than generally known, for many factories declined to respond to his inquiries. In a single county whose industrialists reported no accidents this official knew of five boilers that had burst within a year.[8]

In addition to accidents, the work involved long hours. Sam Patterson wrote his mother that the Odell mill ran from 6 A.M. to noon and from 12:40 to 6:55 P.M., "the same number of hours they work at home [in Salem]." According to one superintendent a few mills "began work at four o'clock in the morning and stopped at twenty minutes past six in the evening," and a Cumberland County mill ran from 5:45 A.M. to 7 P.M., with forty-five minutes off for lunch at noon. Prominent industrialists like D. A. Tompkins claimed that the number of hours worked was gradually and steadily diminishing. But data from the 1890s showed a range of ten to twelve hours per day and one and a half or one day of work on weekends. Even in the depression year of 1894 most cotton mills kept up an eleven- or twelve-hour day. These schedules meant that sixty-six to seventy-five hours per week were typical.[9]

Some bosses made it very clear that these were to be hours of constant and diligent labor. The "Rules Governing Employees in the Winton Knitting Mills" were emphatic and to the point. They described a sober, rather pleasureless day:

> The Mill will start work at 6 A.M.
> All must be present.
> Thirty Minutes will be given for breakfast,
> 7 to 7:30.
> One hour will be given for dinner from 12 to 1 P.M.
> Work will stop at 6:30 P.M.
> No laughing allowed or talking except on business.
> No smoking allowed during work hours.[10]

For their many hours of labor the workers received little, for employers had the advantage of a buyer's market and knew it. With agriculture so depressed, people like Cora Mitchell were writing to "the boss or head man," seeking work and saying, "we want to wo[r]k in the cotton mills or knitting mills it doesn't make much diffrence." Cora asked to know "how much we can make a month"; the answer she received, if any, is unknown. But employers were in such a strong position that often they did not feel it was necessary to specify the potential wages. In recruiting a worker in 1889, H. F. Schenck merely wrote, "I will say I will give you fair wages."[11]

For workers with few resources and no alternatives, that meant low wages. Robert G. Lindsay recalled that in the early days of the Mountain Island Mill, started in Gaston County before the Civil War, typical wages ranged from 25¢ to 40¢ per day for men and 5¢ to 25¢ per day for children. At the end of the century wages had not risen greatly for many workers. The superintendent of a large factory could earn $3.00 per day or more and "2nd bosses" or highly skilled workers $1.50 or so. But in the 1890s few ordinary workers earned as much as $1.00 a day; wages for the typical operative ranged from 40¢ to 75¢, depending on the mill and the job. Children's wages could dip as low as 10¢ or 15¢ per day. A mill owner calculated that the greatest expense for a factory capitalized at $60,000 was machinery, with the cost of buildings trailing far behind. Profit, anticipated to be $18,000 per year for a "1st Class Mill to produce 3000 yds Sheeting per day," exceeded the expected yearly wage bill.[12]

As long as economic conditions in agriculture were deteriorating or weak (and they remained so for many years into the twentieth century), there seemed to be no upward pressure on wages. A large pool of potential operatives who would work for little was readily available. In 1895 a state official noted that textile mills were prosperous, "running night and day," and demanding so much new machinery that many orders had to go to England after the capacity of New England machine-makers was exhausted. Yet, "while the majority of the mills have been making 'big' money this year, the wages of the operatives have remained practically the same. Of the many that cut wages last year, when the . . . 'financial depression' reigned supreme, only a few have raised them to the standard that existed before the reduction was made . . . wages paid are very low."[13]

In any mill wages varied according to three factors: gender of the worker, age of the worker, and the worker's job. (Race was not a factor, because only whites were employed.) Skilled jobs could command as much as twice the pay of comparatively simple tasks, occasionally more. Men earned close to twice as much as women. In a compilation of data for 1890, daily wages for skilled men ranged from 90¢ to $2.50 compared to 30¢ to $1.00 for skilled women. Unskilled workers, who made up the bulk of employees, earned substantially less—30¢ to $1.00 per day for men (with 75¢ typical) compared to 25¢ to 75¢ per day for women (with 40¢ to 50¢ most common). Children (a few of whom were as young as six) earned the least of all, carrying out unskilled tasks that paid 25¢ to 40¢ per day. D. A. Tompkins's handbook for mill builders calculated wages that ranged, on the average, between 58¢ and 83¢ per day.[14]

These wages were so meager that in practice they constituted a "family wage"—one on which people could live only if the whole family worked. It obviously benefited a poor family financially to have more workers contributing to total income, especially in the case of children who might earn almost as much as their unskilled mother did. Employers acted upon this knowledge both implicitly and explicitly. "I would like to know how many working hands you can furnish," wrote John Schenck to one man. In another instance he was more direct: "State how many children you have, whether they are girls or boys, and give the age of each. If you wish to come here, and your family suits me, I will take you at once.... I cannot hold the place open many days. Quite a number of other families have in their applications."[15]

To obtain better wages, workers watched for better opportunities and were willing to move frequently. Indeed, this pattern of occasional shifts from one employer to another occasioned considerable complaint by mill owners. J. M. Rhodes of Cherryville in Gaston County asserted that employers needed to "get the operatives in our mills to stay longer and not move so often." J. N. and W. H. Williamson of Raleigh complained that "mill hands . . . are continually shifting around, owing to so many mills going up. They do not stay, as a rule, long enough to make themselves useful or try to advance themselves. They should be encouraged to remain a long time at a mill, and to become identified with it and . . . have the interest of the mill at heart."[16]

But the employers themselves were responsible for some of this "shifting around." Rhodes admitted that too many factories employed labor recruiters who worked at "getting them dissatisfied," and superintendents sometimes bragged to the owners about their success in obtaining labor. "I got the 2 Berry girls back," wrote one manager. "Allred had got them [for his mill]. But i downd him."[17] Moreover, altering the composition of the work force, given the wage structure that existed, was an important way to manage costs. By switching to cheaper workers, which would force those let go to seek work elsewhere, the mills reduced their wage bill and increased profits. In 1897 a superintendent assured his employer that he understood this basic arithmetic: "Yours of 26th at hand and I note what you say about economizing. whitch [which] I know all about as I never did any thing else. I have been weaving with 3 Girls and only let the men work when I need them."[18]

There is evidence that employers were varying the composition of the work force more systematically as time went on, in order to hold down costs and insure profits. The evidence, which is statistical, runs counter to the professed opinions of mill owners. Child labor was much discussed and received frequent criticism from those employers who were asked to make public statements about it. "We do not want to work [children]," declared an owner in 1890, "but their parents force them in." The next year several other owners agreed, saying "if we refuse to work them, . . . the parents say they will go to some other mill." By 1894 most owners who responded to an inquiry asserted that they opposed child labor and favored compulsory schooling for the young. The general manager of Charlotte's Alpha Mill, for example, came out in favor of a statute "to prohibit children under fourteen years of age from working in the mills." And leaders of the industry such as D. A. Tompkins and J. M. Odell argued that objectionable features, such as night work or child labor, were steadily diminishing and would "soon" disappear in accord with "the tendency of the human race itself to improve and go forward."[19]

Yet the figures describing the textile work force told a different story. Data reported to the North Carolina Bureau of Labor Statistics in 1890 showed that 39.1 percent of textile workers were men, 51.3 percent were women, and 9.6 percent were children under fourteen. These figures were nearly the same in 1891. The percentage of children declined in some years, but there was no downward trend. By 1900, in fact, the proportion of lower-paid women and children had increased slightly, and the percentage of children had more than doubled. At the turn of the century 38.8 percent of mill workers were men, 41.5 percent were women, and 19.7 percent were children under fourteen. In the state's manufacturing sector as a whole, the United States Census for 1900 found that 14.7 percent of the workers were children under sixteen.[20] Child labor had not disappeared, and in North Carolina's textile industry it seemed to be increasing.

Perhaps D. A. Tompkins identified one reason for this in a candid speech delivered in New York in 1906. Although "every Southern cotton mill man," according to Tompkins, was working to eliminate labor by children under fifteen "as fast as he knows how," he admitted that he favored some work by children even younger. Tompkins declared that children needed to be protected not only from "overwork" but also from "excessive indulgence." "Light work, in my opinion, is not bad for children, but, on the contrary, it is good for them and we ought to take them earlier . . . [in] an apprenticeship." Tompkins "particularly desire[d] that they be brought to us at twelve . . . not for the purpose of working them for profit, but . . . for the purpose of education" in the factory part of the year and in the schoolroom the remainder of the time. Such a practice would build character and develop "an early knowledge of what work is."[21] Another Charlotte industrialist stated publicly that children over twelve were not hurt by work in a mill, and a tobacco manufacturer, whose industry employed mostly blacks, said "No child's health was ever injured by working in a tobacco factory."[22]

Mill owners also insisted that child labor was caused by lazy parents who made their children labor for them, but mill workers offered another explanation. One worker from the town of Maiden in Catawba County declared, "there are poor people who would not be able to send their children to school and [still] make a living for them." A Cumberland County operative explained, "We have a public school here, but the factory people cannot spare their children from the mill to attend it. They are too poor. If they were able to send them it would be against the wishes of the managers for them to do so, as they need the children's labor in the mill." Similarly, a Randolph County worker believed that "the capitalists would kick against [compulsory school] laws, because it would deprive them of a great quantity of cheap labor."[23]

Analyzing the reasons for child labor further, a Raleigh man argued that children "are generally employed because they work for less wages," and another worker agreed that ending child labor would raise the level of pay, because "better wages would have to be paid for men and women." Whatever the actual wishes of mill owners may have been in regard to children's education, they frankly conceded that the rock-bottom "family" wage made it impossible for many operatives to send their children to school. H. F. Schenck gave, as a humanitarian reason *not* to enact child-labor legislation, the fact that "about one-half of the families in my employ would not make ends meet if you stopped children who are under fourteen years of age from working. . . . You would cut off the means of support of a good many families . . . deprive families of a large portion of their income." And a man from Charlotte voiced his anxiety that ending child labor would increase the county's welfare bill, because "often . . . their father [is] not sufficiently skilled to earn more than seventy-five cents per day. This will not support the family."[24]

Owners and managers maintained that mill workers were well satisfied with their situation. "Our people are happy and contented," declared John L. Schenck; "Our people all seem to be satisfied and are doing well," echoed Caesar Cone. "Good feelings exist between employer and employees . . . we have had no trouble at all with our help," agreed William H. Williamson, owner of the Pilot Cotton Mills in Raleigh. G. Rosenthal, secretary and treasurer of Raleigh's Juanita Cotton Mills, used superlatives: "Cotton mill employees are well satisfied with their condition. . . . The relations between them and their employers are the very best, and all they want is to be let alone." Alamance County's J. N. Williamson reinforced this assertion by stating that the laborer was "in such a healthful state that there is no remedy needed at all."[25]

Other mill owners emphasized the intangible aspects of life in their factories and mill villages. Conscious policies designed by management were responsible, they said, for good results. "The morals of our operatives are good," stated one official who explained: "We allow no man who drinks to remain. Nor do we have any disreputable women. We have Sabbath-school every Sabbath . . . [and] two of the stockholders, the President and Treasurer, teach in the Sabbath-school." In similar fashion a Mecklenburg County mill was careful to exclude "loose women and drunken men, or bad men and boys." One of its officials praised the effects of an employee savings bank, which had made the hands "cheerful and satisfied—[they] take pride in themselves and in their work." In all, according to the employers, the morale of workers was enviable, and "unfair and obviously untrue" criticisms came only from "'sorehead' mill-help (men probably doing nothing themselves)."[26]

In the late 1880s and 1890s the North Carolina Bureau of Labor Statistics sought the opinions of textile workers. Operating on a budget of only two or three thousand dollars, the bureau lacked the resources to contact every worker systematically. It had to rely mainly upon questionnaires sent by mail to a few operatives whose names and addresses were furnished by their employers. The bureau urged owners and superintendents to supply the names of their "most intelligent, unprejudiced, and reliable workers."[27] Employers probably expected these trusted individuals to echo the glowing descriptions provided by management. What they said, however, was quite surprising and hinted at an enormous amount of dissatisfaction in the anonymous ranks of workers.

Things were not all for the best in the mills, even according to these selected workers. They specified a wide range of problems, but probably nothing attracted more complaint than the excessively long hours of work. "Twelve hours a day is too long for any one to work in a mill," declared a worker in Gaston County who favored legislation requiring an eight- or nine-hour day. "Nine hours is long enough to work in the dust and lint of a factory." A Lincoln County worker agreed that "twelve hours per day is too long to keep operatives at work, especially women and children."

Another factory hand said, "Lessen the hours of labor" and supplied a very practical reason for his recommendation: "The way it is now is cook, eat and sleep, and no time for enjoyment or anything else." When asked about books, a mill hand in Mecklenburg County who had twenty-three years experience said, "I have no time to read them. We have to go to work [at] fifteen minutes to six in the morning and work till seven in the evening; you can judge how much time we have to teach our children." This man believed that even a ten-hour day would be "large help" to workers because it "would give them some time to be with their families, and teach their children."[28]

Even an overseer with twenty-four years of experience judged ten hours "long enough" and said, "I have worked under the twelve hour system all my life, and find it hard." An engineer who helped build mills in Alamance County saw "a very decided opposition" to long hours "among the cotton-mill people" and supported their view by saying, "There is no other class of laborers in this section who work over ten hours per day." "Farm laborers only work from sun to sun and rest when they get ready," wrote a Pitt county agriculturalist who agreed that farmers were lucky compared to the mill hands. At least "farm laborers invariably have Saturday afternoon for rest and recreation."[29]

The mill hands were concerned about health as well as recreation. "The long confinement . . . under the twelve-hour system," wrote a speeder-tender, "keeps us so nearly exhausted at the close of the week and on the Sabbath day, that we don't gain the rest our bodies require." An employee who had recently arrived from Philadelphia favored a sixty-six hours law to assure "every manufacturer an equal chance, and also labor the benefit of the short hours to refresh themselves, which I think they need badly, taking appearance into consideration." Thos. G. Moses of Guilford County declared that a ten-hour law "would be the best thing for the laboring class that has ever been done. You don't know how it is killing up the women and children. It is ruining their health and breaking down their constitutions." Another mill hand wrote, "The confinement is destroying the very life of the people. You can tell any one who works in a cotton mill; they are always a tallow-faced, sickly set of people." And an employee of the Mountain Island mill warned, "In a few years, unless we get shorter hours in cotton mills, you will see a State full of dwarfs and invalids."[30]

Workers felt that the wages they received for such long hours of labor were inadequate. "I think it is very hard for a woman to work 12½ hours a

day for 40¢," wrote one person, and another worker called on the employers to "give the hands better wages. . . . When we make forty cents per day
we can *live*, and that's about all." The Mecklenburg operative quoted
above believed that "Shorter hours and good pay is the best thing . . . to
better their condition. . . . The wages they have to work for will not feed
and clothe them properly." Even a superintendent who had forty years of
experience to his credit asserted that he earned "but little more than a
support. I believe this should be changed."[31]

The anxiety of mill workers for their children came from the heart; they
wanted their children to have a better future but feared they would not.
Perhaps some adults, as mill owners charged, cared little for their children
or their education and lived off the labor of their sons and daughters. But
it was obvious that many factory workers were not that type. Part of the
parents' concern arose from questions of health. "The effect of working
children in mills or other industries," wrote one man, "is injurious to
health, education and morals for self-evident reasons. . . . Fifteen is early
enough for any child to work in a factory." Another mill hand, who admitted to being "not accustomed to express my thoughts in writing,"
nevertheless said, "I will try to inform you with few words how some are
treated. There are children working in factories at the age of eight years,
and are confined there from before day until after dark. This is too long
for older people to be compelled to work. It surely is an injury to the
health and growth of children under fourteen years of age."[32]

But parents voiced even deeper feeling about the question of education,
which meant the chance of greater opportunity for their sons and daughters. The superintendent whose earnings after forty years were still barely a
support was very outspoken. "If our children have to work all their lives in
a cotton mill," he declared, "they should not be required to work more
than ten hours for a day's work. . . . In my forty years' experience I have
known hundreds of poor children who have grown up in perfect ignorance; they could neither read nor spell. They had no chance to learn. . . .
They could not go to night school, for they began work at four o'clock in
the morning, and stopped at twenty minutes past six in the evening."
Guilt and grief plagued the thoughts of a mother who worked in a mill: "I
am a widow, with three children—two boys and one girl. I am not able to
send my children to school. I have to work and have them work. This is a
cause of grief to me, as they are bright children, and would be smart in
books if they had a chance. I will do my best for them, and I daily ask God
to help me discharge my duty to them." A worker in the town of Spray

exclaimed to all who would believe it, "There are boys in this mill fourteen years old that cannot count one hundred." And a mill hand in Randolph County, who believed that child labor "dwarf[s] their aspirations for anything higher," predicted that "the total ignorance of the poor white children" was going to make compulsory education "almost inevitable."[33]

Indeed, the best evidence of factory workers' concern for education was probably the fact that mill owners began to provide school facilities. In 1890 North Carolina had more illiterate whites than any other state and 36 percent illiterate in its whole population; it was one of only fifteen states that had failed to enact a compulsory attendance law. But in 1896 James W. Cannon proudly reported to the Bureau of Labor Statistics that, "We have built a good school room exclusively for our operatives and the same is supported by taxation." The bureau's commissioner also praised Major John Schenck for building a three-hundred-book library for his employees and lauded Captain J. M. Odell, among others, for paying "particular attention to the moral, religious, and secular condition of his operatives."[34]

Odell also had the good sense to make an effective gesture of paternalism in his Concord mill, according to the bureau. Its 1895 report stated that, "A few years ago when objections were raised to his employees attending an up-town church, of which he was a member, he withdrew from that church, built a church exclusively for his operatives, became its chief supporter, and a laborer and teacher therein."[35] Such an event had real potential to create some common feeling between the workers and the owner. In many other, less meaningful ways owners used paternalistic gestures to try to ease relations in the factory. Workers took from these gestures whatever benefit they contained, but the veneer of paternalism did not blind them to fundamental aspects of their condition.

That condition had additional defects, according to the workers. They complained of deficiencies in a number of areas, especially housing. A Buncombe County mill hand protested, "Our houses are small and inconvenient in arrangement. Rent is too high. . . . The water we drink is unhealthy on account of filth." A worker from Cumberland County likewise complained, "Location not healthy. We do not get any pure water." Another in the same county described "house room" for his family as "Very scarce indeed," and a supervisor said, "I know several families that have from six to eight [members] that are living or staying I should have said, in houses 16 x 26 feet and only one fireplace." Workers in Richmond County agreed that "many of the hands have to live in one room, and a good many families have to live in a house with another family." In addition, some people said their houses were "very old and dilapidated" or "roomy enough but . . . not sufficient to keep us warm and dry."[36]

A grievance that was both economic and psychological was the practice, common in some mills, especially prior to 1890, of paying in scrip that had to be redeemed for goods at a company store. A sawyer from Randolph County observed in 1888 that, "The operatives in all the cotton mills trade at the company store. If they could get their money each week, they could do much better." A mill hand in Lincoln County said flatly, "The check system ought to be stopped" and enlarged upon his reasons with this example: "A girl works for fifty cents per day, has three in family to support, gets a check each day for work, and buys her supplies from the company's store. When the fours weeks are ended she has no checks and will get no cash. Just so long as they give us checks and pay once a month, they will keep us on the grind-stone, and we cannot get justice." The "prices for goods" at the company store were a problem, for they were generally "much higher than regular cash retail prices"; if hands had "a chance to trade where they pleased" they could "get better bargains."[37]

But the scrip system was also a psychological burden because it dramatized the employer's control over his operatives. Just as overseers could be "too exacting and domineering" in exercising their authority, the powerful mill owner could use his power too blatantly. The use of scrip tended to throw in the workers' faces the fact that they were not able to provide for themselves and had become dependent on an employer. That is why one mill worker wrote that cash payments would help to make him "more cheerful" and why another said with feeling, "This scrip business . . . is a curse to any country, and ought to be an unlawful thing." Even an overseer with twenty-four years experience thought "all mills ought to pay cash for labor and have regular pay days." That method "would suit us well"; it would preserve more dignity and allow more independence.[38]

The greater the control of an owner over his mill village and the more visible his dominance, the more galling was the situation to workers who came from a self-reliant, yeoman background. And the owner's control, in North Carolina's hierarchical society which had almost no local democracy, could be very encompassing indeed. The Schenck family possessed such control through its influence in Cleveland County and through the fact that some of its mills had been built out "in the country." The Schencks accordingly had been obliged to build the entire factory village from scratch, and they owned every stick of wood within it. In 1898 H. F.

Schenck wrote a letter to a political official that showed his tremendous power.

The problem that spurred Schenck to write was a bridge near the family's factory—"our bridge," as he put it. Young people from the mill village were gathering on the bridge to pass the time, watch the water slip by, and smoke cigarettes. The possibility of fire worried Schenck, but he was particularly irritated that the situation had arisen at all. "A couple of years ago," he explained with impatience, "the legislature passed an act at my request that no person should travel faster than a walk across any bridge in Cleveland County, and I know that young men frequently strike this bridge in a lope and go in a very rapid pace across it." A local oligarch's power was being flouted, and Schenck was determined that no one would smoke or run across his bridge without his permission. He asked the county commissioners to ban smoking on the bridge and to post signs advertising the earlier law, which carried a penalty of ten dollars or thirty days' imprisonment. Plainly, workers had to be careful where they relaxed, smoked, or ran in his mill village.[39]

Such intrusive power must have grated on many workers' self-respect and offended their democratic assumptions about what was right. They combatted it by protecting themselves and their interests as much as possible. Mill owner G. Rosenthal encountered this behavior when he tried "several experiments" to "help" workers. "I have reluctantly come to the conclusion," Rosenthal wrote, "that the less employees are interfered with, the more content they are. I find employees in cotton mills an exceedingly clannish set, who resent promptly whatever they consider interference with their affairs, whether it is meant for their good or not." Rosenthal was relatively perceptive. Other employers merely decided, like E. W. Worth, that "there is a great lack of gratitude" and a willingness to listen to the "agitator," the "chronic grumbler and kicker."[40]

Occasionally the evidence that a hand was angry could be very dramatic, as in a news item which said that, "Wm. Brown, recently an employee in the Orange cotton factory near Hillsboro, was arrested last week for attempting to burn the factory building by setting fire to the lint room. He had some difficulty with the proprietor and sought his revenge in this way."[41] More often, however, workers with responsibilities to spouses, children, or other relatives could not act so directly on their feelings of injustice.

It was clear, though, that such feelings lay beneath the surface. Even some officers of mills admitted that workers "believe that they are badly treated," "that they are not receiving their proportion of the profits made," and that "as a rule they look on the mill-owners as their oppressors." A Columbus County mechanic observed, "The laboring classes believe themselves oppressed." Even a self-described "Old Superintendent" argued that labor should get "an equal part of the products of labor. . . . As it is, capital gets the lion's share which makes the rich richer and the poor poorer."[42] And the workers' comments on "capitalists," "justice," fairness, and "the laboring class" indicated that they had a clear awareness of social class and power.

Most often, due to the difficulties by which they were surrounded, mill workers had to endure rather than protest. They dealt with life in the mill through a number of strategies. In the first place, they did not sever their connection with rural life and farming. They had come from the farm, and they usually had many relatives and friends who still lived in rural areas and followed agriculture. Mill workers could visit these people on holidays and for family celebrations and preserve a connection with the community from which they had come. Children could stay with grandparents or cousins to work out a problem or benefit from an opportunity. And dissatisfied workers sometimes reversed their migration, like "Mike Councelman [who] left off work" at the Holt mill "to crop with Bill Dickey." By the same token those in the countryside could use their relatives in the mill as a resource for finding factory work, if and when that became necessary.[43]

In the factory village operatives maintained a direct, personal connection with nature: they planted gardens and sometimes kept a few animals. D. A. Tompkins preached to aspiring mill owners that the cardinal rule in "providing attractive and comfortable habitations for . . . operatives" was to remember "that they are essentially a rural people. . . . The old instincts cling to them." Therefore, he recommended space for garden plots as a way "to preserve the general conditions of rural life" and cautioned only against providing so much ground that operatives with "scant time" would be unable to manage it.[44] Most mills had plenty of space for gardens, and workers continued to plant, weed, harvest, and preserve according to rural traditions.

How important gardening could be for workers was revealed by the recurring references to it in Henderson Monroe Fowler's diary. The limited cultivation that he did was very significant to him as a source of interest and satisfaction, as well as food. "John Tinnin brought my hogs," he related one month, and a few weeks later he wrote that he had set out six young apple trees and twelve peach trees—thus starting an orchard that carried the promise of fruit in years to come. His accounts of factory matters continued to be sprinkled with entries such as "Fixed my watermelon patch," "Ploughed my garden," and "Just the best rain."[45] Obviously machine time was not the only kind of time that had importance to Fowler; the rhythms of rural life ran along with the factory and reminded him when to plough and when to harvest.

Time books from cotton mills furnish some evidence that the rigid, hurried schedules we tend to associate with machine production were considerably looser and more flexible in nineteenth-century textile mills. Plainly, too, the wishes of the operatives had much to do with variations in the schedules. Because farmers, as the Bureau of Labor Statistics noted, could "rest when they get ready," it was not surprising that hands who had been farmers sometimes pressed for breaks in the factory routine. An early time book contains the words "Shut down Oct. 1st for Camp Meeting," and Henderson Monroe Fowler's frequent descriptions of a "Camp Meeting" or "Protracted Meeting" on a workday suggest that these were important to Alamance County workers and that some attended. On the occasion of an employee's wedding Fowler noted that "all [were] cutting up some," and he was not surprised that when the factory ran on Easter Monday, which "never was the case before," the hands were "all mad & not much good done that day."[46]

Flexibility extended to the length of the work week in the case of many employees. The pay roll of the Willard Manufacturing Company, which operated six days a week in 1899, listed many who had worked less than a full week, some as little as ¾ of a day. The Fayetteville Cotton Mills in 1894 paid most workers for 5½ or 6 days work, but quite a few put in only 4½ days; the same was true of both the Pilot Cotton Mills in Raleigh from 1893 through 1896 and L. Banks Holt's cotton mill in Belmont, Alamance County. The latter, from 1897 to 1900, often paid workers for ½, 1½, 2½, 3½ days, or other amounts less than the full 6½ day work week.[47]

Such variation allowed for sickness, family responsibilities, or possibly a break from the routine. To the owners it offered the advantage of a relatively easy way to alter the size of the work force and total output, as conditions required. For example, at Raleigh's Pilot Cotton Mills from the middle of April through the middle of July 1893, more than a third of those working put in four days or less as the size of the work force grew from twenty to ninety-three. During a similar period in 1896 the number of workers ranged from seventy-four to eighty-nine and 15.2 percent worked four days or less.[48] Those who had to labor unremittingly faced an exhausting regimen, but a sizable minority worked only part time. It is likely that some individuals combined farming or some other job with intermittent work in a mill.

According to historian Sydney Nathans, workers insisted on some flexibility in daily work patterns. As a result, until the end of the nineteenth century the routine on the factory floor "offered slack time for breaks or sociability." Children could play outside for a few moments, and adults could talk while they worked. Nathans quotes one female worker, who recalled, "You had time to fraternize with your fellow workers. You could get up when you had to, sit down when you wanted to. . . . It was no[t] pressure . . . killing you all the time. We were more like just one big happy family."[49]

In a very basic way the mill workers were like a family, for most of them were part of family groups whose members all worked in the mill. Nine families comprised the core of the Pilot Cotton Mills' workers in 1893, and fourteen families encompassed a total of forty-five workers in 1896. The same pattern appeared in the time book of L. Banks Holt's mill in Belmont. Thus Willie and Minnie Thrower worked together in the spinning room, while Andy and Alice Thrower both earned wages as weavers. Parents and children, sisters and brothers saw each other and worked together. They also discovered that in unity they had the strength to defend one person whose interests were threatened. In 1886, a worker and father named "John Allred took 7 hands out of [a Holt] Mill Monday morning . . . on ac[count] of a little fuss between his son John and Webb." Because seven experienced workers were a lot for the factory to lose, its management soon resolved the problem. The Allreds were only "out side of the mill about a day."[50]

Given the state of the economy in the 1880s and 1890s and the nature of North Carolina's social system, workers were not in a strong position. They were relatively powerless, and they knew it. Yet, with the defiant individualism and determination that had caused trouble for the elite in the 1850s and 1860s, ordinary Tar Heels fought against injustice in the mills. They challenged orders, staged brief work stoppages, and occasionally precipitated strikes when they believed change was necessary.

At the Holt's Alamance factory, according to Fowler's diary, disputes between workers and management were not uncommon. Occasionally William Holt himself "turned [a hand] out of the mill," and dissatisfied workers quit, with their relatives, when they did not win adjustment of their grievances. Proof that the workers did not silently accept whatever they were told to do stood out from a comment by Fowler in 1883: "More fus[s] & disturbance with the hands the second week in January . . . than ever was known here."[51]

In February 1887, Fowler noted that "Emily Boggs['] hands left the mill Monday. . . . going to Sweptsonville." Either the operatives there were resistant or Emily Boggs helped them focus their dissatisfactions, because in May there was a "Strike at Sweptsonville" on the first day of the month. Another strike occurred "at Osipie about the same time" and more workers also left the Holt factory. H. F. Schenck observed in a letter to his partner J. E. Reynolds that "sometimes matters turn up that we cannot control, such as the strike we had." Schenck lamented that "three of our first-rate hands" left as a result of the conflict, and the correspondence of other mill owners reveals evidence of protests and strikes by operatives.[52]

The 1880s were a time of considerable unrest, and the decade offered a preview of future conflict. The Knights of Labor grew rapidly in North Carolina, becoming "as strong . . . as they were anywhere in the South, with the possible exception of Virginia." Mechanics in the Raleigh-Durham area formed the heart of the Knights' membership, and they were so well organized that they were able to elect their state leader to Congress in 1886 as an Independent. Democratic papers immediately attacked the Knights with charges that they opposed white supremacy and wanted to put Negroes in charge of the state. In reply the Knights denied the Democrats' criticisms and increased their efforts to appeal to unhappy farmers, thus aiming at an alliance of workers and agrarian elements.[53]

Textile workers joined the Knights in numerous mill towns of the piedmont. They belonged to local assemblies of the organization in Graham, Company Shops, and Swepsonville (all in Alamance County), and in Fayetteville, Mount Holly, Lowell, Mountain Island, Winston, Greensboro, and probably Concord, Salisbury, and Henderson. The operatives in Company Shops were eager to strike; they wanted to close the mills because they felt, "we have got to come down to 11 hours per day." Though dissuaded from striking in 1886, the operatives who joined the Knights in Company Shops probably led an unsuccessful walkout against the Falls of the Neuse Manufacturing Company in 1887.[54]

More significant was the political support the Knights in Alamance County gathered by connecting their discontent with others' grievances. Thomas M. Holt, scion of the county's most powerful family, had been

Thomas M. Holt

Alamance's representative in the state house and served as speaker in 1885. As the 1886 election approached Holt ritually declined to run, pleading the pressure of his business interests, but in fact he had his eye on higher office and gladly accepted renomination "in obedience to the unanimous wish of the [Democratic] party." A second member of his wealthy family was on the ticket for local office. But there were men in Alamance who were angry about the stock law; they favored independent political action. A former sheriff defected to the Republican party, and Independents were gaining strength in the state, partly because many voters still believed that county commissioners should be elected by the people. Poorer voters in Alamance were growing restive under the Holt family's long dominance.[55]

Holt's supporters were worried and defensive. They condemned independent movements and declared that "advocacy of any movement tending to destroy the organization of the Democratic party is treason." The *Alamance Gleaner* praised Thomas Holt's honesty and ability and argued that his success in business was no "reason why he should not be elected to the legislature." To answer charges that "the Democratic party is not the friend of the workingman . . . [whereas] the Republican is his special friend," the paper insinuated that Republicans favored black workers over white workers. County government, claimed the *Gleaner*, was a stale, dead issue.[56]

But these grievances were not dead, they were growing, as shown by the election returns. The votes of mill workers helped the Knights of Labor carry Alamance for its successful congressional candidate. Master Workman John Nichols defeated John Graham, the Democratic nominee. And despite the immense resources of the Holt family, Thomas Holt nearly lost his bid for reelection. By less than a hundred votes out of 2,349 he returned to the North Carolina House.[57]

Chastened by his narrow escape, Holt in 1887 introduced a bill to establish the ten-hour day and reduce the work week to sixty-six hours. He also "moved that a joint committee . . . consider the question of the appointment of a railroad commission." Although Holt's personal experience had sensitized him to the discontent among poorer Tar Heels, his party was less willing to adjust; the railroad commission was defeated and the ten-hour bill tabled. Yet Holt's personal wealth gave him one more card to play. His family's mills had since 1883 been making the expensive but highly productive conversion to steam power; in 1886 L. S. Holt had "adopted the 11 hour system" and early in 1887 W. E. Holt even "advanced 25 per cent on wages." Thomas Holt accordingly reduced the hours in his mill, too, a step that helped him become lieutenant governor in 1888 amid cries that he was "the workers' friend."[58]

Factory workers in the New South did not share the industrialists' satisfaction with the status quo. Their discontent was growing, and as the brief influence of the Knights showed, it had the potential to combine with the protest of farmers, whose plight brought them increasing anguish. Thomas Holt had made a personal response to pressure, but his party had refused to move. If the Democrats refused to respond to stronger demands for change, their only alternative was repression. That choice approached with the 1890s. Fifty years of conflict between poor but democratically minded Tar Heels and a wealthy, rigid elite were building toward a climax.

DEMOCRATIC CHALLENGE,
UNDEMOCRATIC SOLUTION

More than two decades of problems for North Carolina's farmers set the stage for a climactic challenge to the power of the elite and the Democratic party. The self-annointed "better half," including planters, merchants, professionals, and most of the state's industrialists, remained satisfied with a version of the New South that enhanced their position while inhibiting social and economic progress for others. Suffering farmers found that their problems only deepened, and many of them went into political rebellion with the aid of black and white Republicans. Their challenge unleashed egalitarian forces so threatening to the elite that the Democratic party again resorted to fraud and force to safeguard its power and then designed a final, undemocratic political and social solution. This solution—segregation and disfranchisement—eviscerated the coalition of poorer whites and blacks and insured that established interests would not be threatened in the future.

As the 1880s advanced into the 1890s relief seemed unavailable to the farmers. Their successful battle in 1889 against the jute-bagging trust, which had tried to boost prices on the cloth that encircled cotton bales, only reminded them of the continuing exactions of railroads and other monopolies and corporations. Deflation, scarce credit, and the crop-lien made it impossible for most to earn a profit. The harvest of 1891 brought the "poorest crop ever made. The most of the farmers will be brought in debt," wrote John F. Flintoff, who felt "very sorry for my children and all the farming community." The next year Flintoff recorded another "poor crop" and then in 1893 came the "worst financial crisis I ever saw," a nationwide depression more severe than any the United States had yet experienced. Few could muster up the ironic humor of one old farmer who said, "If Miss Prosperity has made her appearance in this section, she certainly has appeared wrong end forward, for there never has been, since Adam was a boy, such weeping, wailing and gnashing of teeth . . . among the poor."[1]

Increasingly the mood of many Tar Heel agriculturalists grew angry and class conscious. Their bitter experience had convinced them that they were a class—they often described it as the laboring class—whose very existence was threatened by corporations, merchants, banks, and capitalists. Though yeomen farmers and tenants preferred to define themselves by independence, they saw that circumstances were forcing them into a corner. "Farming pays in this country," observed one, "but, on account of high interest and scarcity of money, it pays the wrong man." A Caldwell County resident wrote that "the money men have closed in on us . . . again." Asserting that their purpose was "to make slaves of the farmers," he favored a marked expansion of the currency through free and unlimited coinage of silver. Others saw the same confrontation in society. "The farmer has arraigned himself against the capitalist, and the capitalist against the farmer," wrote a man who feared that the capitalists "will crush the farmer, and bring lots of them to be tenants."[2]

To avoid such an outcome, many believed that, "We need better laws for the protection of the masses against the [upper] classes." Class injustice during the "extra hard times" sparked one man's outrage. "Call it socialism or what you please," he wrote; "Damn a country where there is nobody prosperous but the bond-holder and the money-lender." Such conditions, farmers believed, violated Jeffersonian ideals and the traditional vision of a democratic America. The same conviction that economic and political realities were morally wrong came out in the statement of J. A. Wilson, who lived in a strongly Presbyterian section of Mecklenburg County: "Owing to legislation in favor of monopolies our lands are gradually slipping from the hands of the wealth-producing classes and going into the hands of the few. I do not believe God ever intended that a few should own the earth, but that each should have a home. . . . Three-fourths of our population are tenants, and are not able to buy land at present prices; they are the men who create the wealth and pay the taxes."[3]

Many dissatisfied farmers felt that salvation lay in the Farmers' Alliance, an organization which grew rapidly from the late 1880s to include one hundred thousand in North Carolina and close to three million throughout the South and West. In many communities throughout the South the Alliance offered farmers their only real hope of escaping endless debt and ruin. It also offered many of them their first experiences in collective action. In the Alliance farmers met with each other, discussed difficulties, saw that their problems were not caused by individual failure, and debated strategies for change. This process created awareness of the Alliance's potential power and renewed individuals' self-respect. Through the Alliance traditionally individualistic farmers began to act together in purposeful unity.[4]

In North Carolina, too, membership in the Alliance sparked hope in formerly despairing agriculturalists. It helped them see a future of potential as well as problems. "I hope they will be a power for good," wrote a fervent John Flintoff, and another man explained, "We hope the Alliance will do something to relieve the laboring class." North Carolina's farmers realized that major changes were needed; their difficulties went beyond the state level. "There will have to be changes in the policy of our National Government before we get much relief," observed one. But the Farmers' Alliance, in the eyes of many, seemed capable of being the instrument of reform. Thus Alliance men moved into politics, and in 1890 "Alliance-backed candidates by the hundred were swept into office in both West and South," including thirty-eight staunch supporters in Congress.[5]

In North Carolina as in other southern states, however, Alliance men were reluctant to establish a separate political organization in competition with the Democratic party. For decades the Democrats had inculcated white loyalty to their party and insisted that independent voting was racial treason. As the Alliance grew in North Carolina, Democratic papers predictably sounded familiar themes. "The success of the Democratic party should not be endangered," trumpeted the *Greensboro Southern Democrat*. "All good citizens" would oppose "any" effort to divide white voters and thus make possible "a Republican victory . . . the rule of the negro." Similarly, the *North Carolina Intelligencer* asserted that there was no "greater calamity" than Republican rule and approved a formula publicized by South Carolina's Democrats: "White Supremacy is the bulwark of our civilization, and can only be secured by Democratic unity."[6]

Thomas Jarvis wanted Democratic unity also, but he was one of the few who admitted that there were more ways to achieve this than compelling farmers to bend their knees before the party. The Democratic organization could bend too. In 1890 Jarvis advised Samuel A'Court Ashe, then editor of the *Raleigh News & Observer* and a party leader, that "we had better keep in with the Alliance people because they are the bone and sinew of the party and we cannot afford to split with them." Jarvis knew that popular discontent was deep-rooted and significant. In fact, anticipating that a split would hurt the Democrats most, he advised: "If some of us have to take back seats for awhile it is better than to turn the politics of the State over to the Radicals." Jarvis frankly declared that "the main purpose of the [Alliance] is right" and added, "I am in full sympathy with them in their fight against Corporate [power? (page torn)] as well as in many other [things]."[7]

Unfortunately most Democratic leaders lacked Jarvis's sympathy and his willingness to accommodate party interests to the needs of farmers. A breach opened in 1890 when Senator Zebulon B. Vance refused to support the Alliance's subtreasury plan. The subtreasury was the key element in the entire Alliance program and a radical yet simple solution to farmers' financial problems. Saddled with debts and bound to furnishing merchants who exacted high profits on any credit advanced, farmers needed easy credit at reasonable rates and an end to the deflationary spiral of prices. The subtreasury idea proposed at one stroke to expand the currency and finance farmers' operations by advancing them money on crops stored in government warehouses. It promised to create a flexible money supply, end deflation, and open a path of escape from debt and dependency.

Tar Heel Alliance men, led by the vigorous and regionally prominent Leonidas Lafayette Polk, set their hearts on congressional enactment of the subtreasury plan. They persuaded Senator Zebulon Vance to introduce the subtreasury bill in Congress, and many farmers thought he was committed to support it. But Vance, to their surprise, opposed the plan as unconstitutional and asserted, "I never gave any one reason to suppose that I would support the Bill, and only introduced it because in courtesy I could not refuse to do so." Vance maintained that he cared about "the wants of the farmer," but after this apparent betrayal few Tar Heel Alliance members believed him. One of their officers noted tersely that some of the senator's views were "in open opposition to the Alliance."[8]

Moreover, other elements of the Democratic party were even less attuned to the farmers' ideas than Vance. Some local Democratic activists, full of partisan zeal, were eager to punish "[Alliance president L. L.] Polk and his ilk" for showing a "tendency . . . to disrupt the [D]emocratic party." Planters, furnishing merchants, and bankers, who derived benefit from the conditions the farmers deplored, were hostile to reform. Industrial interests, which had become prominent in party councils, were distinctly uninterested in the Alliance's economic proposals. Ed. Chambers

Smith, the chairman of the Democratic Executive Committee in 1890, revealed the weight of industrialists' influence when he told Samuel A'Court Ashe that Democratic victories and white control were "essential to the development of our industries and the promotion of all social advancement." And David Schenck, who earned so much as a railroad attorney that he was willing to forgo the seat on the North Carolina Supreme Court that he previously had sought, supported "Democratic principles and organization" rather than reform innovations.[9]

Alliance success within the party alarmed conservatives in 1891. So strong was the Alliance that four of the state's Democratic congressmen elected in 1890 belonged to it, and a majority in the state's general assembly was pledged to support both the party and the Alliance. This "farmers' legislature" of 1891 achieved a series of breakthroughs in reform at the state level. It "chartered many new banks," increased taxes for schools, established new educational institutions for blacks and for women, and created a Railroad Commission. Under the law this commission was to have power to set rates and to enforce a prohibition on "'rebates and unjust discriminations of any kind.'" Alliance leader and newspaper editor Marion Butler expected it to "stand as a just bar against flagrant outrages of railroads on the people."[10] This commission constituted a strong intrusion upon business in the procorporation climate of Gilded Age America.

Then, in 1892, elements opposed to the farmers asserted themselves, and the growing conservatism of the Democratic party alienated members of the Alliance. With "most of the North Carolina Democratic leaders . . . hostile," progress in the legislature stopped; the national Democratic party, also moving in a conservative direction, nominated Grover Cleveland for president. Some Alliance men began to believe that a separate party was necessary. "Discord May Be a Duty," declared Marion Butler, who was angry that Democratic papers criticized the farmers as "quacks, hayseeders, and wild-cat schemers, who are plotting to ruin the country." The commotion about "fiat money, third party, 'nigger in the wood-pile,'" he said, amounted to a demand that the farmer "put [his] neck under the party yoke, and vote the ticket even if the monopolist and money sharks write the platform and the devil is made the nominee." Determined to have justice, Butler warned, "If Southern Democracy cannot secure justice for its people without a fuss, then it [is] its highest duty to have a quarrel in camp."[11]

When the Alliance fielded a separate People's party (or Populist) slate of candidates in 1892, Democratic leaders saw red. Furnifold M. Simmons,

Marion Butler

chairman of the state executive committee, dispatched a "Confidential" letter to party workers telling them that the 1892 ballot was the most important election since 1876. "It is too clear to require any argument," he declared, that the Populist effort would "help the Republican party." This raised the danger that "our present system of county and town government would . . . be abolished and we would be remanded to the conditions which prevailed during the days of reconstruction."[12]

The Populist ticket did pull some votes from the Democrats, and in retaliation after the election the Democratic legislature punished the farmers "by circumscribing the Alliance charter so as to prohibit its business activities." These activities—principally the operation of cooperative stores—had been extensive and, because they supplied needed commodities at rock-bottom prices, had been very important to hard-pressed farmers. They saw the legislature's behavior as an act of vengeance that did nothing to alleviate farmers' problems. Meanwhile, the severe depression made their situation even worse while it seemed to make President Cleveland more conservative. Moreover, North Carolina's Democratic governor, Elias Carr, enraged farmers and critics of business by leasing the state-owned North Carolina Rail Road to J. P. Morgan's Southern Railway system for ninety-nine years. Carr was a past president of the state Alliance who had refused to join the Populist party. Now he had conferred a precious state asset on America's best-known banker and financier. The rupture widened, and Populist leaders began to organize a "fusion" or joint ticket with the Republicans for 1894.[13]

The pent-up frustrations of farmers, blacks, and ordinary North Carolinians whose interests had been ignored by the Democratic party exploded in the 1894 state elections. The fusionists won a major victory, sweeping a total of seventy-four legislators into the general assembly compared to the Democrats' forty-six. With this impressive majority they elected Marion Butler to a full term in the United States Senate and chose Republican Jeter C. Pritchard to fill the two-year term created by the death of Senator Vance. Then the Populist-Republican majority set about the task of effecting what historians have called "a virtual revolution in North Carolina politics."[14] It was a revolution sensitive to the reforms sought by farmers. But it also was notable for its focus on democratic procedures that had long been denied. The majority's desire for democracy and equality was making itself felt.

For Populists the fusion legislature restored the powers of the Alliance charter and even liberalized its provisions. To address the serious problems of credit and high interest rates that oppressed farmers, the lawmakers "set the legal rate of interest per annum at 6 percent." It was obvious, too, that this new legislature was ready to ease the tax burden on workers and farmers by raising taxes on railroads and businesses.[15] As far as the powers of state government allowed, farmers received a sympathetic hearing and relief.

To broaden opportunity for the state's people, the fusionists reversed the post-Reconstruction Democratic pattern of starving public institutions for revenue. The public schools, from the elementary level through colleges, received "substantially increased state appropriations," despite the nationwide depression. The legislature encouraged local school districts to increase their support of education and set up teacher training institutes for local schools. In addition, the lawmakers appropriated more money for state charitable and penal institutions.[16]

To infuse democracy into North Carolina's aristocratic political system, the legislature threw out the 1877 statute of the "Redeemers" that had put county government in the hands of appointees similar to the antebellum "squirarchy." Popularly elected county commissioners regained power from appointed justices of the peace. For the first time since the years 1868–76, North Carolina's voters could elect their local officials, an opportunity that had been desired by many white as well as black voters. In addition, the legislature enacted what was, according to one historian, "probably the fairest and most democratic election law in the post-Reconstruction South." After the Democrats overthrew Reconstruction in 1876, they had framed "partisan election laws that enabled Democratic registrars to disfranchise voters on the flimsiest pretext." The 1889 election law, which allowed considerable discretion to local registrars, especially had worked against the rights of black citizens. In place of these laws the new measure "permitted one election judge from each party to be present when the ballots were counted, limited the registrars' powers to disqualify voters capriciously, made partisan challenges against voters more difficult, and helped illiterates by allowing colored ballots and party insignia on the ballots."[17]

Those who favored hierarchy and believed that only a few were fit to rule were certain to be outraged. When new faces replaced the accustomed officials, many elite North Carolinians were sure to cry out, as a man from Wilmington did in 1896, that "the board elected by the people were in the opinion of everyone utterly incompetent." But to remove possible complaint and allow even these conservative elements a voice in government, the new law provided that upon the petition of two hundred voters a judge could appoint two additional commissioners to a county board.[18] Thus in every sense the law was very liberal in spirit.

But this fact did not mollify its opponents, and the economic ideas of the national Populist party distinctly alarmed big business. In its Omaha Platform the Populist party had taken strong stands against corporate power and had reached out to workers, inviting industrial laborers to unite their cause with that of farm laborers. "Wealth belongs to him who creates it, and every dollar taken from industry without an equivalent is robbery," declared the platform; it continued, "The interests of rural and civic labor are the same; their enemies are identical." For workers the Populists demanded an eight-hour day and the dismantling of Pinkerton armies used against strikers. In regard to corporations, the Populists opposed "any subsidy or national aid to any private corporation for any purpose." They called for government ownership of the telegraph and telephones, insisted on an expanded currency, and said, "the time has come when the railroad corporations will either own the people or the people must own the railroads."[19]

When Populist-Republican fusion elected Republican Daniel L. Russell governor in the election of 1896, this economic radicalism came home to North Carolina. Russell, despite his personal wealth, quickly declared war on the Southern Railway's lease and sought to have it annulled. Thoroughly reformist in his orientation, Russell was no McKinley Republican. He peppered his public statements with denunciations of "railroad judges" who allied themselves with "railroad kings, bank barons, and money princes" and called for a staggering increase in the taxes paid by railroads. Russell declared that the people were not "the serfs and slaves of the bond-holding and gold-hoarding classes"; he put himself on the side of the "producer and the toiler," not the "coupon-clipper."[20]

This was not, by any means, the kind of rhetoric that Tar Heel planters, businessmen, and industrialists favored. As the power of Populist and Republican reformers grew, mill owners especially maintained with one voice that no government supervision of their enterprises was needed or desirable. "Our people are happy and contented," insisted John F. Schenck, "and the only thing we specially need is to be left alone." G. Rosenthal, the secretary and treasurer of a Raleigh cotton mill, declared that "any interference" in the affairs of workers "is productive of no good." Caesar Cone advised the state's Bureau of Labor Statistics that it could be most helpful "by advocating a 'let-alone' policy by the State

Daniel Russell

Legislature." "I believe it is wrong for a State to undertake to regulate labor in mills," wrote H. F. Schenck. "The Legislature has no business with my contracts and my employees." Indeed, a bureau agent who praised mill owners like those quoted above as "conscientious Christian gentlemen who have the best interests of their employees at heart" nevertheless admitted that others refused to cooperate with him at all. Their typical comment was, "The State has nothing to do with my business."[21]

The industrialists gave different reasons in support of their position. Some claimed that employees' rights were at stake, for "Our employees are opposed to any legislation that in any way interferes with labor in cotton mills; they are fully aware that fewer hours means less pay, which they cannot afford." Workers "should be free to work as they please," argued H. F. Schenck, and action by "the Legislature to abridge their rights in this matter . . . does more harm than good." An employer in Randolph County warned that legislation about factories would "create an antagonism between employer and employee, which is a thing most undesirable."[22]

L. B. Bynum, who owned a Chatham County textile mill, emphasized that regulation was unnecessary. Competition in the industry was real and vigorous, he said, "and it will take care of itself and its interests. There is no combination or wage trust on the part of mill owners throughout all North Carolina, and mill folks can work when and where they please." Similarly, J. M. Odell prophesied that natural forces, plus owners' benevolence, would take care of any problems. After working for forty years "to solve the labor question for myself," Odell said

> I am now fully persuaded that the mill owners have the welfare of the operatives at heart more than any other persons.
>
> I am of the opinion that if there are no labor laws enacted it will not be very long before North Carolina will be the foremost State in this Union. We will have the most contented labor, and the time will soon come when no child under twelve years will be working in the mills, and none that cannot read and write.

Whether all industrialists were as sanguine as Odell or not, most probably would have agreed with Thomas H. Webb of Hillsboro. He opposed labor legislation "because if it is ever once started there is no telling where it will end."[23]

Thus fusion's tide of reform directly challenged both the undemocratic, hierarchical system of power in North Carolina and the economic institutions that benefited from it. It was not surprising that established interests openly denounced a democracy that had long been unfamiliar in the state. Both Josephus Daniels's *Raleigh News & Observer* and the *Charlotte Observer* of D. A. Tompkins and J. P. Caldwell opposed Populism and fusion and diagnosed their danger in the same terms. The *News and Observer* denounced lawmaking by "low-born scum and quondam slaves," whereas the Charlotte paper feared "the rule of Negroes and the lower class of whites." Nor was it surprising that most "railroads, bankers, and manufacturers heavily subsidized" the Democratic party as the foe of change.[24]

It was clear that the forces unleashed by fusion constituted a fundamental and severe threat to the traditional order. The Populists and Republicans were winning. They controlled 62 percent of the seats in the legislature in 1894 and 78 percent of the seats in 1896. Local democracy had been established and elected officials, who had not been appointed by the Democratic legislatures, were beginning to take office at the local level. The new and democratic election law was in place. Moreover, some Tar Heels who had had little to say about government were responding to their new opportunity, as the participation rate by voters rose to a high of 85.4 percent in 1896.[25]

In a number of ways the success of Populism and fusion was even more significant than the period of Republican victories in Reconstruction. Though the Republican majorities before the 1870 defeat were real enough, it remained true that so-called Radical Reconstruction had initially been imposed from outside, whereas Populism and fusion were indigenous products, the fruits of years of building resentment and dissatisfaction on the part of farmers, blacks, and poorer Tar Heels. From the outset Radical Reconstruction had seemed illegitimate to many whites, whereas the conflict of the 1890s involved opposing camps that had come independently to their own highly critical views of each other. Populists and Republicans of the 1890s also seemed less likely to make the mistakes committed during Reconstruction, and years of battle had honed their sense of purpose.

It hardly detracts from the Populists' significance to argue, as sociologist Dwight Billings recently has, that their leaders were "land owners . . . representatives of a lower level of the landed upper class."[26] As Lawrence Goodwyn has pointed out, "the humiliating conditions of life" against which southern agriculturalists struggled were "pervasive in their impact" and "penetrated into every farm and hamlet of the South." Landowning farmers knew that they, too, would become tenants unless conditions rapidly changed. The leaders of social movements have almost always been more privileged than their followers, and the predominant influence of elite figures is no surprise to social theorists. Who the Populist leaders were matters less than what they stood for, and their demands were very radical for their time. (To some national corporate leaders, free silver alone meant the end of western civilization.)[27]

Farmers, black and white, who previously had not cooperated with each other politically saw pressing reasons to do so during the 1890s. A black man who had always been a straight-ticket Republican declared that it was necessary to cooperate with the Populists in order to bring "justice to the people" and block the powerful business interests "who want to enslave the country by a single gold standard." Even more eloquently, a white Democrat who was preparing to bolt to the Populists described the central class issue in terms reminiscent of those used by Randolph County's Emsley Beckerdite in the 1860s: "The issue confronting the American people to-day is the liberty of the laboring people, both white and black, an issue of vastly more importance than the enslavement or freedom of the negro ever was."[28]

It was clear to Democrats that their power was gravely threatened. Thomas Jarvis was one of the first to see that "the 3rd Party will poll a much larger white vote than our friends think," and he suggested increasing "the fund for Common Schools" as a way of winning the black votes "that it is *absolutely necessary* for us to get . . . to get through." As the Democrats' problems deepened, Jarvis urged "straight out" support for free silver because "the people will not tolerate any foolishness on that question." With growing desperation he began to ridicule Populists as "cranks" promoting "many impractical" ideas. In addition, Jarvis, who had advised against the lease to the Southern Railway, urged Governor Elias Carr not to sign any more railroad leases, for "we are not in a position to take on any new issues."[29]

To save themselves, however, Democratic leaders saw that they would have to make a favorable issue, one that could block the democratic thrust of fusion. Race was the tool most obviously at hand—it had worked during Reconstruction, and the party had relied on it in many lesser crises since then. Accordingly, the Democrats began laying plans for the most massive white supremacy campaign the state had ever seen. In addition they looked to the power of money, fraud, and force to turn back the democratic challenge.

Just how far socially elite Democrats were willing to go was demonstrated in Wilmington, where a bloody coup d'état against the city's Republican government and black population took place on 9 and 10 November 1898. This was not racial violence arising spontaneously from prejudiced lower-class whites, whose need to be superior to blacks has seemed to some scholars to be the dominant force behind Jim Crow laws. Instead it was an organized revolution carefully planned "for a period of six to twelve months" by elite whites in Wilmington's business and political communities.[30]

In October, reported the *Wilmington Semi-Weekly Messenger*, several "conservative business" leaders called on Governor Russell to arrange the "suppression of a [R]epublican ticket" in the county, which was done. But that was not enough, for the Republican city government, which included four blacks among ten aldermen, was not facing reelection that year. Led by former congressman Alfred Moore Waddell, prominent whites called other white citizens out into the streets on the night of election day. Violence did not come then, as one of those who responded to arms explained. "Every [white] man you chanced to meet on the street had a Winchester rifle on his shoulder and a white handkerchief tied on his left arm. . . . I didn't see five negroes on the street all night and I was out a good part of the night reconnoitering. But the streets were lined with the whites. . . . The business men, are at present, holding a big meeting to take steps to run the mayor and some prominent negroes out of town."[31]

At that "Remarkable Meeting" a thousand whites adopted resolutions saying that the founding fathers never intended that the ignorant should vote or rule and demanding the banishment of an outspoken Negro editor and the ouster of the city government. That night whites burned the editor's newspaper building and fought with black citizens, some of whom resisted while others were simply victimized. The Wilmington Light Infantry Company established its dominance with a "rapid fire Colt gun" mounted upon a horse-drawn carriage. The *Semi-Weekly Messenger* reported the deaths of seven blacks, although historians note that other "contemporary accounts estimated between eleven and thirty." The revolution succeeded, and Alfred Moore Waddell headed a new city government of white Democrats.[32]

The men who overthrew democratic government in Wilmington emphasized racial motives, declaring, "we will no longer be ruled, and will never again be ruled by men of African origin." They blamed black people for various ills, including the fact that the city had not grown to 50,000 "at least." But behind their coup and the entire white supremacy campaign was the old aristocratic notion that only certain people had a right to power. "Intelligent citizens . . . owning 95 percent of the property" and paying 95 percent of the taxes should rule, the Wilmington whites declared in a resolution.[33] Statewide the Democrats were determined to prevent supposedly unqualified whites and blacks from having power.

The political virtue of a vicious white supremacy campaign was that it could generate enough emotion to split ordinary white farmers and blacks whose alliance was taking power from the Democrats. This in turn would protect the interests of the privileged "better half" whom Democrats represented, especially industrialists, businessmen, professionals, and successful planters. So Josephus Daniels and other Democratic editors whipped up racial hate with charges of "negro rule" caused, supposedly, by the Populists, fusion, and Governor Russell's appointment of a few blacks to patronage positions. Furnifold M. Simmons, chairman of the Democratic Executive Committee, captured the frenzied tone of the 1898 campaign with an "Appeal to the Voters of North Carolina." Imploring them to "restore the state to the white people," Simmons and the Democrats made exaggerated charges about

NEGRO CONGRESSMEN, NEGRO SOLICITORS, NEGRO REVENUE OF-FICERS, NEGRO COLLECTORS OF CUSTOMS, NEGROES in charge of white institutions, NEGROES in charge of white schools, NEGROES holding inquests over white dead. NEGROES controlling the finances of great cities, NEGROES in control of the sanitation and police of cities, NEGRO CONSTABLES arresting white women and men, NEGRO MAGISTRATES trying white women and white men, white convicts chained to NEGRO CONVICTS, and forced to social equality with them.

Summing up the appeal, Simmons declared, "North Carolina is a WHITE MAN'S STATE, and WHITE MEN will rule it, and they will crush the party of negro domination beneath a majority so overwhelming that no other party will ever again dare to establish negro rule here."[34]

In case the Democratic majority was not overwhelming, party leaders made sure that Democratic totals "were considerably padded through frauds," a fact admitted by "a prominent North Carolina clergyman . . . in a national magazine shortly after the election." Another way to render the outcome more secure was to intimidate black voters and thus reduce the opposition's total. To achieve this end Red Shirt Clubs began to demonstrate in communities around the state, especially in southern and eastern

Furnifold M. Simmons

Josephus Daniels

counties. These clubs, according to J. G. de Roulhac Hamilton, were composed of "respectable and well-to-do farmers, bankers, schoolteachers, and merchants." They paraded to show their force and broke up Populist and Republican meetings.[35]

The Democrats did not overlook money, always a useful political tool. Because industrial and business interests strongly favored conservative Democratic policies over Populist and fusion reforms, there was abundant cash to be had. Here Thomas Jarvis paid a small, personal price for his loyalty to party; although he had written to Governor Carr that "[Furnifold M.] Simmons, as you well know, is an *enemy* of mine," it fell to Jarvis to assist Simmons in raising money. The two successfully solicited funds "from many of the bankers, railroad executives, lawyers, and manufacturers in the state and promised that the Democrats would not raise corporation taxes if they regained power."[36]

The vital role of business interests in the white supremacy campaign of 1898 appeared also in the vigorous personal involvement of a number of industrialists. H. F. Schenck made himself a party stalwart and hosted large fish fries to aid the cause. As he saw it, "the salvation of this country depends upon the result of to-morrow's ballot." When the election "terminated favorable for White supremacy," Schenck rejoiced that "the white property owners of North Carolina" would not "be ruled by a parcel of ignorant negroes." Mill owner E. H. Williamson also worked hard to break what he called "the Rep[ublican]—Pop[ulist] shackles," and the *Charlotte Observer* declared editorially that "the business men of the State are largely responsible for the victory. Not before in years have the bank men, the mill men, and the business men in general—the backbone of the property interest of the State—taken such sincere interest. They worked from start to finish, and . . . spent large bits of money."[37]

Although the Democrats won only 52.8 percent of the votes in the single statewide race of 1898, they carried an overwhelming majority into the new general assembly. What they did with that majority helps to identify the basic issues that had been contested. Promptly the legislature rewrote the fair and democratic election law that the fusionists had passed in 1895. Under the new statute the Democratic general assembly assumed control of the state election board and, through it, of local election officers; all voters had to register anew before registrars who enjoyed considerable discretion; a multiplicity of ballot boxes made it difficult for any uneducated voter who did not benefit from an election official's help to cast a valid ballot; and, to avoid possible federal interference, the date of the state election was changed from November to August.[38]

In addition the legislature abridged local democracy once more. The new law was very complicated, with provisions either for election or appointment of various county officers; sometimes additional county commissioners were created, and the provisions varied from county to county. But, in the end, "only thirty-two counties were left undisturbed in the enjoyment of local self-government"; even that number, observed historian Helen Edmonds, was "a tribute to the popularity and idealism of Fusion county government." Restrictions on democracy in the other sixty-five counties went far beyond the supposed purpose of muzzling the sixteen "black counties." That fact, reasoned Edmonds, "showed rather conclusively that an important objective was party centralization and Democratic perpetuation. The Negro served as an effective smoke screen behind which the Democrats seized control of white Republican as well as Negro counties."[39]

Indeed, the legislature wanted to insure that North Carolina's poorer voters, who the *Charlotte Observer* said had been "saved again by the Democratic party," would "stay with it hereafter" and not "run off after Farmers' Alliances and populism." Or, as a Democratic state senator candidly declared, the legislature sought "a good square, honest law that will always give a good Democratic majority."[40] The ultimate and surest way to accomplish that was to disfranchise black Tar Heels, and possibly some poorer whites. Disfranchisement would decimate the strength of the coalition that had challenged the Democrats. By removing half of the potential opposition voters, Democrats could make it virtually impossible for a serious challenge to arise again.

Easily ignoring the pledge of their chairman, Furnifold Simmons, that "the [D]emocratic party does not intend to take away the negro's right to vote," the Democrats and Simmons prepared a disfranchising constitutional amendment. Its "chief engineer," according to the *News and Observer*, was Francis D. Winston, a member of the elite, a well-educated lawyer and Episcopalian who claimed an aristocratic Virginia lineage. The chairman of the House Constitutional Amendments Committee was another wealthy, high-status lawyer and politician of impeccable education and old family. This individual, George Rountree of New Hanover County, had been prominent in the Wilmington coup and viewed lower-class whites in much the same way that he viewed blacks. Adopting the most temporary grandfather clause possible, the disfranchisers evidently valued the idea of a hierarchy itself as deeply as they did white supremacy.[41]

They were determined to put a stop to challenges from lower-class whites and Negroes. As disfranchisement facilitated that arithmetically, so segregation helped achieve it psychologically. The purpose of an 1899 Jim Crow law covering trains and steamboats was in major degree to stigmatize the Negro race and thereby stigmatize all cooperation with Negroes. Decades of white supremacist rhetoric obviously had not done that, for as Furnifold M. Simmons acknowledged to the party in 1900, the problem was that "the white people will not always stand together and vote together."[42] An expanding system of segregation, however, placed blacks in an official pariah caste. If it also gave lower-class whites a feeling of superiority, that result came as a by-product of putting distance between the two groups.

Knowing that this distance was not yet safely established, the Democrats again strained every nerve to exploit racial loyalty in the voting on the disfranchisement amendment in 1900. "Do you want the negro to vote?" screamed the *Alamance Gleaner* in an article addressed "to White Men Only." The Democrat's chief speaker and gubernatorial candidate, Charles B. Aycock, argued that those whites who opposed the amendment were "public enemies" and deserved the "contempt of all mankind." In addition to powerful racial rhetoric, the Democrats felt other tools were necessary. Red Shirts and White Supremacy Clubs appeared once more, and Alfred Moore Waddell urged whites who found "the Negro out voting" to warn him to leave, and "if he refuses, kill him, shoot him down in his tracks." Fraud also was used, continuing a curious pattern in which the Democrats' "largest and surest majorities," as one Republican put it, "were obtained or manufactured in the negro counties and negro districts."[43]

This battery of weapons successfully demolished the remnants of an open, democratic political system in North Carolina. According to the most skillful study of disfranchisement in the South, the 1898 election law significantly reduced black voting, and intimidation and fraud helped white supporters of disfranchisement to roll up huge majorities in the heavily black counties. With fewer North Carolinians voting in 1900 than in 1898, the amendment passed by a margin of 59 percent to 41 percent.[44] Black men had lost their right to vote. Opposition movements like Populism had lost any realistic chance of constructing a majority that could defeat the Democrats. North Carolina had returned to an undemocratic political system that guaranteed the powerful in society effective means of protecting their power. The state's elite minority was secure against democratic challenges once more.

The effects of this drastic restructuring of the political system soon were apparent. Not only did the number of eligible voters drop, but also at the next gubernatorial election in 1904 voter participation fell to 50 percent. In later years it would decline further still in North Carolina as in the rest of the South, for with Democratic victories certain there was little reason to vote. The powerful interests that had helped the Democrats achieve control consolidated their dominant position within the party. As one historian has observed, Tar Heel Democrats "elected the Southern Railroad's candidate to the United States Senate in 1903, a corporation lawyer to the governorship in 1904, and felt quite comfortable with the conservative Alton B. Parker as presidential candidate in that year." Of the state's few "Progressive" reforms passed early in the twentieth century "none . . . protected workers or trade unions." In a vain attempt to become competitive, North Carolina Republicans "adopted a lily-white line" and sought to be more probusiness than the Democrats.[45] The lower classes and reformers advocating their interests had been stripped of power, of influence, and almost of a voice.

It was not surprising, then, that 1900 witnessed a major victory by owners over workers in the textile industry. Strikes occurred at three mills owned by Thomas M. Holt on the Haw River. A union had organized in the area after manufacturers did not share huge profits of 60 percent in 1899, but this union was hardly a socialistic one. It advocated traditional yeoman values and emphasized mutual aid to help the workers regain their independence as "free men and free women." Trouble began when a foreman accused a female weaver of too many trips away from her machine. With the defiant individualism and self-respect that had always characterized North Carolina's yeomen, the woman answered that she "would go when she pleased and where she pleased." After the foreman fired the woman and ordered someone else to take her place, other workers came to the defense of the weaver and criticized her firing. The next day workers stopped the machines, and management quickly closed all three mills.[46]

After meeting together, the mill owners of Alamance County posted notices that said, "after the 15th day of Oct, 1900, this mill will not employ any operative who belongs to a Labor Union." All union workers were ordered to vacate their homes by the fifteenth.[47] Ownership had clearly indicated that it would not adjust the cause of the dispute or have anything to do with unionized workers. The industrialists' membership in the Southern Cotton Spinners Association made it easy for them to coordinate their response.

To the editor of the *Alamance Gleaner*, this seemed unfair. Being careful to say that the union was wrong first because the weaver had deserved firing, the *Gleaner* nevertheless declared that it "could not see why one has not the same liberty to organize as the other. . . . Neither is to be condemned for organizing." This position, contradicting as it did the owners' assumptions about their proprietary rights, was a rather independent one for any Alamance paper to take. Hoping for a compromise, the *Gleaner*'s editor described the owners' help as "those who served them" and issued an appeal to the owners. As "citizens of large wealth," could they not "be more liberal"?[48]

The industrialists, heartened by their large inventories, refused to take a broader view. To "yield to such demands," they held, would be "to give up entire control of the mill." By 1 November one thousand workers had staged a rally at Burlington, and the county's out-of-work textile operatives included five thousand union members. On 8 November the *Gleaner* reported the situation "unchanged—both sides are holding out firmly." On 15 November there was not "the least sign of yielding on the part of either" side. But one week later, after the companies had started evictions, some of the unionized workers returned to their jobs. "A large number, the great majority, remain[ed] firm," but "many" were also "moving away—to Georgia, South Carolina and Virginia."[49]

With their superior resources, the owners were able to hold out longer. They broke the strike, found new operatives if they needed them, and insisted to the end on their power over the mills. Many workers, more than one hundred from the town of Graham alone, left the state rather than submit to the rigid dominance of powerful owners. Many others, however, had to stay and learn to live with powerlessness. They had been defeated, as had the fusionists, Populists, open-range advocates, freedmen, and others before them. In a comment on the departing strikers, the *Alamance Gleaner* used words that could stand as an epitaph to the spirit and plight of many ordinary North Carolinians, black and white, between 1850 and 1900: "Among them are a great many excellent people who prefer to go elsewhere rather than surrender rights and privileges which they as citizens deem their own and should enjoy."[50]

AFTERWORD

People learn from their history. Unfortunately, several generations of ordinary North Carolinians had learned through repeated painful experience that their society was not a democracy. They had learned that it was not democratic either in the sense of being governed by the people's will or of displaying equality and respect for the individual within the community.[1] They had learned that those who held power were determined not to share it and were willing to use extreme measures to protect their dominance.

The undemocratic system inherited from the eighteenth century met with frequent challenge in the nineteenth century. The fifty years from 1850 to 1900 especially saw major social, economic, and political changes that brought opportunities to advance the people's interests. Events permitted, encouraged, and at times demanded powerful challenges to the pattern of elite rule. But by 1900 all these democratic challenges had been beaten back and pointed lessons given in powerlessness.

The elite taught these lessons. The mill owners of Alamance County, by their adamant opposition to the workers' strike, taught that they intended to have complete control. Other industrialists in the state did not overlook opportunities to make the same point. In a Labor Day speech in 1901, for example, D. A. Tompkins told a crowd of workers in Charlotte that they must not join unions, strike, or otherwise "make unlawful demand to control property which they do not own to usurp the powers and functions of the officers." In his textbook on cotton mills, Tompkins delivered an indirect but clear threat to those who advocated maximum-hours legislation. Noting that South Carolina had prohibited more than eleven hours of work per day, he added, "Before this law went into effect, the mill companies did not charge rent on operatives houses. Now, however, they charge," requiring rents that Tompkins's calculations showed to be 5 percent of an average worker's wage.[2]

Similarly, the white military companies of Wilmington labored in 1898 to teach black citizens that they did not have rights. "We are just shooting to see the niggers run," said some white men, and by "going gunning for niggers" they made a point. "The object of the whole persecution," wrote Jane Cronly, a white woman who felt "ashamed" over the coup, was "to make Nov. 10th a day to be remembered by the whole race for all time."[3] The object of the white supremacy campaign, with its apocalyptic rhetoric, intimidation, and fraud was not merely to insure Democratic power but to make poorer whites and blacks remember that they should not challenge recognized power again. Similar lessons had been taught to humble Tar Heels before, on many occasions between 1850 and 1900.

Thus ordinary citizens of North Carolina learned that dissent was not welcome and that it was unwise to challenge the established order except from a position of power. Because that condition was usually beyond the reach of powerless people, many had to learn to cope with unpleasant realities while searching for areas of life in which satisfaction could be obtained. Often such areas remained family or religion, dimensions of life that had always been important for North Carolinians. Or perhaps the search for satisfaction led to some field of recreation in which an individual could achieve through his own efforts. Whatever it was, it had to be a separate realm largely controllable by the individual. It had to be sheltered from politics and society's power, for politics and government to many people meant danger and loss.

The distrust of government was deeply ingrained in ordinary people by experiences in which an elite bent government to its will. These experiences showed that politics had winners and losers: powerful groups used government to advance their interests whereas blacks and whites of low status received little sympathy and less assistance. Ordinary Tar Heels learned to suspect government as hostile, controlled by others, and unlikely to have their welfare at heart. Such attitudes remain very real today.

An illustration of the desire of ordinary people to keep government at bay arose in 1980, when four hundred angry citizens attended a hearing in Gaston County. Their purpose was to oppose plans to rezone land around Crowders Mountain in order to protect it as a state wilderness park. These opponents of the park voiced attitudes of wariness and distrust that were traditional among many common people. They displayed a determination to protect their own lives from interference by a government that often had served the interests of others. In Jeffersonian fashion they viewed their land or farm as the foundation of their independence.

Katherine Busha declared in protest that she had bought land near

Crowders Mountain "specifically to escape zoning requirements and re-strictions. I wanted [to be] out where nobody could tell me what to do." Another speaker charged that, "we have set here for years and the county's never done anything for us, or even knew we were here." Why, he wanted to know, should that unconcerned government now interfere with their lives? And in a statement that drew applause, Mrs. Busha condemned the plan as a violation of "fundamental rights. 'I wanted my land so I could put what I want to on it,' she said. 'If I want to raise some chickens, it's my right. If I want to raise me some meat, it's my right. I'm entitled to this.'"[4] Her words showed her to be the spiritual descendant of yeomen who had opposed fence laws or fought the Confederate government.

Was Mrs. Busha caught in the past and wrong about the present? Did the undemocratic politics of the era from 1850 to 1900 still have any relevance? With economic development and the racial and social progress of recent decades, the South is not the region it once was. Perhaps distrust of government is now an anachronism. How much have things changed? Have aristocratic attitudes faded away?

The influence of history can be long-lasting, and this was especially true of the events of the 1890s. For elite Democrats did more than beat back the challenge of the Populists, disfranchise black people, and stigmatize cooperation between poorer Tar Heels of both races. They imposed an undemocratic electoral system so complete and effective that all future political discourse had a restricted character. The new system excluded a large segment of the population from participation and thereby eliminated a broad spectrum of opinion. Subsequent generations learned their poli-tics within a highly constricted, conservative frame of reference. In this way the events of the 1890s froze political thought and kept it from evolving for decades.

To insure that future generations absorbed a view of reality congenial to the elite, leaders like D. A. Tompkins quickly set about the task of revis-ing, and distorting, the history of the period from 1850 to 1900. Return-ing to accents of paternalism, they labored to put a better face on the brutal repression of democracy that had taken place. They needed, too, to soften the iron control that industrialists had over working-class whites, to cover the fact with a more attractive garment. So they turned to assertions of concern and fellow-feeling, the "proto-Dorian bonds" that some schol-ars later accepted as real.[5]

Tompkins preached the New South orthodoxy many times, seeking to instill a false memory of harmony and interclass unity that had never existed. In a typical claim, he said that "the effort to help the operatives began at a time when everybody in the South was on absolutely the same level of poverty. . . . The warm ties of friendship and affection and love, which had been generated during the period of reconstruction and poverty and equality, made every man desirous of doing as much for his operatives as for himself." Suggesting the view of capital formation and investment that Broadus Mitchell was to repeat, Tompkins declared that, "the man who undertook to build a cotton factory was simply put forward many times without his consent, to help do the most promising thing looking to ameliorating the condition of the people in the country."[6]

Appealing to common history, common feeling, and fear of outsiders, Tompkins also linked the supposed brotherhood of owner and worker to white supremacy. Given the triumph of disfranchisement, this was a theme that would echo again and again in an effort to bind whites together and lessen the dissatisfactions of their lower-class members. According to Tompkins and many others, "Change for the better was brought about by the men who lived in the old times as hard and poor as you did. . . . The improvement has been made by you and your home people who fought with you the battle of white rule in North Carolina."[7]

For all these reasons, it should not be surprising that old antidemocratic attitudes have a way of persisting, despite impressive economic advances. In Charlotte, for example, contemporary forces had transformed the quiet backwater visited by Juliana Margaret Conner into a dynamic city of more than three hundred thousand in 1980. Financial institutions and the regional offices and distribution centers of major corporations anchored what had become a modern economy. Still, one section of the city, the affluent suburbs of its southeast section, dominated local government. It was not unusual for most elected officials to live in the southeast, where they belonged to the same clubs and attended the same churches. The financial resources of businessmen and lawyers from the southeast helped them to dominate a City Council elected at large. The persistence of old attitudes amid change became highly visible in 1975 when some Charlotteans suggested district representation for the City Council, a plan supported by blacks and neighborhood groups from other parts of the city.

The established leadership threw its weight against this idea. The mayor and most councilmen voted to block district representation, and a long line of former mayors and former officeholders warned of the deterioration in local government that would result. To arguments that minorities and neglected neighborhoods would gain a voice through district representation, opponents replied that "you can't get capable candidates to run if you have districts" and that "well-qualified candidates might be prevented from being elected because they happen to live in the wrong district."[8] After a petition drive resulted in the adoption of districts in 1977 and the election of a City Council containing three blacks and four women, many influential Charlotteans "were horrified." They told an incumbent who won reelection that "his job was to hold the line," for many feared power that was not safely in the hands of the established elite.[9]

Four years later prominent conservatives tried, unsuccessfully, to return to the old system. The comments of typical citizens whose votes beat back the attempt showed how clearly they knew that the at-large system of city government had served the wealthy, white business leadership that lived in the southeast suburbs. Voters in a northeast precinct explained "proudly and firmly" why they had supported districts. "I was raised in Charlotte," said a truck driver named William Stinson, "and everything was run from the [south-]east side." Frances Jackson agreed: "Before we had district representation, this side of town had fairly well been neglected." And William Galloway, a black contractor, said, "Most of the people who . . . voted [for] at-large are in southeast Charlotte. Most are white people and most of the people on the council would have been white. . . . We don't want . . . somebody the white establishment may wish to put in office."[10]

Time has brought substantial changes. The civil rights movement inaugurated an era of protest that reversed disfranchisement and ended legal segregation. The rhetoric of Tompkins and other leaders about the noble cause of white supremacy has at last disappeared, although racial code words are still part of politics. In many communities it is evident that a great deal has been done to improve race relations. Charlotte, for example—despite its resistance to district representation—has elected a black man, Harvey Gantt, as mayor. Because racism was deeply rooted, there is, however, still much progress that needs to be made.

This book has shown another dimension of the challenge that faces North Carolina. Undemocratic attitudes and practices more fundamental even than racism were also deeply rooted in the state's history. They, too, must be overcome if the Old North State is to become, as its official toast proclaims, a place where "the weak grow strong and the strong grow great."[11]

NOTES

ABBREVIATIONS USED IN NOTES

SHC, UNC-CH   Southern Historical Collection, the University of North Carolina at Chapel Hill

NCDA&H   North Carolina Division of Archives and History, Raleigh, North Carolina

Duke   Manuscripts Department, Perkins Library, Duke University, Durham, North Carolina

O.R.   U.S. War Department, *The War of the Rebellion: A Compilation of the Official Records of the Union and Confederate Armies*, 130 volumes (Washington, D.C.: Government Printing Office, 1880–1901)

USBRFAL   United States Bureau of Refugees, Freedmen, and Abandoned Lands

NAMP   National Archives Microfilm Publication

PREFACE

1. Quoted in Edmund S. Morgan, *American Slavery, American Freedom,* p. 239; A. Roger Ekirch, *"Poor Carolina."*

2. Hugh Talmage Lefler and Albert Ray Newsome, *North Carolina*, pp. 323, 421; V. O. Key, Jr., *Southern Politics*, chap. 10.

3. Juliana Margaret Conner Diary, SHC, UNC-CH, pp. 4, 7, 10.

4. Ibid., pp. 9, 38, 16.

5. Ibid., pp. 7, 38.

CHAPTER I

1. Conner diary, SHC, UNC-CH, pp. 6, 20, 15–16, 11, 7, 30–32, 10.

2. U.S. Bureau of the Census, *The Statistical History of the United States*, p. 32; Guion Griffis Johnson, *Ante-Bellum North Carolina*, chap. 2 and p. 117.

3. Conner diary, SHC, UNC-CH, p. 55; Johnson, *Ante-Bellum North Carolina*, chap. 2 and pp. 40–41.

4. Johnson, *Ante-Bellum North Carolina*, pp. 55, 59–73. What follows in this study represents some modification of Johnson's description of the social structure.

5. The influential view that southern planters had a seigneurial life-style originated, of course, with Eugene D. Genovese in *The Political Economy of Slavery*.

6. Lefler and Newsome, *North Carolina*, p. 318 and chap. 24.

7. John M. Morehead to Thomas Ruffin, 23 Nov. 1861, in J. G. de Roulhac Hamilton, *Papers of Thomas Ruffin*, 3:194–95. See also William S. Ashe to Thomas Ruffin, 8 Dec. 1861, ibid., p. 203.

8. Lewis C. Harvie to Thomas Ruffin, 28 Nov. 1863, ibid., pp. 346–47; W. F. Leak to Thomas Ruffin, 15 May, 27 Nov., and 7 Dec. 1868, ibid., 4:200, 214, and 215–16; Jean Anderson, "Paul Carrington Cameron as Planter," p. 119.

9. Worth's correspondence with relatives and with manufacturers such as P. H. Winston, Jr., G. W. Swepson, and J. W. Odell about his investments is extensive. For wartime shifting of his assets see Hamilton, *Correspondence of Jonathan Worth*, 1:233, 264–66, 295, 327–28, 399, 302–4, 399–400, 401–3, 428–29, 341–42. For Worth's interest in industrial associations, see Jonathan Worth to L. W. Gilbert, 4 Jan. 1867, ibid., 2: 851–52.

10. Rufus Lenoir Patterson to Samuel Finley Patterson, 20 Oct. 1867, 4 and 21 Mar. 1866, in Jones and Patterson Papers, SHC, UNC-CH; J. Monroe Leigh to Rufus Lenoir Patterson, 17 Nov. 1863, in Patterson Papers, NCDA&H; and Rufus Lenoir Patterson to Samuel Finley Patterson, 3 Dec. 1861 and 30 Aug. 1868, in Samuel Finley Patterson Papers, Duke. For another example of the broadly based entrepreneurial activity of the elite, see Kenneth Rayner to Thomas Ruffin, 5 July 1869, in Hamilton, *Papers of Thomas Ruffin*, 4:221–25. Thomas M. Holt in the postwar period embarked on both agricultural and industrial ventures. See Thomas M. Holt to "Uncle Carrigan," 12 Jan. 1867, 8 Mar. 1870, in James W. White Papers, SHC, UNC-CH.

11. See Thomas Ruffin's many and prominent correspondents in volume 3 of Hamilton, *Papers of Thomas Ruffin*; see also the guide to the Josiah Collins Papers, NCDA&H, and Rufus Lenoir Patterson to his daughter, 22 Jan. 1873, in Samuel Finley Patterson Papers, Duke. See Dwight B. Billings, Jr., *Planters and the Making of a "New South,"* pp. 75–91 for an examination of other family connections among the elite.

12. U.S. Bureau of the Census, 1860, Agriculture and Population schedules; Johnson, *Ante-Bellum North Carolina*, p. 65. Antebellum Democratic leader William Holden once estimated that 110,000 people could not vote for state senator because they owned fewer than the required fifty acres. See Lefler and Newsome, *North Carolina*, p. 377. Professor Gail O'Brien, in her manuscript, "War and the Legal Fraternity in the Creation of the Modern South," estimates that almost 50 percent of the household heads in Guilford County were landless. This estimate was based on the federal population census. A. Jane Townes, "The Effect of Emancipation on Large Land Holdings," pp. 403–12, cautions that census records are less accurate than tax records (see pp. 405–6). Unfortunately few tax

records from the period survived for use in this study. County governments drew up lists of taxables, but these appear generally to have been lost. One group of documents, for Randolph County in 1848, contained returns for nine of thirteen tax districts and revealed that 25.4 percent of the taxables owned no land.

13. Johnson, *Ante-Bellum North Carolina*, p. 65; Gavin Wright, *Political Economy of the Cotton South*, pp. 62–74. Arthur C. Menius III, "James Bennitt: Portrait of an Antebellum Yeoman," pp. 311–12.

14. John F. Flintoff Diary, entries for 1841, 2 Jan. and 15 July 1843, 10 Oct. 1844, 6 and 14 May and 3 June 1845, 15 Dec. 1846, 7 Dec. 1848, 15 Apr. 1853, 1 July and 8 and 10 Oct. 1854, 25 Dec. 1859, and 1 July 1860, NCDA&H.

15. Clement Eaton, *Mind of the Old South*, pp. 147–50.

16. For statistics on the yeomen's economic position, see Wright, *Political Economy of the Cotton South*, p. 36.

17. Flintoff diary, Aug. 1845, NCDA&H; Eaton, *Mind of the Old South*, pp. 147–50.

18. According to the 1860 census, 27,263 people were in skilled trades and crafts; some of these surely owned land, but other landless people labored or followed a trade in towns.

19. This percentage, which is calculated from the U.S. census, represents 37 percent of total farmers and farm workers, or almost twice the "one to four" ratio of farm laborers to farmers that Clement Eaton reported initially in *The Growth of Southern Civilization*, p. 168. Eaton went on to mention the existence of another large class of laborers that, he said, included many Irish ditch diggers and railroad builders, but it appears that he understated the number of landless farm laborers in North Carolina. See also Guion Griffis Johnson, "The Landless People of Ante-bellum North Carolina." These rural laborers are separate from and in addition to the skilled workers mentioned in note 18.

20. See J. Crawford King, Jr., "Closing of the Southern Range: An Exploratory Study" and chap. 7 for more discussion of the importance of the open range for poorer North Carolinians.

21. W. McKee Evans, *Ballots and Fence Rails: Reconstruction on the Lower Cape Fear*, pp. 7, 15.

22. Johnson, *Ante-Bellum North Carolina*, pp. 68–73 is a better description than most.

23. John T. Trowbridge, *Desolate South, 1865–1866*, pp. 171, 117.

24. Sidney Andrews, *South Since the War*, pp. 180–82.

25. See John Hope Franklin, *Free Negro in North Carolina, 1790–1860*.

26. Johnson, *Ante-Bellum North Carolina*, pp. 597, 601; *State v. Newsom*, 1844, in Helen T. Catterall, *Judicial Cases Concerning American Slavery and the Negro*, 2:109–10.

27. Johnson, *Ante-Bellum North Carolina*, p. 599; Catterall, *Judicial Cases*, 2:12–13, including note on p. 13 and p. 1.

28. Paul D. Escott, *Slavery Remembered*, pp. 111–12; George P. Rawick, *The American Slave*, vol. 14, pt. 1, p. 24.

29. Lefler and Newsome, *North Carolina*, p. 323.

30. Ibid., pp. 323, 354–55, 369. On page 377 Lefler and Newsome noted that

"in 1850 about 40 percent of the farms in North Carolina contained less than fifty acres."

31. Ibid.; Donald C. Butts, "A Challenge to Planter Rule: The Controversy over Ad Valorem Taxation of Slaves in North Carolina: 1858–1862," pp. 3–4.

32. Lefler and Newsome, *North Carolina*, p. 323.

33. Ibid.

34. For example see County Court Minutes, Alamance County, Court of Pleas and Quarter Sessions, Sept. 1857, and Mar. 1858, NCDA&H; Jonathan Worth to Alfred G. Foster, 10 June 1858, in Hamilton, *Correspondence of Jonathan Worth*, 1:56–57.

35. William K. Ruffin to Thomas Ruffin, 18 Feb. 1861, in Hamilton, *Papers of Thomas Ruffin*, 3:127–28; the manuscript census returns were the source for data on these individuals' wealth, with the 1860 returns furnishing all data except for two entries, for which 1850 and 1870 were used.

36. Weldon N. Edwards to Thomas Ruffin, 26 July 1859, in Hamilton, *Papers of Thomas Ruffin*, 3:40.

37. Paul C. Cameron to Thomas Ruffin, 10 Sept. [1860], ibid., pp. 90–91.

38. Quoted in Anderson, "Paul Carrington Cameron as Planter."

39. John Stafford to Thomas Ruffin, 15 Jan. 1860, and Weldon Edwards to Thomas Ruffin, 28 June 1860, in Hamilton, *Papers of Thomas Ruffin*, 3:65–67, 85–86.

40. See the *Charlotte Observer*, 9 Jan. 1980, p. B2, for attitudes of citizens protesting a zoning proposal affecting Crowders Mountain. See also Afterword.

41. Paul C. Cameron to Thomas Ruffin, 28 Jan. 1860, in Hamilton, *Papers of Thomas Ruffin*, 3:68–69.

42. John Anthony Scott, "The Movement Toward Universal Suffrage Rights, 1790–1870" (paper in author's possession), p. 1.

43. W. Conard Gass, "'The Misfortune of a High Minded and Honorable Gentleman': W. W. Avery and the Southern Code of Honor," pp. 287, 291–95.

44. Andrews, *South Since the War*, p. 112.

45. U.S. Census, 1860.

46. Lenoir Crescent Methodist Church, Lenoir, N.C., Quarterly Conference Minutes, 1850–1860, NCDA&H; Mount Herman Baptist Church, Orange County, Register and Minutes, 1850–1860, NCDA&H.

47. Mount Zion Baptist Church, Alamance County, N.C., Minutes, Jan. and Sept. 1859, NCDA&H; Mount Olive Baptist Church, Alamance County, Register and Minutes, Mar. and Sept. 1860, Aug. 1861, NCDA&H; Mount Herman Baptist Church, Orange County, Register and Minutes, Feb. 1851, Nov. 1854, July 1858, and Feb. 1855, NCDA&H; Lenoir Crescent Methodist Church, Lenoir, N.C., Quarterly Conference Minutes, Mar. 1851, Mar. 1853, NCDA&H.

48. Mount Zion Baptist Church, Alamance County, N.C., Minutes, Apr.–Sept. 1866, Sept.–Oct. 1859, NCDA&H; Mount Herman Baptist Church, Orange County, Register and Minutes, Oct. 1854, NCDA&H; Lenoir Crescent Methodist Church, Lenoir, N.C., Quarterly Conference Minutes, 26 Mar. 1853, NCDA&H; Mount Zion Baptist Church, Alamance County, N.C., Minutes, May–July 1864, Sept. 1865, NCDA&H.

49. Lenoir Crescent Methodist Church, Lenoir, N.C., Quarterly Conference Minutes, 14 Oct. 1850, 16 July and 9 Oct. 1853, NCDA&H. In addition to the cases discussed, a justice of the peace from Caldwell County appears to have belonged to the conference as well as a man who later became a county commissioner.

50. Robert M. Calhoon, "Faith and Consciousness in Early Southern Culture," a paper prepared for the Symposium in Southern History under the auspices of the Rembert W. Patrick Memorial Lectureship, Guilford College, 28 Mar. 1980, pp. 2, 4, 12, 19, 22, 27. Calhoon's analysis is more complex and subtle than the brief description here can indicate. Both the Lenoir Methodists and Mount Zion Baptists recorded the welcoming of black members, some of whom were clearly identified as slaves.

51. Thomas E. Jeffrey, "The Progressive Paradigm of Antebellum North Carolina Politics"; Thomas E. Jeffrey, "'Free Suffrage' Revisited: Party Politics and Constitutional Reform in Antebellum North Carolina," p. 27, pp. 26–29; Lefler and Newsome, *North Carolina*, pp. 377–78.

52. Jeffrey, "'Free Suffrage' Revisited," p. 38; Lefler and Newsome, *North Carolina*, pp. 378–79; Jeffrey, "Progressive Paradigm," pp. 73–75.

53. Donald C. Butts, "'Irrepressible Conflict': Slave Taxation and North Carolina's Gubernatorial Election of 1860," p. 45.

54. Butts, "Challenge to Planter Rule," pp. 49–50, 55, 60, 71; Butts, "'Irrepressible Conflict,'" pp. 46–47.

55. Ibid.

56. Jonathan Worth to George Little, 20 Feb. 1860, in Hamilton, *Correspondence of Jonathan Worth*, 1:105–6.

57. Daniel M. Barringer to Thomas Ruffin, 18 Apr. 1860, in Hamilton, *Papers of Thomas Ruffin*, 3:79–81.

58. Kenneth Rayner to Thomas Ruffin, 6 Mar. 1860, ibid., p. 72. Italics added for "revolutionize."

59. Butts, "'Irrepressible Conflict,'" pp. 47, 49, 51. Pool's spotty support for internal improvements, which the west favored, was also used against him.

60. Ibid., p. 66; Butts, "Challenge to Planter Rule," pp. 92, 96–97, 99.

61. Butts, "Challenge to Planter Rule," chap. 6.

62. The application of this phrase to North Carolina originated with Kenneth Rayner in the letter cited above, n. 58.

CHAPTER 2

1. John Frederick Mallett Journal, 13 Feb. 1863, Duke.

2. This is a theme of two recent studies, Michael Holt's *The Political Crisis of the 1850s* and Marc Kruman's *Parties and Politics in North Carolina, 1836–1865*.

3. Charles Manly to Thomas Ruffin, 25 Dec. 1859, in Hamilton, *Papers of Thomas Ruffin*, 3:59; Rufus Lenoir Patterson to Col. T. [F.?] W. Alspaugh, 3 Oct. 1860, Patterson Papers, NCDA&H; Jonathan Worth to J. J. Jackson, 29 Nov. 1860, in Hamilton, *Correspondence of Jonathan Worth*, 1:124–25.

4. Lefler and Newsome, *North Carolina*, pp. 447–48.

5. Ibid.

6. Paul C. Cameron to Thomas Ruffin, 12 Oct. 1860, in Hamilton, *Papers of Thomas Ruffin*, 3:99.

7. Rufus Lenoir Patterson to Col. T. [F.?] W. Alspaugh, 3 Oct. 1860, Patterson Papers, NCDA&H. For Holden's shift see William K. Boyd, *Memoirs of W. W. Holden*, pp. 10–17, and Jonathan Worth to [?], undated but probably 1860, in Hamilton, *Correspondence of Jonathan Worth*, 1:125–26.

8. Charles Manly to Thomas Ruffin, 16 Jan. 1861, and Paul C. Cameron to Thomas Ruffin, 21 Jan. 1861, in Hamilton, *Papers of Thomas Ruffin*, 3:112, 114–15; remarks of Jonathan Worth in the N.C. Senate on a proposal to call a convention, January 1861, in Hamilton, *Correspondence of Jonathan Worth*, 1:128–29.

9. Report of N.C. Commissioners to the Peace Conference, 27 Feb. 1861, in Hamilton, *Papers of Thomas Ruffin*, 3:134–37; Bartholomew F. Moore to Thomas Ruffin, 7 Mar. 1861, ibid., p. 138.

The Peace Conference proposed amendments to sanction slavery south of latitude 36°30', guarantee the return of fugitive slaves or provide monetary compensation for any fugitive slaves lost through violence, and protect slavery in the District of Columbia; these proposed amendments would address southern grievances. The conference also proposed amendments to prohibit slavery north of latitude 36°30', prohibit the importation of slaves, and require a four-fifths majority for the admission of any new state; these proposals were designed to ease northern fears. In addition controversial parts of the Constitution were to be exempted from future change except by unanimous consent.

10. Kenneth Rayner to Thomas Ruffin, 25 Dec. 1860, and Matthias E. Manly to Thomas Ruffin, 2 Dec. 1860, ibid., pp. 108–9 and 104–5; Jonathan Worth to J. J. Jackson, 17 Dec. 1860, in Hamilton, *Correspondence of Jonathan Worth*, 1:126–27.

11. Lefler and Newsome, *North Carolina*, p. 450.

12. Jonathan Worth to Dr. C. W. Woolen, 17 May 1861, in Hamilton, *Correspondence of Jonathan Worth*, 1:145–48; John F. Flintoff Diary, 12 Apr. and 10 June 1861, NCDA&H.

13. Charles Manly to Thomas Ruffin, 16 Jan. 1861, in Hamilton, *Papers of Thomas Ruffin*, 3:112; Jonathan Worth to Gaius Winningham, 20 May 1861, and to D. G. Worth, 15 May 1861, in Hamilton, *Correspondence of Jonathan Worth*, 1:149, 144–45; Rufus Lenoir Patterson to Col. T. [F.?] W. Alspaugh, 3 Oct. 1860, Patterson Papers, NCDA&H; Flintoff diary, 28 July 1861, NCDA&H.

14. John Christopher Schwab, *The Confederate States of America*, p. 297; Lefler and Newsome, *North Carolina*, p. 456. The high desertion rate of North Carolina troops has been questioned by Richard Reid in "A Test Case of the 'Crying Evil': Desertion among North Carolina Troops during the Civil War." This author, however, has seen research by William Auman that is more complete and contradicts much of Reid's conclusion. Auman has presented part of his work to the Southern Historical Association and is preparing it for publication.

15. Jonathan Worth to [?], [1860], in Hamilton, *Correspondence of Jonathan Worth*, 1:125–26; Louisa Morehead Patterson to Mrs. Samuel Finley Patterson, 27 May 1861, Samuel Finley Patterson Papers, Duke.

16. Lefler and Newsome, *North Carolina*, pp. 466, 468.

17. Paul D. Escott, *After Secession*, chap. 3. In North Carolina, as opposed to other southern states, secessionists tended to be strong supporters of Davis and former Unionists critics of Davis. Elsewhere the fire-eaters were so ideological that they quickly condemned Davis for his centralizing measures. The secessionists in North Carolina, however, knew that opposition to Confederate policies easily could become opposition to the Confederacy itself. They knew that they had to support the administration down the line and did so.

18. D. A. Montgomery to Mrs. Thomas Ruffin, Jr., 30 Apr. 1861, in Hamilton, *Papers of Thomas Ruffin*, 3:149; Emory M. Thomas, *Confederacy as a Revolutionary Experience*, pp. 109–11.

19. J. C. Harper to Samuel Finley Patterson, 23 Nov. 1864, Samuel Finley Patterson Papers, Duke; Thomas Ruffin, Jr., to Thomas Ruffin, 20 May and 16 Aug. 1861, in Hamilton, *Papers of Thomas Ruffin*, 3:157, 181. Wealthy men, like Jos. H. Hyman of Edgecombe County, often raised their own companies.

20. B. Hazell to Thomas Ruffin, 9 Aug. 1861, Jacob Garrett to Thomas Ruffin, 3 Dec. 1861, George M. Foust to Thomas Ruffin, 18 July 1864, James W. Lea to Thomas Ruffin, 9 Aug. 1864, Edward J. Hardin to Thomas Ruffin, 19 Sept. 1864, and Thomas Ruffin, Jr., to Thomas Ruffin, 14 Oct. 1862, in Hamilton, *Papers of Thomas Ruffin*, 3:180, 199, 402, 413, 423, 261–63.

21. W. Buck Yearns and John G. Barrett, *North Carolina Civil War Documentary*, chaps. 3 and 4.

22. Thomas Bragg Diary, 1861–1862, 17 Feb. 1862, and 18, 20, 16, 19, 25, and 14 Feb. 1862, SHC, UNC-CH.

23. Zebulon B. Vance to Jefferson Davis, 25 Oct. 1862, and Zebulon B. Vance to Weldon N. Edwards, 18 Sept. 1862, cited and discussed in Escott, *After Secession*, pp. 89, 123, 109.

24. Resolution of the General Assembly, in *Public Laws of the State of North Carolina passed by the General Assembly at its Session of 1862–1863*, p. 49; William J. Clarke to Mary Bayard Clarke, 4 Apr. 1863, in possession of Mrs. Graham Barden.

25. Beth Gilbert Crabtree and James W. Patton, *"Journal of a Secesh Lady": The Diary of Catherine Ann Devereux Edmondston, 1860–1866*, pp. 303, 309, 311, 415, 435, 630, 633, 636, 647–50; Jonathan Worth to Gaius Winningham, 23 May 1862, and Jonathan Worth to Jesse G. Henshaw, 23 July 1863, in Hamilton, *Correspondence of Jonathan Worth*, 1:171–73, 245–46; Marc Kruman, "Dissent in the Confederacy."

26. May Spencer Ringold, *Role of the State Legislatures in the Confederacy*, p. 61; Jonathan Worth to A. G. Foster, 9 Dec. 1861, in Hamilton, *Correspondence of Jonathan Worth*, 1:159; B. F. Moore to Thomas Ruffin, 15 and 27 Sept. 1861, in Hamilton, *Papers of Thomas Ruffin*, 3:187, 189.

27. B. F. Moore to Thomas Ruffin, 15 Sept. 1861, Weldon N. Edwards to Thomas Ruffin, 24 Aug. 1861, and Charles Manly to Thomas Ruffin, 25 Dec. 1862, in Hamilton, *Papers of Thomas Ruffin*, 3:187, 185–87, 282.

28. Yearns and Barrett, *North Carolina Civil War Documentary*, pp. 182–83. In 1865 the convention directed the legislature to establish a scale against which the value of debts incurred in the depreciated currency of wartime could be measured.

The legislature did so, affording obviously necessary relief to anyone, especially merchants, who had bought on credit during that period of rampant inflation. See *Public Laws of the State of North Carolina . . . 1866*, pp. 97–99.

29. James Cherry to "My dear Sister," 6 Mar. 1864, Lunsford R. Cherry Papers, Duke; Walter MacRae to "Dear Don," 22 Jan. 1864, and John C. MacRae to "Dear Don," 5 Mar. 1864, Hugh MacRae Papers, Duke. Don MacRae was a businessman and financier from New Hanover County. These complaints of poor clothing arose despite the fact that North Carolina clothed its soldiers and provided for them better than the Confederacy and other states did for other southern soldiers.

30. John W. Brodnax to Thomas Ruffin, 17 July 1862, in Hamilton, *Papers of Thomas Ruffin*, 3:256; [?] Parpatharkies to Josiah Collins III, 19 May 1863, Josiah Collins Papers, NCDA&H.

31. Tracy Whittaker Schneider, "Institution of Slavery in North Carolina, 1860–1865," pp. 128–29, 136.

32. Rawick, *American Slave*, 14:24, and Schneider, "Institution of Slavery in North Carolina," pp. 165–66.

33. Schneider, "Institution of Slavery in North Carolina," pp. 165–66, 205; Kenneth Rayner to Thomas Ruffin, 12 July 1862, and 8 Apr. 1863, in Hamilton, *Papers of Thomas Ruffin*, 3:253, 311.

34. Joe A. Mobley, *James City*, pp. 10–11, 14, 29; Schneider, "Institution of Slavery in North Carolina," pp. 177–78, 228–29. U.S. soldiers often displayed hostility toward the newly freed slaves. See H. G. Spruill to Josiah Collins III, 16 March 1863, in Josiah Collins Papers, NCDA&H.

35. Schneider, "Institution of Slavery in North Carolina," pp. 178–80, 239, 245, 272–73; Hugh MacRae to W. A. Eaton, 9 June 1863, Josiah Collins Papers, NCDA&H.

36. Lefler and Newsome, *North Carolina*, pp. 466–67; Kenneth Rayner to Thomas Ruffin, 27 July 1862, in Hamilton, *Papers of Thomas Ruffin*, 3:256–57.

37. Kenneth Rayner to Thomas Ruffin, 23 Nov. 1862, in Hamilton, *Papers of Thomas Ruffin*, 3:271–72; Bragg diary, 6 Mar. 1862, SHC, UNC-CH.

38. Jonathan Worth to J. J. Jackson, 5 Jan. 1863, in Hamilton, *Correspondence of Jonathan Worth*, 1:221–22; Schneider, "Institution of Slavery in North Carolina," p. 264; O. Goddin to Zebulon Vance, 27 Feb. 1862, in Yearns and Barrett, *North Carolina Civil War Documentary*, pp. 97–99.

39. W. D. Pender to Major W. H. Taylor, 23 Apr. 1863, in *O.R.*, ser. 1, vol. 25, pt. 2, pp. 746–47; Escott, *After Secession*, p. 133; Flintoff diary, 1 Aug. 1863, NCDA&H.

40. William T. Auman and David D. Scarboro, "Heroes of America in Civil War North Carolina," pp. 331, 332–34, 336.

41. *Raleigh Standard*, 17 July 1863. See also the *Raleigh Daily Progress*, 15 July 1863.

42. Edgar Estes Folk, "W. W. Holden, Political Journalist," p. 569; Horace W. Raper, "William W. Holden and the Peace Movement," p. 502; Resolutions of a public meeting held in Guilford County, 15 Aug. 1863, in *North Carolina Standard*, 25 Aug. 1863.

43. Escott, *After Secession*, p. 200.

44. Ibid., pp. 155, 200, 201.

45. Zebulon B. Vance to David L. Swain, 2 Jan. and 22 Sept. 1864, in Vance Papers, NCDA&H.

46. Jonathan Worth to Daniel L. Russell, 16 Feb. 1864, to John Pool, 6 Feb. 1864, and to D. H. Starbuck, 30 Jan. 1864, in Hamilton, *Correspondence of Jonathan Worth*, 1:297–98, 288–89, 283–85.

47. Auman and Scarboro, "Heroes of America," p. 347; David Schenck Diary, 19 Feb. 1864, SHC, UNC-CH; A. C. Cowles to Calvin Cowles, 18 Aug. 1863, in Calvin J. Cowles Papers, NCDA&H.

48. W. W. Holden to C. J. Cowles, 18 Mar. 1864, in W. W. Holden Papers, NCDA&H.

49. Jno. D. Hyman to Zebulon Vance, 17 Feb. 1864, in Vance Papers, NCDA&H; Wm. W. Mimson to Zebulon Vance, 27 June 1864, in Governor's Papers, Zebulon B. Vance, NCDA&H.

50. John A. Gilmer to Zebulon Vance, 14 Apr. 1864, in Vance Papers, NCDA&H.

51. J. M. Leach to Zebulon Vance, 8 Mar. 1864, and "To the Soldiers of the 7th Congressional District," 5 Apr. 1864, in Vance Papers, NCDA&H; J. T. Leach to Governor Vance, 6 June 1864, in Governor's Papers, Zebulon B. Vance, NCDA&H.

52. Escott, *After Secession*, p. 202; E. D. Macadin to Zebulon B. Vance, 20 June 1864, in Governor's Papers, Zebulon B. Vance, NCDA&H.

53. John A. Gilmer to Zebulon Vance, 14 Apr. 1864, in Vance Papers, NCDA&H.

54. Escott, *After Secession*, chap. 3; Lefler and Newsome, *North Carolina*, p. 466.

55. Escott, *After Secession*, p. 203.

56. W. W. Holden to [?], 29 July 1864, in W. W. Holden Papers, NCDA&H (only ten days earlier, in a letter to C. J. Cowles on 19 July 1864, same collection, Holden had expected a majority); B. S. Gaither to Zebulon Vance, 30 Mar. 1864, Vance Papers, NCDA&H; Kenneth Rayner to Thomas Ruffin, 1 Apr. 1864, in Hamilton, *Papers of Thomas Ruffin*, 3:381. See also W. H. Lenoir to Zebulon Vance, 4 Apr. 1864, in Vance Papers, NCDA&H.

57. P. K. O. G. to Zebulon Vance, 6 Aug. 1864, in Governor's Papers, Zebulon B. Vance, NCDA&H. See also W. W. Hampton to Zebulon Vance, 10 Aug. 1864, ibid., and Kenneth Rayner to Thomas Ruffin, 22 July 1864, in Hamilton, *Papers of Thomas Ruffin*, 3:405–6.

58. P. K. O. G. to Zebulon Vance, 6 Aug. 1864, in Governor's Papers, Zebulon B. Vance, NCDA&H.

59. Escott, *After Secession*, chap. 8; see Robert F. Durden, *Gray and the Black*.

60. Schenck diary, 7 Dec. 1864, SHC, UNC-CH; David L. Swain to Zebulon Vance, 21 and 25 Jan. 1865, in Vance Papers, NCDA&H; Jonathan Worth to Joseph A. Worth, 12 Nov. 1864, in Hamilton, *Correspondence of Jonathan Worth*, 1:333–34; Schneider, "Institution of Slavery in North Carolina," pp. 330–43.

61. Durden, *Gray and the Black*, p. 138 and p. 173, which quotes William A. Graham to David L. Swain, 28 Jan. 1865.

62. Escott, *After Secession*, pp. 222–23.

63. Ibid., pp. 222–24; S. F. Phillips to Rufus L. Patterson, 1 Mar. 1865, in Patterson Papers, NCDA&H; John A. Gilmer to Zebulon Vance, 1 and 14 Feb. 1865, in Vance Papers, NCDA&H.

64. Flintoff diary, 13 Apr. 1865, NCDA&H; Rufus L. Patterson to Mary Fries, 3 Mar. 1865 (see also 7 May 1865 to his parents, Samuel Finley Patterson Papers, Duke), Jones and Patterson Papers, SHC, UNC-CH; Samuel Finley Patterson to Rufus Lenoir Patterson, 15 May 1865, Patterson Papers, NCDA&H.

65. Jonathan Worth to Jesse G. Henshaw, 23 July 1863, in Hamilton, *Correspondence of Jonathan Worth*, 1:245–46; Rufus L. Patterson to his parents, 7 May 1865, in Samuel Finley Patterson Papers, Duke; A. M. McPheeters to Rufus L. Patterson, 10 June 1865, in Patterson Papers, NCDA&H; Yearns and Barrett, *North Carolina Civil War Documentary*, p. xv; Janie Smith to Janie Robeson, 12 Apr. 1865, in Lenoir Family Papers, SHC, UNC-CH; Mrs. [Catherine Douglas DeRosset] Meares to her mother, 28 Mar. 1865, in Meares-DeRosset Papers, SHC, UNC-CH.

66. Flintoff diary, 26 Apr., 1 May, and 17 Aug. 1865, NCDA&H.

67. See Escott, " 'Cry of the Sufferers.' "

68. Yearns and Barrett, *North Carolina Civil War Documentary*, p. 215; Escott, *After Secession*, pp. 122–23, 106–7; Thos. L. Cotten to E. J. Hale & Sons, [1864], in Vance Papers, NCDA&H.

69. Escott, *After Secession*, pp. 109, 66–67; W. D. Sidwell to Zebulon Vance, 7 Aug. 1864, in Governor's Papers, Zebulon B. Vance, NCDA&H; Zebulon Vance to James A. Seddon, 21 Dec. 1863, quoted in Escott, *After Secession*, p. 111.

70. Lefler and Newsome, *North Carolina*, p. 456; O. Goddin to Zebulon Vance, 27 Feb. 1863, in Yearns and Barrett, *North Carolina Civil War Documentary*, pp. 97–99; Escott, *After Secession*, pp. 65, 109, 143; see also A. T. Davidson to Jefferson Davis, 22 July 1863, in Letters Received, Confederate Secretary of War, 1861–1865, Record Group 109, NAMP M 437, roll 90, frames 343–47.

71. Flintoff diary, 21 July 1862, 20 May and Dec. 1863, 22 Mar., 20 July and 17 Aug. 1864, and other entries listing prices.

72. Walter Gwynn to Thomas Ruffin, 13 June 1862, and Kenneth Rayner to Thomas Ruffin, 12 July 1862, in Hamilton, *Papers of Thomas Ruffin*, 3:246, 253; Jos. A. Worth to Jonathan Worth, 23 Jan. 1863, in Jonathan Worth Papers, NCDA&H.

73. Escott, *After Secession*, pp. 105–7; Nancy Jordan to Zebulon Vance, 12 June 1864, and Private C. P. Gibson to Governor Vance, 9 June 1864, in Governor's Papers, Zebulon B. Vance, NCDA&H; Isaac M. Broyles and Wm. E. Piercy to Zebulon Vance, 19 Apr. 1863, in Jonathan Worth Papers, NCDA&H. See also A. B. Chapin to Bryan Tyson, 20 June 1864, in Bryan Tyson Papers, Duke.

74. Nancy Jordan to Zebulon Vance, 12 June 1864, and Private C. P. Gibson to Zebulon Vance, 9 June 1864, in Governor's Papers, Zebulon B. Vance, NCDA&H; Isaac M. Broyles and Wm. E. Piercy to Zebulon Vance, 19 Apr. 1863, in Jonathan Worth Papers, NCDA&H; Escott, *After Secession*, p. 132.

75. Escott, "Poverty and Governmental Aid for the Poor in Confederate North Carolina," pp. 467–69.

76. Report of Committee of Finance of settlement with county for indigent soldiers' families, 1863–1865, Randolph County, Miscellaneous Civil War

Records, NCDA&H; County Court Minutes, Caldwell County, Jan. 1864, Apr. 1864, NCDA&H.

77. Escott, "Poverty and Governmental Aid," pp. 469–71.

78. Escott, "'Cry of the Sufferers,'" pp. 235–37; Escott, "Poverty and Governmental Aid," pp. 472–77.

79. William Frank Entrekin, Jr., "Poor Relief in North Carolina in the Confederacy," pp. 64, 73–75.

80. Escott, "Poverty and Governmental Aid," pp. 477–80.

81. Entrekin, "Poor Relief," p. 120.

82. Ibid., pp. 22, 87; Escott, *After Secession*, p. 135.

CHAPTER 3

1. Escott, *After Secession*, pp. 96–97.

2. W. R. Denny, Joel Shoffner, A. E. Enniss to Thomas Ruffin, 30 Mar. 1861, in Hamilton, *Papers of Thomas Ruffin*, 3:142.

3. William K. Ruffin to Thomas Ruffin, 14 Feb. 1862, ibid., pp. 215–16.

4. [Elvira Worth Jackson] to Fannie Long, 15 Mar. 1862, in Jonathan Worth Papers, NCDA&H; Auman and Scarboro, "Heroes of America," p. 333.

5. Rufus Lenoir Patterson to Samuel Finley Patterson, 6 Feb. 1862, in Samuel Finley Patterson Papers, Duke.

6. William S. Tarlton, "Somerset Place and Its Restoration" (a report prepared for the Division of State Parks, N.C. Department of Conservation and Development, 1954), p. 42, NCDA&H; B. B. Hinsley to Josiah Collins III, 4 May 1863, and Geo. W. Spruill to Collins, 16 May 1863, in Josiah Collins Papers, NCDA&H.

7. H. G. Spruill to Josiah Collins III, 11 Mar. 1863, Girard W. Phelps to Josiah [?] Collins, 14 Mar. 1863, and Joseph W. Murphy to Josiah Collins III, 30 May 1863, in Josiah Collins Papers, NCDA&H; Josiah Collins Account Book, entries for 1856: July, pp. 3, 7; 1858: Aug., p. 85 and Sept. 4; in Josiah Collins Papers, NCDA&H; U.S. War Department, Compiled Service Records of Volunteer Union Soldiers Who Served in Organizations from the State of North Carolina, NAMP 401, roll 1 and roll 3; Tarlton, "Somerset Place," p. 43.

8. Broadside in the form of a letter dated 24 Sept. 1862, written by Bryan Tyson, and A. K. Pearce to Bryan Tyson, 9 May 1864, in Bryan Tyson Papers, Duke.

9. Auman and Scarboro, "Heroes of America," pp. 327–45.

10. Nathan Stafford to Bryan Tyson, 13 Nov. 1864, Israel Lowdermilk to Gen. Wessels, 26 Dec. 1864, and A. K. Pearce to Bryan Tyson, 25 Nov. 1863 (see also Wm. Newant to his father, 11 June 1862), all in Bryan Tyson Papers, Duke.

11. William Newant to his father, 11 June 1862, John M. Tomlinson to Bryan Tyson, 25 Oct. 1863, and A. K. Pearce to Bryan Tyson, 25 Nov. 1863, all in Bryan Tyson Papers, Duke.

12. William T. Auman, "North Carolina's Inner Civil War: Randolph County," p. 131.

13. Escott, *After Secession*, p. 133. See also David L. Swain to Zebulon Vance,

26 Sept. 1864, in Vance Papers, NCDA&H.

14. *Salisbury Carolina Watchman*, 23 Mar. 1863.

15. Ibid.

16. Eric Hobsbawm, *Bandits*, p. 13.

17. Charles Tilly, "Charivaris, Repertoires, and Politics"; Natalie Zemon Davis, *Society and Culture in Early Modern France*, chaps. 4 and 5; see also Tilly, *Formation of National States in Western Europe*, chap. 6.

18. A. C. Cowles to "Dear Bro Calvin [Cowles]," 29 Mar. 1864, in Calvin J. Cowles Papers, NCDA&H; Escott, *After Secession*, p. 128.

19. Yearns and Barrett, *North Carolina Civil War Documentary*, p. 106; [?] to Miss Sarah J. Lenoir, 22 Jan. 1865, in Lenoir Family Papers, SHC, UNC-CH.

20. Jonathan Worth to Zebulon Vance, 3 Apr. 1863, in Hamilton, *Correspondence of Jonathan Worth*, 1:230–31; Col. Wm. F. Foushee to Captain Marmaduke Robins, 20 May 1863, Geo. Sipte [?] to S. [?] G. Worth, 4 Sept. 1863, Special Order No. 1, 12 Sept. 1863, Governor Vance to S. G. Worth, 12 Oct. 1863, and R. L. Gatlin to S. [?] G. Worth, 19 Oct. 1863, all in Marmaduke Robins Papers, SHC, UNC-CH; Auman, "North Carolina's Inner Civil War," chaps. 4 and 5.

21. D. G. W[orth] to [?], 30 Aug. 1863, and J. H. Foust to Zebulon Vance, Dec. 1863, in M. S. Robins Papers, SHC, UNC-CH; Anonymous to Governor Vance, Sept. 1864, and J. L. Henry to Governor Vance, 12 Aug. 1864, in Governor's Papers, Zebulon B. Vance, NCDA&H; Auman, "North Carolina's Inner Civil War," pp. 150–54.

22. Wm. Church and others to Governor Vance, 9 June 1864, and Wm. Horton and citizens of Watauga County to Governor Vance, 20 June 1864, in Governor's Papers, Zebulon B. Vance, NCDA&H; J. H. Haughton to Governor Vance, 9 Aug. 1864, in Vance Papers, NCDA&H.

23. W. F. Leath to Governor Vance, 11 Aug. 1864, and Thos. Miller to Vance, 22 Aug. 1864, in Governor's Papers, Zebulon B. Vance, NCDA&H; S. R. Hawley to Governor Vance, 8 Sept. 1864, in Governor's Papers, Zebulon B. Vance, NCDA&H; Geo. A. Foust to M. S. Robins, 6 Oct. 1864, and J. M. Odell to M. S. Robbins [*sic*], 17 Oct. 1864, in Marmaduke Robins Papers, SHC, UNC-CH; Jonathan Worth to [?], 8 Jan. 1865, in Hamilton, *Correspondence of Jonathan Worth*, 1:338; Ed. W. Jones to Governor Vance, 24 Jan. 1865, and A. C. Murdock to Zebulon Vance, 18 Feb. 1865, in Vance Papers, NCDA&H; S. S. Jackson to Jonathan Worth, 25 Feb. 1865, in Jonathan Worth Papers, NCDA&H; David Dick to R. P. Dick, 28 Feb. 1865, in Marmaduke Robins Papers, SHC, UNC-CH.

24. J. M. Worth to Jonathan Worth, 16 Feb. 1865, in Jonathan Worth Papers, NCDA&H; Louise Norwood to [?], [probably Apr. 1865], in Lenoir Family Papers, SHC, UNC-CH; Will Hicks to Governor Vance, 25 June 1864, in Governor's Papers, Zebulon B. Vance, NCDA&H; J. M. Hendrix to Mr. Coles, 22 Mar. 1865, in Calvin J. Cowles Papers, NCDA&H; D. MacRae to his brother, 17 Mar. 1865, in Hugh MacRae Papers, Duke; John C. MacRae to Don MacRae, 3 Apr. 1865, in Hugh MacRae Papers, Duke; Home Guard General Orders No. 1, 3 June 1865 (Edgecombe County), B. F. Knight Papers, Duke; Zebulon Vance to General Johnston, 28 Mar. 1865, and M. Q. Waddell and others to Zebulon Vance, 3 Mar. 1865, in Vance Papers, NCDA&H; Jonathan Worth to J. J. Jackson, 31 Mar. 1865, in Hamilton, *Correspondence of Jonathan Worth*, 1:373–75.

25. Harry Eckstein, "On the Etiology of Internal Wars," p. 134. Eckstein notes that internal war has taken a variety of forms, but its central feature is the fact that a resort to violence is the means to achieve some kind of change within a political system. The purpose of those waging internal war could be to change policies, officeholders, or a constitution, but whatever the purpose, all these goals could in theory be achieved without the use of violence. Eckstein adds that all varieties of internal war "presuppose certain capabilities for violence by those who make the internal war and a certain incapacity for preventing violence among those on whom it is made. All tend to scar societies deeply and to prevent the formation of consensus indefinitely."

26. Ibid., p. 144.

27. Ibid.

28. These percentages were calculated from population statistics in the U.S. Census returns for 1850 and 1860 and from election returns in John L. Cheney, Jr., *North Carolina Government, 1585–1974*.

29. See Paul D. Escott and Jeffrey J. Crow, "The Social Order and Violent Disorder."

30. "Some Account of the Trials and Travels that Thomas Hinshaw, with others, have had to pass through while kept in the Confederate Army. Written by Thomas Hinshaw, 5 August 1863," in Thomas Hinshaw Papers, Duke.

31. Schneider, "Institution of Slavery in North Carolina," pp. 31–40.

32. Nereus Mendenhall to Jonathan Worth, 31 Mar. 1866, in Hamilton, *Correspondence of Jonathan Worth*, 1:523–24; K. H. Trogden to Bryan Tyson, 9 Jan. 1865, in Bryan Tyson Papers, Duke.

33. Charity Robins or Sarah F. Robins [?] to Marmaduke Robins, 19 Sept. 1864, in Marmaduke Robins Papers, SHC, UNC-CH; W. P. Byrum to Zebulon Vance, 7 May 1864, in Vance Papers, NCDA&H; see also A. K. Pearce to Bryan Tyson, 21 May 1864, in Bryan Tyson Papers, Duke.

34. Escott, *After Secession*, p. 115.

35. Auman, "North Carolina's Inner Civil War," pp. 46–48, 92.

36. Escott, *After Secession*, pp. 113–22, and O. Goddin to Governor Vance, 27 Feb. 1863, quoted in Yearns and Barrett, *North Carolina Civil War Documentary*, pp. 97–99.

37. G. Holmes to Governor Vance, 20 June 1864, in Governor's Papers, Zebulon B. Vance, NCDA&H.

38. *State v. Thomas Dougan* for using language in favor of federal government, see Randolph County, Miscellaneous Civil War Records, NCDA&H; charges against William S. Ward, Barney Yeargin, Loton Williams, Alfred Kivett, and others in ibid.

39. Phebe Crook to Governor Vance, 15 Sept. 1864, in Governor's Papers, Zebulon B. Vance, NCDA&H.

40. Thos. S. Willborn to Calvin Cowles, 25 May 1864, in Calvin J. Cowles Papers, NCDA&H.

41. Eckstein, "On the Etiology of Internal Wars," p. 151.

42. J. W. Rawley to J. Cowles and C. J. Cowles, 8 Dec. 1864, in Calvin J. Cowles Papers, NCDA&H.

43. Thomas Settle to Zebulon Vance, 4 Oct. 1864, in Yearns and Barrett, *North

Carolina Civil War Documentary, pp. 103–5.

44. Phillip Shaw Paludan, *Victims*; A. K. Pearce to Bryan Tyson, 3 Dec. 1863, and H. K. Trogdon to Bryan Tyson, 3 Apr. 1864, also Alex K. Pearce to Tyson, 24 Oct. 1864, all in Bryan Tyson Papers, Duke; Auman, "North Carolina's Inner Civil War," p. 154; Paludan, *Victims*, pp. 21–22; Jonathan Worth to [?], in Hamilton, *Correspondence of Jonathan Worth*, 1:338.

45. Escott, *After Secession*, chap. 6, especially pp. 189–93; Emsley Beckerdite to M. S. Robins, 21 Jan. 1865, in Marmaduke Robins Papers, SHC, UNC-CH.

46. S. R. Hawly to Zebulon Vance, 8 Sept. 1864 in Governor's Papers, Zebulon B. Vance, NCDA&H (the location of this writer is given as Blockersville, but the author has not been able to determine its county); Mrs. Kate E. L. Virdin to Governor Vance, [Feb. or Mar. 1865], in Vance Papers, NCDA&H; John C. MacRae to Don MacRae, 3 Apr. 1865, in Hugh MacRae Papers, Duke; Home Guard General Orders No. 1, Tarboro, Edgecombe County, 3 June 1865, in B. F. Knight Papers, Duke.

47. Richard Anderson to Zebulon Vance, 19 Sept. 1864, and A. C. Cowles to Vance, 5 Oct. 1864, in Vance Papers, NCDA&H.

48. S. A. Sharpe, Colonel Commanding Forces, to Governor Vance, 5 and 14 Sept. 1864, and Anonymous to Governor Vance, Sept. 1864, in Governor's Papers, Zebulon B. Vance, NCDA&H (this concerns A. C. Cowles's county).

49. Yearns and Barrett, *North Carolina Civil War Documentary*, pp. 107–8.

50. Some of the best-known works on "moral economy of the crowd" are E. P. Thompson, *Whigs and Hunters*; E. P. Thompson, "Eighteenth Century Crime, Popular Movements and Social Control"; and Hobsbawm, "Social Criminality."

51. Ed. W. Jones to Governor Vance, 24 Jan. 1865, in Vance Papers, NCDA&H; Will Hicks to Governor Vance, 25 June 1864, in Governor's Papers, Zebulon B. Vance, NCDA&H; Louise Norwood to [?], [April 1865], in Lenoir Family Papers, SHC, UNC-CH; Rufus Lenoir Patterson to Mrs. L. M. Fries, Feb. 1865, in Patterson Papers, NCDA&H.

52. Rufus L. Patterson to Samuel Finley Patterson, 4 Mar. 1865, in Jones and Patterson Papers, SHC, UNC-CH; County Court Minutes, Caldwell County, "In Vacation," Mar. 1865; Samuel Finley Patterson to Rufus Lenoir Patterson, 19 Apr. 1865, in Patterson Papers, NCDA&H.

53. County Court Minutes, Caldwell County, resolution of special session called by Samuel Finley Patterson on 22 Apr. 1865.

54. J. M. Worth to Jonathan Worth, 16 Feb. 1865, in Jonathan Worth Papers, NCDA&H. For background see J. M. Worth to Governor Vance, 9 Aug. 1864, in Governor's Papers, Zebulon B. Vance, NCDA&H, and M. M. McMasters to M. S. Robins, 16 Feb. 1865, in Marmaduke Robins Papers, SHC, UNC-CH.

55. J. M. Worth to Jonathan Worth, 16 Feb. 1865, in Jonathan Worth Papers, NCDA&H; Jonathan Worth to John M. Worth, 20 Feb. 1865, in Hamilton, *Correspondence of Jonathan Worth*, 1:354–55; J. M. Worth to Jonathan Worth, 28 Feb. 1865, in Jonathan Worth Papers, NCDA&H; J. M. Worth to Jonathan Worth, 6 and 9 Mar. 1865, in Jonathan Worth Papers, NCDA&H.

56. Elvira Worth Jackson to Mrs. Worth, 16 Mar. 1865, in Jonathan Worth Papers, NCDA&H; Samuel Finley Patterson to Rufus Lenoir Patterson, 2 June 1865, in Patterson Papers, NCDA&H.

57. Gavin Wright, *Political Economy of the Cotton South*, pp. 36, 62–74.

58. E. Beckerdite to Marmaduke Robins, 21 Jan. 1865, in Marmaduke Robins Papers, SHC, UNC-CH. Beckerdite was the local postmaster.

59. Ibid.

60. John Shelton Reed, *One South*, chap. 13.

61. [I. H. Foust] to Jonathan Worth, 2 Mar. 1865, in Jonathan Worth Papers, NCDA&H. Foust was a merchant and cotton manufacturer (see Hamilton, *Correspondence of Jonathan Worth*, 1:74).

62. A. C. Cowles to Calvin Cowles, 18 Aug. 1863, in Calvin J. Cowles Papers, NCDA&H.

63. Schenck diary, p. 41 (Apr. or May 1865), SHC, UNC-CH; W. H. Jones to Zebulon Vance, 26 June 1865, in Vance Papers, NCDA&H; George P. Collins to Anne Cameron Collins, 5 June 1865, in Anne Collins Papers, SHC, UNC-CH.

64. R. C. Kise [?] to Wm. Lafayette Scott, 15 July 1865, in Wm. Lafayette Scott Papers, Duke; W. W. Holden to Archibold McSean, E. S. Pemberton, R. M. Orrell, K. R. Black, Jas. R. See, and M. McKrion, 16 June 1865, and S. H. Stilson to Commanding Officer, Fayetteville, 18 June 1865, in Governor's Papers, W. W. Holden, Letter Book, NCDA&H; Jonathan Worth to Mrs. J. J. Blankard, 30 Apr. 1866, in Hamilton, *Correspondence of Jonathan Worth*, 1:567.

CHAPTER 4

1. Samuel Finley Patterson to Rufus Lenoir Patterson, 15 May 1865, in Patterson Papers, NCDA&H; Jonathan Worth to James Kyle, 29 Oct. 1866, and to W. L. Springs, 22 Sept. 1866, in Hamilton, *Correspondence of Jonathan Worth*, 2:827, 791–92.

2. Jonathan Worth to Edward Bright, 12 and 15 Feb. 1867, W. H. Bagley to Parsley & Company, 28 Feb. 1867, and Worth to Rev. Drury Lacy, 21 Mar. 1867, in Hamilton, *Correspondence of Jonathan Worth*, 2:886–87, 904, 917–18. See related correspondence on pp. 901, 916, 927–28, 931–32, and 935.

3. A. Tilley to Samuel McDowell Tate, 20 Jan. 1868, in Samuel McDowell Tate Papers, SHC, UNC-CH; W. Hastings to Wm. J. Clarke, 15 May 1868, in William Clarke Papers, SHC, UNC-CH; F. Nash to Samuel A'Court Ashe, 11 Mar. 1867, in Samuel A'Court Ashe Papers, NCDA&H.

4. Resolution of Union meeting in Surry County, 6 June 1865, in William Lafayette Scott Papers, Duke.

5. Auman, "North Carolina's Inner Civil War," chap. 4; Auman and Scarboro, "Heroes of America," pp. 351–52; minutes of citizens' meeting, held at Asheboro Courthouse, 20 June 1865, in W. W. Holden Papers, NCDA&H; petition to M. Robins, 26 Jan. 1864, in Marmaduke Robins Papers, SHC, UNC-CH. The identity of magistrates was ascertained through county court records at NCDA&H, and data on their wealth holding came from the U.S. Census of 1860. Further information on Unionists and Confederates and their economic backgrounds and motives is in Auman, "Neighbor against Neighbor: The Inner Civil War in the Randolph County Area of Confederate North Carolina."

6. Paul C. Cameron to Thomas Ruffin, 27 Nov. 1865, Thomas Ruffin's applica-

tion for pardon, and Thomas Ruffin to E. J. Hale, 5 June 1866, all in Hamilton, *Papers of Thomas Ruffin*, 4:42, 16–21, 60–61; Jonathan Worth to B. G. Worth, 11 Sept. 1865, in Hamilton, *Correspondence of Jonathan Worth*, 1:417; R. J. Powell to W. W. Holden, 6 Sept. 1865, in Governor's Letter Book, W. W. Holden, NCDA&H. Paul Cameron put his losses at $700,000 in hard money in a letter to Samuel Finley Patterson, 25 Dec. 1865, in Jones and Patterson Papers, SHC, UNC-CH. In the same collection is a letter from Rufus Lenoir Patterson dated 12 Jan. 1865 [1866], in which he tells his father that Francis and Henry Fries lost three thousand bales of cotton or $600,000 in greenbacks.

7. W. W. Lenoir to Sarah J. Lenoir, 2 Jan. 1865, in Lenoir Family Papers, SHC, UNC-CH.

8. Calvin Wiley to Zebulon Vance, 24 Jan. 1865, in Vance Papers, NCDA&H.

9. Ibid.

10. *Raleigh Daily Sentinel*, 22 Aug. 1865.

11. Edgar Estes Folk and Bynum Shaw, *William Woods Holden*, pp. 101–2.

12. Jonathan Worth to Messrs. Long and Sherwood, 22 Mar. 1859, and Jonathan Worth to Wm. F. Fries, 15 Apr. 1859, in Hamilton, *Correspondence of Jonathan Worth*, 1:68–69, 71.

13. David L. Swain to Thomas Ruffin, 13 Nov. 1865, in Hamilton, *Papers of Thomas Ruffin*, 4:37–39.

14. Lossie [?] to Louis DeRosset, 30 June 1865, in DeRosset Family Papers, SHC, UNC-CH.

15. Schenck diary, 8 Sept. 1880, SHC, UNC-CH. In this diary entry Schenck recounts a conversation that he had with Holden.

16. W. W. Holden to Rufus Lenoir Patterson, 18 June 1865, in Patterson Papers, NCDA&H.

17. Information about Holden's appointments and about the personnel of earlier years was gleaned from the minutes of the county courts, which are on microfilm at NCDA&H. No records for the early months of presidential reconstruction survived in the case of Alamance County.

18. Ibid. See also minutes of citizens' meeting, held at Asheboro Courthouse, 20 June 1865, in W. W. Holden Papers, NCDA&H, and Auman and Scarboro, "Heroes of America," p. 352.

19. Proclamation by Provisional Governor W. W. Holden, 12 June 1865, in W. W. Holden Papers, NCDA&H; J. G. de Roulhac Hamilton, *Reconstruction in North Carolina*, pp. 151–52, 181.

20. W. W. Holden to Major General Cox, 26 June 1865, in Governor's Letter Book, W. W. Holden, NCDA&H; Holden to Justices of the Peace of the County of Yadkin, 13 Sept. 1865, ibid.; U.S. Major J. M. Prince to W. W. Holden, 12 Sept. 1865, ibid.; Jonathan Worth to J. C. Skeen, 9 Sept. 1865, in Hamilton, *Correspondence of Jonathan Worth*, 1:416–17; W. W. Holden to the Sheriff and Justices of the Peace of Randolph County, 16 Sept. 1865, in Governor's Letter Book, W. W. Holden, NCDA&H.

21. Samuel Finley Patterson to Rufus Lenoir Patterson, 7 and 17 Sept. 1865, in Patterson Papers, NCDA&H. For background on this election see C. C. [?] Jones to "Dear Cousin Rufus," 29 June 1865, and C. J. Cowles to Rufus Lenoir Patter-

son, 1 July [?] 1865, ibid. The following year Rufus became sick, decided to resign his seat in the convention, and proposed to his father that he take the place. This time Samuel Finley Patterson was challenged, but on a rainy day he prevailed, 121 votes to 35. See Rufus Lenoir Patterson to Samuel Finley Patterson, 17 Apr. 1866, Rufus Lenoir Patterson to "My dear Brother," 28 Apr. 1866, and Samuel Finley Patterson to Samuel L. Patterson, 20 May 1866, in Jones and Patterson Papers, SHC, UNC-CH.

22. Citizens of Cleveland County to W. W. Holden, 14 July 1865, and W. W. Holden to W. A. Albright, Clerk of Alamance County Court, 31 Aug. 1865, both in Governor's Letter Book, W. W. Holden, NCDA&H; William K. Boyd, *Memoirs of W. W. Holden*, p. 62.

23. Andrew Johnson to W. W. Holden (telegram), 22 Aug. 1865, and Holden's reply, 26 Aug. 1865, both in Governor's Letter Book, W. W. Holden, NCDA&H; Hamilton, *Reconstruction in North Carolina*, p. 117; R. J. Powell to W. W. Holden, 6 Sept. 1865, in Governor's Letter Book, W. W. Holden, NCDA&H.

24. David L. Swain to Thomas Ruffin, 15 Sept. 1865, and Nathaniel Boyden to Thomas Ruffin, 16 Sept. 1865, in Hamilton, *Papers of Thomas Ruffin*, 4:29, 31.

25. Evan Smith to W. W. Holden, [1865], in Governor's Papers, W. W. Holden, NCDA&H.

26. Jonathan Worth to J. L. Bason, 12 Aug. 1865, and to R. S. French, 18 Aug. 1865, both in Hamilton, *Correspondence of Jonathan Worth*, 1:388, 393–94 (see also pp. 413–14); Rufus Lenoir Patterson to Samuel Finley Patterson, 9 Oct. 1865, and Rufus Lenoir Patterson to his wife Mary, 10 Oct. 1865, in Jones and Patterson Papers, SHC, UNC-CH; S. S. Jackson to M. S. Robins, 11 Oct. 1865, in Marmaduke Robins Papers, SHC, UNC-CH. Rufus Lenoir Patterson suspected Holden of desiring repudiation. See Rufus Lenoir Patterson to Samuel Finley Patterson, 11 Oct. 1865, in Jones and Patterson Papers, SHC, UNC-CH.

27. *Raleigh Daily Sentinel*, 29 Aug., 27, 29, and 30 Sept., and 5 Oct. 1865. See also Otto H. Olsen and Ellen Z. McGrew, "Prelude to Reconstruction."

28. Hamilton, *Reconstruction in North Carolina*, p. 151; *Raleigh Daily Sentinel*, 5 Sept. and 8 Aug. 1865; Eric L. McKitrick, *Andrew Johnson and Reconstruction*, pp. 184–208; Hamilton, *Reconstruction in North Carolina*, pp. 130–31. As McKitrick points out, Andrew Johnson failed to give the South clear and correct signals in regard to what was required of the region. Before long he began to give the South quite an inaccurate idea of what the northern public expected of defeated Confederates.

29. Jonathan Worth to Calvin Wiley, 11 Aug. 1865, to D. Starbuck, 30 Aug. 1865, to John Pool and Lewis Thompson, 16 Oct. 1865, and to John Pool, 17 Oct. 1865, in Hamilton, *Correspondence of Jonathan Worth*, 1:387, 404–6, 429–31, 432; Folk and Shaw, *William Woods Holden*, pp. 201–2; Richard L. Zuber, *Jonathan Worth*, pp. 204–6.

30. E. E. Jackson to M. S. Robins, 23 Oct. 1865, in Marmaduke Robins Papers, SHC, UNC-CH; Jonathan Worth to C. B. Dibble, 27 Nov. 1865, and to F. E. Shober, 21 Oct. 1865, in Hamilton, *Correspondence of Jonathan Worth*, 1:454–55, 443.

31. Jonathan Worth to A. B. Hill, 6 Dec. 1865, in Hamilton, *Correspondence of*

Jonathan Worth, 1:455–56; Zuber, *Jonathan Worth*, pp. 207–8.

32. Jonathan Worth to Jesse G. Henshaw, 23 July 1863, in Hamilton, *Correspondence of Jonathan Worth*, 1:245–46; Andrews, *South Since the War*, p. 135; Lefler and Newsome, *North Carolina*, p. 485; R. D. W. Connor, *Manual of North Carolina*, pp. 999–1001.

33. Jonathan Worth to Thomas Ruffin, 18 Jan. 1866, in Hamilton, *Papers of Thomas Ruffin*, 4:48, and to R. R. Heath, 2 Apr. 1866, and to J. J. Jackson, 15 Apr. 1866, in Hamilton, *Correspondence of Jonathan Worth*, 1:524–25, 538–40. J. C. Harper of Burke County also expressed fear that the public favored debt repudiation; see a letter to Samuel Finley Patterson, 13 June 1866, in Jones and Patterson Papers, SHC, UNC-CH.

34. Calvin H. Wiley to Jonathan Worth, 30 March 1866, in Hamilton, *Correspondence of Jonathan Worth*, 1:520–21.

35. Information about Worth's appointments and about the personnel of earlier years was gleaned from the minutes of the county courts, which are on microfilm at NCDA&H.

36. Jonathan Worth to A. G. Foster, 28 Apr. 1866, in Hamilton, *Correspondence of Jonathan Worth*, 1:564–65; Gail W. O'Brien, "War and the Legal Fraternity," pp. 82–83, 178–79.

37. D. F. Caldwell to Jonathan Worth, 31 July 1866, in Hamilton, *Correspondence of Jonathan Worth*, 1:564–65 and 2:711–15.

38. Worried about Caldwell's disaffection, Worth wrote John A. Gilmer and urged that "the boys" treat Caldwell with more respect so that his talents could be gained for defeating the Radicals. See Jonathan Worth to John A. Gilmer, 8 Sept. 1866, ibid., 2:772, and O'Brien, "War and the Legal Fraternity," p. 179.

39. Jesse Parker Bogue, Jr., "Violence and Oppression in North Carolina during Reconstruction, 1865–1873," abstract and pp. 55–62, 84, 85–87, 100, 103, 127–29, 132, 197–98; Jonathan Worth to George Howard, 12 Jan. 1867, Jonathan Worth to W. T. Faircloth, 12 Jan. 1867, B. S. Hedrick to Jonathan Worth, 23 July 1866, A. S. Merrimon to Jonathan Worth, 7 June 1866, and D. F. Caldwell to Jonathan Worth, 31 July 1866, all in Hamilton, *Correspondence of Jonathan Worth*, 2:867, 867–68, 690–91, 1:601–2, and 2:711–15.

40. Andrews, *South Since the War*, pp. 116, 112; John Richard Dennett, *South as It Is, 1865–1866*, pp. 144–45.

41. Jonathan Worth to George Howard, 12 Jan. 1867, Worth to W. T. Faircloth, 12 Jan. 1867, B. S. Hedrick to Worth, 22 June 1866, and Worth to Hedrick, 25 July 1866, all in Hamilton, *Correspondence of Jonathan Worth*, 2:867–68, 870, 1:644–45, and 2:693–94.

42. B. S. Hedrick to Jonathan Worth, 22 June 1866, and Jonathan Worth to B. S. Hedrick, 4 July 1866, in Hamilton, *Correspondence of Jonathan Worth*, 1:644–45 and 2:665–67.

43. Hamilton, *Reconstruction in North Carolina*, p. 172.

44. Ibid., pp. 174–75; Andrews, *South Since the War*, p. 135.

45. Edward Conigland to Thomas Ruffin, 26 June 1866, in Hamilton, *Papers of Thomas Ruffin*, 4:61–62.

46. Thomas Ruffin to Edward Conigland, 2 July 1866, ibid., pp. 62–71.

47. Ibid.

48. Ibid.

49. *Raleigh Standard*, 1 Aug. 1866, anonymous author in *Old North State*, 24 July 1866, letter from B. F. Moore in *North Carolina Standard*, 12 Sept. 1866, and article by "Orange" in *Raleigh Daily Sentinel*, 30 July 1866, all in Hamilton, *Papers of Thomas Ruffin*, 4:107–14, 84–90, 120–30, 99–107.

50. Thomas Ruffin to Edward Conigland, 6 Aug. 1866, and article by William A. Allen of Kenansville in the *Wilmington Journal*, 23 July 1866, ibid., 4:114–16 and 80–84. For more information on conservative's fears, see Edward Conigland to Thomas Ruffin, 2 and 27 Aug. 1866, ibid., pp. 92–93, 118–20.

51. Hamilton, *Reconstruction in North Carolina*, p. 176, and Cheney, *North Carolina Government*, p. 844, for votes.

52. William Clark to Jonathan Worth, 18 Nov. 1866, in Hamilton, *Correspondence of Jonathan Worth*, 2:839–41.

53. E. J. Warren to Alfred E. Willard, 25 Aug. 1866, in Alfred E. Willard Papers, SHC, UNC-CH; Jonathan Worth to D. H. Starbuck, 29 Sept. 1866, and Jonathan Worth to J. J. Crawford, 5 Sept. 1866, in Hamilton, *Correspondence of Jonathan Worth*, 2:794–99, 761–63; Hamilton, *Reconstruction in North Carolina*, pp. 173, 181.

54. Weldon Edwards to Thomas Ruffin, 11 Oct. 1866, in Hamilton, *Papers of Thomas Ruffin*, 4:133; J. C. Harper to Samuel Finley Patterson, 13 June 1866, in Jones and Patterson Papers, SHC, UNC-CH; Matthias E. Manly to Thomas Ruffin, 4 Dec. 1866, in Hamilton, *Papers of Thomas Ruffin*, 4:136–37.

55. Schenck diary, 12 Aug. 1867, in SHC, UNC-CH.

56. W. F. Leak to Thomas Ruffin, 20 Jan. 1868, in Hamilton, *Papers of Thomas Ruffin*, 4:186–87 (emphasis added to "as well as to others"); Jonathan Worth to H. G. Leisering, 7 Jan. 1869, and Jonathan Worth to A. M. Tomlinson & Sons, 11 Apr. 1868, in Hamilton, *Correspondence of Jonathan Worth*, 2:1257, 1185.

57. Jonathan Worth to B. S. Hedrick, 2 June 1868, Jonathan Worth to William Clark, 16 Feb. 1868, Jonathan Worth to B. S. Hedrick, 11 May 1868, all in Hamilton, *Correspondence of Jonathan Worth*, 2:1218, 1154–56, 1200–1201. In his letter to Clark, Worth underlined his feelings about democratic tendencies by saying, "I use the word democratic in its proper—not its party—sense."

CHAPTER 5

1. Record Book of Manchester N. Weld, Agent, USBRFAL, Duke. The United States Census, 1860, Manuscript slave schedule for Moore County shows on page 16 the slaveholdings of W. D. Harrington. Of the twenty-one slaves listed, without names, two entries are the right age and sex for the boys Benjamin Harrington was concerned about, and other entries present likely parents although, again, no names are given.

2. Theodore Brantner Wilson, *Black Codes of the South*, pp. 24, 27.

3. *State v. Evans*, I Haywood N.C. 289, Apr. 1796, *State v. Farrier*, I Hawks 487, Dec. 1821, in Catterall, *Judicial Cases*, 2:13, 43.

4. *State v. Pemberton and Smith*, 2 Devereux 281, Dec. 1829, ibid., pp. 57–58; Rawick, *American Slave*, 14:362.

5. Catterall, *Judicial Cases*, p. 1.

6. Willie Lee Rose, *Documentary History of Slavery in North America*, pp. 219–24. In 1835, Superior Court Judge William Gaston rejected Ruffin's view in an opinion that overturned the conviction of a slave for murder of his overseer. Gaston declared, "It is confidently contended that a master [and by extension the overseer] has not, by the law of the land, the right to kill a slave for a simple act of disobedience, however provoking may be the circumstances under which it is committed."

7. Johnson, *Ante-Bellum North Carolina*, p. 543.

8. *State v. Woodman*, 3 Hawks 384, 1824, in Catterall, *Judicial Cases*, 2:48 upheld the 1794 act.

9. Catterall, *Judicial Cases*, p. 4.

10. Catterall, *Judicial Cases*, 2:31, case of *Richardson v. Saltar*. A higher court granted the plaintiff a new trial on the grounds that Saltar had no right to patrol by himself, but the decision of the jury is more revealing here of community sentiment.

11. *Tate v. O'Neal* in Catterall, *Judicial Cases*, 2:40–41.

12. *State v. Tackett*, ibid., pp. 39–40.

13. *State v. Jowers*, ibid., p. 151.

14. Andrews, *South Since the War*, p. 157; John Richard Dennett, *South as It Is*, pp. 115, 119, 120; Whitelaw Reid, *After the War*, p. 34; and Dennett, *South as It Is*, p. 133.

15. Andrews, *South Since the War*, pp. 181, 154; John T. Trowbridge, *Desolate South*, p. 312; Dennett, *South as It Is*, p. 157; Reid, *After the War*, p. 33.

16. Andrews, *South Since the War*, pp. 117–18; Dennett, *South as It Is*, pp. 109–11.

17. Dennett, *South as It Is*, pp. 119, 167–68, 146.

18. Ibid., pp. 180–81.

19. Wilson, *Black Codes*, p. 44.

20. Schenck diary, 18 June 1866, in SHC, UNC-CH; Lon Taylor to Samuel Finley Patterson [?], 12 Feb. 1866, in Jones and Patterson Papers, SHC, UNC-CH; Jonathan Worth to William Clark, 28 Dec. 1867, in Hamilton, *Correspondence of Jonathan Worth*, 2:1095–96. By May 1868 (pp. 1214–15), Worth feared that it would be "a long time" before black people died out. For evidence that such expectations were widespread in the South, see George M. Fredrickson, *Black Image in the White Mind*.

21. Jonathan Worth to W. F. Craig, 4 May 1866 and to B. G. Worth, 26 Dec. 1867, in Hamilton, *Correspondence of Jonathan Worth*, 1:570 and 2:1094–95; W. W. Lenoir to Sarah J. Lenoir, 2 Jan. 1865, and G. W. Harper to W. W. Lenoir, 21 Jan. 1866, in Lenoir Family Papers, SHC, UNC-CH.

22. Paul C. Cameron to Thomas Ruffin, 27 Nov. 1865, in Hamilton, *Papers of Thomas Ruffin*, 4:42 (see also R. M. Abbott to Thomas Ruffin, 7 Dec. 1865, ibid., p. 47); *Raleigh Daily Sentinel*, 21 Aug. 1865; Andrews, *South Since the War*,

pp. 157–58; Kemp P. Battle to Zebulon Vance, 19 Sept. 1865, in Vance Papers, NCDA&H.

23. The fragile and self-serving nature of planters' paternalism is also discussed in James L. Roark, *Masters Without Slaves*.

24. Paul C. Cameron to Thomas Ruffin, 11 May and 11 Aug. 1865, both in Hamilton, *Papers of Thomas Ruffin*, 3:451–52, 464; Paul C. Cameron to Tod R. Caldwell, 17 Aug. 1865, in Tod R. Caldwell Papers, SHC, UNC-CH.

25. Hamilton, *Papers of Thomas Ruffin*, 3:449–50.

26. Paul C. Cameron to Tod R. Caldwell, 17 Aug. 1865, in Tod R. Caldwell Papers, SHC, UNC-CH; Paul C. Cameron to Thomas Ruffin, 11 Aug. 1865, in Hamilton, *Papers of Thomas Ruffin*, 3:464; Paul Cameron to Thomas Ruffin, 27 Sept., 4 Oct., and 20 Nov. 1865, all in ibid., 4:33–34, 35, 40–41.

27. Paul C. Cameron to Samuel Finley Patterson, 25 Dec. 1865, in Jones and Patterson Papers, SHC, UNC-CH. Cameron used the word "family" in his letter to Tod R. Caldwell, 17 Aug. 1865, in Tod R. Caldwell Papers, SHC, UNC-CH. Jean Anderson's "Preliminary Report" on Stagville and the Cameron operations, available at NCDA&H, provides information on the white lessees. I also appreciate the assistance of Sydney Nathans, who is completing a study of the Cameron slaves and their descendants.

28. Rawick, *American Slave*, 15:334, 86.

29. John M. Morehead to Thomas Ruffin, 12 Oct. 1865, in Hamilton, *Papers of Thomas Ruffin*, 4:36–37; sharecropping terms of Thomas J. Lenoir, 27 May 1865, and Thomas J. Lenoir to Rufus T. Lenoir, 14 Aug. 1865, in Lenoir Family Papers, SHC, UNC-CH; Edward Conigland to Thomas Ruffin, 4 Dec. 1865, Jacob F. Cline to William K. Ruffin, 18 Mar. 1868, and R. M. Abbott to Thomas Ruffin, 25 Mar. 1868, all in Hamilton, *Papers of Thomas Ruffin*, 4:45, 195–96, 197–98.

30. Rufus Lenoir Patterson to Samuel Finley Patterson, 12 Jan. 1865 [1866], Jones and Patterson Papers, SHC, UNC-CH.

31. Rufus Lenoir Patterson to his daughter, 1 June 1872, in Samuel Finley Patterson Papers, Duke.

32. John MacRae to Don M. MacRae, 22 June 1865, in Hugh MacRae Papers, Duke; A. M. Waddell to Governor W. W. Holden, 18 June 1865, W. W. Holden to General J. [?] D. Cox, 22 June 1865, General Cox to W. W. Holden, 23 June 1865, and W. W. Holden to General Cox, 24 June 1865, all in Governor's Letter Book, W. W. Holden, NCDA&H; W. W. Holden to Mayor and Commissioners of Wilmington, 15 July 1865, in Governor's Letter Book, W. W. Holden, NCDA&H; L. L. Clements and J. Peace to Governor Jonathan Worth, 6 Aug. 1866, in Hamilton, *Correspondence of Jonathan Worth*, 2:731, 744–45; Manchester N. Weld to Col. M. Cogewell, 16 Sept. 1867, in Record Book of Manchester N. Weld, USBRFAL, Duke; Robert Vance to Zebulon Vance, 12 July 1865, in Vance Papers, NCDA&H.

33. Reid, *After the War*, p. 51; Dennett, *South as It Is*, p. 109; James A. Leach to Col. Whittlesey, 22 Sept. 1865, in USBRFAL, NAMP M 843, roll 8, Letters Received.

34. Circular no. 1, 16 Feb. 1866, USBRFAL, NAMP M 843, roll 20, Issuances; report from Raleigh Sub-District, 30 Oct. 1866, ibid., NAMP M 843, roll 22, Reports of Operations. This pattern was present in other states as well. See Escott, *Slavery Remembered,* p. 133, and Rebecca Scott, "The Battle Over the Child."

35. Circular no. 5, 16 Feb. 1867, USBRFAL, NAMP M 843, roll 20, Issuances; report from Plymouth, 25 Sept. 1867, ibid., NAMP M 843, roll 22, Reports of Operations (and see also report from New Bern, 30 Oct. 1866, ibid.); see also Friday Williams Freedman to Governor W. W. Holden, undated, Governor's Papers, W. W. Holden, NCDA&H, and Jonathan Worth to Daniel L. Russell, 29 and 31 Oct. 1866, and Daniel L. Russell to Jonathan Worth, 4 Nov. 1866, in Hamilton, *Correspondence of Jonathan Worth,* 2:827, 828, 832–33.

36. Roberta Sue Alexander, "North Carolina Faces the Freedmen," pp. 58, 50, 51.

37. Andrews, *South Since the War,* pp. 121–25. Frenise A. Logan in "Black and Republican" corrects Andrews on Harris's first name and prewar status.

38. Andrews, *South Since the War,* pp. 128–29.

39. Ibid., pp. 129–30; Dennett, *South as It Is,* pp. 175–76; Reid, *After the War,* p. 52.

40. Alexander, "North Carolina Faces the Freedmen," pp. 59, 64, 94.

41. Andrews, *South Since the War,* p. 161.

42. Card of B. F. Moore, candidate for constitutional convention, in *Raleigh Daily Sentinel,* 29 Aug. 1865.

43. *Raleigh Daily Sentinel,* 1, 11, 14, and 21 Sept. 1865.

44. Report from Raleigh, 13 Sept. 1865, USBRFAL, NAMP M 843, roll 22, Reports of Operations, and Col. E. Whittlesey to Maj. Clinton A. Cilley, 9 Aug. 1865, ibid., rolls 1–2, Letters Sent, report from Raleigh, 9 Oct. 1865, report from Henderson, 25 Dec. 1867, report from Capt. Bolenius, 28 July 1867, all in ibid., roll 22, Reports of Operations.

45. Report from Raleigh Sub-District, 30 Oct. 1866, USBRFAL, NAMP M 843, roll 22, Reports of Operations; Assistant Commissioner Bomford to General O. O. Howard, 6 Oct. 1866, ibid., rolls 1–2, Letters Sent.

46. Col. Whittlesey to Col. J. A. Campbell, 8 Jan. 1866, ibid., rolls 1–2, Letters Sent [emphasis added]; report from Raleigh Sub-District, 30 Oct. 1866, ibid., roll 22, Reports of Operations; Bogue, "Violence and Oppression," pp. 84, 100, 132; report of 5 Feb. 1867, USBRFAL, NAMP M 843, roll 33, Reports of Outrages and Arrests.

47. Report from Plymouth, 30 Sept. 1867, USBRFAL, NAMP M 843, roll 22, Reports of Operations; General Orders no. 75, 7 Aug. 1867, ibid., roll 20, Issuances.

48. 2 Aug. and 22 Dec. 1865 and 5 Apr. 1867, ibid., roll 5, Registers of Letters Received.

49. Bogue, "Violence and Oppression," p. 144; General Thomas H. Ruger to Governor W. W. Holden, 1 Aug. 1865 and reply of 14 Aug. 1865, in Governor's Letter Book, W. W. Holden, NCDA&H. The Reports of Operations, 7 Aug.

1865, also describe police brutality in Orange and Johnston counties, USBRFAL, NAMP M 843, roll 22.

50. Registers of Letters Received, entry for 19 Sept. 1865, also Col. E. Whittlesey to General O. O. Howard, 23 Mar. 1866, in Letters Sent, and reports from Raleigh Sub-District, 30 Oct. 1866, and from Lt. Thomas Hay in Warren Sub-District, 25 Sept. 1867, both in Reports of Operations, USBRFAL, NAMP M 843, rolls 5, 1–2, and 22 respectively.

51. Jonathan Worth to J. A. Worth, 30 Apr. 1866, Jonathan Worth to William A. Graham, 12 Jan. 1866, and William A. Graham to Jonathan Worth, 26 Jan. 1866, all in Hamilton, *Correspondence of Jonathan Worth*, 1:566–67, 467, 481–82.

52. B. F. Moore to Thomas Ruffin, 22 Sept. 1865, in Hamilton, *Papers of Thomas Ruffin*, 4:31; A. C. Cowles to Isaac Jarratt, 3 Dec. 1865, in Jarratt-Puryear Family Papers, Duke.

53. In *Public Laws of the State of North Carolina Passed by the General Assembly at the Session of 1866*, p. 99; Jonathan Worth to James L. Orr, 19 June 1866, in Hamilton, *Correspondence of Jonathan Worth*, 1:635; Wilson, *Black Codes*, pp. 105–7. Later in 1866 the convention had to remove the discrimination on rape and repeal six sections of the 1854 code.

54. J. H. Young to J. W. White, 5 Aug. 1867, in James W. White Papers, SHC, UNC-CH; Fredrick Lynn Childs to Samuel A'Court Ashe, 11 Jan. and 28 Oct. 1866, in Samuel A'Court Ashe Papers, NCDA&H.

55. Edward Conigland to Thomas Ruffin, 20 July 1886 [1866], in Hamilton, *Papers of Thomas Ruffin*, 4:76–77; Jonathan Worth to C. C. Clark, 1 Oct. 1866, and A. V. Sullivan to Jonathan Worth, 19 Sept. 1866, in Hamilton, *Correspondence of Jonathan Worth*, 2:806–7, 787–88; Weldon Edwards to Thomas Ruffin, 11 Oct. 1866, in Hamilton, *Papers of Thomas Ruffin*, 4:132–34.

56. Andrews, *South Since the War*, p. 154; Michael Les Benedict, *A Compromise of Principle*, p. 115; Jonathan Worth to Joel Lucas, 18 Feb. 1868, and Jonathan Worth to J. W. Martin, 31 Dec. 1867, in Hamilton, *Correspondence of Jonathan Worth*, 2:1158–60, 1097.

57. Richard Sutch and Roger Ransom, "Sharecropping: Market response or mechanism of race control?," pp. 51–70; Mary C. R. to "My dear sister," 17 July 1865, in Tod R. Caldwell Papers, SHC, UNC-CH; Kate Meares to her mother, 28 Mar. 1865, in DeRosset Family Papers, SHC, UNC-CH; Schenck diary, 24 July 1865 and Apr. 1865 (pp. 42–43), in SHC, UNC-CH; [?] DeRosset to Louis DeRosset, 20 June 1866, in DeRosset Family Papers, SHC, UNC-CH.

58. Mary C. R. to "My dear sister," 17 July 1865, in Tod R. Caldwell Papers, SHC, UNC-CH; Don MacRae to "Dear Julia" (his wife), 4 Sept. 1865, in Hugh MacRae Papers, Duke.

59. Schenck diary, 7 June 1865, SHC, UNC-CH; Escott, *Slavery Remembered*, pp. 143–48; Mary C. R. to "My dear sister," 17 July 1865, in Tod R. Caldwell Papers, SHC, UNC-CH; Herbert Gutman, *Black Family in Slavery & Freedom*, chap. 1; Mary Ann Starkey to Edward W. Kinsley, 7 Oct. 1864, Edward W. Kinsley Papers, Duke; memoir by Jane M. Cronly, "After the War," Cronly Family Papers, Duke; Kate Meares to Cousin, 18 May 1865, in DeRosset Family Papers,

SHC, UNC-CH; population figures from U.S. Census of Population for 1860 and 1870.

60. Don MacRae to "Dear Julia" (his wife), 4 Sept. 1865, in Hugh MacRae Papers, Duke; Schenck diary, p. 58 (headed "The close of 1865"), SHC, UNC-CH; printed Circular no. 3, 15 Aug. 1865, USBRFAL, in William Lafayette Scott Papers, Duke.

61. Alexander, "North Carolina Faces the Freedmen," pp. 658–64.

62. Schenck diary, 13 May 1866, SHC, UNC-CH; Mary L. Peabody to Edward W. Kinsley, 22 Mar. 1863, in Edward W. Kinsley Papers, Duke; report from Office of Superintendent of Education, 31 Oct. 1866, USBRFAL, NAMP M 843, roll 22, Reports of Operations.

63. Alexander, "North Carolina Faces the Freedmen," pp. 398–416.

64. Schenck diary, 14 June 1865 (also see 16 Aug. 1865), SHC, UNC-CH; M. C. Avery to Samuel Finley Patterson, 21 Feb. 1866, in Jones and Patterson Papers, SHC, UNC-CH.

65. Schenck diary, 13 Mar. and 1 Sept. 1866, and 1 Sept. 1868, in SHC, UNC-CH; Jonathan Worth to Thomas Ruffin, 29 Mar. 1867 and Jonathan Worth to William Clark, 26 Oct. 1867, in Hamilton, *Correspondence of Jonathan Worth*, 2:923–24, 1062–66.

CHAPTER 6

1. John L. Emmory to Amy Morris Bradley, 13 Feb. 1877, in Amy Morris Bradley Papers, Duke.

2. Record for Year 1867, entries for 17 and 30 Jan., 10 Feb., 2 Mar., and passim; Diary, Letterbook and Scrapbook, 1870–71, entry for 28 Nov. 1870; *The Lighthouse*, Nov. 1882; *The Lighthouse and Tileston Recorder*, Jan. 1885, all in Amy Morris Bradley Papers, Duke. Bradley encountered obstacles and grew discouraged, but she worked on in Wilmington until 1891, when ill health forced her to resign.

3. Testimony of Dr. John A. Moore in *State v. William Andrews et al.* and testimony of John W. Long in *State v. Thomas Gray*, in Ku Klux Klan Papers, Duke.

4. H. H. Foster to Major General N. A. Miles, 16 May 1867, in Hamilton, *Correspondence of Jonathan Worth*, 2:956–57; William K. Ruffin to Samuel A'Court Ashe, 7 Feb. 1867, in Samuel A'Court Ashe Papers, NCDA&H; and Jonathan Worth to William A. Graham, 27 Feb. 1868, in Hamilton, *Correspondence of Jonathan Worth*, 2:1165–67.

5. J. J. Jackson to Jonathan Worth, 9 Aug. 1866, in Hamilton, *Correspondence of Jonathan Worth*, 2:739–43; Schenck diary, June 1867, p. 83, in SHC, UNC-CH; Braxton Craven to Jonathan Worth, 6 June 1867, in Hamilton, *Correspondence of Jonathan Worth*, 2:976; petition to William W. Holden, 2 May 1868, in W. W. Holden Papers, NCDA&H; W. A. Patterson to Governor W. W. Holden, in Governor's Papers, W. W. Holden, NCDA&H.

6. M. McRae to Jonathan Worth, 16 May 1867, in Hamilton, *Correspondence of*

Jonathan Worth, 2:952–54, and W. F. Leak to Jonathan Worth, 23 May 1867, in ibid., pp. 963–64; J. M. Edmunds to J. Henry Harris, 26 Mar. 1867, in James Henry Harris Papers, NCDA&H; *Raleigh Republican*, 30 Nov. 1867, clipping in Charles N. Hunter Papers, Duke; Schenck diary, 24 May 1867, SHC, UNC-CH.

7. Jonathan Worth to W. H. McRae, 9 Sept. 1867, to B. G. Worth, 28 June 1867, and to A. M. Tomlinson, 26 Sept. 1867, in Hamilton, *Correspondence of Jonathan Worth*, 2:1047–48, 987–88, 1050–51.

8. Jonathan Worth to B. S. Hedrick, 26 Feb. 1867, to James L. Orr, 22 Feb. 1867, to his brother, 8 May 1867, to R. P. Dick, 7 July 1867, to B. S. Hedrick, 8 July 1867, to General D. E. Sickles, 9 July 1867, to D. G. Worth, 24 Oct. 1867, to J. C. Pass, 25 Oct. 1867, to William A. Graham, 28 Oct. 1867, to James Rush, 25 Mar. 1868, to A. M. Tomlinson & Sons, 11 Apr. 1868, all in ibid., 2:899–900, 897, 949, 995–96, 996–97, 999–1000, 1058–59, 1061–62, 1066–67, 1174, 1185 (see also his letters to Thomas Ruffin, 23 Mar. 1867, and to William A. Graham, 3 Jan. 1867, ibid., 4:175, and 2:848–49). In December 1866 W. W. Holden recognized that "the present State governments will be obliterated." See W. W. Holden to his wife, 9 Dec. 1866, in W. W. Holden Papers, NCDA&H.

9. A. M. McDonald, Alex McDonald, James R. McDonald, Alexander Hodge [?], and John W. McDonald to W. W. Holden, 10 May 1868, in W. W. Holden Papers, NCDA&H; Hamilton, *Reconstruction*, pp. 79, 200, 223, 262–63.

10. William P. Heath to W. W. Holden, 29 June 1868, in W. W. Holden Papers, NCDA&H; John Hays H. O. A. to Holden, 7 Oct. 1868, in Governor's Papers, W. W. Holden, NCDA&H; Lucius M. Duckworth to Tod R. Caldwell, 22 Nov. 1868, in Tod R. Caldwell Papers, SHC, UNC-CH.

11. E. J. Warren to Alfred E. Willard, 7 Oct. 1866, in Alfred E. Willard Papers, SHC, UNC-CH; Henry T. Clark to Jonathan Worth, 6 May 1867, in Hamilton, *Correspondence of Jonathan Worth*, 2:944–46; E. G. Reade to Mary Bayard Clarke, 20 July 1868, in William J. Clarke Papers, SHC, UNC-CH. Records of the County Court and County Commissioners in Edgecombe County show that William H. Knight, Robert Norfleet, and John Norfleet managed to stay in office.

12. William J. Clarke Diary, entries in 1868 for 10 Mar., 2 and 26 May, 23, 27, and 28 June, 12, 14, and 20 July, 5, 13, 17, and 26 Aug., and 24 Dec.; also notes for a speech on back of a letter page, all in SHC, UNC-CH.

13. Hamilton, *Reconstruction*, pp. 253, 265–70, and 273–78.

14. Quoted in M. C. S. Noble, *History of the Public Schools of North Carolina*, pp. 290–91. Hood gave another reason for his stand, a reason that proved prescient. "Make this distinction in your organic law," he said, "and in many places the white children will have good schools at the expense of the whole people, while the colored people will have none or but little worse than none. If the schools are to be free to all, the colored children will be insured good schools in order to keep them out of white schools."

15. Ibid., pp. 286, 349, and *Wilmington Journal*, 27 Mar. 1868. Hamilton rightly points out that General Canby's regulations disfranchised eleven thousand white voters (see pages 286 and 236), but that disfranchisement did not cause the Conservative defeat—the cooperation of black and white Republican voters did. Because New Hanover records were missing, the names of county commissioners

were taken from *Branson's North Carolina Business Directory*, editions for 1869, 1872, and 1877–78. Tax lists for 1856, 1865–66, 1869, 1871, and 1877 were found and utilized. The wealth of some of the new commissioners rose during Reconstruction, and for that reason both initial and overall averages are described.

16. Tax lists were consulted if they existed, but almost all of the data on wealth came from manuscript census records for 1860 and 1870. The commissioners were Austin C. Cobb, John Crawford (no data found), John W. McCauley, Samuel J. Crawford, and Simpson F. Vestal in Alamance County; McCaleb Coffey, C. W. Clarke, R. G. Tuffle, Allen Laxton (no data), and Lewis S. Hartley in Caldwell; Robert Norfleet, R. M. Johnson, Thomas Newton, Benjamin Norfleet, and William H. Knight in Edgecombe; and B. A. Sellars, Obed Osborne, J. A. Blair, J. H. Johnson, and John Robbins in Randolph. The commissioners already described for New Hanover were E. M. Shoemaker, James Wilson, Rufus Garris, Stephen Keys, and Elijah Hewlett.

17. It was not coincidental that the areas of Republican strength in the piedmont and mountains corresponded to areas of previous disaffection with the Confederate government. For an analysis of these voting patterns, see Allen W. Trelease, "Who Were the Scalawags?," especially pp. 132–39 and the map on p. 135, which shows considerable white Republican strength in such piedmont counties as Randolph, Moore, Montgomery, Cleveland, Chatham, Alamance, Lincoln, Guilford, and Mecklenburg.

18. Board of County Commissioners, Minutes, Alamance County, NCDA&H, 26 Sept., 15 and 16 Oct., and 16 Dec. 1868, 9 Jan. and 7 Aug. 1869.

19. Ibid., 16 Dec. 1868, 15 Nov. 1869, and 17 Jan. 1870.

20. Schenck diary, 22 Mar. 1869, March 1867, and 22 Mar. 1872, in SHC, UNC-CH.

21. Weldon N. Edwards to Thomas Ruffin, 15 Mar. 1867, in Hamilton, *Papers of Thomas Ruffin*, 4:172; *Wilmington Journal*, 29 Nov. 1867, 24 Jan., 10 Oct., and 7 Feb. 1868.

22. *Tarboro Weekly Enquirer*, 25 Nov. 1871.

23. Sade [Sarah J.] Lenoir to Walter W. Lenoir, 3 Nov. 1866, in Lenoir Family Papers, SHC, UNC-CH.

24. Schenck diary, 21 Nov. 1868, SHC, UNC-CH; Richmond Pearson to William Lafayette Scott, 16 July 1868, in William Lafayette Scott Papers, Duke; petition of Allison Winckoff, dated 30 Nov. 1869, in Rowan County Estate Papers, NCDA&H (the author thanks Terrell Armistead Crow for bringing this document to his attention); Schenck diary, 1 Jan. and 21 Nov. 1868, SHC, UNC-CH.

25. W. [?] Ray to Samuel McDowell Tate, 4 June 1867, in Samuel McDowell Tate Papers, SHC, UNC-CH; W. F. Leak to Thomas Ruffin, 17 Mar. 1868, in Hamilton, *Papers of Thomas Ruffin*, 4:193–94; George Washington Finley Harper Diary, 15 Aug. 1867, in George Washington Finley Harper Papers, SHC, UNC-CH; Jonathan Worth to W. F. Leak, 5 Jan. 1867, in Hamilton, *Correspondence of Jonathan Worth*, 2:859–60; Schenck diary, 4 Jan. 1867, also spring 1869, p. 133, SHC, UNC-CH; *Wilmington Journal*, 6 Mar. 1868; Jonathan Worth to Joel Lucas, 18 Feb. 1868, in Hamilton, *Correspondence of Jonathan Worth*, 2:1158–60.

26. True Bill of grand jury in Halifax County Court of Pleas and Quarter Sessions, Feb. 1868, in John Devereux Papers, NCDA&H; Schenck diary, 24 Mar. 1868, SHC, UNC-CH.

27. Yeomen were still clinging to their tradition of subsistence farming, avoiding the cash-crop economy that would put their self-reliant status at risk. U.S. Census figures for 1870 show that the level of production of most crops had fallen compared to 1860. Cotton planters managed to maintain virtually the same output, but two other important cash crops, rice and tobacco, had fallen to approximately one-third of the 1860 level. Food crops also had fallen, though not quite as drastically.

28. "Many Republicans" of Thomasville, Davidson County, to Governor W. W. Holden, 13 July 1868, in Governor's Papers, W. W. Holden, NCDA&H; Rufus Lenoir Patterson to his wife, 21 Feb. 1868, in Jones and Patterson Papers, SHC, UNC-CH; C. C. Jones to Tod R. Caldwell, 27 Feb. 1868, in Tod R. Caldwell Papers, SHC, UNC-CH.

29. Jonathan Worth to William A. Graham, 27 Feb. 1868, in Hamilton, *Correspondence of Jonathan Worth*, 2:1165–67; Otto H. Olsen, "The Ku Klux Klan: A Study in Reconstruction Politics and Propaganda," p. 351; *Wilmington Journal*, 28 and 22 Feb. 1868; Silas N. Stilwell to Governor W. W. Holden, 14 July 1868, in Governor's Papers, W. W. Holden, NCDA&H; R. B. Bogle to Tod R. Caldwell, 16 Nov. 1868, in Tod R. Caldwell Papers, SHC, UNC-CH.

30. Schenck diary, 28 Apr. 1868, SHC, UNC-CH; Eugene Morehead Diary, pp. 34–35, SHC, UNC-CH; see also the testimony to the U.S. Senate of T. F. Lee, who said, "A man differing in political sentiment from the old inhabitants there, was to a great extent, ostracised in his business, and almost excluded from society." Asked to explain what he meant by "old inhabitants," Lee answered: "I mean what is called the best society in the country . . . the intelligent and educated portion of our community." U.S. Congress, Senate Reports, 42d Congress, 1st session, report no. 1, p. 72.

31. John C. MacRae to Don MacRae, 17 Mar. 1867, in Hugh MacRae Papers, Duke.

32. *Wilmington Journal*, 29 Aug. 1868; *Tarboro Southerner*, 27 Aug. 1868; *Wilmington Journal*, 21 Feb. and 27 Mar. 1868.

33. Miles Welch to Governor W. W. Holden, 12 Sept. 1868, Governor's Papers, W. W. Holden, NCDA&H; *Tarboro Southerner*, 27 Aug. 1868; *Wilmington Journal*, 1 Nov. 1867, 7 Aug. 1868; O. A. Giles to W. W. Holden, 23 June 1868, Holden Papers, NCDA&H; John Pool to W. W. Holden, 9 May 1868, Holden Papers, NCDA&H. Of course, blacks were economically dependent elsewhere, as shown by a threat appearing in the *Salisbury Examiner*, 30 June 1869: "You have to look to Democrats for labor and for bread."

34. Deposition of Henry Baker, 24 Sept. 1868, Governor's Papers, W. W. Holden, NCDA&H. In the restricted space of a city like Wilmington, superior white resources were potentially effective; over a large countryside in which whites were in the minority, violence was unreliable. Allen W. Trelease notes in *White Terror*, pp. 189–91, that in the east the Klan usually went by the name Constitutional Union Guard.

35. See Gordon B. McKinney, "Southern Mountain Republicans and the Negro, 1865–1900." McKinney points out that anti-Negro attitudes were prevalent in the mountains.

36. J. R. Bulla to Governor W. W. Holden, 15 July 1868, Governor's Papers, NCDA&H (see also E. Fullings to Holden, 15 July 1868, J. W. Schenck, Jr., to Holden, 15 July 1868, and John Frey to Holden, 16 July 1868, all in ibid.); John W. Stephens to Governor W. W. Holden, 20 June 1868, and Jordan Chambers to W. W. Holden, 20 May 1868, both in Holden Papers, NCDA&H; Henry Little to W. W. Holden, 27 June 1868, Governor's Papers, NCDA&H.

37. Anonymous to W. W. Holden, n.d., Governor's Papers, W. W. Holden, NCDA&H.

38. U.S. Congress, Senate Reports, 42d Congress, 2d sess., no. 41, pt. 2, pp. 89–99.

39. Testimony of Dr. John A. Moore in *State v. William Andrews et al.*, Ku Klux Klan Papers, Duke; Trelease, *White Terror*, p. 202.

40. Testimony of John W. Long, 30 Aug. 1870, in *State v. Thomas W. [?] Gray*, Ku Klux Klan Papers, Duke.

41. Testimony of William Tickel in *State v. William Lowe [?] et al.* and testimony of John W. Long, 29 Aug. 1870, in *State v. W. C. Tarpley et al.*, ibid.

42. U.S. Congress, Senate Reports, 42d Cong., 2d sess., no. 41, pt. 2, p. 136; Ku Klux Klan Papers, passim, Duke; Robert M. Martin to W. W. Holden, 25 May 1868, Holden Papers, NCDA&H; Bogue, "Violence and Oppression," pp. 212–56; Trelease, *White Terror*, pp. 205, 213–14; Olsen, "Ku Klux Klan"; Schenck diary, 1 Mar. 1881, SHC, UNC-CH.

43. The author agrees here with Olsen, "Ku Klux Klan"; U.S. Congress, Senate Reports, 42d Congress, 2d sess., no. 41, pt. 2, pp. 72–82, 13–14, 118, 146, 112, 82–84, 132–33.

44. U.S. Congress, Senate Reports, 42d Cong., 2d sess., no. 41, pt. 2, pp. 136–39, 13–14, 9; Testimony of Sandy Sellers, *State v. William Andrews et al.*, Ku Klux Klan Papers, Duke; U.S. Congress, Senate Executive Documents, 42d Cong., 1st sess., testimony of Alonzo B. Corliss, Report no. 1, pp. 144–50.

45. U.S. Congress, Senate Reports, 42d Cong., 2d sess., no. 41, pt. 2, p. 48; Testimony of John W. Long, 29 Aug. 1870, in *State v. W. C. Tarpley et al.*, testimony of John W. Long, 30 Aug. 1870, in *State v. Thomas W. [?] Gray*, testimony of Dr. John A. Moore in *State v. William Andrews et al.*, testimony of William Tickel in *State v. William Lowe [?] et al.*, testimony of James E. Boyd in *State v. William Andrews et al.*, all in Ku Klux Klan Papers, Duke.

46. Testimony of James E. Boyd in *State v. William Andrews et al.*, testimony of John W. Long in *State v. W. C. Tarpley et al.*, testimony of John W. Long, 30 Aug. 1870, in *State v. Thomas W. [?] Gray*, testimony of James E. Boyd in *State v. William Andrews et al.*, all in Ku Klux Klan Papers, Duke.

47. John L. Cheney, Jr., *North Carolina Government, 1585–1974*, pp. 1035–36; testimony of Capt. Elis P. Euliss and testimony of James E. Boyd in *State v. William Andrews et al.*, testimony of John W. Long, 29 Aug. 1870, in *State v. W. C. Tarpley et al.*, and testimony of Peter Hughes in *State v. Thos. W. Gray*, all in Ku Klux Klan Papers, Duke.

48. U.S. Congress, Senate Reports, 42d Cong., 2d sess., no. 41, pt. 2, pp. 29, 89–99, 136, 139, 141–43, 159; Olsen, "Ku Klux Klan," pp. 354, 360. Gail O'Brien found the same pattern in Guilford County. See O'Brien, "War and the Legal Fraternity," pp. 235–37, n.43.

49. U.S. Congress, Senate Reports, 42d Congress, 2d sess., no. 41, pt. 2, pp. 30, 123–25, 144, 146, 212, 363–64, 386; testimony of James E. Boyd and testimony of Dr. John A. Moore in *State v. William Andrews et al.*, Ku Klux Klan Papers, Duke; Olsen, "Ku Klux Klan," p. 358.

50. U.S. Congress, Senate Reports, 42d Cong., 1st sess., no. 1, p. 10; the data presented on the individuals listed were compiled by drawing up a list of klansmen (and their offices in the organization), as identified in the two Senate reports cited and in the Ku Klux Klan Papers at Duke, and by comparing that list with a list of officials, drawn from county court records, Cheney, *North Carolina Government*, and from *Branson's North Carolina Business Directory*.

51. Testimony of Capt. Elis P. Euliss and of James E. Boyd in *State v. William Andrews et al.*, Ku Klux Klan Papers, Duke.

52. These data were gathered by using the lists described in note 50 in conjunction with the manuscript census records of the United States for 1860 and 1870. The adjacent listings in the manuscript census of some klansmen suggest that their farms adjoined each other.

53. Testimony of William R. Tickel, 2 Sept. 1870, in state's case against several individuals for assaulting William Long, colored, in October 1869, and testimony of John W. Long, 30 Aug. 1870, in *State v. Thomas W. [?] Gray*, both in Ku Klux Klan Papers, Duke.

54. W. A. Patterson to Governor W. W. Holden, 14 Mar. 1870, and Paul R. Hambrick to Holden, 12 Mar. 1870, both in Governor's Papers, W. W. Holden, NCDA&H; Joel Asheworth to Governor W. W. Holden, 28 Oct. 1870, U.S. Congress, Senate Reports, 42d Cong., 1st sess., no. 1, p. 64. On 20 Mar. 1870, David Schenck confidently had predicted, "Radicalism is doomed in this State now; the summer solstice will be fatal to it." Schenck diary, SHC, UNC-CH.

55. Edward W. Kinsley to Governor John Andrew of Massachusetts, 9 Feb. 1864, in Edward W. Kinsley Papers, Duke; Richard L. Zuber, *North Carolina During Reconstruction*, pp. 20–21; Hamilton, *Reconstruction in North Carolina*, chap. 11; Schenck diary, 28 Dec. 1868, SHC, UNC-CH; C. C. Jones to Governor W. W. Holden, 11 Mar. 1870, in Governor's Papers, W. W. Holden, NCDA&H.

For illustrations of the widespread interest in railroads see Schenck diary, 18 May 1873, SHC, UNC-CH, and various correspondence between Rufus Lenoir Patterson and his father in the Jones and Patterson Family Papers, SHC, UNC-CH. Another typical sentiment was voiced by Joseph Addison Worth to Jonathan Worth on 14 June 1866: "This town must go down to a poor affair if the Western [Rail]road is not extended to Greensboro." Hamilton, *Correspondence of Jonathan Worth*, 1:622–24.

56. W. A. Patterson to Governor W. W. Holden, 14 Mar. 1870, in Governor's Papers, W. W. Holden, NCDA&H.

57. Quoted in *Salisbury Examiner*, 18 Aug. 1869, also 18, 20, and 30 Aug. and 8 Oct. 1869.

58. State tax data was culled from *Public Laws of North Carolina*, volumes covering 1858–75, also 1879; county tax data was taken from Minutes of the Boards of County Commissioners—for Alamance County, 1869–83; Edgecombe County, 1869–80; Caldwell County, 1870–80; and Randolph County, 1874–76, 1880. Records for 1869 were missing for Caldwell County; for 1869–73 and 1877–79 for Randolph; and no records for the period survived for New Hanover County.

Republican support for taxes was stronger than Democratic support, as shown in Allen W. Trelease, "Republican Reconstruction in North Carolina: A Roll-Call Analysis of the State House of Representatives, 1868–1870." Hamilton, *Reconstruction in North Carolina*, p. 277, is misleading about the homestead exemption. The 1866–67 legislature did establish a homestead exemption, but it was only $100 on personal property and $250 for the maimed and for widows.

59. Board of County Commissioners for Alamance, Edgecombe, Caldwell, and Randolph counties; Mother to [?], 12 Jan. 1868, in DeRosset Family Papers, SHC, UNC-CH; *Wilmington Journal*, 5 June 1868; [?] to Tod R. Caldwell, 3 Aug. 1871, in Tod R. Caldwell Papers, SHC, UNC-CH.

60. E. J. Warren to "Friend Willard," 21 Sept. 1867, in Alfred E. Willard Papers, SHC, UNC-CH; John Alfred Williams to Governor W. W. Holden, 24 Apr. 1868, in Holden Papers, NCDA&H.

61. W. A. Patterson to Governor W. W. Holden, 14 Mar. 1870, and Robert Yell to Governor W. W. Holden, 12 Mar. 1870, both in Governor's Papers, W. W. Holden, NCDA&H.

62. The letter of Paul R. Hambrick to Governor W. W. Holden, 12 Mar. 1870, in Governor's Papers, W. W. Holden, NCDA&H, illustrated the kind of appeal that must have put Holden under pressure to act.

63. Hamilton, *Reconstruction in North Carolina*, pp. 483, 485–86; Zuber, *North Carolina During Reconstruction*, p. 33; William L. Scott to his wife, 3 July 1870, to "My dear Payne," 18 July 1870, and to his wife, Ella, 21 July 1870, in William Lafayette Scott Papers, Duke.

64. William L. Scott to his wife, Ella, 21 July 1870, in William Lafayette Scott Papers, Duke; D. MacRae to "Dear Brother," 23 July 1870, in Hugh MacRae Papers, Duke.

65. William J. Clarke to Willie, 9 Sept. 1870, in family papers owned by Mrs. Graham Barden and generously made available to the author; Schenck diary, August 1870, SHC, UNC-CH; John K. Ruffin to William K. Ruffin, 23 Aug. 1870, in Hamilton, *Papers of Thomas Ruffin*, 4:233; testimony of E. M. Holt, U.S. Congress, Senate Reports, 42d Cong., 1st sess., no. 1, pp. 251–56.

66. Silas L. Curtin and fifteen others to Governor W. W. Holden, 11 Oct. 1868, in Governor's Papers, W. W. Holden, NCDA&H; C. Happoldh [?] to Tod R. Caldwell, 29 Nov. 1868, in Tod R. Caldwell Papers, SHC, UNC-CH.

67. Schenck diary, August 1870, SHC, UNC-CH; Hamilton, *Reconstruction in North Carolina*, pp. 521–22, 537–58, and 558 (quotation).

As the 1870s advanced, the term "Democrat" became standard instead of Conservative. Before that time, however, the Conservative label was useful for a number of reasons. It made cooperation with Democrats more palatable for former Whigs, and sometimes could be used to signal to voters that candidates were former Whigs instead of Democrats. Both terms had some currency.

68. Hamilton, *Reconstruction in North Carolina*, pp. 565, 567; Schenck diary, pp. 231–32; J. W. Berry to Tod R. Caldwell, 21 Feb. 1871, and Charles I. Grady to Caldwell, 24 Feb. 1871, in Tod R. Caldwell Papers, SHC, UNC-CH.

69. Hamilton, *Reconstruction in North Carolina*, pp. 563, 571, 591–93; Zuber, *North Carolina During Reconstruction*, p. 47.

70. *Tarboro Weekly Enquirer*, 30 Sept. 1871; *Wilmington Journal*, 19 Aug. 1870; John L. Holmes to Samuel A'Court Ashe, 2 Apr. 1872, in Samuel A'Court Ashe Papers, NCDA&H.

71. Schenck diary, p. 234 (about 4 Aug. 1871), and 4 July 1872.

72. *Raleigh Weekly Republican*, 2 July 1874; Charles N. Hunter to the editor of the *New National Era*, clipping in Charles N. Hunter Papers, Duke; *Alamance Gleaner*, 16 Feb. 1875.

73. R. Y. McAden to Samuel McDowell Tate, 20 Feb. 1875, in Samuel McDowell Tate Papers, SHC, UNC-CH.

74. Hamilton, *Reconstruction in North Carolina*, pp. 605–6.

75. *Alamance Gleaner*, 27 July, 20 Apr., and 22 June 1875.

76. Ibid., 15 and 22 June, and 20 and 27 July 1875. For a spirited Republican rejoinder, see the *Monroe Enquirer*, 20 July 1875.

77. Ibid., 27 July and 10 and 17 Aug. 1875; Hamilton, *Reconstruction in North Carolina*, p. 635.

78. *Amendments to the Constitution of North Carolina Proposed by the Constitutional Convention of 1875*; Hamilton, *Reconstruction in North Carolina*, p. 643.

79. These data were compiled from examination of county court minutes and minutes of the succeeding Boards of County Commissioners for the counties named. In the case of Randolph County, records for congressional Reconstruction existed only for 1869, 1872, and 1874–76; similarly, for New Hanover County the only surviving records of the commission era were for 1868, 1871, and 1876.

80. Data on occupations were drawn from manuscript census reports.

81. *Lexington Central*, 2 Sept. 1876; *Roan Mountain Republican* (in Bakersville, N.C.), 8 July 1876. On 29 July 1876, the *Roan Mountain Republican* asked, "Union Men are you willing to vote for the men who wished to destroy your property and drag you from your homes?"

82. *Albemarle Stanly Banner*, 1 June 1876; *Raleigh Daily Sentinel* quoted in *Randolph Regulator*, 5 Apr. 1876; *Randolph Regulator*, 16 Aug. 1876 and the *Raleigh Daily Sentinel* quoted in this same issue.

83. *Albemarle Times* quoted in *Albemarle Stanly Banner*, 28 Sept. 1876; "Supplement White Slavery in North Carolina—Degradation Worse Than Death," in Vance Papers, NCDA&H; *Albemarle Stanly Banner*, 5 Oct. 1876.

84. Schenck diary, 25 June 1876; Hamilton, *Reconstruction in North Carolina*, p. 654.

85. Frenise Logan, *Negro in North Carolina, 1876–1894*, pp. 49–50.

CHAPTER 7

1. *Wilmington Journal*, 20 Aug. and 8 Oct. 1875, 27 and 6 Oct. 1876.

2. *Raleigh Daily Sentinel*, 4 June 1875 and 16 Mar. 1872.

3. Paul M. Gaston, *New South Creed*, chap. 2, especially pp. 48–54.

4. Ibid., chap. 1.

5. S. P. Smith to his wife, 22 Jan. 1888, in Simpson-Biddle Family Papers, NCDA&H.

6. John Milton Cooper, Jr., *Walter Hines Page*, pp. xix–xxi, 69, 78.

7. Speech to a boys' graduating class, undated, by Richmond Pearson, in Richmond Pearson Papers, SHC, UNC-CH; speech by Major W. M. Robbins, quoted in the *Lenoir Topic*, 14 June 1882.

8. *Lenoir Topic*, 11 Apr. 1883, 13 Feb. and 26 Mar. 1884, and 4 Oct. 1882; *Caldwell Messenger*, 25 Sept. 1875; *Littleton Courier*, 1 Sept. 1892; *Monroe Enquirer*, 22 June 1875.

9. *Pittsboro Home* quoted in the *Alamance Gleaner*, 15 Jan. 1885; *Alamance Gleaner*, 22 Jan., 26 Feb., 3 Apr., and 21 May 1885.

10. *Randolph Regulator*, almost any issue for 1876, for example, 13 Dec. 1876; *Salem People's Press*, 1877 passim.

11. Lefler and Newsome, *North Carolina*, p. 545; Stuart Noblin, *Leonidas LaFayette Polk*, pp. 98–99.

12. Wright, *Political Economy of the Cotton South*, pp. 93–98; Noblin, *Polk*, pp. 98–99; Lawrence Goodwyn, *Populist Moment*, pp. 20–25.

13. The U.S. Census of 1870 shows that there was no overall change in the pattern of crop production for North Carolina, except for sizable declines in virtually all kinds of livestock and crops except cotton. Unfortunately, the county-by-county data for 1870 has been lost, so detailed county analysis is not possible.

14. All data on agricultural production came from the U.S. Censuses for 1860, 1870, 1880, and 1890. Except for 1870, county-level data are extant. (The names, in order, of the publications for these respective years are: *Agriculture of the United States in 1860*; "Productions of Agriculture in the United States," which is table 3 in *The Statistics of the Wealth and Industry of the United States*, 1870; *Report on the Productions of Agriculture*; and *Report on the Statistics of Agriculture in the United States at the Eleventh Census, 1890*.)

15. Ibid.

16. Ibid. The categories expressing location are based solely on physiography and land forms. In a few cases different criteria conceivably could be used; for example, Surry County might be considered mountainous because its western portion is such, and Warren County could be ranked as eastern in terms of cultural patterns and economic activity. But throughout this book the physiographical measure is used consistently.

17. Ibid.

18. Noblin, *Polk*, p. 196, table.

19. Lefler and Newsome, *North Carolina*, pp. 524–26.

20. Ibid., p. 522.

21. John F. Flintoff Diary, 8 Apr. 1890, NCDA&H.

22. *Third Annual Report . . . 1889*, North Carolina Bureau of Labor Statistics, p. 258; speech by J. E. O'Hara, probably 17 Nov. 1879, in Charles N. Hunter Papers, Duke.

23. *The Monthly Elevator*, 16 Mar. 1876, in Charles N. Hunter Papers, Duke; *Raleigh State Chronicle*, 15 Sept. 1883, 26 Jan. 1884; W. C. Coleman to Washing-

ton Duke, 20 June 1896, in Washington Duke Papers, Duke; Logan, *Negro in North Carolina, 1876–1894*, pp. 98–100; *Raleigh Evening Visitor*, 2 Oct. 1888, in Charles N. Hunter Papers, Duke.

24. *Raleigh State Chronicle*, 12 Apr. 1884; J. C. Price to Edward A. Oldham, 21 Aug. 1890, in Edward A. Oldham Papers, Duke; and August Meier, *Negro Thought in America, 1880–1915*, pp. 80–82.

25. Schenck diary, 4 July 1873, SHC, UNC-CH; Frenise A. Logan, "Legal Status of Public School Education for Negroes in North Carolina, 1877–1894"; Lefler and Newsome, *North Carolina*, pp. 534–35; on lodges and other organizations see many newspaper clippings in Charles N. Hunter's scrapbook, Charles N. Hunter Papers, Duke.

26. Newspaper articles of 18 and 19 Oct. 1877, in Charles N. Hunter Papers, Duke (these clippings do not include the name of the newspapers and the date had to be determined from internal references and the calendar); *Journal of the Fourth Annual Meeting of the North Carolina State Teachers' Educational Association*; Neil Fulghum of the North Carolina Museum of History kindly provided the author with three compilations of information on black officeholders: "Black Legislators in the North Carolina General Assembly, 1868–1901," "North Carolina's Black Congressmen, 1875–1901, House of Representatives," and "A Listing of Black Senators and Representatives in the 1877 General Assembly of North Carolina" (the last two of these include valuable biographical sketches).

27. Schenck diary, 13 Mar. 1876, SHC, UNC-CH; Lefler and Newsome, *North Carolina*, pp. 543–44; Jeffrey J. Crow, "Cracking the Solid South: The Fusionist Interlude in North Carolina, 1894–1901," in Lindley S. Butler and Alan D. Watson, *North Carolina Experience*, p. 335.

28. Data compiled from Neil Fulghum's lists—"Black Legislators in the North Carolina General Assembly, 1868–1901," "North Carolina's Black Congressmen, 1875–1901, House of Representatives," and "A Listing of Black Senators and Representatives in the 1877 General Assembly of North Carolina." See also Eric Anderson, *Race and Politics in North Carolina, 1872–1901*.

29. Report by Charles N. Hunter printed in *The Era*, concerning excursion on 25 June 1874, Charles N. Hunter Papers, Duke; Eric Anderson, "A Black Perspective on Redeemer Politics: The Career of James E. O'Hara," a paper delivered at the meeting of the Southern Historical Association, November 1979; "A Card to the Public," a newspaper clipping, unidentified, in Charles N. Hunter Papers, Duke.

30. Articles on State Colored Educational Convention, 18 and 19 Oct. 1877, in Charles N. Hunter Papers, Duke; *Salisbury North Carolina Herald*, 19 Oct. 1887, reprinting an article from the *Charleston News and Courier*; *Journal of the Fourth Annual Meeting of the North Carolina State Teachers' Association*, records of the first day.

Similar differences about strategy and tactics arose for blacks who were active within the Republican party. An interesting view of the problem in the context of party affairs is afforded by Jno. C. Dancy to James H. Harris, 16 Mar. 1880, in James Henry Harris Papers, NCDA&H, and a clipping from *The Banner*, 25 June 1881, in Charles N. Hunter Papers, Duke.

31. Robert G. McCloskey, *American Supreme Court*, pp. 115–21, 210.

32. Summary of address by Professor E. Moore, in *Journal of the Fourth Annual Meeting of the North Carolina State Teachers' Association*; Logan, "Legal Status of Public School Education," pp. 346–48; *Fourth Annual Report . . . 1890*," North Carolina Bureau of Labor Statistics, p. 166.

33. Clipping from *Raleigh News and Observer*, 9 Feb. 1880, in Charles N. Hunter Papers, Duke; Logan, "Legal Status of Public School Education," pp. 348–53.

34. Logan, "Legal Status of Public School Education," pp. 354–56; *First Annual Report . . . 1887*, North Carolina Bureau of Labor Statistics, p. 69.

35. Logan, *Negro in North Carolina, 1876–1894*, pp. 58–63; clipping from *Wilmington Post*, probably 1881 or later, in Charles N. Hunter Papers, Duke.

36. *Journal of the Fourth Annual Meeting of the North Carolina State Teachers' Association*, pp. 19–24.

37. *Salisbury North Carolina Herald*, 12 May 1887; *Monroe Enquirer*, 2 Nov. 1875; *Alamance Gleaner*, 6 Apr. 1875; William B. Shepard Account Book, NCDA&H (time records for February 1873 show wages for black laborers of 50¢ per day); Farming Account Book, vol. 9 in Grimes Family Papers, SHC, UNC-CH (wages in 1878 were 50¢ per day, no rations, for men and 30¢ per day, no rations, for women).

38. *Asheville Citizen*, 2 Dec. 1886, in Negroes in North Carolina, four volumes of clippings at the North Carolina Collection, UNC-CH.

39. Schenck diary, 25 Aug. 1873, 4 Sept. 1874, SHC, UNC-CH.

40. Ibid., 8 Sept. 1865, March 1869, 12 June 1862, and 28 May 1873; circular by Richmond Pearson and reply by Johnstone Jones, undated but 1885 or 1886, also clippings from *Asheville Citizen*, 2 and 9 May 1886 and other papers as distant geographically as the *New York Times*, all in vol. 2 of Richmond Pearson Papers, SHC, UNC-CH; J. S. Penland to Thomas Jarvis, 26 June 1883, Robert B. Vance to Thomas Jarvis, 26 June 1883, Thomas Jarvis to Joseph S. Adams, 19 July 1883, Judge J. C. L. Gudger to Thomas Jarvis, 8 May 1884, Joseph D. Crisp to Thomas Jarvis, 4 June 1884, all in Thomas Jarvis Papers, examined in typescript by the author at NCDA&H.

41. See J. Crawford King, Jr., "The Closing of the Southern Range: An Exploratory Study;" Charles Flynn, *White Land, Black Labor*, and Stephen Hahn, *Roots of Southern Populism*, pp. 239–68. The *Revised Code of North Carolina*, compiled and enacted in 1854, codified the traditional rule: "Every planter shall make a sufficient fence about his cleared ground, under cultivation." Under the new system, as an 1873 statute stated, "It shall not be lawful for the owner or manager of any horse, mule, swine, sheep, goat or neat cattle . . . to permit the said animals to run at large beyond the limits of their own land." *Public Laws of the State of North Carolina . . . Session 1872–1873*, pp. 314–17.

42. Petition from Cabarrus County Commissioners to the North Carolina General Assembly, [?] January 1873, Legislative Papers, NCDA&H; *Alamance Gleaner*, 8 Jan. 1885; petition of sixteen residents of Fulton Township, Davie County, to the general assembly, no date but filed with other 1879 petitions, Legislative Papers, NCDA&H; petition from citizens of Steel Creek Township, Mecklenburg County, 13 Jan. 1873, Legislative Papers, NCDA&H.

43. See, for example, *Public Laws of the State of North Carolina . . . Session 1870–1871*, pp. 282–83; ibid., *Session 1872–73*, pp. 314–17; ibid., *Session 1873–74*, p. 108; *Laws and Resolutions of the State of North Carolina, Session of 1874–75*, p. 70; ibid., *Session of 1879*, pp. 252–57; ibid., *Special Session of 1880*, p. 56; ibid., *Session of 1881*, pp. 140, 149, 244, 283, 329, 468, 491, 540, 559, 566, 576, 587; and similar statutes in succeeding sessions; *North Carolina Farmer*, quoted in the *Lenoir Topic*, 26 Apr. 1882; H. A. Foote to M. J. Hawkins, 18 Jan. 1887, in Marmaduke James Hawkins Papers, NCDA&H.

44. The author thanks Wayne Durrill of the University of North Carolina at Chapel Hill for his generosity in sharing his knowledge about Union County and guiding the author to relevant sources. See the *Monroe Enquirer*, 15 June and 3 Aug. 1875, 28 Jan. 1877, 28 Feb. 1880.

45. *Monroe Enquirer*, 19 Apr. 1879, 28 Jan. 1877; *Laws and Resolutions of the State of North Carolina . . . Special Session of 1880*, p. 56.

46. Petition from [four or five dozen] residents of Gaston County, River Bend Township, 14 Feb. 1879, Legislative Papers, House Petitions, NCDA&H; petition from forty-nine citizens of Alexander County, 3 Feb. 1879, ibid.; petition from seventy-eight citizens of Morgan Township, Rowan County, 28 Jan. 1879, ibid.; petition from four to five dozen citizens of Pasquotank County, 19 Feb. 1879, ibid.

47. Petition from four to five dozen citizens of Pasquotank County to the House, 19 Feb. 1879, ibid.; petition from citizens of Caswell County, Milton Township, 18 Feb. 1879, ibid.; two petitions from residents of South Point Township, Gaston County, containing 100 and 363 names respectively, no date [but 1879], ibid.; petition from 44 residents of Edgecombe County, no date [but 1879], ibid.; petition from 121 residents of Edgecombe County, 26 Feb. 1879, ibid.

48. Petition from 49 citizens of Alexander County to the general assembly, 3 Feb. 1879, ibid.; petition from [approximately 200] citizens of Caswell County, 11 Feb. 1879, ibid.; petition from citizens of Burnsville Township, Anson County, 2 Jan. 1883, ibid.; petition from [approximately 80] citizens of Whitaker Mill Township, Nash County, 12 Feb. 1879, ibid.

49. J. W. Hinshaw to his father, [?] March 1883, in Mebane Hinshaw Papers, Duke.

50. *Randolph Sun*, 13 July 1878.

51. Ibid.

52. *Lenoir Topic*, 11 Jan. 1882, 31 May 1882; Schenck diary, 15 Jan. 1881, 25 Apr. 1881; announcement of "Grand Mass Meeting" of Independent Democrats in Buncombe County, on 21 July 1888, in Richmond Pearson Papers, SHC, UNC-CH; H. A. Foote to M. J. Hawkins, 10 Nov. 1886, Marmaduke James Hawkins Papers, NCDA&H.

Another source of complaint by ordinary citizens was road work, which was assigned by the county boards and often benefited relatively well-to-do farmers who were engaged heavily in the market, though the labor was usually performed by small landholders or landless residents. See, for example, a petition from about seventy-five citizens of Mitchell County to the legislature, 15 Feb. 1879, in Legislative Papers, House Petitions, NCDA&H. These petitioners complained that the board of commissioners had assigned them such a large and onerous job that it would require four-fifths of the laborers in the area three months of work each in the next twelve months.

53. Speech by Governor Thomas Jarvis, 17 Nov. 1879, reported in the *Journal of Industry*, 19 Nov. 1879, and another speech by Jarvis at the Colored Fair, reported by the *Raleigh News and Observer*, 2 Oct. 1880, both in the Charles N. Hunter Papers, Duke; Thomas Jarvis to G. M. Hardy, 16 Mar. 1883, in Thomas Jarvis Papers, typescript, NCDA&H. See also A. J. Ellington to Thomas Jarvis, 8 May 1883, Thomas Jarvis to A. J. Ellington, 9 May 1883, and T. A. Watts to Thomas Jarvis, 17 Oct. 1883, Thomas Jarvis Papers, NCDA&H, for cases in which Jarvis did not seem eager to use state troops against black strikers.

54. Thomas J. Jarvis to Frederick W. Griffin, 18 Aug. 1883, and text of Jarvis's speech in Boston on 5 Sept. 1883, both in Thomas Jarvis Papers, typescript, NCDA&H. These papers contain many continuing references to the development of mineral resources.

55. Thomas J. Jarvis to the Legislature, 3 Jan. 1883, and Thomas Jarvis to William Dossey Pruden, 18 May 1886, ibid.

56. Thomas J. Jarvis to William L. Saunders, 20 Feb. 1888, Thomas Jarvis to Elias Carr, 25 Nov. 1889, and Thomas Jarvis to T. F. Davidson, 4 Nov. 1887, all in Thomas Jarvis Papers, typescript, NCDA&H. William L. Saunders's reply of 28 Mar. 1885, in the same papers, showed sympathy to the problem.

57. Lefler and Newsome, *North Carolina*, p. 542.

58. Thomas J. Jarvis to William L. Saunders, 20 Feb. 1888, and 3 Mar. 1888, in Thomas Jarvis Papers, typescript, NCDA&H.

CHAPTER 8

1. *Raleigh State Chronicle*, 15 and 29 Sept. 1883, 3 May 1884, 12 and 19 Apr. 1884, 22 Sept. 1883, 13 and 27 Oct. 1883, and 3 May 1888.

2. Ibid., 22 Sept. 1883; J. P. Caldwell to William Brandreth, 10 May 1881, in Richard M. Eames Papers, NCDA&H; *Raleigh State Chronicle*, 1 Dec. 1883.

3. *Alamance Gleaner*, 28 Aug. 1886.

4. U.S. Census: for 1890 the census of Population, reel 8, Manufactures; and for 1900, reel 3, report no. 130, Manufactures, North Carolina.

5. Ibid.

6. *Alamance Gleaner*, 23 July 1885; George Tayloe Winston, *A Builder of the New South, Being the Story of the Life Work of Daniel Augustus Tompkins*, p. 232; *Salisbury North Carolina Herald*, February–April 1887.

7. Richard W. Griffin, "Reconstruction of the North Carolina Textile Industry, 1865–1885," especially pp. 35–36, 47, and 49; J. Carlyle Sitterson, "Business Leaders in Post-Civil War North Carolina, 1865–1900," especially pp. 111–18.

8. Ibid., with quoted passages taken from Sitterson, p. 111.

9. James G. Moore to Thomas Ruffin, 13 July 1861, in Hamilton, *Papers of Thomas Ruffin*, 3:172. Other letters that illuminate the varied business activity of

the verbally paternalistic Ruffin include William W. Vass to Thomas Ruffin, 11 Aug. 1860, Charles F. Fisher to Thomas Ruffin, 18 Sept. 1860, and William A. Wright to Thomas Ruffin, 19 Dec. 1860, all in ibid., pp. 88, 92–93, 108.

10. *Raleigh State Chronicle*, 6 Oct. 1883.

11. Dwight B. Billings, Jr., *Planters and the Making of a "New South,"* pp. 63–65.

12. J. M. Odell to F. M. Fries, 27 Mar. 1888, H. E. Fries to Sam Patterson, 13 July 1888, and Sam Patterson to his mother, 22 July 1888, all in Patterson Papers, NCDA&H.

13. Paul M. Gaston, *New South Creed*, pp. 48–53.

14. Winston, *Tompkins*, pp. 93, 84, 295, 289.

15. Ibid., pp. 298–99, 303.

16. David L. Carlton, *Mill and Town in South Carolina, 1880–1920*, pp. 72–74.

17. Broadus Mitchell, *Rise of Cotton Mills in the South*, pp. 132, 135, 106. Mitchell may have hoped to spur an improvement of conditions at the time he wrote by comparing them unfavorably to previous attitudes. But if so, he exaggerated.

18. Ibid., p. 135.

19. Ibid., pp. 161, 188, 233; Holland Thompson, *From the Cotton Field to the Cotton Mill*, pp. 51–52. As we have seen, the white population was not homogenous in outlook, values, or way of life. Mitchell's assertion repeated a tenet of the ideology of white supremacy but did not accurately describe reality.

20. In fact this interpretation originated with politically self-interested industrialists and advocates of white supremacy, a fact that will be discussed in chapter 10.

21. Fred Hobson, *South-Watching*, pp. 67–68.

22. Winston, *Tompkins*, pp. 358–59 and chaps. 1–4.

23. D. A. Tompkins to his fiancée, Harriet Brigham, 14 June 1874, in D. A. Tompkins Papers, SHC, UNC-CH; D. A. Tompkins to Harriet Brigham, 4 and 26 July 1874, in D. A. Tompkins Papers, Duke.

24. D. A. Tompkins to Harriet Brigham, 8 Aug. 1874, D. A. Tompkins Papers, Duke. In the same collection is a letter to Miss Brigham dated 9–12 Oct. 1874, in which Tompkins almost diagnosed his problem. He noted that in his native South "every country bumpkin was . . . familiar" to him, but he felt "a lack of dignity" in the North and was disturbed that there "all the refinement and emotional parts of one's nature" were "expected to be shown."

25. Henry Buisse to D. A. Tompkins, 17 Mar. 1878, D. A. Tompkins Papers, SHC, UNC-CH; Harriet Brigham to D. A. Tompkins, 7 Oct. and 19 July 1874, Harriet Brigham to D. A. Tompkins, 23 Aug. 1874, and 22 Sept. 1874, and correspondence between the two around Christmas, 1874, all in D. A. Tompkins Papers, Duke; D. A. Tompkins to E. St. John, 14 Jan. 1896, in D. A. Tompkins Papers, SHC, UNC-CH.

26. J. M. Odell to F. M. Fries, 27 Mar. 1888, Sam Patterson to his mother, 25 March [?] 1888, and Sam to his mother, 16 Apr. 1888, all in Patterson Papers, NCDA&H. In April 1888 the Odells also invited Sam's brother Drew to visit them while Drew was on a trip to Charlotte.

27. Sam Patterson to his mother, 3 May 1888, and 6 Jan. and 5 May 1889, in

Patterson Papers, NCDA&H. Sam explained to his mother that the cut in wages was the result of economic hard times. Yet, in a letter to her (in the same collection) dated 2 Feb. 1889, Sam stated, "We declared a good dividend despite the hard times."

28. Sam Patterson to his mother, 3 and 24 Mar. 1889, Patterson Papers, NCDA&H.

29. Sam Patterson to his mother, 23 Mar. 1891, Patterson Papers, NCDA&H.

30. *Raleigh State Chronicle*, 3 May 1884; Sam Patterson to his mother, 27 Apr. 1888, Patterson Papers, NCDA&H; *Asheboro Courier*, 30 May 1895; D. A. Tompkins to "My dear Arthur," 25 Mar. 1878, D. A. Tompkins Papers, SHC, UNC-CH.

31. Henderson Monroe Fowler Diary, July–August 1872, 3 and 17 July 1874, and 11 May 1876, SHC, UNC-CH.

32. For examples see ibid., 26 Feb. 1878, 16 Dec. 1879, Mar. 1880, and other passages.

33. Ibid., entries for 16 July 1878, 11 and 16 Dec. 1879, 22 Jan., March, and 11 and 18 May 1880.

34. H. F. Schenck to J. E. Reynolds, 19 Aug. 1889; John F. Schenck to H. M. Craven, 20 Sept. 1898, both in H. F. Schenck Papers, Duke.

35. H. F. Schenck to J. E. Reynolds, 28 Jan. and 4 Feb. 1889, H. F. Schenck to T. A. Davis, 27 May 1889, and H. F. Schenck to J. E. Reynolds, 11 Feb. 1890, all in ibid.

36. H. F. Schenck to J. E. Reynolds, 8 Oct. 1898, and 18 Nov. 1889, ibid.

37. D. A. Tompkins, *Cotton Mill, Commercial Features*, pp. 35, 116.

38. Quoted in Billings, *Planters and the Making of a "New South,"* p. 103, also pp. 103–7, 38.

39. E. M. Holt to J. W. White, 30 Oct. 1873, in James W. White Papers, SHC, UNC-CH; Minutes, Worth Manufacturing Company, 2 Oct. 1884, 4 Oct. 1886, and 6 Oct. 1887, in Leward Cotton Mills, Inc. Papers, Duke; see letters from 1893 concerning the Big Falls Mills in Alamance, the Pineville Cotton Mills in Mecklenburg County, and the Renwood Cotton Mills in Gaston County, in the Marmaduke James Hawkins Papers, NCDA&H; see also a 7 Mar. 1894 letter concerning the Oakdale Manufacturing Company in Concord in Marmaduke James Hawkins Papers, NCDA&H.

40. E. M. Holt to Carrigan, 25 Apr. 1871, in James W. White Papers, SHC, UNC-CH; W. A. Moore to M. J. Hawkins, 25 Sept. 1894, in Marmaduke James Hawkins Papers, NCDA&H; Henderson Monroe Fowler Diary, entries for 20 and 21 Apr. 1874, 6 July 1885, 1 July 1886, SHC, UNC-CH. In October 1883, Fowler wrote that the factory had begun "runing with Steam."

41. H. F. Schenck to T. H. Risdon and Company, 22 Mar. 1889, H. F. Schenck to J. E. Reynolds, 18 and 25 Nov. 1889, and H. F. Schenck to D. A. Tompkins Company, 23 Mar., 15 Nov., and 2 Dec. 1889, all in H. F. Schenck Papers, Duke.

42. Sam Patterson to his mother, 7 and 9 Sept., 14 Nov., 3 Jan., 16 Dec., 2 Feb. 1889, 26 Jan. 1890, all in Patterson Papers, NCDA&H.

43. Sam Patterson to his mother, 9 Nov. 1891, 23 Sept. 1897, and 17 June 1898, in ibid.

44. Sam Patterson to his mother, 23 Mar. 1891, Rufus L. Patterson, Jr., to his mother, 4 Apr. 1892, Sam Patterson to his mother, 20 Jan. and 24 Feb. 1889, W. R. Odell to Rufus L. Patterson, Jr., 25 Jan. 1893, Rufus L. Patterson, Jr., to his mother, 27 Apr. 1896, 1 Dec. 1897, 4 June 1898 and 27 May 1900, all in Patterson Papers, NCDA&H.

45. John L. Patterson to his mother, 24 Feb. 1898, in Patterson Papers, NCDA&H; D. A. Tompkins to R. H. Edmonds, 27 Mar. 1899, in Tompkins Papers, SHC, UNC-CH. Tompkins, of course, was a prime mover in the establishment of the textile school at North Carolina State University. For information on Duke Power, see Robert F. Durden, *Dukes of Durham*, chap. 9. Tompkins spoke of his plans for water power in a letter to Lemuel Bannister, 4 May 1897, in Tompkins Papers, SHC, UNC-CH.

46. Sam Patterson to his mother, 31 Mar. and 14 Apr. 1889, in Patterson Papers, NCDA&H; Worth Manufacturing Company Minutes, in Leward Cotton Mills, Inc. Papers, Duke.

47. F. J. Murdoch to William Alexander Smith, 10 Jan. 1895, in William Alexander Smith Papers, Duke; Trenton Cotton Mill Papers, reports of Apr. 1895, 1896, 1898, 1899, and 1901, in NCDA&H; Durden, *Dukes of Durham*, pp. 129, 139; Tompkins, *Cotton Mill*, pp. 172, 51. Tompkins recommended that of the 15 percent profit, 5 percent be reinvested and 10 percent distributed as a dividend. In the Stowesville Cotton Factory Account Book, 1856–1874, there are detailed estimates of the costs of building and operating cotton factories, and an entry mentioning 1874 costs predicts "an average profit of 30 per cent," in Stowe Family Papers, Duke.

48. *Salisbury North Carolina Herald*, 14 Apr. 1887, pp. 1 and 3.

49. Ibid.

50. Ibid., plus *Branson's North Carolina Business Directory*, 1884 and 1890 editions.

51. *Salisbury North Carolina Herald*, 14 Apr. and 21 Dec. 1887; *Branson's* for 1884 and 1890.

52. *Salisbury North Carolina Herald*, 17 Aug. 1887.

53. Ibid., 19 Oct. 1887.

54. Ibid., 30 Nov. and 14 and 21 Dec. 1887.

55. Mitchell, *Rise of Cotton Mills*, pp. 132, 135, 106.

56. Ibid., pp. 161, 188, 233, 235; D. A. Tompkins to A. W. McAllister, 7 Nov. 1898, in D. A. Tompkins Papers, SHC, UNC-CH; Winston, *Tompkins*, p. 150.

57. Sam Patterson to his mother, 10 and 31 Mar. and 3 Apr. 1889, all in Patterson Papers, NCDA&H.

58. William Alexander Smith to F. J. Murdoch, 9 Aug. 1895, in William Alexander Smith Papers, Duke. Smith is an example of an industrialist whose family had considerable wealth in land and who moved into mercantile and industrial enterprises.

59. Durden, *Dukes of Durham*, pp. 128–45.

60. Data were drawn from the county Records of Incorporation, at NCDA&H; from *Branson's* directories for 1884 and 1896, and, to a small extent, from data in the 1880 and 1900 U.S. manuscript censuses. In the calculation of 71.3 percent,

six non-North Carolina investors were excluded from consideration.

61. William Alexander Smith Papers, Duke. (See description accompanying the collection.)

62. Data were drawn from *Branson's* directories for 1884 and 1896. In regard to total mill growth in the state, the *Thirteenth Annual Report* of the North Carolina Bureau of Labor Statistics gave these figures for numbers of mills: 1880, 49; 1890, 91; and 1899, 181. The *Fourteenth Annual Report* showed 224 in 1900.

CHAPTER 9

1. *Fifth Annual Report . . . 1891*, North Carolina Bureau of Labor Statistics, pp. 130, 135. The state's industrial workers were almost all white. The one exception, which followed antebellum practice, was in tobacco manufacturing. The *Annual Report* for 1887 noted on page 2 that most workers in tobacco manufacturing were black.

2. *Third Annual Report . . . 1889*, pp. 75, 46, 73; *Fifth Annual Report . . . 1891*, p. 50; *Second Annual Report . . . 1888*, pp. 398, 416.

3. *First Annual Report . . . 1887*, J. W. B. of Stanly County, pp. 70–74; *Fourth Annual Report . . . 1890*, p. 34; *Fifth Annual Report . . . 1891*, p. 171.

4. *Fifth Annual Report . . . 1891*, p. 23, emphasis added.

5. Quoted in C. Vann Woodward, *American Counterpoint*, p. 279.

6. Henderson Monroe Fowler Diary, 17 Feb. 1872, 5 and 11 Apr. 1879, 6 Jan. and 11 May 1876, and 14 July 1877, in SHC, UNC-CH. See also 8 Dec. 1879, 1 May 1882, 4 Sept. 1887, and June 1883 for information on accidents. Em Shoffner's first day in the factory was 30 Dec. 1875.

7. H. F. Schenck to Fidelity and Casualty Company, 3 Nov. 1898, in Schenck Papers, Duke.

8. *Ninth Annual Report . . . 1895*, Bureau of Labor Statistics, p. 290. See also the introduction to the *Annual Report* for 1893, in which the commissioner voices his suspicion that matters were worse than reported.

9. Sam Patterson to his mother, 25 Mar. [?] 1888; *Second Annual Report . . . 1888*, Bureau of Labor Statistics, statement by a superintendent who has worked forty years, p. 122; ibid., 1891, pp. 166–67. The tables given in the *Annual Reports* during the 1890s and 1894 are very valuable. D. A. Tompkins asserted that "Movements for amelioration and betterment are . . . well established. . . . The betterment of humanity in Southern cotton mills is going on apace." Winston, *Tompkins*, pp. 265–66. In Tompkins's own *Cotton Mill*, pp. 38, 114, and 116, he predicted an end to night work, regulation of child labor, and the end of mill villages.

10. "Rules Governing Employees in the Winton Knitting Mills," in Winton Knitting Mills Papers, 1896–97, part of the James L. Anderson Papers, NCDA&H.

11. Cora Mitchell to "Dear Sirs," 29 July 1896, in ibid.; H. F. Schenck to Harvey Jones, 20 Mar. 1889, in Schenck Papers, Duke.

12. A recollection of the history of Mountain Island and Gaston County, in the

Robert Goodloe Lindsay Papers, SHC, UNC-CH; *Annual Report*, Bureau of Labor Statistics, for the years 1890, 1892, tables; Pay Roll, Willard Manufacturing Company, 3 Apr. 1899, in Sidney Willard Holman Papers, NCDA&H; Fayetteville Cotton Mills, Account Book, 1894, 1896, in NCDA&H; A. P. Rhyne to Mrs. Lawrence, 23 Dec. 1876, and draft of speech (around or shortly after 1872) in Stowesville Cotton Factory Account Book, both in Stowe Family Papers, Duke. The wage bill was $59.83 per day for 300 days, or $17,949.

13. *Ninth Annual Report . . . 1895*, Bureau of Labor Statistics, p. 61.

14. *Fourth Annual Report . . . 1890*, table, p. 23; *Eighth Annual Report . . . 1894*, pp. 64–65; Tompkins, *Cotton Mill*, pp. 55–68.

15. John F. Schenck to Kell Richy, 10 Sept. 1898, Schenck Papers, Duke; John F. Schenck to Mrs. S. Hawkins, 10 Oct. 1898, ibid.

16. *Twelfth Annual Report . . . 1898*, Bureau of Labor Statistics, p. 40; *Tenth Annual Report . . . 1896*, p. 85.

17. *Twelfth Annual Report . . . 1898*, p. 40; A. C. Schumaker to M. J. Hawkins, 11 May 1895, in Marmaduke James Hawkins Papers, NCDA&H. See also W. A. Moore to Hawkins, 24 Aug. 1895, in ibid.

18. W. S. Allred to M. J. Hawkins, 29 Jan. 1897, in Marmaduke James Hawkins Papers, NCDA&H. As this letter implicitly reveals, Hawkins by this time had succeeded in removing Allred's competition by hiring Allred to work for him.

19. *Fourth Annual Report . . . 1890*, Bureau of Labor Statistics, p. 43; *Fifth Annual Report . . . 1891*, p. 141; *Eighth Annual Report . . . 1894*, pp. 64–65; *Eleventh Annual Report . . . 1897*, p. 248; *Tenth Annual Report . . . 1896*, p. 93; Winston, *Tompkins*, pp. 267, 264–67, 275–76.

20. *Fourth Annual Report . . . 1890*, Bureau of Labor Statistics, p. 23, *Fifth Annual Report . . . 1891*, p. 127, *Fourteenth Annual Report . . . 1900*, p. 175; U.S. Census, 1900, reel 3, report no. 130, Manufactures, North Carolina. Due to the destruction of much of the 1890 census, comparison of census data from 1890 to 1900 is impossible. The Bureau of Labor data, which showed a substantial rise in employment of children between 1899 and 1900, were not as complete as the census data. In 1890, for example, reports to the Bureau of Labor of the state covered 43.5 percent of the cotton mills in operation.

21. Winston, *Tompkins*, pp. 275–77.

22. *Fourth Annual Report . . . 1890*, Bureau of Labor Statistics, pp. 50, 51, 109, and 105.

23. *Fourth Annual Report . . . 1890*, p. 42; *Tenth Annual Report . . . 1896*, p. 71; *Fifth Annual Report . . . 1891*, pp. 167, 177–78. See also *Tenth Annual Report . . . 1896*, between pages 75–80; *Thirteenth Annual Report . . . 1899*, pp. 243, 250. There might have been some truth in the owners' accusation. It is easy to imagine that some men who once were independent farmers may have found the factory situation so disagreeable and earned so little that they hunted or worked outdoors rather than join their families in the mill.

24. *Eleventh Annual Report . . . 1897*, pp. 250 and 249–50; *Thirteenth Annual Report . . . 1899*, pp. 233, 244.

25. *Twelfth Annual Report . . . 1898*, p. 398; *Thirteenth Annual Report . . . 1899*, p. 241; *Twelfth Annual Report . . . 1898*, p. 402; *Eleventh Annual Report . . . 1897*,

p. 247; and *Thirteenth Annual Report . . . 1899*, p. 229.

26. *Fifth Annual Report . . . 1891*, p. 136; *Fourth Annual Report . . . 1890*, p. 49; *Fifth Annual Report . . . 1891*, p. 130.

27. *Fifth Annual Report . . . 1891*, p. 131; *Seventh Annual Report . . . 1893*, introduction.

28. *Third Annual Report . . . 1889*, "Reports of Laboring Men," pp. 281, 282; *Fourth Annual Report . . . 1890*, p. 85; *Fifth Annual Report . . . 1891*, p. 177.

29. *Fifth Annual Report . . . 1891*, p. 180; *Second Annual Report . . . 1888*, p. 55; *Eleventh Annual Report . . . 1897*, p. 257.

30. *Fifth Annual Report . . . 1891*, p. 170; *Tenth Annual Report . . . 1896*, p. 69; *Eighth Annual Report . . . 1894*, p. 77; *Tenth Annual Report . . . 1896*, pp. 76, 75.

31. *Fifth Annual Report . . . 1891*, pp. 168, 172, 177; *Second Annual Report . . . 1888*, p. 122. An Alamance County engineer stated his opinion that employers got away with excessively long hours because, "as the labor is mostly females and boys, the thing is not much agitated."

32. *Fourth Annual Report . . . 1890*, pp. 75, 78. A tobacco-factory worker added this comment on page 115: "Children have no business in factories, or anyone else, until fully grown. Have been in factory for ten years and have noticed this: a cutter never lives more than ten years, where he works daily and steadily."

33. *Second Annual Report . . . 1888*, p. 122; *Fifth Annual Report . . . 1891*, p. 169; *Eighth Annual Report . . . 1894*, p. 80; *Tenth Annual Report . . . 1896*, p. 80.

34. *Thirteenth Annual Report . . . 1899*, p. viii; *Tenth Annual Report . . . 1896*, p. 70; *Ninth Annual Report . . . 1895*, pp. 1, 60. The author does not see here, as Billings did, a significant disposition on the part of manufacturers to support types of progress that aided their own interests. Perhaps such an outlook became important later, but the author does not judge it to have been significant before 1900.

35. *Ninth Annual Report . . . 1895*, p. 61.

36. *Fourth Annual Report . . . 1890*, pp. 75, 81, 82, 92; *Fifth Annual Report . . . 1891*, pp. 188, 166–68.

37. *Second Annual Report . . . 1888*, p. 121; *Third Annual Report . . . 1889*, p. 282; *Fourth Annual Report . . . 1890*, pp. 74, 78.

38. *Fourth Annual Report . . . 1890*, pp. 81, 74, 78; *Fifth Annual Report . . . 1891*, p. 180.

39. H. F. Schenck to M. M. Mauney, 9 Nov. 1898, H. F. Schenck Papers, Duke.

40. *Thirteenth Annual Report . . . 1899*, Bureau of Labor Statistics, p. 228.

41. *Lenoir Topic*, 15 Mar. 1882.

42. *Fourteenth Annual Report . . . 1900*, Bureau of Labor Statistics, p. 197; *Eighth Annual Report . . . 1894*, pp. 74, 81; *Seventh Annual Report . . . 1893*, p. 60; *Fourth Annual Report . . . 1890*, p. 117.

43. Henderson Monroe Fowler Diary, 20 Jan. 1876, SHC, UNC-CH. Similar patterns are described in Tamara K. Hareven and Randolph Langenbach, *Amoskeag*. The author gratefully acknowledges the stimulus of ideas suggested by Jacquelyn Hall and her students at UNC-Chapel Hill, whose work explores these themes much more definitively.

44. Tompkins, *Cotton Mill*, p. 117.

45. H. M. Fowler Diary, 6 and 24 Feb. 1874, 6 Apr. 1874, 3 Mar. 1876, and 17 June 1874, SHC, UNC-CH.

46. *Eleventh Annual Report . . . 1897*, Bureau of Labor Statistics, p. 257; Richmond Manufacturing Company [?], a Richmond County cotton factory, Time Book Oct. 1853, Account Book 262, NCDA&H; H. M. Fowler Diary, 26 Oct. 1874, Sept. 1874, 12 Feb. 1880, Apr. 1879, SHC, UNC-CH. The "Protracted meeting" of 26 Oct. 1874 was on a Monday.

47. Pay Roll of Willard Manufacturing Company for week ending 1 Apr., dated 3 Apr. 1899, in Sidney Willard Holman Papers, NCDA&H; Fayetteville Cotton Mills, Account Book, Feb. and Mar. 1894, Account Book 158, NCDA&H; Pilot Cotton Mills, Time Book, 1893–96, NCDA&H; L. Banks Holt Cotton Mill Account Book, Time Book, 1897–1900, NCDA&H.

48. Calculated from Pilot Cotton Mills, Time Book, NCDA&H.

49. Sydney Nathans, *Quest for Progress*, pp. 30, 34. The same point is made in Hareven and Langenbach, *Amoskeag*.

50. Pilot Cotton Mills, Time Book, NCDA&H (the Throwers worked at this mill); Fayetteville Cotton Mills, Account Book, NCDA&H; L. Banks Holt Cotton Mill, Account Book, Time Book, NCDA&H (filmed from the original in the possession of Mr. Ralph Shatterly, Yanceyville, N.C.); H. M. Fowler Diary, Oct. 1886, SHC, UNC-CH.

51. H. M. Fowler Diary, 18 Feb. 1885, Apr. and Jan. 1883, 29 Mar. and 22 Apr. 1880, SHC, UNC-CH.

52. Ibid., Feb. and May 1887; H. F. Schenck to J. E. Reynolds & Co., 11 Oct. 1898, H. F. Schenck Papers, Duke. For an example of other labor disputes, see the letters of Sam Patterson discussed earlier in the chapter.

53. Melton A. McLaurin, *Paternalism and Protest*, pp. 77–85; Melton A. McLaurin, *Knights of Labor in the South*, pp. 98–101.

54. McLaurin, *Paternalism and Protest*, pp. 77–85.

55. Ibid.; *Alamance Gleaner*, 4 Sept. and 4 Nov. 1884, 2 and 24 Sept., 28 Oct., 26 Aug., and 21 Oct. 1886, and 3 Mar. 1887.

56. *Alamance Gleaner*, 21 and 28 Oct. 1886.

57. Ibid., 4 Nov. 1886; McLaurin, *Paternalism and Protest*, p. 81; Nathans, *Quest for Progress*, p. 35. The Knights miscalculated in 1888, failing to recognize the effects of the presidential election held that year, and were snowed under.

58. *Alamance Gleaner*, 20 Jan. and 3 and 10 Mar. 1887; Nathans, *Quest for Progress*, p. 35; H. M. Fowler Diary, 1883 and after, especially 10 Oct. and 7 Dec. 1883, 6 Sept. 1886, and 1 Mar. 1887.

CHAPTER 10

1. Noblin, *Polk*, p. 211; Flintoff diary, entries for 10 Aug. 1891, 15 Oct. 1892, and 1 Oct. 1893, NCDA&H; Robert F. Durden, *The Climax of Populism*, pp. 16–17.

2. *Fifth Annual Report . . . 1891*, Bureau of Labor Statistics, pp. 29, 41, 44.

3. Ibid., 1894, p. 180; 1896, pp. 32–33, 38.

4. See Lawrence Goodwyn's insights on the psychological aspects of building a mass democratic movement in *Populist Moment*, pp. xviii, xxi (note), and chap. 2.

5. Noblin, *Polk*, pp. 206–27; *Fifth Annual Report . . . 1891*, Bureau of Labor Statistics, p. 95. The best accounts of the origins and course of the farmers' revolt are Robert C. McMath, Jr., *Populist Vanguard*; Goodwyn, *Democratic Promise* (and the condensed version, *Populist Moment*); Woodward, *Origins of the New South* and *Tom Watson*; and Durden, *Climax of Populism*.

6. *Greensboro Southern Democrat*, 18 Sept. 1890, which also quotes the passage from the *North Carolina Intelligencer*.

7. Thomas J. Jarvis to S. A'Court Ashe, 14 Feb. and 6 Mar. 1890. The first letter is found in the Thomas Jarvis Papers in typescript at NCDA&H, and the one of 6 Mar. is in the Samuel A'Court Ashe Papers, NCDA&H. Jarvis also urged Alliance leaders to be patient and understanding with the Democratic party. See Thomas J. Jarvis to Elias Carr, 21 Nov. 1890, in Thomas Jarvis Papers in typescript, NCDA&H.

8. Senator Zebulon B. Vance to Samuel A'Court Ashe, 10 July and 29 June 1890, in Samuel A'Court Ashe Papers, NCDA&H; E. C. Beddingfield, secretary of the North Carolina Farmers' State Alliance, to Samuel A'Court Ashe, 11 July 1890, ibid.; Noblin, *Polk*, pp. 240–51. For information on the subtreasury plan, see Goodwyn, *Populist Moment*, pp. 109–13, 301–7.

9. W. W. Carraway to Samuel A'Court Ashe, 30 Oct. 1890, Ed. Chambers Smith to Ashe, 7 Nov. 1890, and David Schenck to Ashe, 28 Nov. 1891, all in Samuel A'Court Ashe Papers, NCDA&H. The *Lenoir Topic*, 10 Oct. 1883, carried Schenck's letter declining a place on the state's highest court. Schenck wrote that, "the necessities of my family forbid that I should make the pecuniary sacrifice which its acceptance would require."

10. Noblin, *Polk*, pp. 248, 251–52; *Clinton Caucasian*, 17 Mar. 1892.

11. Lefler and Newsome, *North Carolina*, p. 547; *Clinton Caucasian*, 14 Jan. 1892.

12. "Confidential" letter from Furnifold M. Simmons to Democratic party activists, 13 Oct. 1892, in William Alexander Smith Papers, Duke.

13. J. Morgan Kousser, *Shaping of Southern Politics*, pp. 184–85; Jeffrey J. Crow and Robert F. Durden, *Maverick Republican in the Old North State*, pp. 79–80; Marion Butler to Richmond Pearson, 22 Jan. and 19 Feb. 1894 (see also letters of 17 May and 12 June 1894), in Richmond Pearson Papers, SHC, UNC-CH.

14. Crow and Durden, *Maverick Republican*, pp. 49–50; Kousser, *Shaping of Southern Politics*, pp. 184–87.

15. Ibid.

16. Ibid.

17. Ibid.

18. W. B. McKoy to Edw. T. Boykin, 31 Dec. 1896, in William Berry McKoy Papers, Duke; Helen G. Edmonds, *Negro and Fusion Politics in North Carolina*, p. 119.

19. Omaha Platform of 4 July 1892, quoted in the *Clinton Caucasian*, 18 Aug. 1892.

20. Crow and Durden, *Maverick Republican*, pp. 104–5, 101, and chap. 6.

21. John F. Schenck to [?] (apparently a draft of his report to the state Bureau of Labor), not dated but between two letters of 28 Sept. 1898, in H. F. Schenck Papers, Duke; *Eleventh Annual Report . . . 1897*, Bureau of Labor Statistics, p. 247; *Twelfth Annual Report . . . 1898*, pp. 398–400; *Thirteenth Annual Report . . . 1899*, p. 233; *Tenth Annual Report . . . 1896*, p. 60.

22. *Twelfth Annual Report . . . 1898*, Bureau of Labor Statistics, p. 402; *Thirteenth Annual Report . . . 1899*, p. 233; *Tenth Annual Report . . . 1896*, pp. 80–85.

23. *Tenth Annual Report . . . 1896*, pp. 72, 93; *Thirteenth Annual Report . . . 1899*, p. 245.

24. Quoted in Kousser, *Shaping of Southern Politics*, pp. 189, 191, 187.

25. Ibid., pp. 186–87 (percentages calculated from the table).

26. Billings, *Planters and the Making of a "New South,"* pp. 183, 185.

27. Goodwyn, *Populist Moment*, p. 20. From Pareto and Mosca to present-day writers, sociology has generated a large literature on elites, and history provides many examples of elite figures furnishing leadership to even the most democratic political and social movements.

28. Quoted in Durden, *Climax of Populism*, pp. 16–17.

29. Thomas J. Jarvis to Samuel A'Court Ashe, 26 Sept. 1892 and 2 Aug. 1894, Thomas Jarvis to Elias Carr, 6 Aug. 1894, Thomas Jarvis to E. C. Smith, 15 June 1896, Thomas Jarvis to the editor of the *Raleigh News and Observer*, 9 Sept. 1895, and Thomas Jarvis to Governor Elias Carr, 30 July 1895 and 10 June 1896, all in Thomas Jarvis Papers, typescript, NCDA&H. Actually, in North Carolina the third party or Populist vote was not as large as in other southern states. It did not need to be, because Republican strength had remained very substantial. But Kousser estimates that virtually all the Populist vote came from the ranks of former Democrats.

30. John W. Cell, *Highest Stage of White Supremacy*, chap. 4, and pp. 88, 103–4; Woodward, *Origins of the New South*, pp. 211–12; Woodward, *American Counterpoint*, pp. 256–57; "Recollections and Memories by Thomas W. Clawson," Thomas W. Clawson Papers, SHC, UNC-CH. Clawson had been editor of the *Wilmington Messenger*.

31. *Wilmington Semi-Weekly Messenger*, 1 Nov. 1898; "Recollections and Memories by Thomas W. Clawson," Thomas W. Clawson Papers, SHC, UNC-CH; Jack Metts [?] to [?], 9 Nov. 1898, in Hinsdale Family Papers, Duke.

32. *Wilmington Semi-Weekly Messenger*, 11 Nov. 1898; "Resolutions and demands," 9 Nov. 1898, in Alfred Moore Waddell Papers, SHC, UNC-CH; Jack Metts [?] to "My dear Miss Elizabeth," 12 Nov. 1898, in Hinsdale Family Papers, Duke; "Recollections and Memories by Thomas W. Clawson," Thomas W. Clawson Papers, SHC, UNC-CH; *Wilmington Semi-Weekly Messenger*, 15 Nov. 1898 (headline says six killed, but article adds that one wounded black person died); Crow and Durden, *Maverick Republican*, p. 135.

33. *Wilmington Semi-Weekly Messenger*, 11 Nov. 1898.

34. Crow and Durden, *Maverick Republican*, pp. 99, 127–32; Lefler and Newsome, *North Carolina*, p. 557.

35. Kousser, *Shaping of Southern Politics*, pp. 188–89; Lefler and Newsome, *North Carolina*, p. 556.

36. Thomas Jarvis to Elias Carr, 9 Apr. 1894, in Thomas Jarvis Papers, typescript, NCDA&H; Crow and Durden, *Maverick Republican*, p. 125.

37. H. F. Schenck to J. H. Sloan, 10 Nov. 1898, H. F. Schenck to J. E. Reynolds and Company, 7 and 12 Nov. 1898, all in H. F. Schenck Papers, Duke; E. H. Williamson to S. H. Webb, 20 Sept. 1898, in Richard D. White Collection (the Samuel H. Webb Letters are a part of the White Collection), NCDA&H; Lefler and Newsome, *North Carolina*, p. 558.

38. Kousser, *Shaping of Southern Politics*, p. 190.

39. Edmonds, *Negro and Fusion Politics*, p. 187.

40. The *Charlotte Observer*, quoted in the *Wilmington Semi-Weekly Messenger*, 15 Sept. 1898; Kousser, *Shaping of Southern Politics*, p. 190.

41. *Wilmington Semi-Weekly Messenger*, 1 Sept. 1898; Kousser, *Shaping of Southern Politics*, pp. 189, 191–92.

42. *Public Laws of . . . North Carolina . . . 1899*, pp. 539–40; Cell, *Highest Stage*, p. 121 (quoting Simmons).

43. *Alamance Gleaner*, 28 June 1900; Aycock is quoted in Kousser, *Shaping of Southern Politics*, p. 192; Lefler and Newsome, *North Carolina*, p. 561; *Alamance Gleaner*, 17 May 1900; Kousser, *Shaping of Southern Politics*, p. 193; letter to voters from Richmond Pearson, 18 Aug. 1896, in Richmond Pearson Papers, SHC, UNC-CH.

44. Kousser, *Shaping of Southern Politics*, pp. 193–94.

45. Ibid., p. 195.

46. Nathans, *Quest for Progress*, p. 36; McLaurin, *Paternalism and Protest*, pp. 156–61.

47. *Alamance Gleaner*, 11 Oct. 1900.

48. Ibid.

49. Nathans, *Quest for Progress*, p. 36; *Alamance Gleaner*, 1, 8, 15, and 22 Nov. 1900.

50. *Alamance Gleaner*, 29 Nov. 1900.

AFTERWORD

1. *American Heritage Dictionary*, New College Edition, p. 351.

2. *Charlotte Observer*, 3 Sept. 1901, p. 6; Tompkins, *Cotton Mill*, p. 118.

3. Memoir or account, noted as probably by Jane M. Cronly, in Cronly Family Papers, Duke.

4. *Charlotte Observer*, 9 Jan. 1980.

5. Paternalism and personalism in owner-worker relations may well have grown *after* 1900. The research for this study turned up relatively few examples of a strongly personal, paternalistic style before 1900. But after that date manufacturers and elite leaders had far more reason to feel both that their power was secure and that there was something to be gained by easing the resentment of poorer whites. The author does not dispute the assertions of historians who see a warm,

paternalistic style as dominant in mills after 1900, but he suggests that the elite may have felt that the cultivation of such relations was particularly desirable after the crushing of democratic protest in 1900.

6. Quoted in Winston, *Tompkins*, pp. 282–83.

7. *Charlotte Observer*, 3 Sept. 1901.

8. Ibid., 9 Mar. 1977, A section, p. 16, 7 Mar. 1977, A section, p. 18.

9. Ibid., 3 Dec. 1979, C section, p. 1. See also various articles from December 1976, February through March 1977, November 1979, January 1980, and February through April 1981.

10. Ibid., 30 Apr. 1981. William Galloway was accurate about voting patterns. An area resembling a pie slice in the southeast portion of Charlotte voted heavily for at-large representation, but all other areas of the city voted to keep the largely district system (seven district seats plus four at-large seats; the proposed change would have restored an *all* at-large system). In Galloway's precinct the vote to keep districts was 748 to 91.

11. John L. Cheney, Jr., ed., *North Carolina Manual, 1981–82*, p. 60.

SELECTED BIBLIOGRAPHY

PRIMARY SOURCES

MANUSCRIPTS

Chapel Hill, North Carolina
    North Carolina Collection, University of North Carolina at Chapel Hill
        Journal of the North Carolina State Teachers' Educational Association
        Negroes in North Carolina
    Southern Historical Collection, University of North Carolina at Chapel Hill
        Thomas Bragg Diary
        W. G. Briggs Papers
        Tod R. Caldwell Papers
        William J. Clarke Papers
        Thomas W. Clawson Papers
        Anne Collins Papers
        Juliana Margaret Conner Diary
        Henderson Monroe Fowler Diary
        Grimes Family Papers
        George Washington Finley Harper Papers
        B. S. Hedrick Collection
        William Alexander Hoke Papers
        Jones and Patterson Papers
        Lenoir Family Papers
        Robert Goodloe Lindsay Papers
        Jacob A. Long Recollections
        Meares-de Rosset Papers
        Eugene Morehead Diary
        John Paris Papers
        Richmond Pearson Papers
        Marmaduke Robins Papers
        William L. Saunders Papers
        David Schenck Diary
        Samuel McDowell Tate Papers
        D. A. Tompkins Papers
        Alfred Moore Waddell Papers
        James W. White Papers
        Alfred E. Willard Papers

Durham, North Carolina
  Manuscripts Department, Duke University
    William Horton Bower Papers
    Amy Morris Bradley Papers
    John L. Bridgers, Jr. Papers
    Lunsford R. Cherry Papers
    Thomas W. Clawson Papers
    Cronly Family Papers
    George F. Davidson Papers
    B. N. Duke Papers
    Washington Duke Papers
    Benjamin P. Elliott Papers
    Gill Family Papers
    Hinsdale Family Papers
    Mebane Hinshaw Papers
    Thomas Hinshaw Papers
    Charles N. Hunter Papers
    Jarratt-Puryear Family Papers
    Edward W. Kinsley Papers
    B. F. Knight Papers
    Ku Klux Klan Papers
    Leward Cotton Mills, Inc. Papers
    William Berry McKoy Papers
    Duncan McLaurin Papers
    Hugh MacRae Papers
    John Frederick Mallett Journal
    John W. Morrow Papers
    Edward A. Oldham Papers
    Rufus Lenoir Patterson, Jr. Papers
    Samuel Finley Patterson Papers
    Addie Price Papers
    H. F. Schenck Papers
    William Lafayette Scott Papers
    William Alexander Smith Papers
    Stowe Family Papers
    D. A. Tompkins Papers
    Bryan Tyson Papers
    U.S. Bureau of Refugees, Freedmen and Abandoned Lands, North Carolina
      Papers
    Shadrack Ward Papers
    W. A. White Papers
    Woodlawn Cotton Mill Day Book, 1874–1875
Raleigh, North Carolina
  North Carolina Division of Archives and History
    Albright-Dixon Papers
    James L. Anderson Papers

Samuel A'Court Ashe Papers
Commutations, Pardons, and Respites, Tod R. Caldwell
Governor's Letter Book, Tod R. Caldwell
Ernest R. and Della G. Carroll Papers
H. T. Clark Papers
Heriot Clarkson Papers
Josiah Collins Papers
Calvin J. Cowles Papers
John Devereux Papers
Richard M. Eames Papers
Fayetteville Cotton Mills, Account Books, 1894–1898
John F. Flintoff Diary
E. J. Hale Papers
James Henry Harris Papers
Marmaduke James Hawkins Papers
W. W. Holden Papers
Governor's Letter Book, W. W. Holden
Governor's Papers, W. W. Holden
Sidney Willard Holman Papers
L. Banks Holt Cotton Mill, Account Book
Thomas Jarvis Papers
Patterson Papers
Edward W. Phifer, Jr. Collection
Pilot Cotton Mills, Time Book
Lucy Williams Polk Papers
Raleigh Banking and Trust Company Papers
Richmond Manufacturing Company, Time Book
Robert W. Scott Papers
Simpson-Biddle Family Papers
Trenton Cotton Mill Papers
Union Manufacturing Company, Account Book, 1871
Zebulon B. Vance Papers
Governor's Papers, Zebulon B. Vance
Richard D. White Collection
Jonathan Worth Papers
Privately Held Papers
William J. Clarke Papers

GOVERNMENT DOCUMENTS

Amendments to the Constitution of North Carolina Proposed by the Constitutional Convention of 1875.
Annual Reports. North Carolina Bureau of Labor Statistics.
First Annual Report . . . 1887. Raleigh: Josephus Daniels, 1887.
Second Annual Report . . . 1888. Raleigh: Josephus Daniels, 1888.
Third Annual Report . . . 1889. Raleigh: Josephus Daniels, 1889.

Fourth Annual Report . . . 1890. Raleigh: Josephus Daniels, 1890.

Fifth Annual Report . . . 1891. Raleigh: Josephus Daniels, 1891.

[No Sixth Annual Report]

Seventh Annual Report . . . 1893. Raleigh: Josephus Daniels, 1893.

Eighth Annual Report . . . 1894. Raleigh: Josephus Daniels, 1894.

Ninth Annual Report . . . 1895. Winston: M. I. and J. C. Stewart, 1895.

Tenth Annual Report . . . 1896. Winston: M. I. and J. C. Stewart, 1896.

Eleventh Annual Report . . . 1897. Raleigh: Guy V. Barnes, 1897.

Twelfth Annual Report . . . 1898. Raleigh: Guy V. Barnes, 1898.

Thirteenth Annual Report . . . 1899. Raleigh: Edwards & Broughton and E. M. Uzzell, 1899.

Fourteenth Annual Report . . . 1900. Raleigh: Edwards & Broughton and E. M. Uzzell, 1901.

Board of County Commissioners Minutes. Alamance County, 1869–83.

Board of County Commissioners Minutes. Caldwell County, 1870–80.

Board of County Commissioners Minutes. Edgecombe County, 1869–80.

Board of County Commissioners Minutes. Randolph County, 1874–76, 1880.

Caldwell County. Miscellaneous Records.

County Court Minutes. Alamance County.

County Court Minutes. Caldwell County.

County Court Minutes. Edgecombe County.

County Court Minutes. New Hanover County.

County Court Minutes. Randolph County.

Edgecombe County. Road Papers. 1840–68, 1869–97.

Laws and Resolutions of the State of North Carolina . . . Session of 1874–1875. Raleigh: Josiah Turner, 1875.

Laws and Resolutions of the State of North Carolina . . . Session of 1879. Raleigh: The Observer, 1879.

Laws and Resolutions of the State of North Carolina . . . Special Session of 1880. Raleigh: P. M. Hale, and Edwards, Broughton & Company, 1880.

Laws and Resolutions of the State of North Carolina . . . Session of 1881. Raleigh: Ashe & Gatling, 1881.

Laws and Resolutions of the State of North Carolina . . . Session of 1883. Raleigh: Ashe & Gatling, 1883.

Laws and Resolutions of the State of North Carolina . . . Session of 1885. Raleigh: P. M. Hale, 1885.

Legislative Papers. 1871–1885.

————. House Petitions. 1879, 1883.

Private Laws of the State of North Carolina passed by the General Assembly at its Session of 1858–59. Raleigh: Holden and Wilson, Printers to the State, 1859.

Private Laws of the State of North Carolina passed by the General Assembly at its Session of 1860–61. Raleigh: John Spelman, Printer to the State, 1861.

Private Laws of the State of North Carolina passed by the General Assembly at its Session of 1862–63. Raleigh: W. W. Holden, Printer to the State, 1863.

Private Laws of the State of North Carolina passed by the General Assembly at its Adjourned Session of 1862–63. Raleigh: W. W. Holden, Printer to the State, 1863.

Private Laws of the State of North Carolina passed by the General Assembly at its

Called Session of 1863. Raleigh: W. W. Holden, Printer to the State, 1863.

Private Laws of the State of North Carolina passed by the General Assembly at its Regular Session of 1864–65. Raleigh: Cannon & Holden, Printers to the Convention, 1865.

Private Laws of the State of North Carolina passed by the General Assembly at its Adjourned Session of 1865. Raleigh: Cannon & Holden, Printers to the Convention, 1865.

Private Laws of the State of North Carolina passed by the General Assembly at the Session of 1866. Raleigh: Wm. E. Pell, Printer to the State, 1866.

Public Laws of North Carolina, 1858–59. Raleigh: Holden and Wilson, Printers to the State, 1859.

Public Laws of North Carolina, 1860–61. Raleigh: John Spelman, Printer to the State, 1861.

Public Laws of the State of North Carolina, passed by the General Assembly at its Session of 1862–63. Raleigh: W. W. Holden, Printer to the State, 1863.

Public Laws of the State of North Carolina, passed by the General Assembly at its Called Session of 1863. Raleigh: W. W. Holden, Printer to the State, 1863.

Public Laws of the State of North Carolina, passed by the General Assembly at its Regular Session of 1864–65. Raleigh: Cannon & Holden, Printers to the Convention, 1865.

Public Laws of the State of North Carolina, passed by the General Assembly at its Adjourned Session of 1865. Raleigh: Cannon & Holden, Printers to the Convention, 1865.

Public Laws of the State of North Carolina passed by the General Assembly at the Session of 1865. Raleigh: Wm. E. Pell, Printer to the State, 1866.

Public Laws of the State of North Carolina passed by the General Assembly at the Session of 1866. Raleigh: Wm. E. Pell, Printer to the State, 1867.

Public Laws of the State of North Carolina passed by the General Assembly at the Sessions of 1861–62–63–64, and One in 1859. Raleigh: Wm. E. Pell, Printer to the State, 1866.

Public Laws of the State of North Carolina passed by the General Assembly at the Sessions of 1866–67. Raleigh: Wm. E. Pell, Printer to the State, 1867.

Public Laws of the State of North Carolina passed by the General Assembly at the Session 1868–69. Raleigh: M. S. Littlefield, State Printer and Binder, 1869.

Public Laws of the State of North Carolina passed by the General Assembly at the Session 1869–70. Raleigh: Jo. W. Holden, State Printer and Binder, 1870.

Public Laws of the State of North Carolina passed by the General Assembly at the Session 1899. No publication data.

Public Laws of the State of North Carolina . . . Session 1870–1871. No publication data.

Public Laws of the State of North Carolina . . . Session 1872–1873. Raleigh: Stone and Uzzell, 1873.

Public Laws of the State of North Carolina . . . Session 1873–1874. Raleigh: Josiah Turner, Jr., 1874.

Public Laws of the State of North Carolina . . . Session 1874–75. Raleigh: Josiah Turner, Jr., 1875.

Public Laws of the State of North Carolina . . . 1899. No publication data.

Randolph County. Miscellaneous Civil War Records.
———. Records of Slaves and Free Persons of Color.
Records (or Articles) of Incorporation. Alamance County.
Records (or Articles) of Incorporation. Cabarrus County.
Records (or Articles) of Incorporation. Caldwell County.
Records (or Articles) of Incorporation. Gaston County.
Records (or Articles) of Incorporation. Guilford County.
Records (or Articles) of Incorporation. Mecklenburg County.
Records (or Articles) of Incorporation. Randolph County.
Revised Code of North Carolina (enacted 1854). Bartholomew F. Moore and Asa Briggs, editors. Boston: Little, Brown and Company, 1855.
Tax List. Edgecombe County. 1866.
Tax List. New Hanover County. 1856, 1865–66, 1869, 1871, 1877.
Tax Records. Caldwell County.
U.S. Bureau of Refugees, Freedmen, and Abandoned Lands. Records of the Assistant Commissioner for the State of North Carolina. National Archives Microfilm Publication M 843.
———. Roll 5. Registers of Letters Received.
———. Roll 8. Letters Received.
———. Roll 20. Issuances.
———. Roll 22. Reports of Operations.
———. Roll 33. Reports of Outrages and Arrests.
———. Rolls 1–2. Letters Sent.
U.S. Bureau of the Census. Published and Manuscript Records for 1850, 1860, 1870, 1880, 1890 (no manuscript census survived), and 1900.
U.S. Bureau of the Census. *The Statistical History of the United States*. With an Introduction and User's Guide by Ben J. Wattenberg. New York: Basic Books, 1976.
U.S. Congress. Senate Reports. 42d Congress, 1st Session. No. 1.
U.S. Congress. Senate Reports. 42d Congress, 2d Session. No. 41, pt. 2.
U.S. War Department. Compiled Service Records of Volunteer Union Soldiers Who Served in Organizations from the State of North Carolina. National Archives Microfilm Publication M 401. Rolls 1, 3. First Infantry.
U.S. War Department. *The War of the Rebellion: A Compilation of the Official Records of the Union and Confederate Armies*. 130 vols. Washington, D.C.: Government Printing Office, 1880–1901.

NEWSPAPERS PUBLISHED IN NORTH CAROLINA

Alamance Gleaner
Albemarle Second Century
Albemarle Stanly Banner
Albemarle Stanly News
Asheboro Courier
Asheboro North Carolina Bulletin
Bakersville Roan Mountain Republican
Brattleboro Advance
Brattleboro Progress
Charlotte Observer
Clinton Caucasian
Company Shops North Carolina National
Danbury The Old Constitution
Graham Tribune

Greensboro Southern Democrat
Laurinburg Scotchman and Observer
Leaksville Dan Valley Echo
Lenoir Caldwell Messenger
Lenoir Rural Chronicle
Lenoir Topic
Lexington Central
Littleton Courier
Littleton True Reformer
Monroe Enquirer
Raleigh Daily Progress
Raleigh Daily Sentinel
Raleigh Farmer and Mechanic
Raleigh Gazette
Raleigh Holden Record

Raleigh Journal of Freedom
Raleigh Standard
Raleigh State Chronicle
Randolph Regulator
Randolph Sun
Salem People's Press
Salisbury Carolina Watchman
Salisbury Examiner
Salisbury North Carolina Herald
Snow Hill Great Sunny South
Tarboro Southerner
Tarboro Weekly Enquirer
Wilmington Journal
Wilmington Semi-Weekly Messenger

CHURCH RECORDS

First Baptist Church, Graham, Alamance County. Minutes. North Carolina Division of Archives and History.

Lenoir Crescent Methodist Church, Caldwell County. Quarterly Conference Minutes, 1850–60. North Carolina Division of Archives and History.

Mount Herman Baptist Church, Orange County. Register and Minutes, 1850–60. North Carolina Division of Archives and History.

Mount Olive Baptist Church, Alamance County. Register and Minutes. North Carolina Division of Archives and History.

Mount Zion Baptist Association, Alamance County. Session Minutes. North Carolina Collection. University of North Carolina at Chapel Hill.

Mount Zion Baptist Church, Alamance County. Minutes. North Carolina Division of Archives and History.

BOOKS

Andrews, Sidney. *The South Since the War*. Boston: Houghton Mifflin Company, 1971 [1886].

Boyd, William K., ed. *Memoirs of W. W. Holden*. The John Lawson Monographs of the Trinity College Historical Society, 11. Durham: Seeman Printery, 1911.

Brooks, A. L. and Hugh T. Lefler, eds. *The Papers of Walter Clark*. 2 vols. Chapel Hill: University of North Carolina Press, 1948.

Chesnutt, Charles W. *The Marrow of Tradition*. Ann Arbor: University of Michigan Press, 1967 [1901].

Dennett, John Richard. *The South as It Is: 1865–1866*. Edited by Henry M. Christman. New York: Viking Press, 1965.

Hamilton, J. G. de Roulhac, ed. *The Correspondence of Jonathan Worth*. 2 vols. Raleigh: North Carolina Historical Commission, 1909.

————. *The Papers of Thomas Ruffin.* 4 vols. Raleigh: Edwards and Broughton Printing Company, 1918–20.

————. With the collaboration of Rebecca Cameron. *The Papers of Randolph Abbott Shotwell.* 2 vols. Raleigh: North Carolina Historical Commission, 1931.

Hundley, D. R. *Social Relations in Our Southern States.* New York: Henry B. Price, 1860.

King, Edmund. *The Great South.* Edited by W. Magruder Drake and Robert R. Jones. Baton Rouge: Louisiana State University Press, 1972.

Rawick, George P., ed. *The American Slave: A Composite Autobiography.* 19 vols. in Series 1, 12 vols. in Supplement, Series 1. Westport, Conn.: Greenwood Press, 1972 and 1977.

Reid, Whitelaw. *After the War: A Tour of the Southern States, 1865–1866.* Edited by C. Vann Woodward. New York: Harper & Row, 1965.

Rose, Willie Lee. *A Documentary History of Slavery in North America.* New York: Oxford University Press, 1976.

Spencer, Cornelia Phillips. *The Last Ninety Days of the War in North Carolina.* New York: Watchman Publishing Company, 1866.

Tompkins, D. A. *Cotton Mill, Commercial Features: A Text Book for the Use of Textile Schools and Investors.* Charlotte, N.C.: published by the author, 1899.

Trowbridge, John T. *The Desolate South, 1865–1866.* Edited by Gordon Carroll. New York: Duell, Sloan and Pearce; Boston and Toronto: Little, Brown and Company, 1956.

Yearns, W. Buck, ed. *The Papers of Thomas Jordan Jarvis.* Vol. 1. Raleigh: North Carolina Division of Archives and History, 1969.

OTHER

Branson's North Carolina Business Directory. Raleigh: Levi Branson Office Publishing Co., 1869, 1872, 1877–78, 1884, and 1896.

Cheney, John L., Jr., ed. *North Carolina Government, 1585–1974.* Raleigh: Department of the Secretary of State, 1975.

————. *North Carolina Manual, 1981–82.* Raleigh: Department of the Secretary of State, 1981.

Connor, R. D. W., ed. *A Manual of North Carolina.* Raleigh: E. M. Uzzell & Co., 1913.

Hood, James Walker. *A Hundred Years of the A.M.E. Zion Church.* New York: A.M.E. Zion Book Concern, 1895.

Sketches of Charlotte, No. 4. Charlotte: Wade H. Harris, 1902.

SECONDARY SOURCES

BOOKS

Anderson, Eric. *Race and Politics in North Carolina, 1872–1901: The Black Second.* Baton Rouge: Louisiana State University Press, 1980.

Barrett, John G. *The Civil War in North Carolina.* Chapel Hill: University of North Carolina Press, 1963.

Billings, Dwight B., Jr. *Planters and the Making of a "New South": Class, Politics, and Development in North Carolina, 1865–1900*. Chapel Hill: University of North Carolina Press, 1979.

Bruce, Dickson D., Jr. *And They All Sang Hallelujah: Plain Folk Camp-Meeting Religion, 1800–45*. Knoxville: University of Tennessee Press, 1974.

Butler, Lindley S. and Alan D. Watson. *The North Carolina Experience*. Chapel Hill: University of North Carolina Press, 1984.

Carlton, David L. *Mill and Town in South Carolina, 1880–1920*. Baton Rouge: Louisiana State University Press, 1982.

Catterall, Helen T., ed. *Judicial Cases Concerning American Slavery and the Negro*. Vol. 1. New York: Octagon Books, 1968 (1929).

Cell, John W. *The Highest Stage of White Supremacy: The Origins of Segregation in South Africa and the American South*. Cambridge: Cambridge University Press, 1982.

Cooper, John Milton, Jr. *Walter Hines Page: The Southerner as American, 1855–1918*. Chapel Hill: University of North Carolina Press, 1977.

Corbitt, David Leroy. *The Formation of the North Carolina Counties, 1663–1943*. Raleigh: State Department of Archives and History, 1950.

Crabtree, Beth Gilbert and James W. Patton, eds. *"Journal of a Secesh Lady": The Diary of Catherine Ann Devereux Edmondston, 1860–1866*. Raleigh: Division of Archives and History, 1979.

Crow, Jeffrey J. and Robert F. Durden. *Maverick Republican in the Old North State*. Baton Rouge: Louisiana State University Press, 1977.

Crow, Jeffrey and Larry E. Tise, eds. *Writing North Carolina History*. Chapel Hill: University of North Carolina Press, 1979.

Daniels, Jonathan. *Prince of Carpetbaggers*. New York: J. B. Lippincott Company, 1958

Davis, Natalie Zemon. *Society and Culture in Early Modern France*. Stanford: Stanford University Press, 1975 [1965].

Durden, Robert F. *The Climax of Populism*. Lexington: University of Kentucky Press, 1966.

———. *The Dukes of Durham, 1865–1929*. Durham: Duke University Press, 1975.

———. *The Gray and the Black: The Confederate Debate on Emancipation*. Baton Rouge: Louisiana State University Press, 1972.

Eaton, Clement. *The Growth of Southern Civilization, 1790–1860*. New York: Harper & Row, 1961.

———. *The Mind of the Old South*. Baton Rouge: Louisiana State University Press, 1964, 1967.

Edmonds, Helen G. *The Negro and Fusion Politics in North Carolina, 1894–1901*. Chapel Hill: University of North Carolina Press, 1951.

Ekirch, A. Roger. *"Poor Carolina": Politics and Society in Colonial North Carolina, 1729–1776*. Chapel Hill: University of North Carolina Press, 1981.

Escott, Paul D. *After Secession: Jefferson Davis and the Failure of Confederate Nationalism*. Baton Rouge: Louisiana State University Press, 1978.

———. *Slavery Remembered: A Record of Twentieth-Century Slave Narratives*. Chapel Hill: University of North Carolina Press, 1979.

Evans, W. McKee. *Ballots and Fence Rails: Reconstruction on the Lower Cape Fear*. Chapel Hill: University of North Carolina Press, 1966.

Flynn, Charles L., Jr. *White Land, Black Labor*. Baton Rouge: Louisiana State University Press, 1983.

Folk, Edgar Estes, and Bynum Shaw. *William Woods Holden*. Winston-Salem: John F. Blair, 1982.

Franklin, John Hope. *The Free Negro in North Carolina*. Chapel Hill: University of North Carolina Press, 1943.

Fredrickson, George M. *The Black Image in the White Mind*. New York: Harper & Row, 1971.

Gaston, Paul M. *The New South Creed: A Study in Southern Mythmaking*. New York: Vintage Books, 1973.

Genovese, Eugene D. *The Political Economy of Slavery*. New York: Knopf and Random House, Vintage Books, 1967.

Goodwyn, Lawrence. *Democratic Promise*. New York: Oxford University Press, 1976.

————. *The Populist Movement*. New York: Oxford University Press, 1978.

Gutman, Herbert G. *The Black Family in Slavery and Freedom, 1750–1925*. New York: Pantheon, 1976.

Hahn, Stephen. *The Roots of Southern Populism: Yeoman Farmers and the Transformation of the Georgia Upcountry, 1850–1890*. New York: Oxford University Press, 1983.

Hamilton, J. G. de Roulhac. *Reconstruction in North Carolina*. Gloucester, Mass.: Peter Smith, 1964 [1914].

Hareven, Tamara K. and Randolph Langenbach, eds. *Amoskeag*. New York: Pantheon, 1978.

Hobsbawm, Eric J. *Bandits*. New York: Dell, 1969.

Hobson, Fred, ed. *South-Watching: Selected Essays by Gerald W. Johnson*. Chapel Hill: University of North Carolina Press, 1983.

Holt, Michael F. *The Political Crisis of the 1850s*. New York: John Wiley & Sons, 1978.

Johnson, Guion Griffis. *Ante-Bellum North Carolina*. Chapel Hill: University of North Carolina Press, 1937.

Key, V. O., Jr. *Southern Politics*. New York: Alfred A. Knopf, Inc., 1949.

Kousser, J. Morgan. *The Shaping of Southern Politics*. New Haven: Yale University Press, 1974.

Kruman, Marc W. *Parties and Politics in North Carolina, 1836–1865*. Baton Rouge: Louisiana State University Press, 1983.

Lefler, Hugh Talmage and Albert Ray Newsome. *North Carolina: The History of a Southern State*. 3d ed. Chapel Hill: University of North Carolina Press, 1973.

Logan, Frenise. *The Negro in North Carolina, 1876–1894*. Chapel Hill: University of North Carolina Press, 1964.

McCloskey, Robert G. *The American Supreme Court*. Chicago: University of Chicago Press, 1960.

McKinney, Gordon B. *Southern Mountain Republicans, 1865–1900*. Chapel Hill: University of North Carolina Press, 1978.

McKitrick, Eric L. *Andrew Johnson and Reconstruction*. Chicago: University of Chicago Press, 1960.

McLaurin, Melton A. *The Knights of Labor in the South*. Westport, Conn.: Greenwood Press, 1978.

_____. *Paternalism and Protest*. Westport, Conn.: Greenwood Press, 1971.

McMath, Robert C., Jr. *Populist Vanguard*. Chapel Hill: University of North Carolina Press, 1975.

Meier, August. *Negro Thought in America, 1880–1915*. Ann Arbor: University of Michigan Press, 1963.

Mitchell, Broadus. *The Rise of Cotton Mills in the South*. Baltimore: Johns Hopkins University Press, 1921.

Mobley, Joe A. *James City: A Black Community in North Carolina, 1863–1900*. Raleigh: Division of Archives and History, 1981.

Morgan, Edmund S. *American Slavery, American Freedom: The Ordeal of Colonial Virginia*. New York: W. W. Norton & Company, 1975.

Nathans, Sydney. *The Quest for Progress: The Way We Lived in North Carolina, 1870–1920*. Chapel Hill: University of North Carolina Press, 1983.

Noble, M. C. S. *A History of the Public Schools of North Carolina*. Chapel Hill: University of North Carolina Press, 1930.

Noblin, Stuart. *Leonidas LaFayette Polk: Agrarian Crusader*. Chapel Hill: University of North Carolina Press, 1949.

Office of State Budget and Management, Research and Planning Services Section. *Profile: North Carolina Counties*. 6th ed. Raleigh: North Carolina State Government, 1981.

Olsen, Otto H. *Carpetbagger's Crusade: The Life of Albion Winegar Tourgee*. Baltimore: Johns Hopkins University Press, 1965.

_____. *Reconstruction and Redemption in the South: An Assessment*. Baton Rouge: Louisiana State University Press, 1980.

Paludan, Phillip Shaw. *Victims*. Knoxville: University of Tennessee Press, 1981.

Prather, H. Leon, Sr. *Resurgent Politics and Educational Progressivism in the New South: North Carolina, 1890–1913*. Rutherford, N.J.: Fairleigh Dickinson University Press, 1979.

_____. *We Have Taken a City: Wilmington Racial Massacres & Coup*. Rutherford, N.J.: Fairleigh Dickinson University Press, 1984.

Reed, John Shelton. *One South: An Ethnic Approach to Regional Culture*. Baton Rouge: Louisiana State University Press, 1982.

Ringold, May Spencer. *The Role of the State Legislatures in the Confederacy*. Athens: University of Georgia Press, 1966.

Roark, James L. *Masters Without Slaves*. New York: W. W. Norton and Company, 1977.

Sanders, Charles Richard. *The Cameron Plantation of Central North Carolina*. Durham: Privately printed, 1974.

Schwab, John Christopher. *The Confederate States of America, 1861–65*. N.p. 1901.

Thomas, Emory M. *The Confederacy as a Revolutionary Experience*. Englewood Cliffs, N.J.: Prentice-Hall, 1971.

_____. *The Confederate Nation, 1861–1865*. New York: Harper & Row, 1979.

Thompson, E. P. *Whigs and Hunters*. New York: Pantheon, 1976 [1975].

Thompson, Holland. *From the Cotton Field to the Cotton Mill*. New York: Mac-Millan, 1906.

Tilly, Charles, ed. *The Formation of National States in Western Europe*. Princeton: Princeton University Press, 1975.

Trelease, Allen W. *White Terror: The Ku Klux Klan Conspiracy and Southern Reconstruction*. New York: Harper & Row, 1971.

Watson, Alan D. *Edgecombe County: A Brief History*. Raleigh: Division of Archives and History, 1979.

Wiener, Jonathan M. *Social Origins of the New South: Alabama, 1860–1885*. Baton Rouge: Louisiana State University Press, 1978.

Wilson, Theodore Bratner. *The Black Codes of the South*. University, Ala.: University of Alabama Press, 1965.

Winston, George Tayloe. *A Builder of the New South: Being the Story of the Life Work of Daniel Augustus Tompkins*. Garden City, N.Y.: Doubleday, Page & Company, 1920.

Woodward, C. Vann. *American Counterpoint*. New York: Little, Brown, and Co., 1971.

———. *Origins of the New South, 1877–1913*. Baton Rouge: Louisiana State University Press, 1951.

———. *Tom Watson: Agrarian Rebel*. New York: Macmillan, 1938.

Wright, Gavin. *The Political Economy of the Cotton South: Households, Markets, and Wealth in the Nineteenth Century*. New York: Norton, 1978.

Yearns, W. Buck and John G. Barrett. *North Carolina Civil War Documentary*. Chapel Hill: University of North Carolina Press, 1980.

Zuber, Richard L. *Jonathan Worth: A Biography of a Southern Unionist*. Chapel Hill: University of North Carolina Press, 1965.

———. *North Carolina During Reconstruction*. Raleigh: Department of Archives and History, 1969.

ARTICLES

Allen, Jeffrey Brooke. "The Racial Thought of White North Carolina Opponents of Slavery, 1789–1876." *North Carolina Historical Review* 59 (Jan. 1982): 49–66.

Anderson, Jean Bradley. "Paul Carrington Cameron as Planter." *Carolina Comments* 27 (Sept. 1979): 114–20.

Auman, William T. "Neighbor against Neighbor: The Inner Civil War in the Randolph County Area of Confederate North Carolina." *North Carolina Historical Review* 61 (Jan. 1984): 59–92.

Auman, William T. and David D. Scarboro. "The Heroes of America in Civil War North Carolina." *North Carolina Historical Review* 58 (Oct. 1981): 327–63.

Bardolph, Richard. "Inconstant Rebels: Desertion of North Carolina Troops in the Civil War." *North Carolina Historical Review* 41 (Apr. 1964): 163–89.

Boyd, W. K. "William W. Holden." *Historical Papers*. Trinity College Historical Society. Series 3 (1899): 39–78. New York: AMS Press, 1970 reprint.

Bromberg, Alan B. "'The Worst Muddle Ever Seen in N. C. Politics': The Farmers' Alliance, the Subtreasury, and Zeb Vance." *North Carolina Historical Review* 56 (Jan. 1979): 19–40.

Butts, Donald C. "The 'Irrepressible Conflict': Slave Taxation and North Carolina's Gubernatorial Election of 1860." *North Carolina Historical Review* 58 (Jan. 1981): 44–66.

Crow, Jeffrey J. "'Fusion, Confusion, and Negroism': Schisms among Negro Republicans in the North Carolina Election of 1896." *North Carolina Historical Review* 53 (Oct. 1976): 364–84.

Eckstein, Harry. "On the Etiology of Internal Wars." *History and Theory* 4 (1964–65): 133–63.

Escott, Paul D. "'The Cry of the Sufferers': The Problem of Welfare in the Confederacy." *Civil War History* 23 (Sept. 1977): 228–40.

———. "The Moral Economy of the Crowd in Confederate North Carolina." *The Maryland Historian* 13 (Spring/Summer 1982): 1–18.

———. "The Perspective of Slaves in North American Plantation Society." *Carolina Comments* 27 (Nov. 1979): 139–46.

———. "Poverty and Governmental Aid for the Poor in Confederate North Carolina." *North Carolina Historical Review* 61 (Oct. 1984): 462–80.

Escott, Paul D. and Jeffrey J. Crow. "The Social Order and Violent Disorder: An Analysis of North Carolina in the Revolution and the Civil War." *Journal of Southern History* (Feb. 1985): forthcoming.

Gass, W. Conrad. "'The Misfortune of a High Minded and Honorable Gentleman': W. W. Avery and the Southern Code of Honor." *North Carolina Historical Review* 56 (Summer 1979): 278–97.

Griffin, Richard W. "Reconstruction of the North Carolina Textile Industry, 1865–1885." *North Carolina Historical Review* 41 (Winter 1965): 34–53.

Harris, William C. "William Woods Holden: In Search of Vindication." *North Carolina Historical Review* 59 (Oct. 1982): 354–72.

Hobsbawm, Eric J. "Social Criminality." *Bulletin of the Society for the Study of Labour History* 25, 1972.

Jeffrey, Thomas E. "'Free Suffrage' Revisited: Party Politics and Constitutional Reform in Antebellum North Carolina." *North Carolina Historical Review* 59 (Jan. 1982): 24–48.

———. "The Progressive Paradigm of Antebellum North Carolina Politics." *Carolina Comments* 30 (May 1982): 66–75.

———. "'Thunder from the Mountains': Thomas Lanier Clingman and the End of Whig Supremacy in North Carolina." *North Carolina Historical Review* 56 (Oct. 1979): 366–95.

Johnson, Guion Griffis. "The Landless People of Antebellum North Carolina." *Carolina Comments* 31 (Jan. 1983): 23–32.

King, J. Crawford, Jr. "The Closing of the Southern Range: An Exploratory Study." *Journal of Southern History* 48 (Feb. 1982): 53–70.

Kruman, Marc W. "Dissent in the Confederacy: The North Carolina Experience." *Civil War History* 27 (Dec. 1981): 293–313.

Linden, Fabian. "Economic Democracy in the Slave South." *Journal of Negro History* 31 (Apr. 1946): 140–89.

Logan, Frenise A. "Black and Republican: Vicissitudes of a Minority Twice Over in the North Carolina House of Representatives, 1876–1877." *North Carolina Historical Review* 61 (July 1984): 311–46.

———. "The Legal Status of Public School Education for Negroes in North Carolina, 1877–1894." *North Carolina Historical Review* 32 (July 1955): 346–57.

———. "The Movement of Negroes from North Carolina, 1876–1894." *North Carolina Historical Review* 33 (Jan. 1956): 45–65.

McKinney, Gordon B. "Southern Mountain Republicans and the Negro, 1865–1900." *Journal of Southern History* 41 (Nov. 1975): 493–516.

Menius, Arthur C., III. "James Bennitt: Portrait of an Antebellum Yeoman." *North Carolina Historical Review* 58 (Oct. 1981): 305–26.

Miller, Robert D. "Samuel Field Phillips: The Odyssey of a Southern Dissenter." *North Carolina Historical Review* 58 (July 1981): 263–80.

O'Brien, Gail W. "Power and Influence in Mecklenburg County, 1850–1880." *North Carolina Historical Review* 54 (Spring 1977): 120–39.

Olsen, Otto H. "The Ku Klux Klan: A Study in Reconstruction Politics and Propaganda." *North Carolina Historical Review* 39 (Summer 1962): 340–62.

———. "Southern Reconstruction and the Question of Self-Determination." In *A Nation Divided: Problems and Issues of the Civil War and Reconstruction*, edited by George M. Fredrickson, pp. 113–41. Minneapolis: Burgess Publishing Company, 1975.

Olsen, Otto H. and Ellen Z. McGrew. "Prelude to Reconstruction: The Correspondence of State Senator Leander Sams Gash, 1866–1867." *North Carolina Historical Review* 60 (Jan. Apr. July 1983): 37–88, 206–38, and 333–66.

Raper, Horace W. "William W. Holden and the Peace Movement in North Carolina." *North Carolina Historical Review* 31 (Oct. 1954): 493–516.

Reid, Richard. "A Test Case of the 'Crying Evil': Desertion among North Carolina Troops during the Civil War." *North Carolina Historical Review* 58 (July 1981): 234–62.

Russ, W. A., Jr. "Radical Disfranchisement in North Carolina, 1867–68." *North Carolina Historical Review* 11 (Oct. 1934): 271–83.

Scarboro, David D. "North Carolina and the Confederacy: The Weakness of States' Rights during the Civil War." *North Carolina Historical Review* 61 (Apr. 1979): 133–49.

Scott, Rebecca. "The Battle Over the Child: Child Apprenticeship and the Freedmen's Bureau in North Carolina." *Prologue* 10 (Summer 1978): 101–13.

Sitterson, J. Carlyle. "Business Leaders in Post-Civil War North Carolina, 1865–1900." In *Studies in Southern History*, edited by J. Carlyle Sitterson, 39:111–21. The James Sprunt Studies in History and Political Science. Chapel Hill: University of North Carolina Press, 1957.

Steelman, Lala Carr. "The Role of Elias Carr in the North Carolina Farmers' Alliance." *North Carolina Historical Review* 57 (Apr. 1980): 133–58.

Sutch, Richard and Roger Ransom. "Sharecropping: Market response or mechanism of race control?" In *What Was Freedom's Price?*, edited by David G. Sansing, pp. 51–70. Jackson: University Press of Mississippi, 1978.

Thompson, E. P. "Eighteenth Century Crime, Popular Movements and Social Control." *Bulletin of the Society for the Study of Labour History* 25, 1972.

Tilly, Charles. "Charivaris, Repertoires, and Politics." Center for Research on Social Organization Working Paper #214.

Townes, A. Jane. "The Effect of Emancipation on Large Land Holdings, Nelson and Goochland Counties, Virginia." *Journal of Southern History* 45, no. 3 (Aug. 1979): 403–12.

Trelease, Allen W. "The Fusion Legislatures of 1895 and 1897: A Roll Call Analysis of the North Carolina House of Representatives." *North Carolina Historical Review* 57 (July 1980): 280–309.

————. "Republican Reconstruction in North Carolina: A Roll-Call Analysis of the State House of Representatives, 1868–1870." *Journal of Southern History* 42 (Aug. 1976): 319–44.

————. "Who Were the Scalawags?" In *Reconstruction in the South*, edited by Edwin C. Rozwenc, pp. 119–44. 2d ed. Lexington, Mass.: D. C. Heath and Company, 1972.

Yates, Richard E. "Governor Vance and the Peace Movement." *North Carolina Historical Review* 17 (Jan. and Apr. 1940): 1–25, 89–113.

DISSERTATIONS AND THESES

Alexander, Roberta Sue. "North Carolina Faces the Freedmen: Race Relations during Presidential Reconstruction, 1865–1867." Ph.D. dissertation, University of Chicago, 1974.

Auman, William T. "North Carolina's Inner Civil War: Randolph County." Masters thesis, University of North Carolina, Greensboro, 1978.

Bogue, Jesse Parker, Jr. "Violence and Oppression in North Carolina during Reconstruction, 1865–1873." Ph.D. dissertation, University of Maryland, 1973.

Butts, Donald C. "A Challenge to Planter Rule: The Controversy over Ad Valorem Taxation of Slaves in North Carolina, 1858–1862." Ph.D. dissertation, Duke University, 1978.

Entrekin, William Frank, Jr. "Poor Relief in North Carolina in the Confederacy." Masters thesis, Duke University, 1947.

Folk, Edgar Estes. "W. W. Holden, Political Journalist, Editor of *North Carolina Standard*, 1843–1865." Ph.D. dissertation, George Peabody College for Teachers, 1934.

O'Brien, Gail W. "War and the Legal Fraternity in the Creation of the Modern South: The Guilford Experience, 1848–1882." Manuscript for a book based on a Ph.D. dissertation, University of North Carolina, Chapel Hill, 1974.

Schneider, Tracy Whittaker. "The Institution of Slavery in North Carolina, 1860–1865." Ph.D. dissertation, Duke University, 1979.

INDEX